Donn Piatt

ADST-DACOR DIPLOMATS AND DIPLOMACY SERIES

Series Editor: Margery Boichel Thompson

Since 1776, extraordinary men and women have represented the United States abroad under all sorts of circumstances. What they did and how and why they did it remain little known to their compatriots. In 1995 the Association for Diplomatic Studies and Training (ADST) and DACOR, an organization of foreign affairs professionals, created the Diplomats and Diplomacy book series to increase public knowledge and appreciation of the role of American diplomats in world history. The series seeks to demystify diplomacy through the stories of those who have conducted U.S. foreign relations, as they lived, influenced, and reported them. *Donn Piatt: Gadfly of the Gilded Age* by Peter Bridges, 48th volume in the series, recounts the life and times of a multifaceted public man and sometime diplomat in the booming decades of the late nineteenth century.

OTHER TITLES IN THE SERIES

Gordon S. Brown, *Toussaint's Clause: The Founding Fathers and the Haitian Revolution*

Herman J. Cohen, *Intervening in Africa: Superpower Peacemaking in a Troubled Continent*

Charles T. Cross, *Born a Foreigner: A Memoir of the American Presence in Asia*

Brandon Grove, *Behind Embassy Walls: The Life and Times of an American Diplomat*

Parker T. Hart, *Saudi Arabia and the United States: Birth of a Security Partnership*

Edmund Hull, *High-Value Target: Countering Al Qaeda in Yemen*

Dennis Kux, *The United States and Pakistan, 1947–2000: Disenchanted Allies*

Jane C. Loeffler, *The Architecture of Diplomacy: Building America's Embassies*

Terry McNamara, *Escape with Honor: My Last Hours in Vietnam*

William B. Milam, *Bangladesh and Pakistan: Flirting with Failure in Muslim South Asia*

Robert H. Miller, *Vietnam and Beyond: a Diplomat's Cold War Education*

Ronald E. Neumann, *The Other War: Winning and Losing in Afghanistan*

David D. Newsome, *Witness to a Changing World*

Richard B. Parker, *Uncle Sam in Barbary: A Diplomatic History*

Nicholas Platt, *China Boys: How U.S. Relations with the PRC Began and Grew*

Howard B. Schaeffer, *Ellsworth Bunker: Global Troubleshooter, Vietnam Hawk*

James W. Spain, *In Those Days: A Diplomat Remembers*

James Stephenson, *Losing the Golden Hour: An Insider's View of Iraq's Reconstruction*

Ulrich Straus, *The Anguish of Surrender: Japanese POWs of World War I*

Jean Wilkowski, *Abroad for Her Country: Tales of a Pioneer Woman Ambassador in the U.S. Foreign Service*

DONN PIATT

Gadfly of the Gilded Age

❦ · ❦

PETER BRIDGES

The Kent State University Press
Kent, Ohio

ADST-DACOR Diplomats and Diplomacy Series

© 2012 by The Kent State University Press, Kent, Ohio 44242
ALL RIGHTS RESERVED
Library of Congress Catalog Card Number 2012013502
ISBN 978-1-60635-116-1
Manufactured in the United States of America

LIBRARY OF CONGRESS CATALOGING-IN-PUBLICATION DATA
Bridges, Peter, 1932–
Donn Piatt : gadfly of the Gilded Age / Peter Bridges.
p.   cm. — (ADST-DACOR diplomats and diplomacy series)
Includes bibliographical references and index.
ISBN 978-1-60635-116-1 (hardcover : alk. paper) ∞
1. Piatt, Donn, 1819–1891. 2. Statesmen—United States—History—19th century—
Biography. 3. Journalists—United States—Biography.
4. United States—History—19th century. 5. Ohio—Biography. I. Title.
F496.P58B75 2012
070.92—dc23
[B]
2012013502

16 15 14 13 12   5 4 3 2 1

For our grandchildren

Amanda, Peter, Devlin,

Gigi, Penny, and Roland

with hope that during their lives

the words of Shelley may come true:

"The world's great age begins anew,

The golden years return. . . ."

Who shall speak for the people?

who has the answers?

where is the sure interpreter?

who knows what to say?

—Carl Sandburg

The man who has no enemies has no following.

—Donn Piatt

CONTENTS

ACKNOWLEDGMENTS

I am indebted to many people for the help they have given me with this book. I am deeply grateful to the Kent State University Press and its director, Will Underwood, for agreeing for a third time to publish a work of mine. Joyce Harrison, the acquisitions editor of the Press, has been unfailingly helpful and, beyond that, good natured, no matter how many complications were offered her by a dour and sometimes forgetful fellow. I am equally grateful to managing editor Mary Young and marketing manager Susan Cash for their kind help and applied wisdom.

I owe a great debt to Margaret Piatt and Jim White of the Piatt Castles for opening to me both the Castles and their rich (and well-ordered) archives. As I sat there many days in an upstairs room, going over letters, poems, scrapbooks, and the very books that young Donn had read, I felt sure I was coming closer to a vanished age. (Incidentally, spelling and capitalization of these houses' names have varied over the years, and even Donn Piatt was not consistent. Originally, the whole property was known as Mac-o-cheek. Today the two so-called Castles are Mac-O-Chee and Mac-A-Cheek.)

Daniel W. Crofts of the College of New Jersey read an early draft and pointed out a number of gross errors I had made. John W. Hubbell, professor emeritus of Kent State University and former director of its press, whom I hope I may call not just friend but mentor, read two later drafts and called my attention to a number of mistakes and lacunae. I also profited greatly from the comments, both critical and careful, made by the press's two anonymous academic readers.

I have written previously that I believe archivists and librarians to be one of the best classes of human beings. My work on this book has reconfirmed this belief. Every request I made of an archive or library was promptly answered, and some people went out of their way to help me. Lynda Lasswell Crist, editor and project director of the Papers of Jefferson Davis at Rice University, located for me a number of letters exchanged between Piatt and the old Confederate president that I would otherwise never have found. Kristina Eleyet, president of the Logan County, Ohio, Genealogical Society, worked late on the only day I could spend in Bellefontaine to find for me the surviving court records dealing with Piatt. Jane Thomas and Bob Puglisi of the Old Rock Library in Crested Butte, Colorado, made it possible for me to receive many old volumes on interlibrary loan in a small mountain town. Dale Flick, librarian of the Cincinnati Literary Club, pored through the old club archives to find the warm letter Piatt sent to the club president in 1890. Nan Card, the curator of manuscripts in the Rutherford B. Hayes Presidential Center in Fremont, Ohio, spent much time locating for me all the correspondence relating to Piatt and his friend the president. John P. Richardson kindly shared with me a number of press articles relating to Piatt that he had come across during his own research on Alexander Shepherd. The staff of the Library of Congress, and particularly the people of the Manuscript Division, continued the kind help I began to receive from them a decade or more ago.

Not least, I am grateful to my wife, Mary Jane, for hearing me out when, so many times, I needed to share something about Piatt and his contemporaries, and for urging me so many times to keep in mind the need to produce a book that was not only accurate but readable.

While I have profited from the help of many, what mistakes may be found in this book are all mine.

INTRODUCTION

This is the story of a once famous man with an always rare name: Donn Piatt. As he matured, America moved toward civil war; both before and during the war he served the republic well; after the war he prospered in that booming yet corrupt time that his sometime friend Mark Twain named the Gilded Age. Those decades were later pictured by historians as a dark time, but they were also decades of progress and development.[1] In that age, Donn Piatt became famous across America for his fierce criticisms of people, ranging from presidents he had befriended to swindlers he despised.

Piatt was a gentleman from Ohio and a man of many accomplishments. After his death in 1891 his biographer Charles Miller called him a diplomat, historian, journalist, judge, lawyer, orator, poet, politician, soldier, statesman, and even theologian. Not least, he was a patriot. He was also a lobbyist, a novelist, a playwright, and a humorist who was once called in to replace Mark Twain when Twain's humor failed him. Many laughed at what Piatt wrote about others; many laughed at him. Sometimes he even laughed at himself—when he was not wielding his sharp pen.

Among all these occupations it was as a Washington insider, a journalist and editor, that he made his national name, after serving as both a diplomat in powerful Paris and a Union officer in tough battles. In 1869 Rutherford B. Hayes, future president, wrote his friend Donn Piatt that he thought Piatt's true vocation was to be a "disturbing element," and that it was a vocation in which he could do great things.[2] Hayes was right, and America needed such an element. In that Gilded Age, the relief that people had felt at war's end soon turned to widespread worry that a president who had been a wartime hero, Ulysses Grant, had gone imperial—and that both Grant's administration and the Congress were corrupt. Washington was becoming more important in America, and at the same time Washington sycophants and lobbyists were becoming more numerous. America looked like a society of haves and have-nots. The American press seemed sometimes somnolent and indulgent in the face of lies and decay. In some ways it was a time like our own.

Donn Piatt was never somnolent. Until days before he died, at seventy-two, in the fine chateau he had built in the quiet Ohio countryside, he continued to attack the wrongs and corruption he saw in America. Piatt was an early American muckraker, although that was not a term used in his lifetime.[3] He told his readers that a man was gauged by his enemies. As he worked on and his health went slowly downhill, he said it was better to wear out than to rust.

Piatt knew everyone who counted in Ohio, and in his time Ohioans filled jobs from the White House down. When he moved east, he became a national gadfly and a scourge of top leaders, who sometimes reacted sharply to his criticism. Of the half dozen presidents he came to know, one cursed him—or at least so he said. Another jailed him—of this there is no question—for inciting riot and rebellion. One day Piatt was knocked down in the Capitol by a promoter he had accused of bribing congressmen. On another day a drunken senator he had ridiculed came gunning for him but went to the wrong newspaper in his search. Piatt afterward published his correct address; he kept regular hours, he said, and he wanted the senator to know his schedule: "We kill Senators on Monday . . . Wednesday we fight members of the House . . . and we protest any intrusion on Friday and Saturday . . . some little time has to be given to editing our insults."[4] Piatt died after reminding the public of a grave fault in an Ohio native and martyred president who had been a close friend, James A. Garfield, and while trying to thwart the aspirations of an Ohio politician named William McKinley.[5]

In the little more than seven decades that Piatt spent on earth, the rural republic on the Atlantic seaboard spread its dominion across the continent and survived four years of bloody civil war. Immigrants and pioneers filled the spaces where Lakota and bison had roamed. Railroads and the telegraph began to provide fast transport and almost instant messaging. Industry and agriculture boomed, while cities grew into places of culture and even grandeur. By the century's end, a few years past Donn Piatt's own end, America was promising to become the world's greatest power.

That century was not just booming and tawdry but exciting—depending on what part you played; few Southern sharecroppers or Northern hod-carriers or cooks, black or white, found life exciting, and women's roles were limited. But if you were a man and you came from the middle or upper classes (and had good health), there were adventures to be had everywhere, at either first or second hand. Piatt may never have seen the Mississippi River, and he certainly never got as far east as the Danube, but he ranged widely through eastern America, sojourned in western Europe, and savored much that he saw. By examining his life we can hope to gain a better understanding of his vanished world.

In Piatt's time, as newspapers became more important in American society, so did the journalists. His friend and fellow editor Horace Greeley became the Democratic candidate for president. Henry Raymond, founder and editor of the *New York Times,* headed the Republican National Committee. Piatt himself was once called the third-best-known man in Washington—after the war heroes Ulysses Grant and William Tecumseh Sherman, both of whom he reviled.

Nineteenth-century America had no single metropolis like Paris or London. Although Washington became more important, a British observer could still scoff that the country really had no capital.[6] Most Americans lived in small towns or the countryside. There was no radio, television, or Internet, but the telegraph made it possible for Donn Piatt's funny quips and biting columns to be reprinted quickly in papers and journals across America. Although many people loathed him, he helped to shape views on the national agenda. It was an important role. It was an interesting life.

Piatt was an independent with a fiery temper from boyhood onward. He respected his father and inherited his occasionally wrathful ways but, as a youth, broke with him on politics; he later followed his father into the law reluctantly. Among Piatt's older friends and colleagues it was only Edwin Stanton, in the years before Stanton became Lincoln's stern war minister, who perhaps became a mentor for Piatt; Stanton continued during the war to be a good friend to this complex person.

Complex, indeed. As the years passed, Piatt mocked both Catholic and Protestant churches, attacked the millionaires and defended the workers, yet he ended as a Catholic and a rich man. He viewed himself as moral, but his ethics—or good sense, at a minimum—came into question after he became a Washington lobbyist while remaining a journalist. There are questions about his actions that this book will not resolve in his favor.

Was there in Piatt an envy of men who became greater personages than he? Was it envy, at least in part, that led him to tackle them so fiercely? One senses that he might have gotten further in government and politics if he had been more amenable to discipline, or at least willing to play up to people in senior positions—most notably in 1860. After Lincoln's election that November there was a brief period when, as a friend of both Lincoln and Piatt wrote, the two men and their wives were as thick as fingers in a mitten.[7] Then, it seems, Piatt said to the president-elect too many words that Lincoln did not want to hear. When the war began, Piatt had won no post and, aged forty-one, enlisted as an army private.

Much time divides us from Donn Piatt; but we who live in an age that has its own share of wars, corruption, and inequity do well to consider this influential and litigious—yet often gentle—American. Too much of our past is lost to write with certainty about all the doings of Piatt and his peers. Still, there should be more than enough here to hold the reader's attention down to the man's end and, indeed, beyond.[8]

⊰ 1 ⊱

BIG FIRE AND HIS FAMILY

Donn Piatt was favored from the beginning. He was born in 1819 into a prosperous family with an honorable past, in an America whose prospects seemed bright— although there were dark clouds. James Monroe had entered the White House in 1817, and for a time an era of good feelings ensued; but the question of admitting Missouri to the Union as a slave state soon reminded Americans that slavery remained the great national problem. There had been economic expansion since the end of war with Britain in 1815, but now came the Panic of 1819. Banks failed, mortgages were foreclosed, and unemployment rose. Still, men like Donn's father, Benjamin Piatt, who was one of the leading citizens of Cincinnati, could read with pleasure of how the country was getting bigger and more modern. Spain had just ceded Florida to the United States. The National Road already stretched west to Wheeling, in the western part of Virginia, and before long it would reach through Ohio and Indiana into the new state of Illinois. Work was progressing on the Erie Canal, which would link the Great Lakes region to the East. Eight years earlier, in 1811, Nicholas Roosevelt[1] and his young wife, Lydia Latrobe, had taken the first steamboat on Western waters down the Ohio and Mississippi rivers to New Orleans. Just now the *Savannah* had become the first steamship to cross the Atlantic.

The name Piatt was never common in America. There is more than one account of when the first of the Piatts came to the New World. This may have been a man who came to New Jersey from the Rhone region of France in the seventeenth century. His name was probably René Piatt, although the first written record of him, a deed for his purchase in 1677 of sixty acres of land at Woodbridge, New Jersey, called him "Rene Piatt alias Lafleur." The family were French Protestants, Huguenots. In America, René married a native of Flushing, New York, named Elizabeth Sheffield.[2]

René and Elizabeth Piatt's great-grandson Jacob Piatt was commissioned as an ensign in the Continental Army at the beginning of the Revolution. He went

1

on the unsuccessful expedition against Quebec in 1775; took part in the battles of Germantown, Brandywine, Short Hills, and Monmouth; was wounded; and at war's end was a colonel with an outstanding record.[3] During the Revolution Jacob Piatt married Hannah Cook McCullough, a native of New Jersey who was described as a woman of great beauty.[4] Their first child, Benjamin McCullough Piatt, father of Donn Piatt, was born in 1779 in Bloomsbury, New Jersey. After the war five more children were born to Jacob and Hannah, and Jacob was granted a large tract in northern Kentucky for his wartime services. He moved his family there from New Jersey in 1795, and above the Ohio he built, in 1804, a huge house he called Federal Hall. Eight decades later he and his now vanished mansion would appear in slightly fictionalized form in stories by his grandson Donn.[5]

Benjamin Piatt was a teenager when the family came to the Ohio Valley. He and his younger brother, John, began their business careers by taking flatboats loaded with produce down the Ohio and Mississippi rivers to New Orleans. The Mississippi was an even wilder, riskier river then than it was a quarter century later, when young Abraham Lincoln worked a flatboat downstream from Indiana to New Orleans. The Piatt brothers succeeded and made money from their venture. Decades later Donn Piatt, with perhaps his adventurous father in mind, was to write a poem he called "The Ohio Boat-Horn," about a sturdy pioneer on a flatboat in the big river.[6]

Later, Benjamin Piatt studied law in Cincinnati. In 1799, aged twenty, he married Elizabeth Barnett, daughter of a wealthy Virginia family that had moved to Kentucky. In 1810 he was named attorney general of the new Territory of Illinois, and the Piatts and their several small children moved west to Kaskaskia, a once French town on the Mississippi River and the territorial capital.[7] After the War of 1812 began, reports reached Kaskaskia that Indians allied with the British might come raiding. A family story tells of Elizabeth Piatt being unable to sleep at night and going to sit in an arbor in the garden with her husband's rifle on her knees.[8] In June 1813 Piatt resigned his post and moved his family back east to Cincinnati.[9] There he became a lawyer, judge, and member of the Ohio legislature.

Benjamin and Elizabeth Piatt's ninth child, Donn, was born in Cincinnati on June 29, 1819, in the family home, a brick house on Main Street between Sixth and Seventh streets. By the time of Donn's birth only four of the older eight children were still living: Jacob Wykoff, the eldest, and three sisters, Hannah, Arabella, and Martha Ann. The Piatts' tenth and last child, Abram Sanders, was born two years after Donn, in 1821.[10]

Benjamin Piatt's brother and former partner on the river, John, founded in Cincinnati the first private bank west of the Appalachians and became a merchant prince.[11] During the War of 1812 he supplied the army with provisions on credit, trusting verbal assurances from the secretary of war that the government would reimburse him. At war's end the government refused to pay him more than the original contract stipulated—though he had had to pay out far more than he made—and insisted he refund the $46,000 he had been driven to pocket from sales. He was hounded by creditors, imprisoned for debt, and died in jail in 1822.[12] His heirs pursued his claim, however, and a half century later, in 1875, the U.S. Supreme Court finally awarded them what they sought. It was an important lesson for his nephew Donn: To get justice you might well have to lobby the government, hard and long.

After the War of 1812 came boom years in much of America, particularly in Cincinnati. It was true that the city had its imperfections. Fanny Trollope recalled Cincinnati in her unflattering best seller *Domestic Manners of the Americans,* published in 1828, as a place that was lacking in culture. Mrs. Trollope had come from England, and she had personal disappointments in Cincinnati; she opened America's first department store there, and it failed. Still, she was relating hard fact when she wrote of how in Cincinnati garbage was thrown into the streets and disposed of by roaming herds of pigs. (Even decades later, immense droves of hogs filled the streets in autumn and early winter, on their way to the city slaughterhouses.)[13] The people had little feeling for art, and the only public amusement place was a theater that was poorly attended. But the city was also, she had to admit, a booming place, where one could see as many as fifteen steamboats tied up at the wharves and fourteen hundred houses were built in a year.[14]

The wide-ranging British traveler Captain Basil Hall visited Cincinnati the year after Fanny Trollope's book came out. His account of his travels across the continent offended some Americans, but few people in Cincinnati could take offense at what he wrote about their city: "Cincinnati is one of the much-cried-up wonders of the West, and not without reason . . . it furnishes a very striking instance of the activity of this bustling people. The town itself . . . is very pretty, and very advantageously situated on the right bank of the Ohio. . . ."[15]

An ambitious and enterprising man in Cincinnati might well acquire a fortune by the time he reached middle age. Donn's father, Benjamin Piatt, and his law partner, Nicholas Longworth, both got rich. In Piatt's case the fortune was based on real estate. He had begun buying land around Cincinnati when it was a small place, and as it expanded, his investments mounted in value.[16]

Years after the Longworth and Piatt partnership ended, a Longworth would marry the daughter of a president, Theodore Roosevelt. Benjamin's son Donn would achieve, over coming decades, quite a different relationship with a succession of presidents.

In 1828 Benjamin Piatt acquired seventeen hundred acres of land in Logan County, Ohio, a hundred miles north of Cincinnati. He retired there the following year at the age of fifty together with his wife and five children, including Donn, who turned ten years old that June of 1829. Some of the land was deeded to Benjamin for legal fees, at $1.50 per acre, by John Enoch, who around 1812 had obtained a tract of three thousand acres in the area. Enoch, like John Piatt, had contracted with the U.S. Army to furnish provisions during the war. When the army refused to buy cattle from Enoch after the war ended, he successfully sued the government with Benjamin Piatt as his lawyer.[17]

The Piatts called their place Mac-o-cheek, from the Mekoche, who had a village nearby and were one of the five Shawnee clans created, according to Shawnee legend, by the old Grandmother after the Great Deluge. Ohio was the earliest known homeland of the Shawnee people.[18]

One of the first whites to be struck by the beauty of this place had been Simon Kenton, a Virginian turned Kentucky frontiersman. In 1778, roaming with another Kentuckian through what later became Ohio, Kenton was captured and his comrade killed by the Shawnees after the two stole Indian horses. As the Shawnees took Kenton toward the center of their nation, in today's Logan County, to be put to death, they forced him to run the gauntlet in several villages, including the one at Mac-o-cheek. Despite broken bones and injuries, the story goes, Kenton was impressed by what fine land it was. He escaped death—saved by that enigmatic character Simon Girty, who had once been his fellow scout[19] but now fought against the Americans alongside the Shawnees.[20]

Donn never forgot that first trip northward from Cincinnati to his new home deep in the country. His father had gone ahead, and it was his mother who took him, his three older sisters, and his younger brother to Mac-o-cheek in a Conestoga wagon pulled by four horses. (One supposes there was also a hired man along as driver.) They spent three nights at inns along the way, and the fourth night camped by the roadside. That, Donn Piatt wrote six decades later, was his most glorious memory of all. He woke at dawn to hear songbirds and the cawing of crows and the calls of wild turkeys; and then he watched in wonder as a buck and two does ran across the woods and into the big trees.[21]

The first white family had settled in what was to become Logan County three decades earlier, only two years before Ohio became a state in 1803. There were still Shawnees there, but they were no longer a threat to settlers. After the Revolution, in 1786, their villages at Mac-o-cheek and nearby had been destroyed by a force of federal soldiers and Kentucky militiamen under General George Rogers Clark and his deputy, Benjamin Logan, for whom the new county was named.[22] When the white farmers came in, the land was still covered with virgin hardwood forest, huge oaks and hickories in the stream valleys and maples and beeches on the uplands. Here and there were little patches of open prairie that perhaps had been glacial lakes or had been burned over by the Indians; there were no roads, just an occasional Indian path.[23]

By the time the Piatts came, the woods were giving way to farms. Just six years later, the first railroad through Logan County was already under construction. It was to stretch from Dayton up to Lake Erie, and Benjamin Piatt was one of its directors.[24] Benjamin Piatt had not retired from the city to lead an idle life in the countryside. With the assistance of his family, farm laborers, and several tenants, he cleared the land, built mills powered by the waters of the nearby creek, and began to develop a large agricultural operation.[25]

Although civilization was arriving, Donn and his brother Abram, who became his close comrade, grew up in a countryside that kept traces of the wilderness. Charles Grant Miller's 1893 biography of Donn says he grew up "passionately fond of the forest."[26]

Old Simon Kenton had moved nearby and would sometimes visit Mac-o-cheek. He died in 1836, aged eighty-one, when Donn was almost seventeen. As a boy, Donn loved to hear Kenton tell the story of how half a century earlier he had run the gauntlet at the Shawnee village that once stood near the Piatts' house. When the Piatts came to Mac-o-cheek, there was still a mixed band of three hundred Senecas and Shawnees in Logan County. In 1830 President Andrew Jackson signed the Indian Removal Act, and the following year the leaders of that band acquiesced in the Treaty of Lewiston, which provided for their final removal to lands in Arkansas and Missouri.[27]

What Donn best remembered, though, was not the Shawnees but a band of Wyandots, who lived—until they, too, were forced to move west, in 1843—on a reservation sixty miles northeast of West Liberty. The Wyandots considered the Shawnees their younger brothers and ranged freely into traditional Shawnee territory. Piatt recalled that "it was a not uncommon event for a number of them to visit our settlement, offering skins and maple sugar for sale. A mingled feeling of fear and curiosity held me in their presence, and having heard very wild stories of their wars . . . I hung about the copper-colored sons of the forest quite fascinated."[28]

As a boy, Donn Piatt was already what might be called a spirited sort. By the time he was eight his father decided to call him Big Fire, from the name of some Indian chief. (Abram was Walk in the Water.)[29] His father, too, although he is described as having been a great gentleman, could show a hot temper. In fact, his son Donn's unusual given name is said to have resulted from a quarrel. The story, which seems credible, is that he was originally named Dunn, the married name of his wife's sister. When Dunn Piatt was still small, his father quarreled with the Dunn family and decided that his son should no longer bear that name—and so he became Donn.[30]

The new Logan County covered 440 square miles. By the time the Piatts moved there in 1829 the population was still modest but growing fast. The county had 3,181 inhabitants at the census of 1820; by 1830 there were 6,432, and 14,013 in 1840. Even then, with just over 30 inhabitants per square mile, it was a quiet rural place, depending on one's perspective. Thomas Jefferson had written earlier that when a region attained a population density of just 10 to the square mile, the inhabitants felt uneasy and began looking for vacant country.[31]

The large double log house that Benjamin Piatt built at Mac-o-cheek was far less pretentious than his father's Federal Hall—at first the rafters were exposed, and there was no plaster on the inside of the log walls—but it felt more comfortable. The family liked to say there were seventeen rooms, but as can still be seen today, some were quite small.[32] There was a good library, much of which remains today, and even a London-made piano, which the family believed was the first such instrument ever transported across the Alleghenies.

Some accounts say that Donn's mother, Elizabeth Barnett Piatt, made the house a station on the Underground Railroad, sheltering slaves during their flight north to freedom. She had been born in 1780 in Fluvanna County, Virginia, to William Barnett, a slave owner, and his second wife, Isabella Harrison, née Woodward.[33] In 1784 William Barnett moved his family and his slaves to a large tract of land he had acquired near Frankfort, Kentucky—and then he liberated his slaves. Later, he taught Elizabeth and his other children that slavery was a heinous crime.[34] Her son Donn said that she was "an earnest Abolitionist, because of her Virginia birth and life, wherein her sensitive nature was pained by the cruel practices of slavery."[35] One wonders how much she really remembered of Virginia, which she had left when she was four. Nor can we document her work on the Underground Railroad—or, for that matter, the work of many others who are said to have taken part. In any case, Donn, who seems to have been exceptionally devoted to his mother, became a strong opponent of slavery. The views of Donn's father on slavery are less clear. It seems that as a lawyer his first concern was that the laws and the Constitution be honored, even though they protected the institution of slavery.[36]

At some point the Piatts returned from the countryside to Cincinnati, to permit Jacob Wykoff, their oldest son, to attend city schools. By the time Donn reached school age they had returned to Mac-o-cheek. He was initially tutored at home by a governess and then went to the local schools, at West Liberty and later Urbana. He was also tutored by a Catholic priest, Father Collins, at Mac-o-cheek.[37] Although the Piatts had been Huguenots, Donn's mother had become a Roman Catholic around the time of Donn's birth. She eventually had a chapel of hewn logs built near the Mac-o-cheek house, where visiting priests could say Mass. She reportedly did this while her husband was away on a visit to Cincinnati. According to one of their grandchildren, when Benjamin, a Presbyterian, returned and saw the new Catholic chapel, "he was so greatly excited that in his anger he told her he would shoot any priest who entered his door."[38] She insisted that the chapel would remain and would be used. Eventually, he acquiesced and then became a Catholic himself.

Donn Piatt is said to have been "of striking personal beauty" when a boy.[39] By the time he was ten he decided to take up hunting. One day he and the younger Abram called on George Martin, a neighbor. Donn told Martin that their father had sent them to borrow his rifle, pouch, and powder horn so their father could kill a pig. The unsuspecting Martin lent them what they wanted. The boys went into the woods after wild turkeys. They found a flock; killed two and wounded another; and in chasing the wounded bird dropped Martin's gun, got lost, and spent the night in the woods. Martin found them at sunrise. As Piatt later told the story, the old hunter was angry at the loss of his rifle, mollified when the boys' father bought him a new one, and less than pleased when Donn began to outdo him in telling tall tales that included, "What boars I killed, what bears I shot, while even Indians in war paint were put to flight." This, said Piatt, led Martin to originate the maxim that "All b'ys are born liars."[40] It was not the end of tall stories told by Donn Piatt.

Donn's love for the woods continued. When he was fourteen, a young lawyer named Nathaniel C. Read came to Mac-o-cheek, on the first of many visits that culminated in his marrying the boys' sister Martha Ann. Nathaniel, Donn, and Abram went hunting, one rifle between the three of them. In the woods, Abram pointed out a wild turkey in a tree. Read grabbed the gun from Donn and got off a shot that missed the bird, which flew off unharmed. Donn berated the older Read for seizing the gun when he, Donn, was the better shot. Donn said Read could not hit a barn at a hundred yards; Read said Donn was afraid to stand at a hundred yards and be shot at. Donn reloaded the rifle, handed it to Read, marched off a hundred yards, and invited Read to blaze away. Read did so but fortunately missed his target. "There," said Donn, or so we are told, "I told you that you couldn't shoot, and now let us hear no more of your contradiction."[41]

Donn Piatt's later life gives every reason to believe the story is true. He was always ready to contest anyone, from presidents on down, whom he thought wrong. He showed both bravery and boldness. Bravery is a virtue—while boldness, virtue or not, can impede a man's prowess. It may well have done so in the case of Donn Piatt.

It was probably in that same year of 1833 that Donn was sent to the Athenaeum, a Catholic school in Cincinnati, predecessor of today's Xavier University.[42] His time there furthered an attraction to Catholicism that resulted in his final turn to the church—but only decades later.

In Cincinnati young Piatt met a number of artists. One, a young sculptor named Hiram Powers, became a close friend. Powers was a Vermonter who had come to Cincinnati as a boy in 1817. By 1827 he was carving wax mannequins for the theatrical version of Dante's *Inferno* put on by Frances Trollope.[43] One imagines young Powers and the still younger Piatt talking not only of art but of slavery, of which both became strong opponents. In 1834 Powers moved to Washington, and three years later to Florence, where he would die decades later. He soon became famous in America for his neoclassical works in marble, above all his 1843 *Greek Slave*, which became a symbol for American abolitionists.

Piatt studied at the Cincinnati Athenaeum for three years. He might have stayed longer, it was said, were it not for "a difficulty with the faculty, that resulted in his pitching the professor of mathematics out of a window."[44] Unfortunately, details

of this interesting posthumous story are lacking. Despite his withdrawal from the
school, he seems to have felt he had received a good education, better than he
would have had in public schools. Indeed, two decades later he denounced the
Cincinnati public schools as "devil's nurseries" that raised children to "commit
murder for five dollars."[45]

When young Piatt eventually returned to Mac-o-cheek, he had dreams of a
literary life. He was already a good writer and reader. When he was thirteen or
so, he had gone with others to the county jail, out of curiosity, to see a notorious
thief and murderer named Byron Cooley. Young Piatt asked Cooley to tell him his
story and afterward wrote an essay that he titled "The Career in Crime of Byron
Cooley," which he sent to the Catholic bishop of Cincinnati, John Baptist Purcell,
who was to figure later in Piatt's life. The essay was so well written that the bishop
did not at first believe it was the boy's work.[46]

Benjamin Piatt did not think his son could hope to make money in the literary
line. He sized Donn up as a fit candidate for legal work and told him he wanted
him to begin reading Blackstone's *Commentaries.* Donn demurred. His father
then suggested that he had better turn to farming.[47] This was not a threat but a
proposal. The Piatt agricultural enterprise was growing, and Benjamin needed
help. He had already decided to be not just a crop grower and animal raiser but
also a processor. Around 1840 he began to build a system of dams and channels on
Mac-o-cheek Creek, to create a headrace. Soon there was a gristmill on the creek,
and later a sawmill and a distillery as well.

Donn did not want to devote his life to farming—better to be a lawyer. He
began to read law at Mac-o-cheek under his father's guidance. We still have his diary for 1840.[48] When it begins, he is reading law in a poorly heated and poorly lit
small building near the front gate of the family property. He has company; there
are two other students, as well, Thomas J. Gallagher and Robert Bruce Warden.
He knows he must be a disciplined person, and—no doubt having read Benjamin
Franklin—he sets down the following:

> Rules.
> 1. Rise at 5 o'clock in winter, 4 in summer.
> 2. Drink no coffee, tea or other hot liquid.
> 3. Eat no meat in warm weather.
> 4. Never be idle one minute.
>   Regulations.
> 1. Write to mother [who was probably in Cincinnati] every Saturday.
> 2. Study law not less than six hours a day.
> 3. Practice music one hour a day.
> 4. Do my duty about the room and assist father.
> 5. Be punctual with my correspondents.
> 6. Write diary and go to bed at nine o'clock.

Piatt found Blackstone's *Commentaries* heavy going—with reason. Anyone making their way through the tedious pages of Blackstone's introductory chapter must agree with the great English jurist, even before reading further, that "the study of the laws is not merely a matter of amusement."[49] Time after time the student set the law aside to read Plutarch or Shelley or a life of Charles I—or to practice shooting, or go hunting or fishing or ride his horse, Robin, through the countryside. He had always been a good reader; often in the big family library he came upon a book that he had read as a child. (Diary for January 13, 1840: "Read Plutarch's life of Pyrrhus—read it when 12 years old, disappointed in the 2nd reading." March 16: "Tried to study—couldn't. Took up Peveril of the Peak. Read it when 10 years old, remembered it all as if red [*sic*] yesterday.")

If Donn's father was displeased that his son could not keep his nose either in books of law or out of Scott's novels, perhaps he did not say so. Years later Robert Warden, who had become a judge in Cincinnati, had fond memories of those years when he, Donn, and Thomas Gallagher were studying under the elder Piatt: "Sweet, unassuming, uniform in his kindness, he seemed our beau ideal of a gentleman, whilst his quaint, humourous remarks reminded one of some of Addison's and Irving's sketches."[50] It appears that Benjamin Piatt did not mind that at twenty his son was, beyond reading Blackstone, also finding time to write articles for publications including the *Catholic Telegraph* of Cincinnati and the *Ohio Statesman* of Columbus.[51]

In the spring of 1840 Donn Piatt was about to turn twenty-one. His eyes were hurting him, and a local doctor warned him that he would lose his vision if he kept on reading in bad light. He took time off for the outdoors and did not go blind, but there were other things to do, too. There were young women in his life.

On April 3 he wrote in his diary, "Talked away the afternoon to a very pretty country girl, intelligent & modest. Drank brandy until half tipsy. Made love for three hours, with the lass upon my lap sang Barbara Allen & Bonny Doon & wound up offering my heart hand & fortune to the lady. She laughed so merrily at it, that I laughed too." Two weeks later, he "saddled Robin and rode up to Zanesfield.—from that went to McGee's—spent the night with Louisa. A simple hearted country girl, who takes all you say in good earnest. Poor innocent Lambs how they suffer."[52]

How many "Lambs" were there? The day after the night with Louisa, he wrote, "Felt very stupid this morning . . . rode over to see Mary G. 'Oh! Whistle & I'll come to you my lad, Tho' Father & Mither and a' should go mad.' And mad I think they would go if they knew all."[53]

Meanwhile, he was finding yet a new interest: politics. The year of 1840 was when William Henry Harrison, the Whig candidate, ran for the presidency against Martin Van Buren, the Democrat. Benjamin Piatt was a Whig and a longtime friend of Harrison.[54] In the previous decade, Jacksonian democracy had empowered common people. Now the Whigs wanted the people to believe that Harrison, who came from a genteel Virginia family and lived in an Ohio mansion, was really a rough frontiersman. Harrison has with reason been called "the first fully packaged presidential candidate."[55]

Benjamin's sons Donn and Abram would have none of this. Despite their Whig father they decided that they were Democrats. That March, Donn went to a political discussion in the town of Urbana, ten miles south. "Col. James . . . called on me for a speech, said I wouldn't, changed my mind, began speaking. . . . Whigs began hissing and Dem. applauding. Told Whigs to go to the Devil."[56] Soon afterward, at Bellefontaine, the county seat, some man asked him to describe the differences between the Whig and Democratic platforms. Donn did so, and the man, he said, "told me, I was the smartest young man he 'knowed on' [and] I would be a great man one day.—pray heaven he prove a prophet."[57]

There were other Democrats in the village of West Liberty, two miles from Mac-o-cheek. Donn and his fellow student of the law Bob Warden decided to start a newspaper there, to be called *The Democratic Club.* It would be a new voice; the only existing newspaper in the county, the *Logan County Gazette,* was pro-Whig. Some friend provided a hundred dollars, a press was obtained, and on May 21, 1840, the paper's first issue appeared. Three decades later, when Piatt was running a larger paper in a larger place, he told his readers that the press they had used was a historic one: "The present Judge Warden, then Bob Warden, came to Logan county with that identical old press upon which Ben Franklin was taught his trade of printer. Franklin bequeathed it to Bob's uncle and the uncle, seeing in Bob another Franklin, gave him the press and enough type to set up one side of a nine by twelve sheet, and with his blessing sent the youth to achieve his fortunes."[58]

One need not believe all that Donn Piatt said in his long life, including his account of Franklin's old press making its way to western Ohio.[59] Piatt also wrote later that he and young Warden saw themselves as "Democrats not by conviction but by birth"—which perhaps he did not realize was not complimentary to his Whig father.

Donn and the *Democratic Club* made a local sensation. He spent two hours handing out copies to people who came to the printing shop. He contributed much of the content, and both in the paper and in speeches he was making he adopted a belligerent style. It was an emotional campaign, and tempers ran high. The paper's office in West Liberty was broken into by a crowd of Whigs, who threw the cases of type out the window. In Bellefontaine, Donn heard, there were people who planned to beat him up if he showed his face there again. He showed his face there, to give evidence in a trial, and was interrupted in the courtroom by the editor of the local *Gazette,* a man named Clark. Piatt followed Clark to his office and "cowhided" him. He was fined ten dollars and wrote happily in his diary that local people paid the fine for him.[60]

Even in West Liberty he and Warden got into fights.[61] Piatt was not deterred; what would life be without enemies? But, he said, what really saved the paper and its staff from further damage was a friend named Jim Moore, well muscled and six feet six inches tall. Moore suggested they make him the "'sponsible ed'tur," which was done. After that, when belligerent Whigs stormed into the office looking for the editor, they encountered the huge Moore—and calmed down.[62] (Whatever fights young Piatt got into, there is no indication that he started more than the one with the editor in Bellefontaine. In his later life he was certainly combative in what he said and wrote but never physically aggressive, although he was physically attacked at least twice.)

Young Piatt made a number of public appearances in Ohio that year, speaking for the Democrats at open-air political debates, including a large meeting at Black's Schoolhouse Grove south of Mac-o-cheek. Afterward he wrote an account of the meeting for the *Ohio Statesman,* a newspaper published in Columbus by Samuel Medary, an outspoken Democrat who was later territorial governor of Minnesota and Kansas. Young Piatt had been outspoken, too, at the meeting. For a time Medary was threatened with a libel suit by a Whig whom Piatt had mocked there.[63]

Piatt's biographer Miller says Donn Piatt was already a practiced speaker as well as writer by the time of the 1840 campaign. He had made his first speech long before, at the age of thirteen, when an atheist came to West Liberty and challenged local ministers to a debate. The clergymen refused to speak, but the challenger was told that if he still wanted a contest, he would be accommodated by an orator. The orator turned out to be young Piatt. The atheist spoke first, from the pulpit of the Methodist church, and while he spoke, Donn took notes. Then came Donn's turn to speak. The boy mounted the pulpit with his notes. He was not very tall, and someone provided a box for him to stand on. He began eloquently, but the box he was standing on gave way and he suddenly disappeared from view. The crowd applauded, and "the boy, confused and stammering, appealed to the judges for their decision, which was, of course, promptly given in his favor."[64]

The Whigs won both Ohio and the White House in the election of November 1840. The Democrats' defeat did not lessen Piatt's interest in politics, although, he wrote in his diary, "State gone to the devil."

Ohio was producing numbers of men prominent in national affairs. If the Commonwealth of Virginia was the Mother of Presidents, the state of Ohio would in the coming decades become the second parent, and not just of presidents but also of statesmen. Piatt met a number of these future stars in Ohio even as he continued to study law. Was the law his own best path? He wanted to see still more of politics and government. In December 1841, aged twenty-two, he took time off from his studies to travel to the city of Washington for the first time in his life.

He took a room at Brown's Hotel, the main resort of politicians in Washington, located at Sixth Street and Pennsylvania Avenue, between the Capitol and the White House. With two friends he called on President John Tyler, who had been Harrison's vice president and had replaced him the previous April when Harrison died, unexpectedly, just a month after his inauguration. Piatt wrote that he was not impressed by "His Accidency," nor by proceedings in the Congress. Listening to the great Henry Clay speak in the Senate, he decided that Clay was an impressive speaker, but a great man only in manner.[65] As for the president, he was "a regular old Virginian—very ugly—with a head of hair that looks as if a comb had never touched it."[66] Tyler told Piatt he was being criticized by both Democrats and Whigs in Congress. "He remarked, among other things, 'You (the Democrats) cut my throat with a keen razor; the Whigs, damn them, do it with a meat ax. Or rather, I am between two millstones, and they grind horribly.' . . . He said he was the President of the people, independent of all party. 'I have no party. They do say, indeed (laughing) that I have a corporal's guard in Congress.'"

Piatt underrated "His Accidency," who was, indeed, a man without a party. Tyler had been a Democratic senator who voted to censure a Democratic president, Jackson, and subsequently agreed to join Harrison's Whig ticket. On Harrison's death, Tyler inherited both his seat and his Whig cabinet; by the time of Piatt's visit all those cabinet members but one—Secretary of State Daniel Webster—had resigned. Nevertheless, although the Whigs turned against him and the Democrats disliked him, Tyler accomplished much. He was a skilled Washington veteran, a man with intense ambition who enjoyed the game of politics and, it has been said, "relied on political success to measure his self worth."[67]

Piatt and friends went from the White House to call on Francis Preston Blair, "Old Blair," a famous friend of presidents from Andrew Jackson onward, in his residence across the avenue from the White House, which we now call Blair House. The young man wrote happily in his diary that they and Blair and his wife and daughter had "talked for an hour or so, eating fruit and drinking wine."[68] Three decades later, Piatt was to return to the nation's capital to become a fierce and public critic of presidents, Congress, and the growing Washington crowd of lobbyists and schemers. Among those whom Piatt would come to scorn was Old Blair's son Montgomery Blair, after he had been postmaster general under a president named Lincoln.

If the young visitor from Ohio had felt honored to meet both the president and Old Blair, he was not impressed by many of the ladies of the national capital: "By the by, what an ugly set of women they have here—yellow faces, scraggy necks, worn out by late hours, ice creams, wines, hot rooms, and night air. Very few pretty ones, such as Miss Woodbury, Miss Spencer, Miss Hill, and one or two others. One can see all the beauty in Washington in half an hour."[69]

Whether she was a beauty or not, Piatt had his head turned by President Tyler's eighteen-year-old daughter, Elizabeth, when he visited the White House a second time to attend the president's New Year's Day reception. Piatt, who was just twenty-two, recalled with pleasure that when he was presented to Elizabeth Tyler, "she told me she was pleased to see Western men in the people's house at this time. 'Miss Tyler,' I replied, bowing, 'you do me proud.'"[70]

One more pleasant moment during Piatt's stay in Washington came when he visited the Library of Congress, then housed in the Capitol, and found there the marble head of Chief Justice John Marshall done by his friend Hiram Powers. He remembered the hours he had spent in Powers's dusty little studio in Cincinnati, "talking of the future, dreaming aspirations, things yet to come. And have they come? Partly, and of the rest time must tell."[71] Powers, then working in Italy, might have tempered Piatt's optimism a little had he seen him in Washington. Congress had paid Powers five hundred dollars for the Marshall bust, but other artists were paid twice as much for busts of other chief justices, and Powers felt ever afterward that doing the bust had cost him the opportunity of doing a full-length statue of Marshall. Indeed, he wrote later, he had "starved out in Washington."[72] Donn Piatt was not going to let that happen to him in the national capital—in time, his name would be made there.

❧ 2 ❧

WRITER, ENVOY, LAWYER, VOICE

Sometime in 1842, after he came back to Ohio from Washington, Piatt satisfied his father that he had mastered the law sufficiently well that he could practice it. In addition to his father, for a time he had as his teacher another able lawyer and prominent Ohioan, Thomas Corwin. At that point Corwin, in his late forties, had already been a lawyer, prosecuting attorney, state legislator, member of the U.S. House of Representatives, and governor of Ohio. In later years he would be a U.S. senator, secretary of the treasury, and minister to Mexico—as well as Piatt's courtroom opponent in a major case in Cincinnati.[1]

Piatt soon moved to Cincinnati and joined the firm of his elder brother, Jacob Wykoff Piatt, and Nathaniel C. Read, who had once fired a rifle at him and was now his brother-in-law. Charles Dickens visited Cincinnati that year and found it "a beautiful city; cheerful, thriving, and animated,"[2] but for young Piatt the law, at least, was hard slogging. His diary for 1843 is in the main a dull compendium of days spent in court, briefs written, and his financial accounts—modest accounts, with often only a dollar or two taken in. Still, he found time to make political speeches in nearby towns and take boxing lessons and attend temperance meetings. If there were to be more afternoons with pretty girls, Piatt decided, they would be without brandy. His turn away from hard drinking lasted him a lifetime; it mirrored the decrease in drinking across the country, which was due in good part to the temperance movement.[3]

That August of 1842 the firm allowed Piatt a long vacation. For the second time in his life he went east. From Cincinnati he returned to Mac-o-cheek, and then, since railroads were still few and far between, he spent a full week traveling from Ohio to New York City by stagecoach, Lake Erie steamer, canal boat, and train. He took a room at the Globe Hotel in Manhattan and then spent a day calling on three young and well-known New Yorkers.[4]

The first of these three, Park Benjamin, had been one of the editors of the *New*

England Magazine, had worked with Horace Greeley on the latter's *New-Yorker,* and was now editing a magazine called the *New World.* The second, Parke Godwin, was a journalist who worked for the *New York Evening Post,* edited by the radical Democrat William Cullen Bryant, whose son-in-law and biographer Godwin was to become. The third young man was Theodore Sedgwick, who after Columbia College had spent a heady year in Paris, dining with the Marquis de Lafayette and drinking with Alexis de Tocqueville. Sedgwick was also a *Post* contributor and had edited the writings of William Leggett, who had worked on Bryant's paper and died after a brief but fiery career. (One historian says Leggett had written "as if his pen were a cutlass" in support of freedom of opinion.)[5] Piatt left no memorandum of his talks with the three New Yorkers, but there is little doubt it was a mind-opening experience. He went home convinced that he must do much more, both in writing and in politics.

In early October 1843, when Piatt was back at work in Cincinnati, a man named Birney left the law firm, and Piatt became a full member of the firm.[6] This may have been James Birney, a son of the famous abolitionist James Gillespie Birney,[7] whom Piatt had befriended while a student in Cincinnati.[8]

In December, Piatt went to Columbus, for the first time visited the state legislature, and went to see an old love, Miss Gwynne. It was not she, however, but two other young ladies whom he squired to Christmas parties. On New Year's Eve he proposed to "Lissy"—was this Miss Gwynne or another?—but she would not have him. His diary for 1843 ends with the conclusion that it had been "a most unfortunate year."

For the next two years Piatt continued to work at the law in Cincinnati. After a number of romances he fell in love with a very attractive young woman, Louise Kirby, the eldest daughter of a wealthy Cincinnati businessman, Timothy Kirby. Born in 1826 and so seven years younger than Donn, she had attended the Academy of the Sisters of Notre Dame, a Catholic girls' school.[9] She is said to have been "not only a brilliant conversationalist, but a fascinating one as well . . . she lived in the English classics. . . . She had a keen sense of humor."[10]

Mr. Kirby was not pleased by Louise's attraction to Piatt. When he heard that the young man was seeing his daughter, he bought up various bills that Piatt owed and showed them to Louise as proof of Piatt's lack of responsibility. She responded that she would read nothing that would prejudice her against her husband—and so Kirby learned that the couple had been married.[11] Donn's brother Jacob Wykoff, who was the part-time clerk of Hamilton County, had issued the marriage license, and a Catholic priest, Father Edward Purcell—brother of the bishop—had married them secretly in August 1847.

Louise's father was eventually reconciled to the marriage but cannot have been pleased when Donn gave up his Cincinnati law practice and took his wife to live at Mac-o-cheek, in a cottage near the house his father had built. Louise found

Mac-o-cheek a paradise of fields and groves, "where wild flowers lift their gor-geous cups—where birds sing and waters sparkle." She loved it all, both sights and sounds: "the heavy rumble of the old red mill . . . the droning of bees, the chirping of crickets, and the ceaseless babbling of the brook."[12]

The couple was delighted when their son was born in 1848. They named him Charles Mac-a-chee Piatt and proudly had calling cards made for him.[13] Two years later, in 1850, the little boy died of cholera, which killed hundreds of people that summer in Cincinnati and other nearby places. Donn and Louise were dis-traught. They were never to have another child.

Piatt found law cases, though he was living in the countryside. The first two were put into his hands by his father; they were important land suits, and he won both of them.[14] Eventually, the law began to pay him fairly well, but what he liked doing best was writing. He wrote poetry, fiction, and even ballads.[15] He and Louise also did more remunerative writing: contributions to the *Cincinnati Commercial,* the *Louisville Journal,* the *Home Journal of New York* (predecessor to today's *Town & Country*), and the *National Era,* which, published in a slave-holding city—Washington—became the leading journal appealing to antislavery Southerners.[16] The editor of the *National Era* was Gamaliel Bailey, who together with James Gillespie Birney had published an antislavery newspaper, the *Philan-thropist,* in Cincinnati before moving to Washington.

It was not easy going for antislavery editors in either city, or in other parts of the country. In 1835 there had been forty-six riots in America directed at aboli-tionists.[17] One night in 1836 a Cincinnati mob broke into the *Philanthropist* of-fices, tore the press apart, and then went looking for Birney. Failing to find him, they looted black neighborhoods.[18] Among those who tried to defend the press from the mob was seventeen-year-old Donn Piatt.[19]

Later, but before his marriage, Piatt joined a Cincinnati "garrison" of volunteer police organized to counter the proslavery mobs that still gathered in the city. One of his comrades in the garrison, James Gillespie Birney's son William, wrote years later:

> The most dangerous mob in Cincinnati was the one in 1841, against the English confectioner, Burnett. He was a zealous abolitionist. . . . Having res-cued a slave girl and sent her safely to Canada, he jeered at the masters and some constables who were seeking for the fugitive. . . . A mob collected on three successive evenings to take Burnett from his house and hang him. . . . Twelve friends helped him and his two sons to defend his house. . . . Donn Piatt . . . was one of the garrison, and the writer personally knows he did his duty. Many of the assailants were severely injured. . . . [20]

Piatt did not restrict his activity on the antislavery front to defending presses and editors from mobs. On February 20, 1846, Francis A. Cunningham, a Democrat who represented western Ohio in the U.S. House of Representatives, presented in the House "A memorial of Donn Piatt and nine hundred and forty-eight others, citizens of Hamilton county, in the state of Ohio, remonstrating against the admission of Texas or any other State into the Union as a slave State."[21] Piatt had organized his fellow citizens, and they had made themselves heard as regarded the future. The memorial came too late to have any effect on Texas, which had formally become a state the day before the petition was presented in the House.

Donn returned, perhaps frequently, from Mac-o-cheek to the city. Cincinnati's population continued to grow fast; it was no longer the smallish place in which his father had made his fortune, the place where Fanny Trollope saw pigs roaming the streets. From the end of the eighteenth century until the 1830s, there were few cities or towns in America that seemed so harmonious and offered so many opportunities—and not just for lawyers like the Piatts. An artisan wrote that Cincinnati was "a fine place for mechanics. . . . Mechanics here can make their fortune in four or five years."[22] The economic boom was slowing, but Cincinnati was steadily becoming a grander city. A dozen years after Trollope's and Hall's accounts, yet another English visitor commented that the city had attained more architectural beauty in its public buildings "than probably any city of the same age on the surface of the globe."[23]

The Piatts were an attractive young couple, and a number of politicians, writers, and artists began to come to their home in the countryside.[24] Among them were Ohioans who had held top public offices, like Tom Corwin. Other prominent visitors included William M. Corry, a Cincinnati lawyer and state legislator whom people called "Citizen" Corry because a stay in revolutionary France in 1848 had given him radical views; Wilson Shannon, who had already been governor of Ohio at the age of thirty-six; William Allen, a former U.S. senator; and Allen's nephew Allen G. Thurman, a member of Congress who later became chief justice of Ohio.

One of the Piatts' more interesting guests at Mac-o-cheek was a young Irish immigrant, Thomas Mayne Reid, who as a U.S. Army officer had been seriously wounded in the charge at Chapultepec in the Mexican-American War. He had pushed on almost alone to the castle walls, under heavy fire in which he was wounded, encouraging his men to follow. Some said Mayne Reid's bravery had made the charge succeed. In the summer of 1848, after he left the army, Mayne Reid went to Newport, Rhode Island, and met the Piatts, who were vacationing there. (One surmises that the Piatts went there because Newport had a growing summer colony of artists, writers, and other intellectuals—though probably not many from Ohio.) The Piatts took a liking to Mayne Reid, who was just a year older than Donn, and invited him to spend the following winter at Mac-o-cheek. He was pleased to accept the invitation, having so far found nothing to do in civilian life but some writing for journals.

Mayne Reid spent several months at Mac-o-cheek and there wrote his first novel, *The Rifle Rangers,* a tale of adventure in Mexico based on his own Mexican service.[25] Both his hosts and their guest seem to have enjoyed one another's company—up to a point. Donn Piatt wrote later that

Mayne Reid . . . had come out of the Mexican War decorated with an ugly wound, and covered with glory as the bravest of the brave in our little army under [General Winfield] Scott.

When not making love to the fair girls of the Mac-o-Chee, or dashing over the country on my mare, he was writing a romance with the scene in Mexico and on our Mexican border. He would read chapters to us of an evening (he was a fine reader), and if the commendation did not come up to his self-appreciation he would go to bed in a huff, and, not touching pen to paper for days, would make my mare suffer in his wild rides. I found that to save [my] bay Jenny I must praise his work, and he came to regard me in time as Byron did Gifford. When told that that ugly critic had pronounced "me lord" the greatest of living poets, Byron said that he was "a damned discriminating fellow."[26]

In coming years Mayne Reid's many adventure novels would sell widely in America and Europe, including Russia. Vladimir Nabokov once recalled how when he was a boy in Russia one of Mayne Reid's novels gave him his first vision of the American West.

Another visitor to Mac-o-cheek who would soon make his name, but not in either prose or politics, was William W. Fosdick. He became a well-known writer of popular songs, including one called "Aura Lee" (the tune of which became Elvis Presley's famous "Love Me Tender" a century later).

Altogether the Piatts were running a kind of rural salon that was perhaps unique in Ohio. Soon they had a stable of not only interesting but influential friends.

By 1848 Piatt had befriended Salmon P. Chase, a native of New Hampshire and graduate of Dartmouth College who had moved to Cincinnati in 1830 to practice law. Chase early made a name for himself as the compiler of three volumes of *Statutes of Ohio*. He also made friends with leading Ohio abolitionists, including Gamaliel Bailey and James Gillespie Birney, and he acted as defense attorney for a number of Ohioans accused of assisting fugitive slaves.[27] By 1848 Chase was the de facto leader of Ohio's antislavery forces, and Piatt was one of many young Ohioans for whom, as one historian put it, Chase was "a shining example and a high ideal."[28]

Slavery remained the major issue in America. Two years earlier, in 1846, Congressman David Wilmot, Democrat of Pennsylvania, had attached to legislation in the U.S. House of Representatives a proviso that any territory won in the just-begun war with Mexico should be free of slavery. The proviso failed to win approval, but it enraged Southern slaveholders. There were already Southerners who could imagine civil war. A decade earlier, for example, a prominent professor of law in Virginia, Nathaniel Beverley Tucker, had published his novel *The Partisan Leader*, which described a revolt by a "Southern Confederacy." People in the North were not oblivious to such sentiment in the South, and many Northerners began to think that the antislavery movement might need to take a new and sharper political form. In Europe, 1848 saw a wave of democratic revolutions, which, though unsuccessful, told some Americans that turmoil could come to this country, too, if wrongs were not righted.

In July 1848 Piatt wrote Chase from Mac-o-cheek to convey what he had heard in talking with many people at political meetings. The most important of the meetings had been the Free Territory Convention, which Chase had urged be held, and which had met in Columbus in late June. A thousand delegates were present, and Piatt was elected one of the seven officers.[29] The next step, it was agreed at Columbus, should be a national convention. Soon antislavery men from across the North had agreed that this convention should be convened in Buffalo, New York, in August.

Piatt did not like slavery, but there were limits to what he wanted done about it. Like many other whites—including Abraham Lincoln—he did not think American blacks were equal to whites and he did not support the cause of abolition, as his friend Salmon Chase did. Piatt wrote years later, "We felt a sorrow that our great man should be engaged in such a vile business as acting and laboring with Abolitionists. To us, as to the community generally, an Abolitionist was not only a negro thief, but an associate of negroes and a disturber of the peace. None the less did we cling to, and seek to give Mr. Chase our protection."[30]

Piatt most recently had been a member of the "Barnburner" faction of the Democratic Party, which supported former President Martin Van Buren and which, broadening Wilmot's idea, opposed the extension of slavery into any new American territories, not only those won from Mexico. The Barnburners had just held a meeting at Utica and nominated Van Buren as their presidential candidate for the November elections. The immediate question for the Ohioans was what should happen at the Buffalo convention.

Piatt wrote Chase that if Martin Van Buren ran for the presidency, he would surely lose. He hoped that Chase would support John McLean, an Ohioan and an associate justice of the U.S. Supreme Court, for president, and John Van Buren, the former president's son, for vice president.

Piatt, together with other Barnburners, soon left the Democrats. At Buffalo it was decided to form a new, antislavery Free-Soil Party. Piatt together with Chase worked for the new party in the 1848 election campaign. Free-Soil did as the Barnburners had done and nominated Martin Van Buren as its presidential candidate.

It was a time when many men changed their party allegiances. Chase had briefly been a Whig and then had joined the antislavery Liberty Party in 1841. In 1848, believing that such a small party built on a single theme could not succeed, he played the leading role in combining Liberty with Ohio's Barnburners in Free-Soil and became the Free-Soil candidate for U.S. senator from Ohio.[31] Piatt stayed with him as elections neared.

The 1848 presidential election was won by Zachary Taylor, the Whig candidate. Lewis Cass, the Democratic candidate, ran a strong second, with almost 43 percent of the popular vote. Piatt had been right about Martin Van Buren, who got only 10 percent. But what of Chase's candidacy for the Senate?

U.S. senators were then elected by state legislatures, not by popular vote. That November Piatt assured Chase that he would be in Columbus at the beginning of the session of the legislature, to lobby for him. He told Chase that he had heard from his brother-in-law N. C. Read, now an Ohio supreme court justice, that the Free-Soil Party could have the Senate seat if the Democrats could have all the state offices in play. The virtuous Chase wrote Piatt that he "hoped the Free Soilers wd. act with conscientious regard to right, & let consequences take care of themselves."[32]

The consequences did not take care of themselves; it was a two-month struggle. On February 22 the Ohio legislature finally elected Salmon P. Chase to the United States Senate. The Democrats backed him after the Free-Soilers agreed that Democrats could take all the state offices and the Democrats agreed to repeal of the state's restrictive Black Laws of 1807—and after what must have been considerable lobbying by Piatt.[33] Chase became the Free-Soil Party's only U.S. senator. Later, he was twice elected governor of Ohio, became secretary of the treasury, and was appointed chief justice of the United States. Piatt and Chase were to remain friends until Chase died a quarter century later. Once, Chase took exception to an article Piatt had written, but then the two exchanged letters reassuring one another of their friendship.[34]

Another frequent visitor to Donn and Louise at Mac-o-cheek was Lincoln's future secretary of war, Edwin M. Stanton. Piatt and Stanton met at Columbus after Piatt's brother-in-law Read, by then a member of the Ohio supreme court, had arranged in 1842 for Stanton to become the court reporter. The job paid only three hundred dollars a year, but it gave Stanton the chance to work not just in Steubenville, his home town of fewer than five thousand people, but also in Columbus, the state capital, where he could get more important law cases and meet more influential people.

Stanton began to spend his vacations with the Piatts at Mac-o-cheek. Piatt later recalled the younger Stanton as far different from the stern war minister he was to become; he had "a most joyous nature . . . a keen sense of humor . . . a laugh . . . hearty and contagious."[35] Stanton, a devoted Episcopalian, told Piatt he was writing a book he would call *The Poetry of God,* describing how the Creator had used the highest imagery in his communications with humans.[36] (The book never appeared.) Piatt and Stanton became very close. Piatt remembered fondly that once, before he had married Louise, Stanton even traveled across Ohio to the town of Zanesville, "to reknit a love affair of mine after I had been jilted by a lovely girl."[37]

This "joyous" Stanton was clearly finding solace at Mac-o-cheek from what was great personal grief. In March 1844 Stanton's wife, Mary, had died, and his ensuing grief is said to have verged on insanity. Two years later, his brother Darwin Stanton took his own life, and Edwin Stanton "began to turn a stern face to the world."[38] Salmon Chase also suffered grievous losses—three wives and four of his six children had died by the early 1850s, as had a wayward, drunken brother, but Chase proved more able than Stanton to concentrate on his public work without family tragedy affecting it.[39]

When the 1850s began, Donn Piatt was still spending much of his time in the Ohio countryside, writing. Occasionally, he would take on a law case; not infrequently, he worked at politics, making speeches around the state and meeting a range of interesting and influential people. He does not seem to have taken much interest in the burgeoning farming and farm-related industries that his father was managing at Mac-o-cheek. Benjamin Piatt, with help from his son Abram and other family members and employees, was raising cattle and swine, growing and processing corn and wheat, and cutting what remained of the virgin forest.

The Piatts were modern farmers. Abram urged members of the Logan County Agricultural Society to increase their yields by planting corn in rows instead of hills. By doing that, the Piatts were producing 140 bushels of corn per acre on good bottom lands when other farmers in the area got no more than 40 bushels per acre. In addition, by 1850 the gristmill, sawmill, and distillery that Benjamin Piatt had built were producing yearly 28,000 barrels of flour, 100,000 feet of lumber, and 18,000 gallons of whiskey, valued altogether at over $16,000 ($400,000 or more in today's prices).[40] That was impressive, but it did not attract Donn to the business.

In 1850 the Free-Soil movement nominated for governor of Ohio the Reverend Edward Smith, with a platform claiming that the federal government had the power to end slavery in the states. That went beyond what Piatt, and other young Ohio Democrats who had become Free-Soilers but not abolitionists, believed was constitutionally possible; their main aim was to prevent extension of slavery to the territories. Piatt returned to the Democrats. His friend George Hoadly, later governor of Ohio, recalled that while many Ohioans were changing their political positions, "Donn Piatt, almost alone of his crowd, stood by his old anti-slavery flag."[41] He also returned from quiet Mac-o-cheek, in the autumn of 1851, to live in Cincinnati and practice law. Soon he had a lucrative practice.[42] That did not preclude more politicking. Piatt campaigned in Ohio for Democratic candidates, including Franklin Pierce, who won the presidency in 1852.

That same year of 1852, Piatt was elected one of the three judges of the court of common pleas of Hamilton County, of which the county seat is the city of Cincinnati. This was in effect the main court for what was now a sizable city. (Cincinnati numbered 115,435 inhabitants at the census of 1850; the next largest place in Ohio, Columbus, had a population of only 17,882; Cleveland came third with 17,034.) When Piatt first went to the bench, there were those who said his election was a joke, that he was young and inexperienced. But he worked hard at the job, and many, though not all, came to admire his work. None of his decisions was reversed by a higher court.[43]

Judge Piatt took a liking to a graduate of Kenyon College and Harvard Law School named Rutherford Birchard Hayes,[44] who was just a year younger than he was. Hayes had come to Cincinnati in 1850 to practice law and had made a slow start; it had taken him six weeks to earn his first retainer, five dollars. In some cases a judge was called on to appoint a lawyer as a defense counsel; many of Hayes's cases were court appointed, by Piatt and his fellow Cincinnati judges. In April 1852 Hayes acted as the assistant defense counsel in the murder trial of James Summons, before a panel of three judges including Donn Piatt. One of the other two judges was Stanley Matthews. There had already been three mistrials in the case. This time, despite Hayes's efforts, Summons was found guilty. (Later he was pardoned by Ohio's governor, Salmon P. Chase.)[45] Nevertheless, young Hayes began to make a name for himself—though little income—as a defender of murderers and runaway slaves.[46] A quarter century later Stanley Matthews would be instrumental in having him declared president of the United States after one of the most fiercely disputed elections in American history; and Hayes as president would name Matthews to the United States Supreme Court. Piatt and Hayes were friends, but Matthews and Hayes had been classmates at Kenyon College and were closer friends.

Piatt was still in his early thirties when he became a judge in Cincinnati. When he visited Washington soon after receiving his appointment, a friend there presented him to the well-known author of *The Scarlet Letter* and *The House of Seven Gables,* Nathaniel Hawthorne, saying, "We have a habit out west, Mr. Hawthorne, of putting our young men on the bench to study law." This, Piatt told a journalist decades later, embarrassed him seriously. After all, even if he was new on the bench, he was not a raw youth; he had been a lawyer for a decade. The distinguished novelist, who was fifteen years older than Piatt and a shy, sensitive man himself, sensed Piatt's discomfiture. He took him aside and spent two hours talking with him. And, said Piatt, this began a friendship that lasted until Hawthorne's death, in 1864.[47]

At about this time—according to one account, the autumn of 1853, when Donn Piatt was far from Ohio—three slaves ran away from a Piatt family that lived near Covington, Kentucky. The three made their way across the Ohio River to Cincinnati, where Levi Coffin, the unofficial president of the Underground Railroad,[48] put them on a train to go north to Sandusky, on Lake Erie. From there they would be able to cross to safety in Canada. But the Kentucky Piatts telegraphed north to a relative living near Bellefontaine—the county seat of Logan County—and the relative had the fugitives taken off the northbound train when it stopped at Bellefontaine. The local abolitionists had the man, presumably Benjamin Piatt, taken to court.

Despite the abolitionists' action, things looked bad for the fugitives. The Fugitive Slave Act of 1850, more draconian than the earlier act of 1793, placed the power of the federal government behind the recovery of slaves who fled their masters. There were harsh penalties both for law officers and for private persons who refused to assist in the recovery. Many Northerners were outraged by this legislation; it had recently led Harriet Beecher Stowe, who had lived in Cincinnati and visited the homes of Kentucky slave owners, to write the new national bestseller, *Uncle Tom's Cabin.*

When court proceedings had gotten under way in Bellefontaine and the court-room was packed with the curious, the abolitionists quietly spirited the three slaves away to the village of Northwood. There, students at a little college called Geneva Hall hid them for two weeks and then got them safely to Sandusky and onto a steamer to Ontario.[49]

There is also, however, a different account. On December 31, 1852 (not 1853), the newspaper that African American leader Frederick Douglass was publishing in Rochester, New York, carried a report of a recent "stampede" among Kentucky slaves, during which a number of them had succeeded in making their escape. Three had gotten onto a northbound train in Ohio and, Douglass reported,

> On the cars they were met by one Don Piatt, an ex judge of the Hamilton Common Pleas Court. He recognized them as the property of a relative. He approached them, made himself known to them, told them that his father, who resides near West Liberty, was in want of laborers, and he assured them that if they would stop with him, that he (Don) and his friends would purchase them, and give them their freedom. The fugitives confided in him—left the cars at West Liberty and took up quarters with old Piatt. After they had been there a few days the arrangement between Don and the fugitives leaked out, and the result was that the friends of the fugitives, who understood the character of the Piatts, sued out a writ of *habeas corpus* requiring old man Piatt to bring them before a judge at Bellefontaine, and to show by what authority he held them. Piatt not being able to show any authority for detaining them, the negroes were declared to be free to go where they pleased. They were immediately taken in charge by some abolitionists and started on their way to Canada—Within two hours after, the Kentucky claimants arrived in hot pursuit of their "property." But they found nobody there to promote their object.

Is Frederick Douglass saying that Donn Piatt played a part in trying to return fugitive slaves to their owners? At the end of 1852 he was not, as Douglass wrote, an ex-judge. He was still on the bench at Cincinnati; but one assumes that he may have met the fugitives on the train when he was returning to Mac-o-cheek for a visit. Piatt was a man who had defended an antislavery editor from a Cincinnati mob and had defended in court persons accused of violating the Fugitive Slave Act; a man who in 1846 had engineered a petition to Congress opposing the ad-mission to the Union of a new slave state. Douglass's account does not, on the face of it, place blame on Donn Piatt. It does leave open the possibility that it was his father, who believed that laws must be obeyed   including the Fugitive Slave Act of 1850—who had sent word to Kentucky relatives about the escaped slaves.

Indeed, Donn Piatt himself said that his father had done so, in a story that he published decades later in a volume of "tales." In the story, the slaves numbered not three but twenty, and they belonged to Donn's grandfather, who had in fact died years earlier but who in the tale "felt very much relieved at their going, and hoped steps might be taken to prevent their return." But even if Donn was telling a tale, at a guess his father really was the man who sent word South that three slaves had reached West Liberty.[50]

Donn Piatt was making a good start as a judge, but he wanted more. His new acquaintance Nathaniel Hawthorne had written a campaign biography of Franklin Pierce, and in 1853 the president appointed Hawthorne American consul at Liverpool, where Hawthorne hoped to have a sizable income from consular fees. Piatt, too, had campaigned for Pierce, and he hoped the president would name him U.S. envoy to Portugal. The United States had no career foreign service at that time, or for decades afterward. It was political connections that counted in the American foreign affairs spoils system—a system that continues today in the United States alone among advanced nations.[51]

Both diplomatic and consular posts were then much sought after. Ohio's governor Reuben Wood, who had named Piatt a judge in 1852, resigned his governorship in 1853 to take a job abroad that had less prestige than the post Piatt hoped for but promised a sizable income: that of American consul at Valparaiso. Alas, Wood wrote Secretary of State William A. Marcy after arrival in Chile, while President Pierce himself had told Wood that the Valparaiso job was worth $18,000 to $26,000—consuls were not paid a salary but lived from fees collected—he had found that the most he could make honestly as consul was only $6,000 a year.[52] That was still a large income for the time.

Why Piatt wanted to go to Lisbon is not known. It was not an exciting place. Portugal had been in decline since the loss of its largest colony, Brazil, three decades earlier, and the American legation at Lisbon was a small post. The American envoy there bore the title of chargé d'affaires, less senior than the rank of minister borne by envoys at larger legations. (The highest level of diplomatic representation is that of an ambassador, whose post is an embassy. Until 1893 the United States had neither ambassadors or embassies, only ministers and legations, on grounds that Americans wanted a relatively low level of governmental involvement with foreign countries.)

Perhaps Piatt asked for Lisbon because he would not seem to be overreaching in asking for the job. In any case, the pay was not bad. Consuls at posts like Valparaiso could expect to make more than some American diplomats did, but the salary of the chargé d'affaires at Lisbon was a good $4,500 a year, and the new chargé d'affaires would receive an additional year's salary as an "outfit" on leaving Washington for his new post plus an "infit" of one quarter's salary on completion of his mission. The previous envoy at Lisbon had been Charles B. Haddock, a New

Hampshireman no more prominent than Donn Piatt. (Haddock did have one distinction; he was the nephew of former Secretary of State Daniel Webster.)

Records in the National Archives indicate that by now Piatt had impressive and extensive connections across the Midwest. He secured recommendations for the Lisbon job that were sent to President Pierce and Secretary Marcy by the governors of Ohio and Michigan, as well as fifty-seven members of the Ohio legislature; several Ohio editors; and several members of Congress, including Senator Stephen A. Douglas of Illinois. But Secretary Marcy also received a letter from Cincinnati Democratic leader Andrew Giffin, expressing hope that Piatt, a "Political, Avaricious Demagogue," would not be given a post.[53] (Giffin did not explain why he thought Piatt a demagogue, but two years later a certain H. S. Thomas wrote the *National Era* that "Piatt and other demagogues" had supported "the foreigners . . . allies of the slave holder and rum-dealer." Editor Gamaliel Bailey replied that Thomas was totally off the mark; the proslavery mobs he had seen in Cincinnati were composed not of immigrants but of native-born Americans.[54] In any case, Piatt was no supporter of slaveholders but was strongly opposed to slavery.)

The Lisbon job went to a better-known Democrat, John L. O'Sullivan of New York, a leader of the Young America wing of the party and the founder of the *Democratic Review*.[55] Still, it seemed something had to be done for the Ohioan. For a time it was proposed to make Piatt the secretary of legation at London. The minister at London was James Buchanan, the former secretary of state, and Piatt as secretary of legation would be Buchanan's deputy. In the end, though, the London job went to a young man named Daniel Sickles, whom Buchanan knew and wanted—and who had not just campaigned for Franklin Pierce, as Piatt had done, but had voted for him as a delegate at the 1852 Democratic convention. Secretary Marcy opposed the nomination of Sickles; President Pierce approved it.[56]

Eventually, Pierce and Marcy agreed to name Piatt the secretary of legation at Paris. The new American minister to France was to be John Y. Mason, a Virginian in his fifties, a Democrat who had been both secretary of the navy and attorney general. Piatt would be Mason's deputy. Even if he would not head the mission, he would hold a position of some prestige in a major capital. The Emperor Napoleon's nephew Louis-Napoleon Bonaparte had been elected president of the French Republic in 1848 and in 1851 staged a coup d'état that made him Emperor Napoleon III. France would undoubtedly continue to play a key role—perhaps the key role—on the European continent.

Aside from the money and the importance of France, the great smoky city of Paris may not have seemed an ideal place for the Piatts. Louise's health was failing. She had spent much of the winter of 1852–53 in Washington, in the hope that the climate there might be better for her than the Ohio valley. She had, however, overtaxed herself in Washington, spending many days listening to debates in the Senate and, inter alia, meeting William Makepeace Thackeray when he visited

Washington after Cincinnati. ("I sat by the side of the eminent Thackeray . . . and he had the kindness to tell me I was a *delightful* woman. I certainly was a delighted one. Yet he does not talk as he writes—not half so charming.")[57] What ailed Louise is not known. One physician has suggested to the author that her heart might have been weakened by rheumatic fever, a streptococcal infection not uncommon in the days before antibiotics.

Nevertheless, in August 1853 Donn, Louise, and her fifteen-year-old sister, Ella Kirby, sailed to France on the steamship *Franklin*.[58] Louise wrote her father that during the Atlantic crossing both Donn and her sister were seasick for some days.[59] Louise, however, was determined not to feel ill and said she missed no meals. In fact, she clearly enjoyed the voyage. There were a number of more or less interesting passengers, including the French minister to Mexico, who could talk for twelve hours straight; the Swedish consul at Charleston, who, despite the rolling seas, for breakfast had a bottle of ale, several cups of coffee and of tea, and ham and eggs without limit; a grandson of John Jacob Astor, who "walks on his toes, talks about the Rhine and tells stale college jokes"; and Mrs. Samuel Ward of New York, "a lady so traveled as to be entirely foreign," and her daughter Genevieve. The two last-named ladies were later to be involved romantically in Europe with the same Russian prince, and their unfounded complaints to various American legations—including Donn Piatt's in Paris—are richly documented.[60] More than twenty years later, Genevieve Ward, by then a well-known singer, was to complain to a Pennsylvania paper that when the Paris prefect of police had demanded her papers, Piatt had given them to him.[61] He had had reason to do so; the Wards caused useless trouble for various European police departments, as well as for American legations. It was not the Wards who had reason to complain.

In some ways the Paris air, smoky or not, proved to be as good for Louise as the sea air had been. A month after her arrival, writing as "Bell Smith," she began to contribute to the *Home Journal* and the *National Era* a series of sprightly, funny pieces on France and the French that later appeared as a book, *Bell Smith Abroad*.[62] Donn, too, sent reports from France to both American and British papers.[63] He did not receive his diplomatic commission until April 1854, after his brother Abram wrote the president to remind him of his promise.[64] It seems possible that the administration had wanted to wait until Mason had arrived in Paris, which he did at the end of January. By now Piatt was reportedly proficient in French—Mason was not—and even before Piatt received his commission, he provided the new minister with what Mason told Secretary Marcy was "valuable service."[65]

Mason's American counterpart across the Alps in Turin was another Virginian. This was a Democratic editor from Richmond named John Moncure Daniel, a fiery fellow, although he was already suffering from the tuberculosis that would kill him before he reached forty.[66] Daniel sometimes went to Paris to consult physicians and to see Mason, whom he considered his mentor. Daniel and Piatt, both of them much younger than Mason, soon became acquainted. Whether they became friends seems doubtful. Conceivably, there was some jealousy on the part of Piatt, who was junior to Daniel in rank although six years older.

Minister Mason's most memorable contribution to American diplomacy was the so-called Ostend Manifesto, the product of his meeting at Ostend on the Belgian coast, in October 1854, with his counterparts from London (James Buchanan) and Madrid (Pierre Soulé). The Manifesto warned Spain that its misrule in Cuba might force the United States to take over the island (which American presidents had long hoped to acquire peacefully by purchase). It did so in a ham-handed way, reinforcing Northern fears about Southern hopes—and there were such hopes—of extending U.S. slaveholding territories southward into the Caribbean.[67] The Manifesto raised ridicule as well as fears in America, while people in Europe saw it as a crude if not atypical example of American diplomacy.

Piatt wrote about Mason's participation in the adventure, or misadventure, years later in an article for *Harper's*. As he said, Ostend did nothing for Mason, but it had a positive outcome at least for James Buchanan: "Southern politicians saw in this man a creature they could mold to their own traitorous purposes— even then clearly defined. They were not mistaken. The Minister who had unhesitatingly appended his signature . . . in the hope of such a reward as was eventually given him, occupied the Presidential chair in stolid indifference for four years; while, to his knowledge, the most active preparations were being made for the destruction of the government that had so honored him."[68]

But that fate remained in the future. More immediately, the French government, angered by the crippling of the French ambassador to Spain by U.S. Minister Soulé in a duel, told Mason after the Ostend meeting that they would not let Soulé, who had gone from Ostend to London, return through France to his post at Madrid. It was not the first time Soulé, who was born in France, had run into trouble with the French authorities; he had been exiled from the country for revolutionary activity and had settled in Louisiana.

Mason sent Piatt to Calais to meet Soulé, who had not heard that he was being refused entry and had already landed at Calais and been forced to return to London. Piatt went on to London, where Soulé told him—as Mason reported to the secretary of state—that "neither by deed, nor by words uttered or written, has he afforded the shadow of a pretence for the wanton measure."[69] Eventually, after Mason protested to the foreign minister, the French relented and let Soulé transit France.[70]

In November 1854 Piatt was sent to Washington with a number of dispatches, notably Mason's report to the State Department on the Ostend meeting. The other big subject of the day, on which the Paris legation did a considerable amount of reporting to Washington, was France's alignment with its ancient enemy Britain in the Crimean War against Russia.[71]

Piatt cannot have enjoyed the prospect of leaving his wife for over a month, but she would be near good friends the Piatts had made in their first year in Paris. If Louise should need to consult a physician, there was an American doctor named

Rawlings, whom John Moncure Daniel consulted on visits from Turin (and who may have been the first to diagnose the tuberculosis that eventually killed Daniels in Virginia, with Rawlings at his side, at thirty-nine).

An Atlantic crossing was always an adventure. Piatt traveled to England and sailed from Liverpool on the *Baltic*, a luxurious paddlewheel steamer of the Collins Line. Just two months earlier the *Baltic*'s sister ship, *Arctic*, had collided with another ship off Newfoundland and over three hundred passengers died. *Baltic* came through and arrived in New York late on November 25.[72]

Piatt went down to Washington for what proved to be a memorable couple of days. He wrote Mason that when he delivered his dispatches to Marcy, the secretary of state said that they had been waiting for them in order to complete the president's report on Ostend. Piatt then went to call on the secretary of war, Jefferson Davis, who "expressed himself delighted in seeing me and immediately went off into praise of the most extravagant character of you and your conduct in the Soulé affair." Later in the day he again saw Marcy, who, he wrote Mason, "said he and the President were pleased by the able manner in which you had conducted the affair."

The next day Piatt called at the White House, where he found that President Pierce was holding a Cabinet meeting. "The President however came out smiling[,] took both my hands and said 'Why[,] you and Judge Mason are heaping honors on us.' He had no time to talk but insisted on my taking dinner with him tomorrow—and said he had a thousand questions to ask—and a vast number of messages to send to his 'dear good friend Judge Mason.'"

Nor was this the end of Piatt's high-level Washington encounters. He saw James Campbell, the postmaster general, who said, "Tell Judge Mason for me by G-d that he has covered himself with glory," and Caleb Cushing, the attorney general, who told him frankly that, as Piatt wrote Mason, "Judge Mason was much blamed at first for his rather kind and flattering course towards the French government—but these events evince the wisdom of it."

Piatt reported to Mason that he had found on his brief visit to Washington that behind the scenes, "the administration is waterlogged, rolling helplessly—and between Marcy and the President exist very ugly and uncomfortable feelings." Nor did Marcy have any love for the envoy at London; Buchanan had been his rival in seeking the election to the White House that Pierce had won.

Piatt continued,

Gov. Marcy said yesterday among other things "they are using the Legation at London for the purpose of giving American passports to political offenders and spreading revolutionary documents over Europe—complaints are continually being made to us—and this made us suspicious of the Soulé affair. It has injured the consultation at Ostend. I did not want Sickles and Sanders [George N. Sanders, the consul at London and a radical, pro-slavery Democrat] mixed up in it." I asked then why Mr. S. [Soulé] had been selected to be the bearer of so important and delicate [an] affair. "God only knows" he answered. "Forney [John W. Forney, clerk of the House of Representatives and, like Buchanan, a Pennsylvania Democrat] . . . arranged everything. The President can say why— I cannot." I asked him why he did not relieve Mr. Buchanan from his heavy labors. He turned sharply and asked me why. "Oh" I said "he complains of these weighty cares that our unfortunate party is forced to put upon—" He looked at me from under those shaggy brows for a moment and then laughed. "Oh you mean he takes great credit to himself?" No[,] I replied, on the contrary he complains of the responsibility.[73]

Within a few days Piatt took ship again for Europe. He was happy to find Louise in fair health. His Washington visit had been a heady experience; it must inevitably have stirred his ambitions.

Soon after Piatt returned to the Paris legation, in January 1855, Minister Mason suffered the first of several strokes. He took off for the warm South of France, hoping to recover. The legation informed the French foreign minister that Piatt "would be in charge of the affairs of the legation."[74] That was not quite the same as being the chargé d'affaires, since Mason was still in the country and therefore, under international law and diplomatic practice, still in charge.

In any case, for four months Piatt ran the post. Before Mason fell sick he had thought well enough of Piatt's work to recommend him to President Pierce for promotion. A similar recommendation had been made by Pierre Soulé, who apparently gave Piatt credit for getting the French to lift their ban on his entering France.

Piatt had immediately reported Mason's illness to Secretary Marcy. In January 1855 Piatt wrote Marcy a further, confidential letter about Mason that would no doubt have infuriated Mason—with good reason—had he learned of it. Piatt reported that Mason was continuing to improve and his mind had not been affected. "I presume," he added, "that the Judge [Mason] will wish to retire to his farm and pass the remainder of his well-spent life quietly. . . . These are speculations of my own only, as the Judge's life, for the present, depends upon his entire exemption from cares of all sort—and a consideration of his private affairs—distressing as they are—would at once be fatal." Piatt then went on to suggest that when the time came for Buchanan to leave London, Marcy might wish to consider sending Mason to London. This was the first time, Piatt wrote, that a public servant had been struck down in the discharge of his duties, and if Mason were to be sent to London, "I think the country would sustain the administration in an act, that would at once recognise his great service and lift him from the pecuniary troubles that may yet embitter his old age. I may be writing indiscreetly—but it comes from impulses which I know you will pardon."[75]

Did Marcy know before he received this letter that Mason's finances were in bad shape (as was the case)? Why did Piatt suggest Mason should retire and then propose he be sent to London? Piatt must have reasoned that if Mason left Paris, either for London or for retirement, he himself would be a good successor as U.S. minister. He was indeed writing indiscreetly. His ambition is all too evident in the self-serving letter, which does not do him credit. Nor did it result in his promotion.

Before Mason fell sick, Piatt had had—or so he wrote later—considerable respect for him. He found Mason peevish and querulous after his strokes.[76] Piatt eventually decided that he could no longer serve under him, resigned, and returned to America in October 1855.[77]

Mason wrote his colleague in Turin, John Moncure Daniel, that Piatt had not even said good-bye, that creditors were complaining that Piatt had left large debts, and that he had degraded his official position. Legation files indicate that Mason's complaints were exaggerated. Piatt left Paris before the lease on his house expired but said he thought the landlord was agreeable to his doing so; he made no farewell visit to Mason but wrote him a perfectly polite letter saying he was leaving suddenly to catch a ship on which he had just been promised a stateroom.[78] (Louise had already returned to America.) He had asked a friend to act as his agent in Paris and forward any bills to him.[79]

The only clear misconduct on Piatt's part while he was in Paris—which Mason was probably not aware of—was his issuance of an American passport to an Italian republican revolutionary named Gaspare Belcredi. In late 1855 Belcredi was arrested in Piedmont by the Sardinian authorities on suspicion of subversive activity. He showed an American passport signed by Piatt in Paris and was released. Minister Daniel heard of this and invited Belcredi to the Turin legation. The man hardly spoke English; Daniel doubted that he was really an American citizen and wrote to Piatt for confirmation of the man's status. Piatt wrote back from Paris that "Belcredi (may he be hung) was I suppose a citizen of my creation."[80]

That was bad enough, but America's minister in London, James Buchanan, who would soon become president, did something of the same, signing a blank passport that ended up in the hands of another Italian revolutionary.[81] Worse, Buchanan imprudently attended a dinner in London given by the consul, George Sanders, that featured as guests almost every prominent European revolutionary, from Alexander Herzen to Giuseppe Mazzini. If this had come out in public, it would have complicated, to say the least, American relations with Europe's monarchical governments. Even if nothing was published about the dinner, it may well have become known to other governments and occasioned one of the "complaints" that Marcy had told Piatt were being made about Buchanan's legation.

Piatt was not the only person to find Mason much changed by his illness; Mason was later viewed in Washington as "impotent from disease."[82] He was also a profligate, who was to die penniless after spending large sums to entertain Napoleon III and his entourage—what Attorney General Cushing had more politely called Mason's "rather kind and flattering course" toward the French. Mason's once considerable estate had also been depleted by financial reverses and by his liability for debts incurred by relatives.[83] One wonders whether such worries helped bring on his strokes.

Among the differences between Mason and his deputy was the fact that Mason was a Virginia slaveholder, while Piatt was strongly antislavery. More immediately, while Piatt and his wife came from well-to-do families, they did not care for the fifteen or so wealthy American families resident in Paris whose members were close to Mason. These were people whose greatest regret, Louise wrote, was that they could not buy themselves titles. In Donn's view they were "an insufferable set of snobs."[84] For their part, the Piatts did what they could to help the American travelers and residents who found themselves short of funds, or otherwise in difficulty, in Paris. Louise, in particular, made friends of a number of American artists who lived there,[85] including George P. A. Healy, who painted Donn's portrait and would later become famous for his many portraits of leaders on both sides of the Atlantic. Aside, perhaps, from the fifteen rich families, Paris Americans liked the young couple from Ohio.[86]

In Paris the Piatts had befriended Horace Greeley, famous founder of the *New York Tribune,* when he went as U.S. commissioner to the Paris exposition of 1855. Soon after they met, Greeley was arrested by the French authorities, on the complaint of a sculptor whose work had not been returned after the recent New York world's fair, of which Greeley had been a director. Lawyer and author Maunsell B. Field recalled how, on a June afternoon, he had seen a fiacre containing Greeley and several French bailiffs draw up in front of the American legation. Piatt came out of the building and had a heated talk in French with the bailiffs, trying to convince them to release Greeley and insisting that he would guarantee Greeley's appearance in court if that proved necessary. Piatt spoke good French, but what he said did not impress the bailiffs. He wrote years later, "It was not wise to rush into that conflict without our diplomatic coat. Could we have added the cocked hat with national tail feathers of the American rooster, it would have been well. The French mind respects the diplomatic position, being a civilized, a polite nation, and finds in the clothes thereunto belonging conclusive evidence of mysterious powers. Now our diplomacy did not get beyond the legs. . . . We might have kicked a French official, but he in return, while respecting our diplomatic legs, could have punched our unofficial head."[87]

Greeley knew no French but nevertheless began shouting at the bailiffs and tried to get out of the carriage. The officers of the law thrust him back into the carriage; then they alighted and tied their tricolor sashes around their waists in a self-important way—leading Piatt to laugh. The bailiffs asked haughtily if the American diplomat was ridiculing the colors of France. Soon Piatt and the bailiffs were shouting at each other, while from inside the carriage Greeley's squeaky voice could be heard saying, "Take me to jail! Take me to jail!" The officers of the law did just that; they climbed back into the fiacre and drove the captive editor to Clichy prison.[88]

Greeley had not been long in his cell when he was visited by the ailing Minister Mason, who seemed to Greeley more worried about the situation than Greeley himself was. Half an hour later arrived Louise Piatt, bringing the editor's wife and son. Greeley's wife told him that Louise had come to see her as soon as she had heard of the arrest, to assure her that she need not worry. Donn Piatt wrote later that it was he who had convinced Mason to intervene with the French authorities on behalf of Greeley and that initially Mason's reaction "was graced with certain hard language, to the effect that said 'Greeley was a black abolition son of a female dog,' or words to that effect."[89]

The prisoner was released on the following Monday, after a judge ruled that he should not have been arrested in the first place, since Piatt had guaranteed his appearance in court.[90] Greeley left for New York at the end of July and never made another trip to Europe.

When Piatt left Paris that autumn, the New York Times reported that he was working on a book on American diplomacy that would describe how the American minister to France had sat, awkward and perspiring, for three hours at a state dinner without speaking or being spoken to.[91] Before leaving, Piatt wrote Greeley to ask him to publish something in the Tribune about the sad state of affairs at the Paris legation. Greeley replied in a friendly letter, declining to do so lest it should appear that some blame should attach to Piatt. He added that he hoped Piatt would look after Greeley's wife and son, who he thought might return to New York on the ship that Piatt was taking; he looked forward to seeing the Piatts in Washington.[92] The friendly though not close relationship between Piatt and Greeley was to continue as years passed.

Piatt's book on diplomacy never appeared. Some years later, though, in a magazine article, he wrote mockingly and indeed accurately of Napoleon III as "a little fellow in gaudy court dress . . . no Bonaparte, nor is he a great man. . . . This man is a sham and a fool." But he described his late chief, Mason, in terms that if critical were far milder than he was capable of using.[93] One senses that he felt a little sorry for Mr. Mason. Still later he would write that before suffering his first stroke, Mason had been "a kind, considerate—I may say, lovable—sort of a man. . . . Ill health transformed Judge Mason from a patient, polite gentleman, to one who was weak, peevish and unreasonable. . . ."[94] (After Piatt left Paris, Mason decided he did not want another Northerner. His next secretary of legation was a fellow Virginian, O. Jennings Wise, whose father was the state's governor, Henry Wise.)[95]

One of the consequences of Piatt's Paris service was debt. His salary as secretary of legation was $2,000 per annum; Mason was paid $7,500 as minister. While Mason was laid up from his strokes, Piatt had seen the need to engage in more representational activity, as the interim head of the American mission. He had also had to pay out of his own pocket for his trip to Washington with the dispatches reporting the Ostend Manifesto. He was not then the wealthy man he would become, and it hurt him to expend thousands of dollars more than he was earning.

Returned from Paris, in the autumn of 1855 Donn joined Louise at Mac-o-cheek. He was distressed to learn in November that the Paris correspondent of the *New York Daily Times* had reported that a gentleman connected with the Paris legation had returned to America suddenly, leaving unpaid bills totaling eight or ten thousand dollars. He fired off a long letter to the paper saying that the reference was clearly to him and the report was untrue. He did not, he said, owe eight or ten thousand; an eighth part of that would pay all he owed in the world; and before leaving Paris he had asked a friend, Charles J. Fleischmann, to be his agent and forward to him any unpaid bills.[96]

Nor, Piatt wrote the *Times,* was it true that he had left Paris suddenly. Since his private affairs had been dragged before the public, he wanted readers to know, first, that "the American honor is yet safe, so far as I am concerned," and, second, that he had been called on to act as chargé d'affaires for half a year, while receiving only his inadequate salary as secretary of legation. He was not, he said, a man of fortune, and in carrying out his official duties he had had to expend eight thousand dollars of his private means.

Gamaliel Bailey's *National Era* published "with pleasure" the full text of the letter from Piatt;[97] there were reports in other papers that Piatt had acted badly. Although the same accusations would be resuscitated by his enemies years later, Piatt would, as earlier, know how to defend himself.

Piatt stayed at Mac-o-cheek until January 1856 and then went to Washington to look for things to write about. Throughout his life it was writing fiction, poetry, and drama that most attracted him; but belles lettres never proved very profitable for him.

At some point Piatt ran into his Ohio friend Edwin Stanton on a Washington street. For a second, he wrote later, Stanton's face lit up with pleasure, but then a sad and gloomy expression took its place and Stanton's manner turned cold. To Piatt it seemed not hostility but a kind of indifference. He walked with Stanton to his room at the National Hotel, and he could see that Stanton was trying, without success, to be pleasant to him. He left Stanton, but in another minute remembered there was a message he wanted to give him, and returned to Stanton's room. When Piatt knocked, there was no answer. He walked in and found Stanton seated at the table, in tears. Piatt wrote, "Shocked and astonished, I stammered out my message. 'Yes, yes,' he said, wiping his eyes, 'It is very kind of you, Donn, but not now, please, not now.'" This was neither the jolly man who had liked to visit the Piatts at Mac-o-cheek nor, Piatt wrote, the future secretary of war, "stern, vindictive, and often in manner brutal." It was a man, Piatt knew, who had suffered the death of his dear companion from youth, his first wife, and he would perhaps never be lighthearted again.[98]

Piatt soon left Washington to go back to Ohio, presumably by the end of March, when William Makepeace Thackeray, already a notable figure among English writers, gave two lectures in Cincinnati during his second American

tour.[99] We are told that Piatt entertained him there "at a notable dinner."[100] Did
Thackeray discuss the question of slavery with Piatt, who strongly opposed it?
On both his visits to America Thackeray toured the South, including Richmond,
Virginia, many of whose inhabitants were slaves. Thackeray's fellow countryman
Charles Dickens had found Richmond a place where, despite pretty villas, the
overall scene was set by the decay and gloom of slavery. In contrast, Thackeray
wrote home to England that the blacks in Richmond, slaves as well as freemen,
were obviously happy and well off.[101] After he returned to England, he wrote *The
Virginians,* a novel set during the American Revolution, as a tribute to those cour-
teous white ladies and gentlemen he had met in Virginia.

In the spring of 1856 Piatt joined two other lawyers in Cincinnati in defending
a number of Irish Americans in federal court, in what Ohioans called the "filibusters case."

For Americans in the middle of the nineteenth century, a filibuster commonly
meant not a long speech to delay legislation but a freebooter carrying on unauthorized military action against a foreign country. Between 1848 and 1860,
American filibusters put together perhaps two dozen plots aimed at taking over
portions of Mexico, and there were similar plots aimed at Central America and
Spanish-ruled Cuba.[102] The most famous of the American filibusters, William
Walker, had invaded Baja California three years earlier and tried to set up a new
republic. Failing in Mexico, in 1855 he invaded Nicaragua with a small force, and
by the time of the trial in Cincinnati, Walker had succeeded in taking over that
Central American republic. The United States government was soon to recognize
his Nicaragua regime, but it did not last. Nor did Walker himself last much longer;
he was shot by a firing squad in Honduras in 1860.[103]

The defendants in the 1856 Cincinnati filibuster trial were members of the Robert Emmet Club, a branch of the Irish Emigrant Aid Association of Ohio. Emmet
was the Irish patriot who had led a rebellion against British rule in Ireland and
was executed in 1803. The Emmet Club had been organized in Cincinnati some
months previously and had a total of only seventy-three members, but it hoped
for the creation of similar clubs across Ohio. The prosecution charged that club
members intended to violate the Neutrality Act of 1818 by organizing an invasion
of Ireland with the aim of securing Irish independence. The last Irish uprising
against the British had occurred not long since, in the revolutionary year of 1848.
It had failed miserably, but that did not end the hopes of Irish nationalists, including many who had come to America.

The filibuster case raised high feelings in Cincinnati, particularly among the
numerous Irish Americans in the city, many of whom thronged to the courtroom.
One imagines that, as a democrat who opposed slavery and oppression and had
recently issued an American passport to an Italian revolutionary, Piatt was happy
to assist in the defense. The federal prosecution team was headed by Tom Corwin,
the former legislator, governor, and law teacher of Donn Piatt. The case went on

for almost a month. It turned out that the main and not very credible witness for the prosecution had been paid a hundred dollars by the British consul in Cincinnati, who had strongly urged that the trial be held. In the end, Piatt and his colleagues beat Corwin and secured the discharge of the defendants.[104]

By now Piatt, though always a democrat, had left the Democratic Party, as had many others. In the summer of 1856 he took an active part in the campaign of John Charles Frémont, the presidential candidate of the new Republican Party, making speeches on Frémont's behalf across Ohio.[105] Piatt felt he had good reason to leave the Democrats. They had been the party of Andrew Jackson, who had done so much to empower common people; but they were also the party of Southern slave owners, and Donn Piatt was, as always, firmly opposed to slavery. In addition, he, like many other Americans, who not seldom choose heroes (or supposed heroes) to be president, was attracted by Frémont as an individual. Frémont was an intrepid explorer of the West and the man who had taken California from the Mexicans. Piatt would initially have liked to see his friend Chase gain the Republican nomination in 1856, but other men more influential in the party found Chase's antislavery views too radical for him to run a strong campaign. Some also said Chase had an excess of ambition—a charge that can probably be leveled at anyone who wants to move into the White House.[106]

It was far from clear that Frémont could, if elected, keep the country together. The debate over the future of slavery in America had become passionate. In 1854 Senator Stephen A. Douglas, Democrat of Illinois, had sponsored the Kansas-Nebraska Act, superseding the old Missouri Compromise, which forbade slavery in new states or territories north of latitude 36 degrees, 30 minutes. The new act permitted the inhabitants of Kansas and Nebraska to decide for themselves whether their territories should be free or slave. Several emigrant aid societies were bringing antislavery Northerners into Kansas, but Southerners were moving in, too. Soon there was guerrilla warfare in Kansas. The initial Kansas constitution made it a slave territory; after more Northerners had moved into the territory, a second constitution was voted that made it free.

In November 1856 Frémont lost the election to James Buchanan, the Democratic candidate. While still serving as the less than illustrious envoy in London, Buchanan had written President Pierce that his plan for the future was that of "closing my mission here . . . & then retiring to my peaceful home."[107] Unfortunately for the United States, he became president instead. But even though a Democrat would occupy the White House for the next four years, the Republican vote had been fairly heavy: Frémont gained 33 percent of the popular vote. (Buchanan got 45 percent; former president Millard Fillmore, running for the Know-Nothings, who were soon to disappear, got not quite 22 percent.)

The Republicans were now the most powerful party in the North, and Republican antislavery leaders like Chase and Seward were increasing their influence. In his inaugural address Buchanan said that all the nation's practical problems had been solved. That was patently untrue. The problems remained, slavery above all, and Buchanan was clearly not the man to solve them. A Republican victory in four more years looked quite possible.

After Frémont's defeat Piatt went to Cincinnati and spent the winter and spring there working on law cases. He took Louise to Rhode Island for the summer of 1857. He was not a wealthy man at this point, but he may have felt flush. That March the Congress had voted to pay him $2,114 for the months he had been chargé d'affaires at Paris, above and beyond the salary he had received at the time.[108] Piatt claimed he had been obliged to spend for official purposes $10,000 more than he had been paid, but even $2,000 was a goodly sum. The congressional action also amounted to vindication of his conduct as a diplomat, despite the complaints that John Mason had made about him.

Together with an older friend, the brave antislavery editor Gamaliel Bailey, Piatt may have used some or all of the money from Congress to buy what he described as "a handsome cottage, on two acres, facing the ocean," at Narragansett in Rhode Island.[109] The Baileys and Piatts vacationed there, near the seaside, from mid-July to mid-September, and then returned to their respective homes in Washington and Ohio.

Later that autumn Piatt traveled from Ohio to Washington, where he tried to convince Bailey that he and his *National Era* should align themselves firmly with that rising antislavery leader, Salmon P. Chase. Bailey would not agree; he wanted to keep his editorial independence.

A year later Bailey was in poor physical and financial health. He wanted to get out of America, to make an extended trip to Europe. Piatt engineered a plan to finance his trip through a company to be headed by Salmon Chase. With the help of Chase's name they would raise $5,000 from Bailey admirers, use that to buy property that Bailey owned in Chicago, resell the property at a profit, and give the money to Bailey. Piatt traveled through Ohio and the Northeast, with encouragement from Chase, to solicit subscriptions for the stock. With most of the amount raised, Bailey sailed for Europe at the beginning of June 1859—and died at sea, at the age of fifty-one.[110]

Donn's oldest sibling, Jacob Wykoff Piatt, had also died, in 1857 in Cincinnati, at the age of fifty-six. It was Wykoff who had taken young Donn into his law firm. Donn revered his older brother and later memorialized his finest feat: the creation, in Cincinnati, of America's first professional fire department in the face of threats to his life from a mob of volunteer firemen.[111]

For three years, until 1859, Piatt followed the same schedule—Narragansett in summer, Cincinnati and the law during most of the other months—and then he and Louise moved back to Mac-o-cheek.[112] He had become a successful lawyer, but he still wanted to be a writer; and he always loved the countryside.

Donn's brother Abram liked writing as much as Donn did, and in 1858 he had started a newspaper at West Liberty that he called the *Mac-a-cheek Press*. The contributors soon included Donn and his younger cousin, the poet John James Piatt, who was also publishing his poetry in the *Louisville Journal* and was soon to marry his fellow poet and fellow contributor, Sarah Bryan.[113]

The Piatt newspaper was an eight-page weekly. Even though it was being published in a small town, it aimed to be important: "A Family Journal—devoted to politics, literature, agriculture, science, art, and general intelligence." The Piatts got copies around the state, and people began to take notice.

Before moving back to Mac-o-cheek, Piatt visited Washington, in February 1859. While there, he was invited to dine one Thursday evening at the home of Daniel Sickles, who several years earlier had gotten the legation job in London that Piatt had expected and was now a member of Congress. The dinner invitation was brought to him, Piatt later recalled, by Francis Barton Key, who offered to lend him a dress coat for the occasion. Key, the district attorney of Washington (and the son of Francis Scott Key, author of "The Star-Spangled Banner"), was a friend of the Sickles but apparently was not going to the dinner. The Sickles house, the so-called Stockton Mansion, stood on Lafayette Square near the White House. Piatt later remembered the Sickles dinner as a brilliant affair, with the guests assembled under the gas lights by glittering silver and gorgeous flowers.

After dinner, Piatt wrote, Sickles invited him and another member of Congress, Anson Burlingame, into his library to smoke.[114] Sickles' daughter came in with his mail, and, with apologies to his two guests, Sickles took a minute to open and peruse the letters. Among them, according to Piatt, was an anonymous letter that told Sickles his wife was cuckolding him. The following Sunday, in Lafayette Square, Sickles shot to death his wife's lover, who was none other than Francis Barton Key. Sickles was exonerated on grounds of temporary insanity—his lawyer was Edwin Stanton—and went on to a career that led a recent biographer to call him an American scoundrel.[115]

What Piatt said he and Burlingame most remembered from that dinner in Washington was the cool and quiet way in which Sickles received the news that his wife had a lover. The two guests followed Sickles back into the drawing room, where the famous actor Dion Boucicault entertained the company with songs and stories. Sickles, Piatt wrote later, "was attentive as if no ugly shot had penetrated his brain. And the following Sunday came the horrible event."[116] (It is not clear how Piatt and Burlingame knew that among the letters Sickles opened that evening was the one reporting his wife's infidelity. The *New York Times* claimed on uncertain authority that Sickles did not receive the letter in question until the following morning.)[117]

The ambitious Donn Piatt turned forty in June 1859. What might he yet accomplish in life? So far he had done interesting things but nothing of great moment. Opposition to slavery had led him like others from the Democrats into the Free-Soil Party; he had gone back to the Democrats; recently he had joined the new Republican Party. He had made at least one well-received speech out in Rhode Island, on behalf of a Republican candidate, and for a moment it seemed possible that he might become the next lieutenant governor of Ohio. His friend Bailey reported in the *National Era* that the Ohio Republicans were soon to nominate candidates for state office, and "Judge Piatt, of Cincinnati, is spoken of as candidate for the Lieutenant Governorship. . . . He has a large heart, a fine intellect, and much political experience."[118] Piatt no doubt possessed all those qualities, but it was another Republican, Robert C. Kirk, who was nominated for lieutenant governor that June and won the 1860 election.

Politics was fascinating but less than all absorbing to Piatt, who never neglected literary matters. The proprietor of Cincinnati's leading bookstore, a young man named Ainsworth Rand Spofford, founded the city's Literary Club in 1849, and Piatt joined in 1852.[119] He found among the members the young lawyer Rutherford Hayes, whom he had befriended when he was a judge. Other club members besides Hayes would one day become prominent in the nation, including Salmon Chase; Stanley Matthews, who had sat on the bench with Piatt and would one day sit on the U.S. Supreme Court; Murat Halstead, whose newspaper would become a force in the Ohio Valley and beyond and who would for a time be Piatt's employer; William H. Smith, future head of the Western News Syndicate, predecessor of the Associated Press; and Alphonso Taft, who would one day be U.S. attorney general and secretary of war. (Taft, unlike Hayes, never made it to the presidency—but his son, William Howard Taft, did.)[120] Spofford, the club's founder, would also go to Washington, in 1861, as a correspondent for the *Cincinnati Commercial*—the beginning of a very successful career in the capital.[121]

In and out of the Literary Club, Piatt knew many or most of the Ohioans who became prominent Republicans. Besides Stanton, Hayes, and Chase, whose protégé Piatt began to consider himself, he had made a friend of Robert C. Schenck, former member of Congress, minister to Brazil, and railroad president. Outside Ohio, Piatt knew a probable presidential candidate, William H. Seward, the Republican senator from New York. Another senator had presented Piatt to Seward one day in the Capitol, and Seward invited him to a stag dinner at his handsome house, where Piatt found him dictating to two clerks and wearing a faded silk gown and slippers, which he kept on at dinner with Piatt, the clerks, and other guests. Piatt wrote that he eventually got to know Seward intimately.[122]

Meanwhile, the national debate over slavery expanded to near crisis. In October 1859 Americans were variously shocked, amazed, inspired, and appalled by "Ossawattomie" John Brown's attack on the arsenal at Harper's Ferry—an enterprise that historians have termed both quixotic and criminal.[123] A federal force led by Lieutenant Colonel Robert E. Lee soon captured the insurgents, and Brown and six of his abolitionist followers were hanged by the federal authorities on December 2.

Sometime later that winter, Donn Piatt was standing in front of his family's old house at Mac-o-cheek when he saw a wayfarer coming down the road—a young but gaunt and worn-looking fellow with long hair. The man walked up to Piatt and said he was Richard Realf, and he thought he was starving. Piatt indicated that the name meant nothing to him. In a low voice the stranger said, "Secretary of state to Ossawattomie Brown's republic."

At that point Piatt remembered the name. Small wonder, Piatt thought, that Realf was announcing himself in a low voice. Most Ohioans opposed slavery, but there were Piatt neighbors who abhorred what Brown had done and would be happy to hang this man from the nearest tree; his name was indeed known in Ohio as elsewhere.

Before the attack on Harper's Ferry, John Brown had held a sort of convention in Chatham, Ontario, which elected a slate of officials for his fantasized future American government. Realf, a young poet who had come to America from England, had joined Brown in the hope he could help free slaves, but, as Piatt put it, "the rough old fanatic had no use for a poet, and so made Richard a piece of fringe-work to his imaginary republic." Realf told Piatt he had been in Texas at the time of Brown's attack on the arsenal; he had been taken in chains to Washington but had not been convicted of any crime. (He had, however, testified before the congressional committee investigating John Brown's acts and had been paid $600 for his time and travel.)

Apparently, Realf had come to Mac-o-cheek because he had heard of Donn Piatt as an antislavery reformer. Just where he had come from was not clear—we know now that he had been in Cleveland and had left there saying he was going to Columbus—but in any case the question was what to do with him. Louise Piatt said they must hide and protect him; Donn's mother agreed; his father favored giving him some money and telling him to move on.

In the end the Piatt family let Realf stay, fed him, and cut his hair and gave him better clothing. They decided to tell any curious neighbors that he was Ralph Richards, a distant relative from the East. Donn even put him to work on the *Mac-a-cheek Press*—after Realf told Piatt he was a poet—and then went to Columbus to tell his friend Salmon Chase, now governor of the state, that he was harboring the poor refugee. Chase said that he supposed the Virginians were satisfied after seeing Brown hanged and would not try to hunt down a secondary figure like Realf.

Realf might have been a good poet, but he proved a poor editor. Piatt dismissed him and let him go, after arranging for him to give a lecture on Shakespeare in West Liberty. Realf left town, Piatt said, with $10.50 and a well-stuffed valise. They never met again.[124]

By early 1860 Abraham Lincoln was increasingly being spoken of as a Republican candidate for the presidency. Piatt would have preferred Salmon Chase but doubted Chase could be nominated and decided to back Lincoln, who had made a number of appearances in Ohio in 1859. However, when the Republican convention opened in Chicago in May of 1860, neither Chase nor Lincoln but Seward was the favorite candidate. Piatt went to the convention as a delegate, but another

Logan County Republican, William H. West of Bellefontaine, contested Piatt's seat and won it.[125] Seward was ahead at the first ballot but soon fell behind. Lincoln was nominated.

Piatt decided to campaign for Lincoln. Immediately after the convention, he went to New York and remained in the East until September, assisting in the campaign plans and in campaign speaking.

The 1860 presidential campaign was not the first time Piatt spoke for a Republican candidate. He had campaigned for Frémont in 1856 and had made Republican campaign speeches in 1859 in Rhode Island, together with several past and present members of Congress, including Anson Burlingame. Several papers reported that he had spoken there eloquently. The *Providence Journal* declared, "Judge Piatt is an orator of unusual power, and expresses his views with force, and enlivened with wit and humor."[126]

In August 1860 Piatt left New York to take his wife to Narragansett again for sea bathing—but a journalist friend reported finding him there "as usual surrounded by politicians. . . . We ate, slept, walked, wrote, sat, drove, fished, and bathed in politics."[127] The members of the company included Piatt's Ohio friend Robert Schenck and a Republican editor from Hartford named Gideon Welles. But August was not just a month at the beach for Piatt. On August 15 he was in Norwich, Connecticut, to speak at a Republican meeting along with Horace Greeley and others.[128] On August 28 he spoke, along with Schenck, to the Young Men's Republican Union, at the Stuyvesant Institute in New York City.[129]

Meanwhile, Schenck offered to go campaigning in Lincoln's home state of Illinois. Lincoln liked Schenck well. The two had served together as Whigs in Congress. After Lincoln's single term ended, he had asked Schenck, who was still in Congress, to help him in what proved to be an unsuccessful attempt to gain appointment as commissioner of the General Land Office. In a speech at Dayton in September 1859, Schenck had been perhaps the first person to recommend in public that the Republicans nominate Abraham Lincoln for president. Schenck made his campaigning offer to Lincoln in two letters he sent him in mid-August. Lincoln quickly replied, "I am very glad you are coming among us. . . . *We really want you.*"[130]

Schenck must have told Piatt that he was going out to Illinois—and Piatt quickly latched on. It was too good an opportunity to miss.

When Piatt first met Abraham Lincoln, and when Lincoln first heard the name Donn Piatt, is not clear; but Lincoln knew the name Piatt well. Piatt County was part of Illinois' Eighth Judicial Circuit, which Lincoln traveled for years to represent clients at the fifteen county seats. Piatt County was named for an early settler, James A. Piatt, who was a cousin of Donn Piatt—the son of Donn's grandfather's brother Abraham Piatt.[131] Beyond that, Lincoln and his law partner William H. Herndon had been engaged only recently, in December 1859, by Donn's brother Abram to bring some ejectment suits on lands in Clinton County, Illinois, a hundred miles south of Springfield.[132]

Lincoln may also have remembered meeting another Piatt two years earlier: Donn's friend and younger cousin, the poet John James Piatt. Young Piatt sat on Lincoln's right at breakfast while they were waiting for a train at Tolono, Illinois, and was embarrassed when he mistook the well-known lawyer, and future president, for a clergyman.[133]

No evidence has been found that Lincoln asked Donn Piatt as well as Robert Schenck to come out to Illinois, although Piatt's biographer Miller claimed that Lincoln did so.[134] In any case, sometime in October the team of Piatt and Schenck began to address electoral meetings in southern Illinois. The *Chicago Tribune* reported that crowds were deeply impressed by Schenck's forceful arguments and by the "genial, witty, argumentative and eloquent" Piatt.[135] It was not an altogether easy assignment. Piatt had been quite ill in New York at the end of September,[136] and one wonders whether he was fully recovered when he traveled west. Piatt recalled later, without mentioning his illness, that the Illinois crowds had been both large and disorderly and that he and Schenck had to compete for attention with a traveling show featuring "fat women, anacondas, invalid beasts, and spangled riders."[137] The two campaigners had a heavy schedule, speaking in nine towns in nine days and then ending their efforts at a rally in Springfield, two nights before the national election.[138] Schenck gave the main speech; Piatt followed with, as he put it, "a cheerful review of the situation, that seemed to amuse the crowd, and none more so than our candidate for the Presidency."[139]

The day before the November election Lincoln invited to tea in Springfield three Ohioans—Piatt, Schenck, and David Cartter—all of whom, Lincoln's chronicler Roy Basler tells us, were being mentioned as possibilities for the Cabinet if Lincoln won and the leading Ohio candidate, Salmon Chase, should decline to join the new administration. Lincoln already knew that he wanted Chase in the Cabinet—but he was especially fond of Schenck.[140] He must also have had good memories of the last time he had seen David Cartter. Cartter had been sent to Springfield that spring, together with other distinguished Republicans, to tell Lincoln that the party had nominated him for the presidency.[141]

Also invited to tea at the Lincolns' that afternoon were four Illinois party leaders Lincoln wanted to put together with the Ohioans, and his new private secretary, John G. Nicolay.[142] Piatt recalled, "I looked at the plain furniture of his humble home, at the tea-table with its frosted pound cake, set upon a molded glass pedestal and flanked by good, old-fashioned indigestion in the shape of jellies and canned fruits—the work of the good lady who poured out the tea, while her husband sat at the head of the table with one boy on his knee and another hanging to his shoulder."[143]

After the tea Lincoln invited both Schenck and Piatt to come back to Springfield if he should win. He won, but had he been serious about inviting Piatt? A telegram from Lincoln's brother-in-law, C. M. Smith, assured Piatt that he was wanted,[144] and he quickly returned to Springfield. Schenck was there, too, and

Lincoln had the two men to dinner one November evening. Mrs. Lincoln was not the greatest of cooks. Piatt wrote years later that "the supper was an old-fashioned mess of indigestion, composed mainly of cake, pies, and chickens, the last evidently killed in the morning, to be eaten, as best they might, that evening."[145]

As they talked, Piatt looked at Lincoln and thought he was the homeliest man he had ever seen. As tall as he was, his hands and feet were so long that they looked out of proportion. He sat, Piatt recalled, with one leg thrown over the other "and the pendant foot swung almost to the floor. And all the while two little boys, his sons, clambered over those legs, patted his cheeks, pulled his nose, and poked their fingers in his eyes, without causing reprimand or even notice."[146]

The three men and Mary Todd Lincoln talked far into the night. Piatt foresaw war. Lincoln said he doubted there would be war; Southern politicians were bluffing and would never give up their stake in the federal government. Piatt recalled Lincoln saying, "They won't give up the offices. . . . Were it believed that vacant places could be had at the North Pole, the road there would be lined with dead Virginians."[147] He also remembered how Mary Lincoln, Southern by birth and upbringing, expressed "an amusing assumption of the coming administration that struck me as very womanly, but somewhat ludicrous. For instance, she said, 'The country will find how we regard that Abolition sneak Seward.' Mr. Lincoln put the remark aside very much as he did the hand of one of his boys when that hand invaded his capacious mouth."

After the evening at the Lincolns', Piatt and Schenck took part in larger meetings with Lincoln at his old law office and at the local party headquarters.[148] One day they also went together to call on Lincoln at the office that had been reserved for the president-elect in the Illinois State House. Hundreds of people were streaming in to Springfield every week to see Lincoln, hoping to get jobs or contracts. Lincoln's law partner Ward Hill Lamon said that the hotels of Springfield were filled for weeks with "gentlemen who came with light baggage and heavy schemes."[149] Piatt found that Lincoln had devised "a jolly good way" of disposing of the office seekers who claimed they they had come simply to seek his advice or his views. He would say, "Ah! You have not read my speeches. Let me make you a present of my speeches." And that would end the conversation. Lincoln was a wily man, and he knew he must also be wary. Piatt recalled later that "Lincoln told us he felt like a surveyor in the wild woods of the West, who, while looking for a corner, kept an eye over his shoulder for an Indian."[150]

The day that Piatt and Schenck went to the State House, the two Ohioans fortunately found Lincoln alone. The three talked, and then, perhaps as others came into the room, Lincoln took Schenck aside for a conversation in low tones.[151] What should Piatt make of that?

Later in November the president-elect invited both Donn and Louise Piatt and Robert Schenck, to travel with him on his first trip to Chicago since the election.

Piatt thought it was Schenck whom Lincoln intended to bring into his Cabinet. If so, what was in store for him? Henry Villard of the *New York Herald* reported—perhaps on the basis of what Lincoln, his friend and confidant, had told him—that Piatt "is hounding Lincoln, and trying to get a promise of something from him."[152] *Vanity Fair* decided to have a little fun with that: "It is quite evident that this writer is making game of the President elect. Observe, in the first place, how he uses the word Hounding, then consider how commonly the name 'Don' is bestowed upon pointers and other sporting dogs; after which nothing can be more natural than the inference that the Don referred to is meant to be represented as making a Dead Set at the old bird of Springfield."[153]

The old bird—Lincoln was then fifty-one—soon heard more than he wanted to from Piatt. Initially, it seems, in Chicago the Lincolns and the Piatts got on very well. Schenck wrote his daughter from the elegant Tremont House, where the party was staying, that "the Lincoln's [*sic*] and Piatts are thick as fingers in a mitten."[154]

Then, however, Piatt was brash enough to tell Lincoln for a second time—in the presence of vice president–elect Hannibal Hamlin, whom Lincoln barely knew—that Lincoln should realize that Southerners were in earnest and were bent on war. Piatt added, still more brashly, that he doubted Lincoln would be inaugurated at Washington the following March. Lincoln said that the fall in pork prices at Cincinnati had affected Piatt. (Cincinnati was the center of the hog and pork trade.) Piatt, now admittedly irritated, said that in ninety days the countryside would be white with army tents. According to Piatt, Lincoln, who was perhaps irritated in turn, then said, "Well, we won't jump that ditch until we come to it. . . . I must run the machine as I find it."[155]

Abraham Lincoln was a poor man's son who as a prominent and successful lawyer still maintained an earthy, homespun way. He was now, however, not just a midwestern lawyer but the president-elect of the United States. At home in Springfield he had brushed off Piatt's frank prediction of war; now, in Chicago, he heard too much. He did not want Donn Piatt working near him in Washington.

There was nevertheless a moment in December when the press reported a rumor that Piatt would be made private secretary to the new president. The rumor does not seem to have originated with Piatt. The *Mac-a-cheek Press* scoffed that "DONN PIATT was unfortunately confined to bed when that specimen of ornithology, known among the French as a *canard,* went flying through the press connecting his name with the position of private secretary to the President."[156] John Hay was engaged to join John Nicolay as a second private secretary; would Lincoln really want three such assistants? That may have seemed doubtful—but three months later, the press reported that Lincoln's friend and law partner Ward Hill Lamon had been offered a position as a third private secretary.[157] Lincoln made Lamon the marshal of the District of Columbia, but he did acquire a third secretary, a young editor he had known in Illinois, William O. Stoddard, who during three years in the White House remained on close terms not only with the president but also with Mrs. Lincoln, who disliked Hay and Nicolay (who in turn disliked her; their code name for the president's wife was "Hellcat").[158]

Lincoln brought into his first Cabinet Piatt's friends Chase, Seward, and later Stanton—as well as Piatt's fellow vacationer at Narragansett, Gideon Welles—but Robert Schenck, despite a rumor that he might be made secretary of the navy,[159] was left out of the Cabinet, and Lincoln did not give Donn Piatt any sort of job. We do not know how many reasons Lincoln had for keeping Piatt out of his new administration. However, besides what Lincoln had heard and seen of Piatt in person, the president-elect had received an anonymous letter from Cincinnati saying that Piatt was boasting he would be made minister to France and that "nothing could bring your administration into greater contempt here than your appointing such a man to office."[160]

In addition, as he wrote to the president-elect in early December 1860, Schenck had learned after he and the Piatts accompanied the Lincolns to Chicago that "much foolish, & some cruel, gossip was rife & current in the 'good society' of that city in relation to my friends, the Piatts."[161] Among other things, Schenck wrote, people claimed that Piatt had returned from the Paris legation in disgrace, and that in Chicago the Piatts had tried to prevent other friends of the Lincolns from gaining access to them. Schenck insisted to Lincoln that the rumors were absolutely untrue; he attached a memo Piatt had written at his request, stating the facts about his Paris service. It did no good.

Aside from whatever Lincoln made of Piatt as a person, Lincoln knew what jobs meant in politics. He saw, for example, the political need to appoint Simon Cameron of Pennsylvania as his first secretary of war, although Cameron's reputation was so bad that Lincoln was warned that it would be a standing offense to the country if he gave Cameron a Cabinet seat.[162] But Cameron counted more in Pennsylvania than Piatt, or Schenck, did in Ohio—and Lincoln had the necessary Cabinet member from Ohio in Salmon Chase.

Although neither Piatt nor Schenck was called to Washington, they would soon be together in the Union army—an army that was exploding in size and needed not just private soldiers but more officers of all ranks than the regular army and its veterans could provide.

⋠ 3 ⋡

A SOLDIER IN THE GREAT WAR

Lincoln kept on denying, in public if not to himself, that civil war would come. His intention, no doubt, was to avoid words or actions that might inflame the country before he entered into his new office. His intention led him to say foolish things. On his way through Ohio to Washington for his inauguration, he could still tell a crowd in Columbus, two months after South Carolina had announced it was seceding—and six other Southern states had followed suit—"It is a good thing that there is no more than anxiety, for there is nothing going wrong."[1] But even if that was patently untrue, even if the Union was not holding, many people in the North did not want to see force used to keep the republic together. Horace Greeley spoke for many when he wrote that "the erring sisters should depart in peace."[2] Over the winter, in the North and the South, many newspaper editorials reflected the belief—or at least the hope—that war could be averted.

The war began, as Donn Piatt had predicted it would, in the spring of 1861. One spring day Piatt's young friend William Dean Howells, who would later become America's greatest man of letters, came to see Piatt at Mac-o-cheek, together with William Douglas O'Connor, another young writer, who several years later would publish *The Good Gray Poet*. (O'Connor's book was a strong defense—perhaps the first strong defense—of his friend Walt Whitman. Piatt may have liked O'Connor, but later he wrote scathingly about Whitman as a poet. Nor did Whitman like Piatt.)

When Howells visited Piatt in 1861, he was feeling on top of the world. Two years earlier, in his early twenties, he had been struggling to make a living. He had lost his job at the *Ohio State Journal,* and his first book of poetry had sold few copies. He had then asked a better-known poet—Donn's cousin John James Piatt—if they might publish their poems together.[3] Eventually, Howells would come to pity the other poet, who had fallen far behind him professionally, but in 1859 Howells was the one who needed help. The next year, though, he wrote a campaign biography of Lincoln, which was published just after Lincoln's nomination for the presidency.

The book was a success, Lincoln was elected, and Howells was rewarded with an appointment as the American consul at Venice.

As Piatt soon learned, David Cartter, the Ohioan who together with Piatt and Schenck had met with Lincoln in Springfield, was also getting his reward, appointment as the American minister to Bolivia. That was not the end of the political plums for Ohioans. Several other Ohioans who had worked for Lincoln were given diplomatic or consular positions or were made judges.[4] Piatt could see by now that there would be no plum for him. Someone, presumably Piatt, wrote in the *Mac-a-cheek Press* of April 15, 1861, after Fort Sumter had surrendered and Lincoln had called for 75,000 volunteers, that Donn had never wanted a job in Washington. He had hesitated to return to Springfield after Lincoln's election, but, the writer went on,

> Donn went, and Mr. Lincoln himself invited our friend to accompany him to Chicago. He did not press Mr. Schenck; he never spoke of Mr. S. or anybody else. But he and the President spent all the time they passed together in telling each other funny stories. They parted, the best of friends, and . . . how could Donn press Schenck for the Cabinet when his other friend Chase had the place. Donn never asked a place of this Administration for himself or any friend, and never wanted one. The place he seeks he is at this moment taking for himself—and that is a place in the ranks of our army, with a musket on his shoulder.[5]

One may question Piatt's insistence that he had not sought, or wanted, a job in Lincoln's administration—but at least the last sentence was true. At the age of forty-one Donn Piatt enlisted in the Union army as a private. His name was first on the roll of volunteers from Logan County.[6] Soon a company was formed at West Liberty, composed mainly of young farmers, and the men elected Piatt their captain. He wanted to form them into a cavalry unit; these were men who worked with horses every day. To formalize creation of the cavalry company he went to Columbus—where he was told by Governor William Dennison that there was no authority for such a unit. Undaunted, Piatt wrote to the War Department in Washington. Pending a reply from Washington, the captain and his men were mustered in as Company C of the 13th Ohio Volunteer Infantry, commanded by his younger brother Abram Sanders Piatt. It was just as well that they were formed as infantry. In May 1861 Donn Piatt received a message from U.S. Secretary of War Simon Cameron: "I regret to be obliged to decline your patriotic offer of a company of cavalry."[7]

Piatt himself must have regretted he could not lead a cavalry unit. His friend Howells, who had watched his company at drill, reported in the *New York World* that they were all splendid horsemen. A riding master who had come from Cincinnati to Mac-o-cheek to teach them watched the "the furious *abandon* with which they managed their steeds" and, Howells said, decided that all he could do was try to restrain them a little.[8]

Donn's younger brother, Abram, wanted as much as any patriotic Northerner to serve the Union. Initially, before the Confederates took Fort Sumter in April and war broke out, he had offered his services for what people understood would be a Union attempt to resupply the federal forts in the South. By the end of March he had decided instead, presumably because of Donn's experience abroad, to seek a diplomatic commission, and wrote the new president, "I have been desirous to be Secretary of Legation to Mexico."[9] But it was instead a military commission as colonel that was given him. He was promoted to brigadier general in 1862 but resigned his commission in 1863 after an injury at Fredericksburg. (It appears that the unstated reason for his resignation was not his injury but concern for the Piatt property in Ohio, which had been left in the care of his and Donn's aged father, Benjamin, who died later in 1863 at the age of eighty-four. When, after setting home affairs aright, Abram tried to regain his commission, Secretary of War Stanton told him that he was sorry that Abram had resigned when he did and that there was no vacancy for him to fill.[10] That ended Abram's military career, and he remained in Ohio as manager of the family enterprises.)

In June 1861 the War Department changed its mind about Company C and authorized the cavalry unit that Donn Piatt wanted. It was too late for that, however. Piatt had accepted an invitation from his friend Robert Schenck, who had recently been commissioned a brigadier general, to become his adjutant general and chief of staff. Earlier the new president had called in Schenck and asked, "What can you do to help me?" Anything, Schenck said. "Can you fight?" He would try, Schenck said. "Well," said Lincoln, "I want to make a general out of you."[11] That was very well, but apparently there was some delay. Schenck telegraphed Lincoln flatly in mid-May, "Will you appoint me Brigadier General."[12] And the answer was yes.

Captain Piatt was with General Schenck that July at the first battle of Bull Run and in August 1862 at the second. Both officers acquitted themselves well in both battles—but before Piatt had joined Schenck, and before First Bull Run, the new general lost a number of men to enemy fire in what the press styled "the lamentable affair at Vienna."[13] The affair had a lasting effect on Piatt as well as on Schenck.

Schenck was not the first member of his family to become a general despite lack of military experience. His father, William C. Schenck, a prosperous surveyor and landowner in Ohio, had served as a general in the War of 1812.[14] After the younger Schenck was commissioned as a brigadier general, he was put in command of the First Regiment, Ohio Volunteer Infantry while a brigade was being formed for him. A scant month later, having completed all the training they were to receive, Schenck and the new regiment were at Washington. Trouble was looming for the new general—an incident that would cement Piatt's feelings for Schenck and confirm his dislike of West Pointers.

Down the Potomac a few miles, the city of Alexandria had been seized by Union forces. It was decided that Schenck should station companies of the First

Ohio along the Alexandria, Loudoun & Hampshire Railroad that stretched from Alexandria into the countryside of northern Virginia. (The rail line, abandoned in the 1960s, is now the forty-five-mile Washington & Old Dominion Trail.)

There were reports of Confederate forces somewhere out the line toward Leesburg. Schenck's superior officer, Brigadier General Daniel Tyler, decided to go see for himself and with several staff officers took a train out the line through the hamlets of Falls Church and Vienna. They stopped three miles beyond Vienna, having seen no sign of the enemy, and returned to Alexandria. Tyler then ordered Schenck to take his regiment and occupy the line.

The following day Schenck and his regiment boarded a train in Alexandria and headed out. The locomotive was at the rear, pushing a half dozen cars. The train stopped to leave six companies along the line near Falls Church and continued west. As it neared Vienna with Schenck and his remaining 180 men, it was fired upon by both Confederate artillery and infantry hidden behind foliage. The train halted quickly, and the troops disembarked. Schenck sent word that the engineer should pull the train back beyond range of enemy fire. Someone or something—one report said a cannonball—uncoupled the engine and one car from the rest of the train, and the engineer started moving. Instead of stopping just down the track, he ran the truncated train all the way to Alexandria, leaving Schenck and men stranded and forced to retreat on foot. Ten men were lost to enemy fire.[15]

It was hardly Schenck's fault that the locomotive engineer had fled the scene. Nevertheless, the new general quickly became the butt of comments about his inexperience, both from career officers and from the press. The *New York Times* said, with reference to the "unfortunate encounter" near Vienna, that "his Brigadier-Generalship seems to be the only qualification which entitles him to lead troops to battle."[16]

Piatt was angered by these attacks on Schenck by officers who were graduates of West Point, and by the failure of another West Pointer, Schenck's commander, Irvin McDowell, to say anything in Schenck's defense. It all induced in Piatt a permanent hatred of and scorn for the military academy and its graduates that was often reflected in his writing.

After Piatt had joined Schenck, his friend Rutherford B. Hayes, who had been commissioned a Union major, served for a time in Schenck's brigade. Hayes found that Piatt always had something funny to say. He wrote his uncle that Piatt told him that at the first battle of Bull Run, when shells whistled around them, he had tried to remember his old prayers but could only recall "Oh Lord, for these and all thy other mercies, we desire to be thankful."[17]

During the battle Schenck's brigade had indeed come under heavy fire. On the morning of that fateful day, July 21, they were stationed where the Warrenton road crossed Bull Run on the stone bridge still to be seen there. The brigade was there as a decoy, to keep the Confederates focused on them while the bulk of the Union force went to the right, to try to turn the Confederate left flank. General William

Tecumseh Sherman, whose brigade was together with Schenck's for much of the day, later wrote his wife that his horse had been shot through the foreleg, his knee had been grazed by a ball, and another ball had hit his collar.[18] Finally, at four o'clock in the afternoon, Piatt wrote later, he suggested to Schenck that it was time to cross the bridge and go to the relief of the Union force that had by now failed to outflank the Confederates. Schenck agreed, but the brigade was hardly across the bridge when the order came to retreat.

The *New York Times* published a letter from Piatt about the battle a month afterward. There were reports of a conversation before the battle between an un-named Union officer and Representative Daniel Gooch, one of the members of Congress who had ridden out to watch the Union forces tromp the rebels. The officer, Piatt wrote, had been himself. He had told Gooch that "we were driving on to a disastrous defeat. . . . Our army was made up of volunteers, only an ag-gravated militia, that could not stand a reverse of any sort . . . in half an hour after a defeat we would have to fall back on Washington with our force resolved back into its original element of mob."[19]

Piatt said that he and Gooch had also met with other prominent civilians who had come out to the field, including Senator Henry Wilson, who chaired the Sen-ate's Committee on Military Affairs. Piatt had told the group that the Union forces were not ready for battle:

I wished them to telegraph our real position to the President, and ask him to give us time, or Gen. Scott. Winfield Scott would have been for us at that mo-ment equal to ten thousand men. I had the best reason in the world for this opinion. I had been assured, late on Saturday night, that Gen. Scott would be with us, and early on Sunday morning I was sent by Gen. Schenck to hurry on the Second Ohio and Second New-York Regiments. Riding through their encampment and along the lines, I told the men we would be under the eyes of the old hero, who had never lost a battle, and their quick, hearty response told me at once of the magic in that name.

Who had told Piatt that the old and grossly overweight general-in-chief would come to the field? There was no chance of that. Instead, came the rout of the federal forces that Piatt predicted to Gooch. The rout should not have been a surprise. Wil-liam Howard Russell of the *Times* of London, who had reported on the bloody war in the Crimea, had lately come to America on assignment. In the Crimea, he had seen terrible bungling and inefficiency in the British Army, but at least there had been discipline and order. Soon after reaching Washington he concluded that the new Union army deployed around the capital was an unprepared, ill-disciplined "rabblement"—while on a visit to South Carolina he had found Confederate mili-tary preparations more formidable than he would have expected.[20]

Still, Piatt wrote later, the Union soldiers had not at first run from the enemy. Many men had become disheartened after the initial engagement with the enemy at Blackburn's Ford on Bull Run, when they tried to use the old Belgian-made muskets they had been issued: "Our men found locks breaking and barrels bursting with far greater damage to themselves than to the enemy we assailed."[21] When an officer remonstrated with a group of retreating volunteers, Piatt reported, one man said, "Give us guns we can shoot, and we'll fight." The officer did a quick check of twenty muskets and found only one in serviceable condition.

Piatt wrote that the defective guns had reportedly been bought for the army by the firm of Weed & Sandford and that the matter should be investigated.[22] There is no indication that this was ever done (Weed was Thurlow Weed, the New York political leader behind Secretary of State William Seward). In any case, it was true in 1861 that the Union forces had few modern arms. The army ordnance department had not only failed to procure an adequate supply of new breech-loading rifles but had also bought various sorts of obsolete arms, when standardization as well as modernization was needed.

Piatt never exaggerated his part in the battle, but when many Union soldiers turned tail and ran, he did not. There is a witness to his bravery. Schenck's fellow brigade commander E. D. Keyes wrote later that when the Union retreat turned into a rout, and when Keyes (not a new soldier but a West Pointer who had spent three decades in the army) had just crossed Cub Run, east of Bull Run, and was leaving the field at what he called "a moderate pace," he saw Piatt standing there and "trying to collect men to stay the retreat."

Piatt alone could not stem the tide. Generals as well as privates were fleeing the field. Keyes admitted that although Piatt had called out to him, he himself had kept on eastward to the point where his brigade had camped the previous night.[23] Where Schenck was at this point is not clear. What is clear is that Piatt stood his ground and tried to get others to do the same.

Two decades later Piatt wrote to the author Donald Grant Mitchell, who was putting together a memorial volume on the recently deceased General Tyler, that at Bull Run "we went into the fight a mob, and came out a mob, falling back in confusion but slowly, and without a panic." The story that there had been a panic was, he said, due to Russell of the London *Times*, who together with other correspondents and a number of members of Congress had been down near Cub Run, in the Union rear, where ammunition and supply wagons were parked. A "handful" of Confederate cavalry had swept down on the site. Then, said Piatt, two cannons of a Union battery commanded by a captain named Ayers "poured a rapid fire of grape and canister into the whole covey of fighting Confederates, struggling teams and wild [Northern] civilians. The whole scrimmage did not last two minutes, but it was of sufficient duration to send Mr. Russell back into Washington, where he described what he had seen as the panic of Bull Run."[24] (The *New York Times* agreed with Russell, saying that "he cannot in the least exaggerate its horrible disorder.")[25]

We do not know what impression was made on Congressman Gooch by Piatt's dire forecast just before the battle; certainly the defeat itself made a deep impression on Gooch. He became a leading member of the Congressional Joint Committee on the Conduct of the War, established in December 1861 after the Bull Run defeat had been followed by the small but disastrous battle at Ball's Bluff on the Potomac River. That committee remains the toughest congressional investigating committee in American history. Its members believed that war was too important to be left to the generals, or indeed to Lincoln's executive branch. Soon, as one historian put it, "to its [the committee's] doors the generals marched like schoolboys summoned for a secret examination."[26] Gooch, a Dartmouth-educated lawyer known for his penetrating examination of witnesses, became its legal expert.[27]

A quarter century after the Civil War had ended, Donn Piatt told a reunion of Union veterans in Ohio that as soon as Schenck returned to Washington from Bull Run, he had composed his report to his immediate commander, General Daniel Tyler, and given it to Piatt to deliver. Piatt said he had not gone a block from the Capitol grounds, where Schenck had found shelter, when he ran into a journalist friend who wanted the latest news from the battle.

"Old man," said Piatt, "I have got it all down here in black and white."

"Let me read it!"

"Read it, thunder, you can have it. Take and print it and be careful to send old Tyler a marked copy."

Afterward, Piatt said, when Tyler read Schenck's report in the *New York Tribune,* he called Schenck in to ask why he had sent his report to the papers and not to him; Schenck called in Piatt and told him to go see Tyler, who was understandably furious and told Piatt he would have him court-martialed.

Piatt told the veterans in 1890 that he had replied, "Well General, my business is not in the Army and if you do that I will have time to write up that Blackburn's Ford affair," in a way not flattering to Tyler. Tyler told him to get out. And yet, said Piatt to the veterans, the fact was that if the top Union commander, General George McDowell, had "followed up that demonstration [at Blackburn's Ford] with a battle immediately, the first Bull Run would in all probability, have been a victory for us."[28]

Shall we believe all this? An Italian would likely comment, *Se non è vero è ben trovato*—even if it's not true, it makes a good story. In fact, it seems clear that Piatt embellished the truth in his talk to his old comrades. Several years earlier, in 1883, he had told Donald Grant Mitchell that he had not given the journalist the original of Schenck's report to Tyler but had gone to a restaurant with the journalist and let him make a copy. Piatt told Mitchell,

I knew that this was in violation of army etiquette, if not of stricter regulations; but this knowledge did not restrain me. I remembered that my General [Schenck] had suffered most outrageously from the press, for having lost six men of his command by the fire of an unexpected piece of artillery while conveying his brigade, in strict obedience to written orders [from Tyler, as we have seen], by rail. I was determined that this same press should have, in advance of other reports, an account of what that General had done at Bull Run, where he proved himself as he did subsequently, one of the bravest and most efficient officers in the field.

Of course I was brought up with a sharp turn for my indiscretion, and General Tyler gave me a piece of his military mind, that, as Dickens said, was about the most disagreeable piece he had on hand. This did not, however, prevent our becoming warm friends not long after.[29]

With Piatt's help, after Bull Run, General Schenck got favorable press coverage. He was generally seen to have acquitted himself well in the big battle, making up somewhat for the earlier incident at Vienna.

Even though Lincoln had found no job for Donn Piatt in his administration, Louise Piatt went to call on Mary Todd Lincoln at the White House at the end of September 1861. It seems the two continued to like one another, and Mary Lincoln valued Louise Piatt's opinion. The previous November, when the Piatts had accompanied the Lincolns to Chicago after the presidential election, Mrs. Piatt had told Mrs. Lincoln that the presidential residence was in shabby condition. Then or later, Mrs. Lincoln decided she would thoroughly renovate the house's furnishings—and that she would spare no expense. Very quickly after her arrival in Washington, people began to see that this lady was "at once avaricious and wildly extravagant."[30] As the president was distressed to learn later, soon she was spending much more on furnishings and decoration than Congress had appropriated for that. And she wanted Louise Piatt to see what she had done.

On September 29, 1861, Mrs. Lincoln wrote to her cousin and close friend Elizabeth Todd Grimsley, "Mrs. Don[n] Piatt calls here in an hour's time. . . . We now occupy the stately guest room—She spoke last winter of the miserably furnished rooms. I think she will be astonished at the change."[31] Indeed, Louise wrote the president's wife after her visit, complimenting her on her taste.[32] Mrs. Lincoln must have been pleased by that letter. One doubts that she shared it with her husband. Given his later anger over his wife's overspending, Louise's letter would not have made him feel more kindly toward the Piatts.

After Bull Run, Schenck and Piatt and their brigade were sent to the Kanawha River in western (now West) Virginia, to serve under General William S. Rosecrans, who had succeeded General George B. McClellan there on July 22, after McClellan was called to Washington to command the Army of the Potomac.

There were both political and strategic reasons that the Union should seize control of this western part of Virginia. The people there were mainly pro-Union, few were slave owners, and their economy was more closely bound to the Ohio Valley than to the rest of Virginia. After the secession of Virginia from the Union was approved at Richmond in May, the Unionists of western Virginia had met in Wheeling and formed a pro-Union Reorganized Government of Virginia, which would eventually proclaim the formation of a new state, West Virginia. The region's strategic importance related largely to the fact that the Baltimore & Ohio Railroad, the rail link between Baltimore, Washington, and the Midwest, ran across western Virginia into Ohio. Already, in May 1861, the Confederates had burned several bridges along the railroad near Grafton, where the line crossed the Monongahela River.

Rosecrans knew the area; he had worked there before the war as a coal company executive. His Confederate opponent, General Robert E. Lee, did not know the area. Worse, Lee had two subordinate commanders, John B. Floyd and Henry A. Wise, who had both been governors of Virginia before the war and who now fought with one another almost more than they fought against the enemy. One of Rosecrans's commanders, General Jacob D. Cox,[33] wrote later, "If [Wise] had been half as troublesome to me as he was to Floyd, I should, indeed, have had a hot time of it. But he did me royal service by preventing anything approaching unity of action between the two principal Confederate columns."[34]

Lee did not enforce his will on his subordinate commanders. He could not do so; he lacked full authority over them. President Jefferson Davis maintained direct contact with them and directed, or tried to direct, the army's movements from distant Richmond. In addition, a long spell of rainy weather made the roads over the mountains impassable for Confederate supply trains, and Lee's force ran short of food and munitions.[35]

Lee's problem with Floyd and Wise did not mean that all went well on the Union side. Piatt took the liberty of writing Horace Greeley's *New York Tribune* that at one point the Union forces had pinned down Floyd and his six thousand men, "the flower of the rebel army. We had his artillery, his horses, his wagons, his pots and pans, his well and sick, his contrabands—in a word, his everything. Our army was wild with delight and eager to get at him." But then, wrote Piatt, Union general Henry Washington Benham had let Floyd escape and "all our fond dreams melted into thin air. The public demands an explanation."[36] The public did not get an explanation—but Rosecrans censured and then got rid of Benham, a West Pointer but an incompetent who was later demoted to lieutenant colonel.

By the end of October 1861 the Union forces had occupied most of what would soon become a new state of the Union. Lee retired to central Virginia, leaving the North to hold a line along the Appalachian ridges in western Virginia for the remainder of the war. With a damaged reputation, the man who would eventually become the South's greatest general was sent south to an inglorious job, strengthening the fortifications of Charleston.

The campaign had, on the other hand, been a considerable success for Rosecrans. In his months in the West, Piatt developed a great admiration for Rosecrans and for one of Rosecrans's wing commanders, General George H. Thomas, that continued—with the exception of some months in 1862—for the rest of his life. In the 1880s Piatt would begin a biography of Thomas intended to prove that the "Rock of Chickamauga" had been the Union's greatest general. Rosecrans also liked Piatt and later recommended him for promotion.[37] But Rosecrans's own military reputation would not prosper.

When Piatt was serving at the legation in Paris, he got to know the American envoy at Turin, John Moncure Daniel, as mentioned in chapter 2. They had not become close friends. For some time in late 1861, during the campaign in western Virginia, they were close enemies, although they cannot have known this. While Piatt was serving in Schenck's brigade, Daniel was at times just several miles away, as the aide-de-camp to Confederate General Floyd.[38]

Although Schenck had served honorably at Bull Run and was doing well in Rosecrans's command, there were other senior officers who did not like him. Someone continued to inspire press attacks on him. Schenck failed to get the promotion to major general and the field command that he was sure he deserved. General Thomas, in particular, had made charges against Schenck that seemed to block his chances. Schenck felt that he had been wronged. In January 1862 he sent Piatt to Washington—which gave Piatt the chance to see his wife—to appeal on Schenck's behalf to the new secretary of war, Edwin Stanton, apparently on the day that Stanton took office. Piatt wrote to Schenck, "He told me to say that the great comfort he has in taking his present position is that he will have it in his power to help his friends and among the first to look after is General Schenck. 'I have full confidence in Schenck he is a man of intellect and courage—he has shown these qualities not only in the field, but in living out the infamous attacks made on him by the press.'"[39]

Piatt went on to say, "As for myself—he is very kind and says he wants to find a place in the Department for me—so as to have me near him." Then came a brief but tantalizing postscript: "P.S. Mrs. Lincoln invited us all to a state dinner on last Friday—It was both imposing and funny." One wonders what the president thought when he saw Donn Piatt on his guest list, presumably put there by Mary Todd Lincoln.

Piatt stayed on in Washington for several weeks, although, as he wrote Schenck, "It does not look creditable to be hanging about Washington while this fighting is going on." (General U.S. Grant, after capturing Fort Henry on the Tennessee River on February 6, was marching eastward to capture Fort Donelson on the Cumberland.)

No record has been found of Piatt's appointments during his stay in Washington, but at least once during the war he met with Secretary of State Seward. Seward, Piatt recalled later, "would rise up solemnly, at intervals, and announce that the war would end in sixty days. . . . I asked him one day what he, in the old Scratch, meant by this absurdity. He replied that he meant it for a foreign market, that I had no idea how ignorant those foreigners were about our real condition, and that in this way he got two months of delay of the European recognition of the Confederacy."[40]

Stanton offered Piatt a chance to stay in Washington for good—"a handsome place in the Department," Piatt wrote Schenck—but to take it he would have had to revert to civilian status, and he did not want to give up his army commission. Piatt reported to Schenck that Stanton then offered to assign him to any staff job in the army he would like to have, other than his current job with Schenck. "But after some reflection I told him my fortunes were yours."[41]

Piatt had been trying to see the president, as well as Stanton, to press Schenck's case. Each time, Lincoln sent back word that he was busy but to come again.[42] On February 8 Piatt wrote Schenck, "I succeeded at last in having an interview with Abraham and was pleased to find that he had quite forgotten the affair and on my recalling it to his mind, he drawled out 'Ah, yes, I remember but they overruled Schenck's motion.' But Mr. President you are the higher court to which General Schenck appeals—of course Genl. Thomas having done wrong will sustain it, if he can. 'Well now I'll tell you what I'll refer the whole matter to Stanton.'"

Stanton dismissed the complaint against Schenck. Piatt soon rejoined Schenck at his new brigade headquarters at Cumberland, Maryland, on the Potomac River, 135 miles by rail from Washington. Piatt had labored and lobbied hard and long for his friend and commander, both with Lincoln and in several meetings with Stanton. Before he left Washington he saw Stanton one more time, to ask the secretary to give Schenck a field command. Stanton said that he wished he could do that, but it was up to the general-in-chief. The general-in-chief was George B. McClellan, a prewar Democrat who, Piatt wrote Schenck, hated both Schenck and Schenck's commander, Rosecrans, as Republicans.[43] If true, a month later it mattered less. McClellan was removed, and Schenck's career opened up again. He was promoted to major general later in 1862 and got the command he wanted.

On February 17, shortly before Piatt left Washington for Cumberland, news reached the capital that Grant had captured Fort Donelson. This meant the loss to the Confederacy of both Tennessee and Kentucky.

The following day Piatt wrote Schenck, "This war is drawing rapidly to a close."[44] It was one of the least prescient things he ever wrote, but perhaps he may be excused for it. At the end of January Lincoln had issued two major orders. February 22 was to be "the day for a general movement of the Land and Naval forces of the United States against the insurgent forces." Perhaps the Union could knock the Confederacy out of the war? Lincoln hoped his orders might stir McClellan to act, but they had no effect. There was no "general movement" or, indeed, any major battle in the east. In the west, in early April, Grant contested successfully the Southern forces led by P. G. T. Beauregard and Albert Sidney Johnston in the huge, bloody battle of Shiloh. It was not a decisive victory. The war would not end for three more years.

After Piatt reached Cumberland, his 1893 biographer tells us, he did major service in helping bring to order a large body of disorganized troops, in a situation complicated by the presence in Cumberland of many sick and wounded men.[45]

Soon Schenck's brigade moved out of Cumberland, crossing the Potomac into Virginia to help oppose the Confederate forces under General Thomas J. Jackson, whose men had baptized him "Stonewall" at Bull Run. The fighting up and down the Shenandoah Valley that May and June ended triumphantly for Stonewall Jackson, but there was one moment when Schenck's force, although outnumbered, charged up Bull Pasture Mountain and dislodged the Confederates from their position. It was a rare occasion of a Union force outfighting Jackson, before he was mortally wounded at Chancellorsville the following year.

The Union forces that fought Jackson in the Valley were under the command of General John Charles Frémont, whom Piatt had campaigned for, up and down Ohio, when he ran for president in 1856. At the beginning of the war, Lincoln had put Frémont in command of the Department of the West. He had then removed him in November 1861, after Frémont without authorization announced the emancipation of slaves of Confederate owners. After Jackson outfought Frémont in 1862, Frémont was put under General John Pope in a new Army of Virginia and decided to resign his commission—but not before Piatt had put in a good word for him with the secretary of war.

During the Valley campaign Piatt accompanied Schenck one day to a meeting at Frémont's headquarters. Piatt wrote a quarter century later that Frémont had told the assembled officers that General McClellan was committing a serious blunder in his campaign to capture Richmond from the sea. (The Army of the Potomac, led by McClellan after he had been removed as general-in-chief, had been transported down Chesapeake Bay to Fort Monroe in March 1862 and was slowly making its way toward Richmond up the peninsula between the James and York rivers.) Frémont, Piatt recalled, told his officers "that our objective point was not Richmond but Lee's army; that if Lee was driven out of Richmond he was driven back on his resources and that the proper line was on the interior where victory meant annihilation of the Confederate force for they would be cut off from their resources and driven into the sea."

Not long after this, at the beginning of July, Piatt was again sent to Washington, bearing dispatches from Frémont to the secretary of war. After he had delivered the dispatches to Stanton, the secretary invited Piatt to tea at his home. Stanton, said Piatt, asked him "how he was 'getting on under that little mountebank of the Mountain Department.' The great war Secretary's lip had a way of curling up from his white teeth in a sneer that was an insult that hurt and humiliated without a word to direct its meaning. I resented this and said that Fremont had more ability in his little finger than McClellan had in his whole body. 'That may be' and the gleam of the white teeth became more intense 'and not say much either. But what has he done to impress you with his ability?'"

Piatt then repeated to Stanton what Frémont had said about the need for an overland attack on Richmond. According to Piatt, Stanton listened to him and said nothing further about Frémont but instead said of McClellan, "This fellow with his gang, is busy as the devil impressing upon the men that he is molding to his purpose that the cabal at Washington as he calls us have abandoned them to death in the swamps of the Chickahominy. We are today in more peril from the Army of the Potomac than from the rebels at Richmond." (The McClellan-inspired vendetta against Stanton continued for some time; fortunately for Stanton, Lincoln eventually weighed in on his behalf.[46] In his 1886 manuscript, Piatt said that Stanton's words about the "cabal" had come back with renewed force since in his posthumous memoir, *McClellan's Own Story*, McClellan had confirmed what Stanton said. The memoir claimed that there had been a "conspiracy of the politicians," whose real object was not the restoration of the Union but the permanent ascendency of their party, who were ready to sacrifice the Union if necessary, and who wanted to ruin McClellan by forcing him into "premature movements.")[47]

The following day, Piatt said, when he went to take leave of Stanton at the War Department, Stanton pulled down a large wall map of Virginia and asked Piatt to repeat what he had heard Frémont say. Stanton then commented, "It has common sense to back it," and, Piatt wrote, that was the idea subsequently followed by Stanton and Lincoln.[48] Subsequently, after McClellan's campaign failed, a Union army under General Ambrose E. Burnside did strike south overland toward Richmond but was stopped at Fredericksburg in December 1862.

Alas, Piatt wrote, if Stanton had only studied the works of a man whom he liked to refer to—Thomas Jefferson—he would have found in *Notes on the State of Virginia* that the direct route south from Washington to Richmond was cut by rivers that would afford a good defense against a Union invader, as Burnside found at Fredericksburg. (Jefferson had written that the Rappahannock River was a good two fathoms—twelve feet—deep as far upstream as Fredericksburg.)

One wonders whether—although Piatt did not claim this—it was what Frémont had said that made Lincoln and Stanton realize not just that the Peninsular campaign was a bad idea, but that the Union's "objective point" was not Richmond but the destruction of Lee's army. The following year, when General Joseph Hooker, commanding the Army of the Potomac, wanted again to move on Richmond, an angry Lincoln told him, "Lee's army, and not Richmond, is your true objective point." After Lee's subsequent defeat at Gettysburg in 1863, Hooker's replacement, George G. Meade, reported proudly that Lee had been pushed off Northern soil. Again Lincoln was furious. It was not a question of liberating territory; Meade should have followed and destroyed Lee's army.

After Piatt concluded his business in Washington, he received a leave of absence, his second in 1862, to go to Cincinnati and see his wife, who was not at all well. One suspects that it was his friend Stanton who personally authorized the leave.

Piatt returned to Washington only in late August, and, because of a lack of trans-port, he did not rejoin Schenck's brigade in northern Virginia until the night of August 29—the second day of the second battle of Bull Run. The battle ended the following day with another Union defeat, but at least this time it was not a rout.

Piatt ended the battle unharmed. Schenck was severely wounded in the right wrist and was taken by ambulance to Washington, to Willard's Hotel. When the am-bulance drew up to the hotel, a passerby looked in and exclaimed, "Why, General, is it you?" Schenck, showing his bandaged arm, replied, "Yes, and they have shattered me, too." He spoke not very distinctly, and as a result the rumor spread around the capital that the general had said the Union army was scattered to the winds.[49]

Although the Union lost that battle, Schenck, with Piatt at his side, and his bri-gade had fought stubbornly and tenaciously. Schenck was not a great general, but he showed bravery that day. His fellow commander John Pope praised him highly, saying, "To his presence and the fearless exposure of his person . . . is largely due the protracted resistance made by this brigade."[50] In the following weeks Schenck's condition improved, but neither he nor Donn Piatt would ever see battle again.

Just two weeks after Second Bull Run, the Union suffered another discourag-ing defeat. The Union force at Harper's Ferry, more than 12,500 men, surrendered to Stonewall Jackson as an army now led by Robert E. Lee was launching its first invasion of the North. It was the largest single capture of federal forces to date; it was to prove the largest such capture during the entire war. In a week a commis-sion was named to investigate the surrender. Its members included Major General David Hunter as president,[51] the judge advocate general, and three other officers plus Donn Piatt, who was called on to write the commission's findings. Stanton commended him for his work on the report, which censured three Union officers, and had Piatt, who until now had remained a captain, promoted to the rank of major.[52] It was still a long way to the top.

Meanwhile, General Schenck had become a Republican candidate for an Ohio seat in the U.S. House of Representatives. In November 1862 he was elected to the House for what would be his fifth term, defeating a two-term Democratic con-gressman, Clement L. Vallandigham, the strongly pro-South Ohio "Copperhead" who the next year would be tried by a Union military tribunal and banished to the Confederacy. Schenck, despite his House victory, stayed on in the army for now instead of returning to Capitol Hill.

That November of 1862, the adjutant general's office in Washington named Pi-att to a new commission to investigate the conduct of General Don Carlos Buell. As commander of the Army of the Ohio, Buell had failed in his attempt to take Chattanooga and had retreated from central Tennessee, then failed to prevent the invasion of Kentucky by a Confederate force under General Braxton Bragg. The members of the new commission included Major Generals Lewis Wallace and Edward Ord, three brigadier generals, and Major Donn Piatt as "Aide-de-Camp, Judge-Advocate, and Recorder."

Lew Wallace, who after the war was to become famous as the author of the novel *Ben-Hur*, wrote to his wife in mid-December that he had found that Piatt was a "sharp, quizzical man of the world—knows everybody and everything."[53] Four decades later, in his 1906 autobiography, Wallace wrote for the first time that Piatt "gave us to understand . . . that we were 'organized to convict'; meaning, as we took him, that Secretary Stanton and General [General-in-Chief Henry W.] Halleck were desirous of getting rid of General Buell, and had selected us to do the work. This we did not believe; but it left Major Piatt stripped of respect."[54]

Piatt was not necessarily following a dictate from Washington in telling the generals—assuming Wallace's recollection was accurate—that they should render a finding against Buell. One wonders whether Wallace had forgotten that Piatt's role as judge advocate was to prosecute the case against Buell.

There could be no question that Buell had serious problems as a commander. He had graduated from West Point in 1841 and had spent the next two decades as a career Army officer, mainly in staff and not line positions. Perhaps, it was suggested years after the war, he was not ready to handle large numbers of troops on the battlefield. Perhaps, too, he failed as a commander to see that the type of "thinking volunteer" who made up most of his command could not be treated as harshly as a soldier of the old regular army.[55] In any case Buell was a strict disciplinarian if not a martinet, and under his command the Army of the Ohio was seriously demoralized.[56] A number of his regimental and brigade commanders took the extraordinary step of signing a petition asking that he be removed.[57]

It was not just a question of command. Buell's very loyalty was in question. The general was certainly not unsympathetic to the South. It can have been no secret in the army that before the war Buell had married a woman of Southern origin who brought eight slaves to the marriage—slaves whom Buell kept in bondage. Just recently, campaigning in Tennessee, in March 1862, Buell had turned all fugitive slaves away from his camp. Supposedly, he thought that showing respect for the institution of slavery might convince Confederates that relatively few Northerners were really opposed to it.[58] He was not, one may say, in tune with the president or the secretary of war.

After Piatt received the order naming him to the commission, he went to Washington, where Secretary Stanton told him that no charges against Buell had been prepared and that Piatt should go see Andrew Johnson, the future president, who was then military governor of Tennessee, and Oliver P. Morton, governor of Indiana, who could furnish him with all the charges necessary.

On November 26, the day before the commission was to convene in Cincinnati, Piatt went to see Morton in Indianapolis. Morton was a worried man. The Republican-dominated Union party had just lost ground to the Democrats in state elections, and antiwar sentiment seemed on the rise. The election results strengthened the governor's determination to see Buell removed from command.[59]

Miller's biography of Piatt reports that the governor told him "that General Buell was in treasonable correspondence and even personal communication with

General Bragg, that the entire movement from Murfreesboro to the Ohio, was planned and conducted for the purpose of giving both Tennessee and Kentucky to the rebels."[60] When, however, Piatt said he would place these charges before the commission, Morton demurred and said what he had told Piatt was only for his own guidance. As for Andrew Johnson, he later sent a deposition, but it stopped short of suggesting treason, although earlier, one historian writes, "The governor's incessant ravings that Buell was a traitor found considerable reception among soldiers desiring a command change."[61]

Piatt himself was convinced of Buell's treason, but, as he wrote later with some bitterness, "Neither Morton nor Johnson could be got to appear before the court and face the man they had been maligning."[62] At the same time, Piatt had doubts about the willingness of Major General Ord, the Marylander who chaired the commission, to see Buell found guilty, no matter what the evidence might show. (Ord and Buell had been students together at West Point.)

Piatt decided that some insubordination was called for. He went around Ord and wrote a confidential letter to Judge Advocate General Joseph Holt, with whom he had worked closely on the Harper's Ferry commission, expressing his lack of confidence in Ord.[63] Before sending the letter he showed it to Wallace, who, according to Piatt, pronounced it correct. Subsequently, Piatt wrote another letter to Holt, which he did not show to Wallace, saying that recently Wallace had been "irritated by a letter gotten up for the 'Commercial' by some penny a liner ridiculing him—he came out in a card eulogizing General Ord. . . . I suspect feeling ugly toward Gen'l Halleck [the army's top commander] for not giving him a command he seeks to throw blame on him for the delay in attacking Chattanooga—I may be mistaken in this—But it looks so."[64] (Halleck was a natural to attack for slowness; many people in Washington viewed him as too timid and hesitating in his conduct of the war.)[65]

In the event, none of the witnesses called before the commission attacked General Buell directly, other than General George E. Thomas. Piatt's admiration for Thomas increased further when, he wrote, "General Thomas quietly, modestly and most incisively cut Buell's ground from under him, and showed the retreat from before Chattanooga to have been one of the absurdest events of the war."[66]

After sessions that stretched over six months, in May 1863 the commission finally concluded its work by issuing an "Opinion" that, while critical of Buell's conduct as an army commander, found "no evidence worthy of consideration" indicating disloyalty.[67]

Soon after the commission adjourned, as Piatt wrote later, he found himself sitting in the War Department together with Brigadier General Daniel Tyler, another commission member.[68] (Two years earlier, Piatt had angered Tyler by giving a journalist a copy of the Bull Run battle report. More recently, he and Tyler had become warm friends despite the difference in their ranks, and they had worked well together on the commission.)[69] President Lincoln walked out of Secretary Stanton's office, saw the two officers, and asked if they had any matter worth reporting to him. Tyler said they did. They had ascertained that Bragg, with just ten thousand men, "drove your eighty-three thousand men under Buell back from before Chattanooga, down to the Ohio at Louisville, marched around us twice, then doubled us up at Perryville, and finally got out of the State of Kentucky with all his plunder." Lincoln asked what the meaning was of all this. Didn't Union men fight as well as the rebels? Yes, said Tyler, but Bragg had his men under control; if a man left ranks, he was punished; if he deserted, he was shot. In contrast, Tyler told the president bluntly, "If we attempt to shoot a deserter, you pardon him, and our army is without discipline. Why do you interfere? Congress has taken from you all responsibility." Lincoln looked at Tyler sadly, and said, "Yes, Congress has taken the responsibility and left the women to howl about me." And he strode away.[70]

At the beginning of 1863 Schenck, now promoted to major general and still suffering from his wound in the wrist, was named commander of the Middle Department, with headquarters at Baltimore. Piatt, his commission work ended, went with him again to be his deputy and chief of staff. Piatt admitted later that he himself was ambitious; he wanted to be a general—but would he ever get there?

For a time Louise joined her husband in Baltimore. She was pregnant, she felt weak, and she was worried that she might not live much longer. She wrote to her younger sister, Ella, who was soon coming to visit them,

> Yes you had better bring my dotted dress—calico with points and buttons— it will be very nice after the baby is born—and it is so hot. I have several houses offered me—I shall not go into them before July. I wish you would hurry on so as to help me decide things—and then you return home to come back. If I have a house I can send for Dr. Murphy to come pay a visit in this part of the country about the 26 of August.[71] If only I had him near I would not think about dying—but I am so terrified for fear something will be wrong and just as I have my baby to hug I will have to go—Donn says it is all nonsense in me—to think any such thing.[72]

The baby was stillborn. By early September, Louise, in feeble health, had returned to Ohio.[73] It was a sad and very trying time for her. The year of 1863 continued to be a trying time in different ways for her husband, too, beyond his distress over Louise, who was now far away.

That June, General Robert E. Lee, preparing to launch his second invasion of the North, which would end at Gettysburg, ordered a corps of his Army of Northern Virginia to attack the Union division at Winchester that was commanded by Major General Robert H. Milroy. Just before that, Schenck had sent Piatt to Winchester to investigate the scene. Piatt decided that Milroy's position was indefensible. After leaving Winchester, and after seeing a telegram from General-in-Chief Halleck stating that most of the troops at Winchester should be withdrawn to Harper's Ferry, thirty miles to the northeast, Piatt telegraphed Milroy that he should "immediately take steps to remove your command from Winchester to Harper's Ferry."

That was not Schenck's understanding of what should be done. Schenck telegraphed Milroy that Piatt had "somewhat exceeded his instructions. You will make all the required preparations for withdrawing, but hold your position in the meantime."[74] Milroy was a man who, Schenck wrote years later, was "always moved by undaunted and impetuous, though rather uncalculating, bravery."[75] Milroy stayed where he was.

Piatt, at Harper's Ferry, was surprised that Schenck had countermanded his order. As Lee's forces were beginning to surround Milroy, Piatt telegraphed Schenck on June 13 in terms certainly franker than most subordinates would use with their general: "Am very sorry that you interfered with me."[76]

There was reason for Piatt to be sorry—and for the president of the United States to be worried. On June 14 Lincoln telegraphed Schenck, "Get Milroy from Winchester to Harper's Ferry if possible. He will be gobbled up if he remains, if he is not already past salvation."[77]

He was past salvation. After a three-day battle Milroy's men hoisted the white flag, and three thousand of them surrendered; Milroy and a few others escaped. Lee then led the Army of Northern Virginia north into Maryland. It seemed possible that Lee would strike east and try to take the city of Baltimore and other points along the vital rail link from Washington to the Northeast. Schenck and Piatt made what preparations they could. They had quick fortifications built along the approaches to Baltimore, using black men as laborers. They also stationed troops along the railroad, and Schenck ordered the commander of the Baltimore naval squadron to have his ships' guns trained on the city, in case the worst should happen.[78]

Lee's army did not turn toward Baltimore but continued north from Maryland into Pennsylvania. After his defeat at Gettysburg in early July, Lee withdrew his forces to Virginia.

Soon after this a military court of inquiry was called to meet in Washington, to investigate the surrender at Winchester. General Schenck was summoned to testify as Milroy's commander. Schenck was understandably worried that blame would attach to him and sent Piatt to see Lincoln and deliver a protest that the court was rigged. Piatt found Lincoln that evening as the president was leaving the War Department to walk back to the White House. He was about to leave for the Soldiers' Home, his favorite place to spend warm summer nights. It had been a long day, and he was clearly not pleased to see Donn Piatt.

As they walked to the mansion Piatt told Lincoln of Schenck's protest. Lincoln asked to see it. Piatt wanted to read Schenck's protest to the president, as Schenck had instructed him to do. Lincoln said he knew how to read, and as they reached the White House he took the paper from Piatt, sat down on the steps and read it, and asked Piatt if he and Schenck were not "squealing like pigs, before you are hurt?" Lincoln continued that he was, after all, the court of appeal; did Piatt think he would permit injustice to be done to Schenck?

Piatt replied that before an appeal could reach the president, Schenck's reputation would "be blasted by a packed court." According to Piatt, Lincoln got an ugly look on his face and said, "Come, now! You and I are lawyers, and know the meaning of the word packed. I don't want to hear it from your lips again. What's the matter with the court?"

"It is illegally organized by General Halleck."

"Halleck's act is mine."

"I beg your pardon, Mr. President, the rules and regulations dictate that in cases of this sort you shall select the court; you cannot delegate that to a subordinate any more than you can the pardoning power."

Piatt then handed the president the book of regulations, which Lincoln admitted he had never had time to read and added that he would read it that evening. (Lincoln spent long evening hours reading in order to master military matters.)[79] Piatt said that unfortunately Schenck would meanwhile be put under arrest. Lincoln thereupon scribbled a note that he handed to Piatt, ordering proceedings of the court suspended until further notice.[80]

In the end Schenck appeared before the court. When the court concluded its work, among its findings was that Schenck had disregarded repeated instructions from General-in-Chief Halleck to maintain only a small force at Winchester. The findings of the court of inquiry went to the War Department and then to the President. Lincoln—no doubt loathe to take action against his old friend Robert Schenck—wrote, "I cannot say that in this case any of the officers are deserving of serious blame. No court-martial is deemed necessary or proper in the case."[81] Piatt, who had tried to get Milroy to abandon his indefensible position, was of course blameless.

Maryland, the heart of Schenck's Middle Department, was still a slave state in 1863, although slavery had been abolished in the nation's capital and, from the Union point of view, had been abolished in the rebel states by Lincoln's Emancipation Proclamation in January 1863. Lincoln had gotten only 2.3 percent of the Maryland vote in 1860—the state had gone for John Breckenridge, the pro-slavery Democrat—and there were still many Southern sympathizers in the state.

At his Baltimore headquarters General Schenck decided he should not countenance disloyal behavior. He ordered that Maryland women who seemed to be spying on Union movements should be detained and then had them sent across to Confederate lines. He forbade Maryland newspapers to put "CSA" after the names of Marylanders killed in the service of the Confederate States Army. On the eve of the Fourth of July, 1863, he issued an order that all houses in Maryland should display the American flag on the Fourth; police were to record the addresses of houses that did not fly the flag.[82]

Chief of Staff Piatt of course had a hand in all this. He had no more liking than Schenck did for the rebel-minded ladies of Maryland. He once recalled how just after the battle of Gettysburg, when he had been in charge during a brief absence by Schenck, a number of women had come to the Baltimore army headquarters for permission to visit the battlefield and look for family members in the Confederate forces who might be dead, wounded, or prisoners there. Schenck had said no to such requests, but Piatt finally gave in and furnished the ladies both passes and transport—and learned later that they had carried with them disguises that permitted a number of prisoners to escape. When the facts came out, Piatt said, he would have been cashiered if Secretary Stanton had not intervened.[83]

Sometime in the middle of 1863 Piatt told Stanton, while on a visit to Washington, that it was time to emancipate the slaves in Maryland. Stanton said he and Schenck should mind their own business and obey orders.[84] Stanton was giving Piatt a friendly warning. In January 1862 Stanton, then legal adviser to Secretary of War Simon Cameron, had drafted a passage for Cameron's annual report calling for freed slaves to be enlisted in the Union army. Lincoln would not have that. He removed Cameron (who in any case was a poor administrator who had been giving contracts to cronies)[85] and named Stanton to replace him, not knowing that Stanton had written the offending passage.

Stanton had become secretary of war at a difficult time. McClellan had been in command of the Army of the Potomac for months but had still not attacked the South. Carl Sandburg repeats in his account of Lincoln's war years a story that Piatt told years after the war—that Stanton, on the eve of joining Lincoln's cabinet, "sat in Donn Piatt's hotel room in Washington replying to a query from Mr. and Mrs. Piatt. 'Yes, I am going to be Secretary of War to Old Abe.' 'What will you do?' was asked. 'Do? . . . I will make Abe Lincoln President of the United States. I will force this man McClellan to fight or throw up.'"[86]

Despite his brave words to the Piatts, Stanton—who never did force McClellan to fight—was concerned both about McClellan as leader of a kind of military aristocracy of regular officers, and about his own standing with the president. In 1855, six years before the war, Abraham Lincoln had traveled to Cincinnati to assist Stanton, the chief defense counsel for John Manny of Rockford, Illinois, who was being sued by Cyrus McCormick for alleged infringement of patents on McCormick's reaper. Stanton spoke of Lincoln insultingly, and apparently in Lincoln's hearing, as an ill-dressed, long-armed ape with whom he did not want to associate. Lincoln, who had worked for months on the case—originally to be tried in Illinois—returned to Illinois disappointed and humiliated.[87] But in 1862 he knew that he needed Stanton in his cabinet, set aside whatever memory he retained of Stanton's insult, and pressed him to become secretary of war.

In 1863, when Stanton warned Piatt about obeying orders, the Union's command problems remained worrisome. McClellan had finally been replaced as commander in November 1862 by Ambrose Burnside, and the next month Burnside had been soundly defeated by Lee at Fredericksburg. In January 1863 Burnside was replaced by Joseph Hooker, who was no more an ideal commander than McClellan or Burnside had been.

Piatt did not heed Stanton's warning to keep still and follow orders. He wanted Schenck to do more with black Marylanders. In late June 1863, Schenck telegraphed Lincoln that he could raise one or even two regiments from among the four thousand blacks, both slaves and freemen, who had already been working hard for the Union, building hurried fortifications at the edges of Baltimore when Lee invaded Maryland.[88]

It was not easy for Lincoln to reach a decision about recruiting Maryland blacks. He telegraphed Schenck on July 4, just as the Gettysburg battle ended, saying, "Your dispatches about negro regiment are not uninteresting or unnoticed by us, but we have not been ready to respond."[89] The response came the following day. Stanton telegraphed Colonel William G. Birney, who was then at Fortress Monroe near Norfolk, that he should report immediately to Schenck in Baltimore in order to begin recruiting a black regiment. Birney responded that he was leaving that evening on the overnight boat to Baltimore and said, "If you will send me to Baltimore two officers drummer & fifer & twenty picked men uniformed & armed from first U.S. Colored troops I can raise a Regt. in less than ten days."[90]

Birney came from an abolitionist family—his father, as mentioned in chapter 2, was James Gillespie Birney, the abolitionist editor and longtime executive officer of the American Anti-Slavery Society—and he had been Piatt's friend for over twenty years. Birney set to work with a will. On July 21 he wrote to Treasury Secretary Chase, his as well as Piatt's longtime friend, that Schenck and Piatt "have rendered me invaluable aid. They are admirably fitted for military government. Every thing now promises success. A sure revolution is going on in popular feeling. I feel sure not only of raising a regiment but of striking a heavy blow at the 'institution' in this state."[91]

Within several days Birney had recruited two companies of black soldiers from among the free blacks of Baltimore. One July evening he assembled them at Fort No. 1 on West Baltimore Street, one of the fortifications built with black labor, to present a new regimental flag to Colonel Piatt. The *Christian Recorder* of Philadelphia wrote that in addition to the new soldiers, "the colored laborers . . . assembled to the number of thousands to witness the presentation."

Piatt went to the meeting to accept the flag on behalf of his command, and he made a stirring speech to the crowd: "Our first act achieved our independence as a nation. This, the last act, proclaims the independence of the man. . . . The Almighty has written upon all his works that a lie cannot live. . . . The war was a necessity. We had attempted to live down the edicts of the Almighty, and the hand of death was upon us. Thomas Jefferson had written that all men were born equal, and in the prophetic agony of his great soul he foretold ruin to his people for the attempt to deny what God had decreed."[92]

Those were heady words to be spoken in the heart of what was still a slave state. They were decidedly not words that the president, worried about the allegiance of white Marylanders, would have approved.

Piatt said after the war that he had learned that large numbers of slaves had been moved out of the District of Columbia to Maryland, in anticipation of emancipation in the District, and were imprisoned in slave pens in Baltimore.[93] Birney believed that his orders permitted him to recruit both slaves and freemen. He went to the slave prisons in Baltimore and freed their inmates, many of them the slaves of white Marylanders serving in the Confederate army.[94] He also sent recruiting parties into the countryside to enlist slaves. White owners were enraged and made their feelings known in Washington. At the beginning of September the War Department telegraphed Schenck, "It is reported on good authority that Col Birneys recruiting agents are creating trouble in the neighborhood of Easton Md by interference with the slaves."[95] Lincoln continued to receive complaints about the recruitment efforts from white Marylanders. Among their reasons for complaint was Birney's use of recruiters who were themselves black. This Lincoln thought a needless affront to the whites. (Stanton, for his part, seems to have had no problem when Birney asked for black soldiers to be assigned to him as recruiters. Perhaps Stanton had said nothing of this to Lincoln.)

At the end of September the president ordered the complete suspension of black recruitment, pending talks with Maryland officials. Stanton argued the need to resume recruitment.[96] The question revolved around the recruitment of slaves, not freemen. At the beginning of October Lincoln telegraphed Birney to ask how many slaves he had recruited. Birney replied, "Between 1250 and 1300 as near as I can judge."[97] Lincoln decided to permit the enlistment of more Maryland slaves, if their masters consented, in which case the master would receive compensation—if he was judged loyal to the Union.

Piatt wrote years later that at some point he had improved on the recruiting orders Birney received from Washington. First, he said, he told Birney that he should recruit only slaves for the new regiments. Birney said he would be happy to do so but would need authority in writing from General Schenck. Piatt tried Schenck, who said such authority could come only from the War Department since Birney was acting directly under its instructions. Piatt could not move him and so waited until Schenck moved himself, going off to Boston to transact some business. With Schenck gone, Piatt was in command, and he ordered Birney that only slaves should be recruited. Piatt claimed that his order effectively made Maryland a free state, that slaves in the countryside heard of the order and fled their owners, streaming into Baltimore to enlist. It was true that in addition to the slaves Birney had taken from Baltimore prisons, a number of slaves in the countryside heard of the recruitment drive and fled their owners to enlist.[98] But many still remained in bondage in Maryland, and the revolution in popular feeling that Birney had described to Chase was still far from universal in that state.

Piatt had been urged to take action by several antislavery Marylanders, including Hugh L. Bond, judge of the Baltimore criminal court, and Henry Winter Davis, a Radical Republican member of Congress. Some other, equally influential Marylanders were opposed to doing anything against the status quo—including Montgomery Blair, who as postmaster general was a member of Lincoln's cabinet, and who had received a letter from Maryland governor Augustus W. Bradford about "the kidnapping of our slaves."[99]

Since the beginning of the war, the president had not wanted field commanders to act on their own on matters relating to either emancipation or the recruitment of black men for the army. He had removed John Charles Frémont from command of the Department of the West in November 1861 after Frémont announced the emancipation of slaves belonging to secessionists.

Piatt wrote that soon after issuing his slave recruitment order, he received a telegram from the War Department asking who was in charge at Baltimore. Piatt responded that he was, in the absence of General Schenck. Quickly came another telegram from the War Department, ordering him to report there. He took the train to Washington and on reaching the War Department was told that the secretary of war was at the White House. Piatt went there and was shown into the presence not of Stanton, as he had expected, but of Abraham Lincoln—a furious Abraham Lincoln.

The president aimed above all to save the Union, with or without slavery. Aside from the outright Southern sympathizers in Maryland, the loyalty of many people in the state was uncertain, and the step Piatt had taken was worrisome. In the autumn of 1862 Lincoln had told visitors he was worried that if he freed slaves in all parts of the country, the fifty thousand Union soldiers from border states might change sides.[100] Even a year later, the *New York Times* commented that Lincoln "has studiously avoided all interference" with slavery in Maryland and the other border states.[101] When in 1863 Lincoln issued the Emancipation Proclamation, freeing only the slaves in the rebel states, Secretary of State Seward, meeting Piatt on the street one day, commented bitterly, "We show our sympathy with slavery by emancipating slaves where we cannot reach them, and holding them in bondage where we can set them free."[102] As late as 1864, Treasury Secretary Chase wrote in his diary that both Schenck and another Ohio general named James A. Garfield "were bitter against the timid and almost proslavery course of the President."[103]

We do not know just what words Lincoln used with Piatt that day in 1863. Piatt said that Lincoln cursed him and that later that night he wrote down just what the president had said. Certainly Lincoln was in a rage. He had not liked Piatt since their initial, friendly days together back in 1860. He would not let Piatt say a word in his own defense, and he threatened to dismiss him dishonorably from the service. Reportedly, Piatt kept his commission only after Stanton and Chase interceded on his behalf.[104]

Lincoln did not often lose his temper, but this is far from being the only example of what one historian politely calls his rare episodes of pique.[105] As Ward

Hill Lamon put it, Lincoln was generally good humored, "but at some times he would burst out."[106] In his Illinois years before becoming president, when he dosed himself with the popular remedy called blue mass, which was full of mercury, Lincoln had had instances of both deep gloom and towering rage. In the White House, too, at times he dealt sharply with visitors. When in September 1861 Jessie Frémont went to see the president on behalf of her husband and spoke to him heatedly—perhaps even whipping her handkerchief across Lincoln's face—he launched into a tirade.[107]

There seems to be no confirmation from other sources that Lincoln had Piatt called down to Washington and cursed him for what he had done in Maryland. On July 23, two weeks after Birney had begun recruiting black soldiers in Maryland, Piatt telegraphed Stanton, "Will you permit me to come to Washington to see you?" Stanton replied the following day, "You have permission to visit Washington," without promising to receive Piatt; but one assumes they met.[108] Why Piatt wanted to see the secretary of war we do not know; it may have had something to with the recruitment question—or with Piatt's personal hopes for the future. It is not impossible that it was on this visit that Piatt met an enraged Lincoln, but it is more likely that the encounter was in August. On August 11, Piatt received a "summons" to appear in Washington and reported there—to whom is not clear—on August 12.[109] Piatt said later that he had waited to issue his order on slave recruitment until Schenck went to Boston; Schenck is known to have been in Boston in August.[110]

There is no doubt that Lincoln's concern over black recruitment in Maryland was increased by reports he received that under Schenck and Piatt, Birney was not so much recruiting slaves as forcibly impressing them into service. The president's secretary John Hay wrote in his diary about Schenck and Birney that "S—'s favorite way, (or rather B—'s, whom S— approves) is to take a squad of soldiers into a neighborhood and carry off into the army all the able-bodied darkies they can find, without asking master or slave to consent. . . . 'The fact is,' the President observes, 'S— is wider across the head in the region of the ears, and loves fight for its own sake, better than I do.'"[111]

Is it conceivable that Piatt fabricated his account—published only in 1887—of what was perhaps the next to last time he saw the president? There were other occasions when, at a minimum, Piatt embellished the truth. In 1887 Lincoln and Stanton were in their graves, but others were still alive who knew the history of the Middle Department, including Robert Schenck and William Birney, who had become the U.S. attorney for the District of Columbia (and died in 1907). No one, so far as the author can find, contested Piatt's account, which he repeated in 1888 in his contribution to a well-publicized volume, *Reminiscences of Abraham Lincoln by Distinguished Men of His Time*. Was his account buoyed by a personal diary? He said that he had written down Lincoln's exact words the night of their meeting. Jeremiah Black, former attorney general and friend of Donn Piatt, knew that Piatt had kept a diary, now vanished, in which he recorded "sayings, doings and surroundings of Mr. Lincoln between the [1860] election and the inauguration."[112] It is not clear whether he was keeping such a diary in 1863.

In any case, slavery was in its last days in Maryland, although the Union authorities tried to mollify pro-slavery Marylanders by providing that a slave owner should receive—if he swore allegiance to the United States—the amount of three hundred dollars for each slave who had been recruited. Slavery was not officially abolished in Maryland until the state adopted a new constitution in 1864. Even then, former slave owners tried to take advantage of an old apprentice law to have black children kept in bondage.

Seven black regiments were recruited in Maryland during the Civil War. By the end of the war the state had furnished 8,700 of the Union's black soldiers, and they fought in many battles and skirmishes. One of these units, the Ninth Regiment Infantry, U.S. Colored Troops, was among the units that marched into Richmond, the capital of the newly defeated Confederacy, in April 1865.[113]

The last time that Piatt saw Abraham Lincoln may have been when the president traveled to Gettysburg to make remarks at the dedication of the battlefield cemetery in November 1863. The presidential train to Gettysburg went through Baltimore, where General Schenck and his staff—with Chief of Staff Piatt presumably among them—boarded at Camden Station. After the train left Baltimore, the president and other members of his party gathered for lunch around a table in the baggage car. Young Wayne MacVeagh, the Republican Party chairman for Pennsylvania, said what seems to have been a few words too many to the president about the need for a more radical party line.[114] One imagines Piatt, if he was anywhere nearby, smiling as he remembered how he himself had first rubbed Lincoln the wrong way, three long years ago.

The procession to the Gettysburg cemetery the next day was headed by a squad of cavalry. They were followed by the cannons of the Fifth New York Artillery, General Schenck and his staff, and then Ward Hill Lamon and his numerous staff of aides. After all this came the president and three of his cabinet members, mounted on fine horses.[115]

Before going to Gettysburg, Schenck had submitted his resignation from the army in order to take the seat in Congress to which he had been elected the previous autumn. The resignation would be effective soon, on December 5. Who would replace him in the Middle Department? Could it be Piatt? That depended on the president.

It seems Lincoln never forgave Donn Piatt for the action he had taken in Maryland—if not for his brash remarks on earlier occasions. Stanton told Piatt after the war that when he took Lincoln a list of officers recommended for promotion to general—and apparently he did that at least twice—Lincoln drew a line through Piatt's name and said, "Knows too much."[116]

How many such recommendations were made to the president is not clear. Rutherford Hayes's wife had written her husband in 1862 that a rumor was circulating that Piatt was to be promoted to brigadier general.[117] More definitely, we know that when General Schenck was about to resign his position at Baltimore in the autumn of 1863, a group of Marylanders called on the president to urge that he promote Piatt to replace Schenck. The governor of the state of Delaware, William Cannon, and his secretary of state, N. B. Smithers, then wrote Lincoln to "cordially join in the request that Col. Piatt be commissioned Brigadier General and put in command in Maryland and Delaware. . . . We beg leave, with our Maryland friends, strongly to urge the appointment."[118]

Congressman Henry Winter Davis, the influential Radical Republican, was one of the Marylanders who wanted Piatt to replace Schenck. Davis wrote to Samuel F. Du Pont of Delaware that when a group of Union men from Maryland—and some from Delaware—went to see the president about this, Lincoln responded that both Schenck and Piatt were "good fellows." But, he added, "[they ran] their machine on too high a level for me. They never could understand that I was boss." Lincoln indicated that he thought that Piatt, in particular, was too radical on the question of blacks and that if he were appointed to head the Middle Department, the result would be violent controversy among Maryland whites. What explicitly the president said, Davis wrote, was that "it would make a Missouri of Md."[119]

Besides the recommendations in Piatt's favor, some of the Marylanders who strongly disliked Piatt made their feelings about him known in Washington. Charles C. Fulton, editor and publisher of the *Baltimore American,* wrote the president that he represented "the respectable and loyal portion of our community" in hoping for Colonel Piatt's "early disappearance from Baltimore."[120]

Piatt might well have proved a competent general. By 1863 he had learned more about warfare than had many other men, North and South, who were promoted above their abilities in armies that were critically short of leaders. His commander, Schenck, had had no military experience when he was made a general. Neither had Piatt, but Piatt soon acquired a sense for strategy and tactics. It was Piatt who saw, when Schenck did not, that Milroy must evacuate Winchester if he was not to lose his division.

Schenck ended the war with a record that was all in all honorable, but it was perhaps fortunate for him that he was never called on to conduct a major battle. One historian tells us that throughout the four years of war, North and South, "No general out of civilian life showed the capacity to direct an army of combined arms—infantry, artillery, cavalry. . . ."[121] One might add, however, that a number of these generals, including Robert Schenck, proved competent in commanding divisions, which were sizable units, and even corps. Piatt himself never made any public criticism of his friend Schenck. After the war he recalled, for example, that at the first battle of Bull Run Schenck "was the only officer of that day who brought off a brigade in order from the field."[122]

Piatt resigned his commission in April 1864 and went home to Ohio to join Louise.[123] He had served, honorably, for three years, and that was more than most men could say. Perhaps he thought, wrongly, that—as he had opined to Schenck two years earlier—the war was winding down.

Piatt would have liked to take his ailing wife to the seaside that summer, but by June it was clear that she was too weak for that, too weak even to go back from Cincinnati to their beloved Mac-o-cheek. Perhaps, he wrote, they could go to the sea the following year.[124] That was not to be. Louise passed away that October, in Cincinnati, at the age of thirty-eight.[125] Donn built a fine stone tomb for her at Mac-o-cheek, inscribed with a poetic epitaph he had written:

> "To thy dear memory, darling, and my own,
> I build in grief this monumental stone;
> All that it tells of life in death is thine,
> All that it means of death in life is mine. . . .

Louise had been much liked and admired. The *New York Times* reprinted an obituary from a Cincinnati paper: "In her death, society loses one of its brightest ornaments, and American literature a gifted contributor."[126]

Donn's close friend and brother Abram had lost his wife, too, just two years earlier. Abram had married a Kentucky cousin, Hannah Piatt, in 1840, and she died in 1861.

Among the letters of condolence that Donn Piatt received was a long one from Horace Greeley, who wrote, "I am not accustomed to regard death as an evil, but this death saddens me, since I know that you can never again have so loving and gentle a companion, nor do I expect to have so devoted and generous a friend. . . . You may possibly marry again, though I think you will not; but in any case the romance of your life is over and cannot be renewed. . . ."[127]

⊰ 4 ⊱

WHAT TO DO IN PEACETIME?

America's civil war finally ended in the spring of 1865. People in Ohio felt joy and relief at the news of Lee's surrender, and then shock and sorrow at the assassination of the president. Looking ahead, though, people mourning both the president and their own dead might hope for a happy future for the country. But could South and North really come together again? Lincoln was replaced by his obscure vice president, and some said Andrew Johnson was no sort of leader, nothing but a drunkard. People were also saying hard things about some of the men who had helped Lincoln to lead the Union to victory—men like Edwin Stanton, who remained secretary of war.

When, that April, Lincoln had been assassinated and Seward attacked and nearly killed, Piatt suddenly recalled that shortly before leaving the Middle Department in Baltimore, a year and a half ago, he had seen an intercepted Confederate letter speaking of the assassination of Edwin Stanton as sure to happen. The plotters had killed the president and seriously injured the secretary of state; was some group still gunning for the secretary of war? Piatt quickly telegraphed Stanton what he remembered of the rebel letter—the fellows involved had been from Maryland and were perhaps still around—and he followed up with a letter saying, "I never dreamed such a horrible thing could occur as this murder—and I now look back in wonder at your escape."[1]

What of Donn Piatt? He had survived the war uninjured, and now he was middle-aged; he celebrated his forty-sixth birthday that June. If he did not deceive himself—and he was not a man to deceive himself—he could not look back and see great accomplishments on his part. He had served honorably in the war, but even though he had known a number of the great war leaders, he himself had not become a top commander. He had been a successful lawyer, but it had been some years since he had practiced law, and he had no practice to return to after leaving the army. He had been a judge but not a very senior one. He had served the nation as a diplomat but not a top one. He was a writer but not a famous one; he had published no books and few if any memorable articles or essays. He was well off economically, but he was not rich; he needed to earn money.

On the other hand, although Piatt had not been named chief of a diplomatic mission, neither had Lincoln's aide John Hay, who was going out just now, after long wartime years at the president's side, to take the very job that a less experienced Piatt had held a decade earlier, secretary of legation at Paris.

Most important, perhaps, Piatt knew a lot of influential men; he knew a lot about American society and government. And he had a lot of energy.

What then should he do with the rest of his life—which might not last for many years more? His father had lived into his eighties, but American men commonly died before they reached sixty, even without war.

Piatt cannot have expected in 1865 that he would live for another quarter century—and would become a familiar name to many millions of readers in America, as well as to many abroad, and a source of dread or loathing to many of his nation's great men.

That autumn of 1865 he gave a speech at Salem Grove in Logan County, to an audience composed in good part of Union army veterans. He spoke mainly about Edwin Stanton, and he spoke with warmth and from a feeling of deep loyalty. It had been the fashion of late, he said, to abuse Stanton: "While he was creating great renown for his country, he was making deadly enemies for himself." Piatt hoped that his fellow citizens, and above all his fellow soldiers, would ensure that history put Stanton in the place where he belonged, "for he has been the true friend of the soldier, the friend of the honest man, and above all the truest friend of his country in its darkest hour."[2]

In fact, if Lincoln had bent the Constitution with harsh wartime measures, Stanton had bent it further. In the first ten months of war, Seward's State Department had had control of military arrests of civilians, and there were almost nine hundred such arrests. Subsequently, Stanton and the War Department had control, and while figures differ, the army probably arrested thirteen thousand civilians from 1862 to 1865.[3]

In October 1865 Piatt also gave a talk in Dayton, to attack Clement Vallandigham. The former Copperhead congressman had made his way back to Ohio in 1864 from his exile in the Confederacy and Canada. Vallandigham was not finished with politics; several years later he was to make one more unsuccessful bid for reelection, this time to the U.S. Senate. Meanwhile, in 1865 he had written to Horace Greeley that he wanted to support President Johnson but was concerned that there might be a reign of terror against those who, like him, had opposed the Lincoln administration.[4] What Piatt used against Vallandigham at Dayton was not terror but mockery. He wondered why anyone paid attention to "this solemn, dull, egotistical fellow." He might be a Democrat, Piatt said, but this was not "the good old Democracy that once ruled the land. I belonged to that glorious old Democracy. . . . But . . . fifteen years since, the Democratic party, finding itself very feeble and failing, went South for its health, and it never got back again. I believe it was killed in this war."

Piatt went on to discuss the question of African Americans, who he did not suppose would give their support to men like Vallandigham. Piatt would continue to interest himself in the plight of black Americans, but this Dayton speech reminds us that Northern whites like him did not think civil rights for former slaves meant that they need become Northerners' friends and neighbors. Piatt's tone seems to have been fully serious, not mocking, when he said, "What we propose doing is, in the reconstruction of the Southern States, to have the negro so secure in his rights that he will be disposed to remain at home, where the climate suits him—where his associations, interest, and family ties are. This will draw them from the Northern States and relieve us from further consideration of their status here. If there is any evil to come of their citizenship, let the South, that, for generations, has enjoyed the profits of slavery, take it as the loss and balance accounts."[5]

Among the reasons that Ohioans could be happy in 1865 was the fact that the bloody war had not made Ohio a battleground, except for the two weeks in July 1863 when John Hunt Morgan's force of 1,800 Confederate cavalrymen swept eastward across southern Ohio, destroying bridges and railroad lines and terrorizing civilians. The state's human losses in the battles elsewhere had been heavy. An estimated 35,000 Ohio men had died in the Union's service—and a few in the Confederacy's.[6] Only New York State had lost more soldiers than Ohio.

Before the war, Ohio had already been a leading agricultural state. The soil and climate were good for crops, and production was steadily increasing. Piatt's Ohio in the late 1800s was not the scene of erosion and played-out land that Louis Bromfield described decades later in *Malabar Farm*.

In the second half of the nineteenth century, Ohio was becoming a leader in industry as well as agriculture. Even in little West Liberty (population 741 in 1870) there were both a manufacturer of carriages and a firm making "Circular and Drag-Saws, Lumber-wagons, Spring-wagons, Horse-rakes, Cultivators, Shovel-plows, Harrows, &c."[7] In Logan County's seat, Bellefontaine, there were still more firms, including the A.J. Miller company, which had begun making horse carriages in 1853 and decades later would turn to the manufacture of horseless carriages—automobiles.[8] The railroad, too, was helping to push progress. The Indianapolis & Bellefontaine Railroad had been chartered in 1848, and even before the Civil War had connected with other lines, which provided Logan County with a rail link to the East Coast. Later, Bellefontaine would be a division point on the Big Four line from St. Louis to New York.[9]

Ohio also continued to produce major players in national politics. In the next quarter century three successive presidents—two of them friends of Donn Piatt—would be Ohioans, while the possible candidacy of a fourth Ohioan began to loom large. Meanwhile, in 1865 Piatt, former lawyer and former judge, became a lawmaker: He was elected to the Ohio state legislature. That was an honorable position but not a great one. He must have wondered whether Columbus was a big enough stage for him. Despite his other attainments, in the world of politics he had been until now at most an attendant player.

Piatt made a campaign speech at West Liberty before his election to the legislature. As in his anti-Vallandigham speech at Dayton, he talked at some length about former slaves. So many had left the South, because they had been oppressed; 25,000 blacks, he said, had crossed the Ohio River into Ohio and Indiana in just ten days. Of his speech a local paper reported, "If the copperheads have their way, said the colonel, the laborers at the North will be over-run by negroes driven from their homes by cruel masters."[10] He had, it seems, no solution to offer for the problem that he described. But were poor Southern blacks really flooding into Ohio?

Certainly, few blacks had settled there up to now. The state's discriminatory Black Laws had been abolished by 1849, but the underground railroad routes that had operated through Ohio had taken almost all the slaves beyond Ohio into Canada. Before the war the Buckeye State had not been a hospitable abode for African Americans. At the last prewar census, in 1860, blacks in Ohio had made up just 1.6 percent of the state's population and numbered just over 3.0 percent of the population of Piatt's Logan County.

Piatt's concern that in the wake of the war Southern blacks might flood into Ohio proved unfounded. At the 1870 census, African Americans were just 2.4 percent of the state's population and in 1880 only 2.5 percent. Nor did many move into other Northern states in those years. Of a Southern black population of several millions, perhaps no more than 68,000 moved north in the 1870s and 185,000 in the 1890s.[11] The sizable black migration to Northern cities came only in the next century. But in 1865 it made good political sense to Piatt to warn of a black wave coming.

Among those who had urged Piatt to seek a seat in the legislature was his old commander Robert Schenck, who was currently representing an Ohio district in the U.S. House of Representatives—and wanted something more. In 1848 Piatt, as a political activist in Columbus, had helped Salmon Chase gain a seat in the U.S. Senate. Schenck's hope now was that Piatt could do the same for him, from within the legislature.[12] (U.S. senators were still being elected by state legislatures; direct popular vote for senators came only in 1913.)

Piatt spent two years representing Logan County as a legislator at Columbus. He spoke frankly there. When a bill was introduced to honor his childhood hero Simon Kenton with a monument above his grave at Urbana, one member objected that Kenton had been a horse thief whose depredations unnecessarily incited the Shawnee to make war on the whites. Piatt rose to object. He had, he said, known Kenton in his old age, and he was "honest, honorable, and in his simple way kind and dignified." Piatt went on to say that Kenton had admittedly played a role in a bloody war that "had no cessation until the Indians were subdued, driven out, and, I may say, annihilated. . . . Of course Kenton considered it right to take their property, as he took their lives, and horses were the most valuable property they had."[13] Piatt failed to convince those opposed to the Kenton monument, which was not erected until 1884. (He notably stopped sort of justifying what the whites had done to the Indians. Later, he was to write a poetic lament for the great Shawnee, Tecumseh, who had been killed fighting the Americans in 1813: "He lived as lives the warrior, in heavy stream of fight. He died as dies the chieftain.")[14]

The member from Logan County introduced a number of bills on subjects that he felt needed to be addressed, even when it was clear they would not pass. One called for the appointment of a state railroad commissioner who would look into the frequent abuses in railroad management. Another called on the state school commissioner to use his influence to stop local school systems from paying women teachers less than men, a practice that continued for decades. One of his more unpopular proposals was to try to reduce corruption in Ohio cities by making local police forces more autonomous, less dependent on elected officials. In addition, he said later in wry fashion, "I made a fight for negro suffrage, and won, by a decreased majority. Then, after spending a couple of winters at Columbus, I quit, by unanimous consent."[15]

Piatt seems to have made a creditable overall record as a state legislator, but it was not the life he wanted, and, as he indicated, the voters agreed that two years was enough. Moreover, even if he had swung his fellow legislators to support black suffrage, in the 1867 state elections Ohio voters overwhelmingly defeated the proposal.[16] African Americans in Ohio would not gain the right to vote until the Fifteenth Amendment to the U.S. Constitution was ratified in 1870.

Did Piatt want to go higher in politics? His biographer Miller says that toward the end of his term a number of leading Ohio Democrats wanted to see him nominated for a seat in the U.S. House of Representatives, "but he discouraged the effort and it was given up. He had no ambition to be one of a class that he held in contempt."[17]

But what about Schenck? Piatt fought hard but failed to get his friend elected to the Senate. At first Schenck's prospects seemed good, but his rival for the post, John Sherman—brother of General William Tecumseh Sherman—had powerful support from Washington: President Andrew Johnson. The "drunken tailor," as Piatt called the president in letters to Schenck, reportedly turned former general James B. Steedman away from support for Schenck by promising Steedman a cabinet seat if he backed Sherman.[18] Later, Piatt would charge outright that votes had been bought to defeat Schenck and elect Sherman. Both John Sherman and his brother the general remained favorite targets of Donn Piatt ever afterward.

Schenck remained in the U.S. House of Representatives until finally he failed of reelection. In 1870 he was named American minister to the United Kingdom. London was a prestigious post, but things would not go well there for him.

Horace Greeley had guessed wrong in thinking that Donn Piatt would never marry again. On July 12, 1866, he married Louise's younger sister, Ella, who as a teenager had lived with them in Paris, a decade earlier. Donn and Ella were married in Cincinnati, by Father Edward Purcell, the Catholic priest who had married Donn and Louise so many years before.[19] Ella turned twenty-eight the month before the wedding, and Donn turned forty-seven.

Alas, Ella was injured in a railroad accident two years after their marriage, when she was returning to Cincinnati after receiving news that her mother had died. One of her legs was left paralyzed—and she had other enduring health problems—for the rest of what turned out to be a long life.

It appears that Donn had some problem with his own health the year after he and Ella married. In July 1867 he wrote a brief will in which he described himself as "being in a doubtful state of health." All of his estate was to go to Ella, with one exception. This was the house where he was born, on Main Street in Cincinnati, which his father had left to him and which he wanted to leave to his brother Abram Sanders Piatt, "that he may extricate himself from his present embarrassments."[20] Whatever the embarrassments were, Abram extricated himself, and he, Donn, and Ella all lived decades longer.

Donn's second marriage would last for many years, until his death. It seems to have been a very happy one. Whether it was more companionate than romantic is not certain. Could either of them ever forget his marriage to Louise? A friend of both Donn and Louise, the well-known writer Gail Hamilton (Mary Abigail Dodge), wrote in a private letter that she wondered what Ella might make of the inscription Donn had placed on Louise's tomb, about his "death in life" after Louise had gone. He had in effect said that he had died with his first wife. Might that not make Ella think that she was now united to a "moist unpleasant body"?[21]

In 1885, after Donn and Ella had been married for almost two decades, the press reported that he was said to have fathered an illegitimate daughter, born to an actress named Mary Burkhauser. A Cincinnati lawyer, Nathan E. Jordan, filed suit against Piatt, alleging that mother and daughter had sought his help until they could reach an amicable settlement with Piatt. Jordan said he had advanced the women $1,100, and he wanted Piatt to repay him. Jordan added that the women had told him that Piatt had, over some years, rented several different houses for them in Washington, D.C., and had "cohabitated" with the girl's mother.[22]

Both Jordan and Piatt must have felt some bitterness about the case. Before the Civil War their respective parents had been neighbors at West Liberty. Nathan Jordan's brother and Donn Piatt's nephew Benjamin Piatt Runkle had been two of the seven cofounders at Miami University of the Sigma Chi fraternity.[23]

Piatt was reported to have said that the Burkhausers were blackmailing him, that the girl was the daughter of a convict and he had taken her from the gutters of Cincinnati, educated her—and given her (but why?) his name. The girl, who was known as Nellie Piatt, and her mother had, he said, tried to extort money from him, but he had refused them.[24] The outcome of the Cincinnati case is unknown. It was followed by two cases brought against Piatt in the court of common pleas at Bellefontaine. Piatt swore in an affidavit on September 26, 1888, that when Nellie was six years old, around 1859, the Purcell brothers, archbishop and priest, had asked him to look after the child; that he had treated her as a foster child, but that she was not his natural child; that he had had her educated in Catholic schools in Kentucky, Indiana, and then Washington, D.C., moving her to a new school when she became "discontented"; and that when she was eighteen, she had for a time lived on Capitol Hill with his cousins John J. and Sarah Bryan Piatt. Later, Donn had agreed to give the girl and her mother sixty dollars a month, half to pay the rent on a small house in Washington and half for expenses. It appears that he stopped the payments after Nellie had proved a profligate in his eyes, spending a huge amount, two hundred dollars, for a sealskin coat.

Things got ugly. Nellie claimed Piatt had come to see her once in Cincinnati and had fallen on his knees and begged her to save him from the penitentiary. Why should he fear the penitentiary? "Well he had ruined me between fifteen and sixteen years of age." Later, after it became clear that she had been led to charge incest by "ill advisers," she admitted the charge was untrue.

Affidavits were exchanged by the parties for at least several years. In 1892, after Donn's death, the writer Celia Logan (Connelly) swore in an affidavit that she was a longtime family friend and that Ella had been deeply disturbed by the lengthy proceedings and finally threatened a separation, until Connelly told Ella all she knew—including the fact that Donn called Nellie his niece. A lawyer named David S. Hounshell swore in an affidavit the same year that Donn had told him "that she was the daughter of his brother Wyckoff Piatt."

It appears that Donn was blameless, that for a number of years he had been looking after the illegitimate child of Jacob Wykoff Piatt, who had died in 1857 and whose memory Donn revered.[25] (Perhaps not coincidentally, in 1888 Celia Logan published a novel called *Her Strange Fate,* in which a woman who has been adopted as a child learns only in adulthood her birth father's identity.)[26]

Donn's other brother, Abram, had been a general, but, thanks to Abraham Lincoln, Donn had not—at least not yet. In May 1866 a friendly member of Congress from Ohio, William Lawrence, wrote Piatt that he had requested the War Department to grant Donn Piatt a retroactive commission as brevet brigadier general. It was not uncommon to grant such commissions. That year hundreds of Union officers who had gone back to civilian life were given retroactive promotions. During the war Piatt had wanted to be a general; now he could have the title. But Piatt was sorry to learn what the congressman had done. He wrote Lawrence to say,

> I could have had, I presume, the brevet you propose, long since, had I desired it. The officers I served under having earnestly urged my promotion to that

rank while in the field would now, I am proud to say, join in any attempt at a
mere compliment, if I wished it. But I do not. On the contrary, I should feel
shamed if such brevet were conferred at the instigation of political friends. The
highest rank that I reached while in the service was that of lieutenant-colonel,
and now, long after that service, to jump up by brevet to brigadier-general, is
to make a farce and a mockery of what I hold sacred, the years of service I gave
to my country on the field.[27]

Piatt also wrote to Stanton, who was still the secretary of war and, like Piatt,
did not like all these honorary postbellum promotions:

> I received by yesterday mail a note from the Hon. Wm. Lawrence that he had
> applied to your Dpt. for "a brevet of Brig. General." You know my opinions
> on this and I have the pleasure to know yours—so I write to assure you that
> the application was made without my knowledge and I beg that it may not
> be complied with. I struggled hard, as you are aware, for promotion while in
> the service. It was I believe an honorable ambition. Rank meant power and I
> fondly believed I could do more service did I possess it. But I am too old,[28] and
> ill and unhappy to care for empty honors. My only stimulant, healthy stimu-
> lant, to success is gone. I fight on now to save myself from thought of myself.
> That is all. There is yet another reason—I have stood by you on all occasions in
> public and private and were I now to receive any thing at your hands this mean
> miserable world would say "Piatt has his reward."[29]

Lawrence's request was therefore not acted on, and Piatt was called Colonel for
the rest of his life, while many others became postbellum generals. Stanton would
no doubt have been happy to recommend his friend for a brevet. Years later, Piatt wrote, "At the end of the late civil war the rush for epaulets was wider-spread
than the gallant enlistment of volunteers during the conflict, and the great war
secretary, Stanton, with a cynical sense of humor peculiar to him, brevetted all
the sutlers, wagon-makers, commissaries, contractors, quartermasters—in a word,
every body soliciting the honor."[30] There were few men who, like Donn Piatt, were
offered a postwar brevet and refused it. There were in any case other possibilities
for Piatt's advancement in rank.

In January 1867 the Republican governor of Ohio, Jacob D. Cox, announced
that he would not run for reelection. His withdrawal from the coming race
opened the field, and at least eight men were spoken of as possible candidates,
including Donn Piatt, Robert Schenck, and Rutherford Hayes.[31] It was Hayes who
became the Republican candidate, and who was elected governor by a narrow
margin. Piatt must have been disappointed. He spoke out for Hayes during the
election campaign in a positive if not enthusiastic tone, saying, "The people will

find his utterances full of sound thought, and his deportment modest, dignified, and unpretending. . . . Possessed of high order of talent, enriched by stores of information, General Hayes is one of the few men capable of accomplishing much without any egotistical assertion of self."[32] Despite his friendship with Hayes, before the campaign ended Piatt crossed party lines to write articles supporting Hayes's Democratic opponent, Allen G. Thurman, who years earlier had visited Donn and Louise at Mac-o-cheek.[33]

Meanwhile, Ella's physical condition was extremely worrisome. In late 1867 she and Donn left Ohio for New York to consult Dr. Charles Fayette Taylor. The doctor and his elder brother, Dr. George H. Taylor, had developed a well-known system of exercise and massage therapy combined with hydropathy and good nutrition, based on a cure invented in Sweden.[34] Within six months Ella had improved to the point that she was no longer in any danger of death, as she apparently had been; but she remained an invalid.[35] Three years later, when Donn took her vacationing at Lake George in the Adirondacks, he wrote a nephew, "Your aunt is yet very feeble."[36]

In New York, Horace Greeley tried repeatedly to get Piatt to join the staff of the *Tribune*.[37] Piatt declined the invitations. Although they had long agreed on the need to end slavery in America, they disagreed on a number of problems, notably trade. Greeley was a protectionist, and Piatt favored free—or relatively free—trade.

Later, Miller tells us, a number of stories circulated about the job negotiations between Greeley and Piatt. The latter had supposedly wanted such a high salary that Greeley responded, "Why, Donn, you don't understand. I don't ask you to become owner of the concern, but merely an editor."

Another version had it that Piatt had applied for work on the *Tribune* and told Greeley that he had printed enough of Piatt's stuff that he must know he could do good work. Greeley replied that what Piatt called good work was not what he wanted. He said, "A certain amount of dullness is necessary to make a newspaper please the masses. The editor of a newspaper can less well afford to be brilliant than stupid." Piatt supposedly replied, "I had not looked at it in that light, but come to think of it, the success of your paper can be accounted for on no other ground. But you don't know me, Horace; you are not aware of the infinite reach of my versatility. I solemnly assure you that, if occasion requires, I can be as stupid as yourself."

Still another story was that Greeley as a joke offered Piatt the position of agricultural editor, warning him that he would be expected to write learnedly about pumpkins and squash. Piatt responded that at the moment he knew nothing about pumpkins and squashes, "but I can soon learn all about them through a study of your editorial corps."[38]

Whether or not any of those stories was true, certainly Piatt liked to make fun of his eccentric friend, just as he had mocked him that day in Paris when Greeley's French failed him. There seems to be an echo of Greeley's offer to make Piatt agricultural editor in an 1871 report that Piatt, by then editor of his own newspaper in Washington, had just spent a day in New York "for the purpose, as he says, of securing Mr. Greeley to contribute to the farming department of THE CAPITAL." Piatt said the report was not quite correct; "It is true that we sought to make the venerable Greeley [at sixty, he was eight years older than Piatt] a contributor to our journal, but what we really did solicit was a series of agricultural articles on *What He does not Know about Farming.*"

Piatt also told the story of a man who took Greeley's hat by mistake at a presidential inaugural ball and, wearing it home, began to have strange hallucinations. The man finally fell asleep and dreamed that the world was a coffee mill and he was grinding it with a crank. Piatt returned to this "crank" theme a number of times, saying that Greeley himself was like a hand organ continually grinding out the same old tunes with a crank.[39]

Although Piatt never went with Greeley's paper, he did, for a time, work as associate editor of the *New York Sun*.[40] The *Sun* had recently been taken over by Charles A. Dana, who had learned journalism under Greeley at the *Tribune*. During the war, readers had been absorbed by news of battles and casualties—never had a war been so well and fully reported—but now something new was required if papers were to keep readers' attention. It was Dana who showed the way, with a simplicity of style coupled with stories of human interest.[41] It is not clear how much time Piatt spent on Dana's paper, but it must have been good experience. However, when in 1868 he was offered another job, in Washington, he and Ella moved there.

Piatt had not achieved greatness, but he had known America's great men when he had visited the capital in earlier years. What could he accomplish now that he was going to live there?

⋇ 5 ⋇

PIATT TO THE CAPITAL

Donn Piatt had long had what might be called a love-hate relationship with the city of Washington. As a young man he had been repelled by the vacuousness and ineptitude he saw in Congress and the White House. Washington was hot and dusty in summer and often frigid and muddy in winter. Even so, Louise Piatt had written as early as 1855 that she sensed from what Donn told her "what a magnificent place it must yet be."[1] Washington's population was to reach 109,000 by the census of 1870. That was twice what it had been a decade earlier, just before the Civil War, but Washington was still only half the size of Cincinnati (1870 population, 216,000), the handsome city where Donn had been born and educated and to which he often returned.

After the war the national capital was all in all still shabby rather than handsome, despite a few grand buildings. Even its greatest thoroughfare, Pennsylvania Avenue, was unpaved. However, the presence of the government, the diplomatic corps, and not least the growing corps of journalists and of lobbyists, made Washington a very interesting—indeed, unique—American city. Nor could anyone who visited there in late April or May ever forget the blooming fruit trees, dogwoods, and azaleas in the city, the broad tidal river stretching down toward the sea, and the green Virginia hills beyond.

Beyond the dogwoods and azaleas, the war had made the federal government the country's largest employer. Now Washington's "fostering hand" was enlarging its role, overriding state governments to give the vote to former slaves; creating a pension system for a million veterans; modernizing and extending taxation; subsidizing the new transcontinental railroad.[2] The new Department of Agriculture, created during the war, was setting up experimental stations and extension services across the country; the National Weather Service began issuing forecasts for the public; and as the country's population grew, so did the nationwide operations of the post office.[3]

At the same time, some people sensed an increase in corruption in America and interested themselves in the cause of reform. For some Northerners this was perhaps a question of turning the old antislavery drive into new channels.[4] For others, though, the end of the war meant there was no more to fear, and there ensued "a season of contentment and of lassitude" in which at least initially there seemed little need for people to interest themselves in national affairs.[5]

Piatt did not believe in lassitude, and he soon found that there was a lot to do in the national capital. He went there in 1868 to become the correspondent of the *Cincinnati Commercial,* which under Murat Halstead became perhaps the most important newspaper west of the Alleghenies. Piatt and Halstead had known each other since before the war and were fellow members of the Cincinnati Literary Club. Unlike Piatt, who had enlisted in the Union army at the age of forty-one, Halstead, ten years younger, had never served in the war.[6] He joined the staff of the *Commercial* in 1853, became editor-in-chief in 1859, and in 1866 took over active control of the paper.

The war had brought many journalists to Washington, and after the war more American newspapers were finding the need for a correspondent based there. It was a time, though, when some journalists tended to refrain from criticism of officialdom; when most newspapers were still what a standard history calls "servile party organs."[7] That did not include either Halstead or his new man in Washington. Piatt named the House of Representatives the "Cave of the Winds" and called the Senate the "Fog Bank." Soon the foibles of statesmen were being mocked without mercy in Piatt's dispatches.

He found good company in the growing Washington press corps. Two of the top political correspondents—one historian calls them the two foremost—were Henry V. Boynton of the *Cincinnati Gazette,* who, like Piatt, had been a Union lieutenant colonel from Ohio, and George Alfred Townsend, who had been perhaps the youngest Civil War correspondent and now wrote for several papers.[8] Both would become close collaborators with Donn Piatt, Townsend soon and Boynton years later.

Piatt wrote to his friend Friedrich Hassaurek, the Cincinnati German American editor who had been Lincoln's envoy to Ecuador, that he was also finding time to write for magazines. He said that what he really wanted was to give up political writing and turn full-time to belles lettres, but that the lack of international copyright agreements kept him from doing so.[9] That seems a stretch. The copyright problem, which was a serious one, does not seem to have deterred many if any other writers. In any case, Piatt was less than fully content to be working under editor Halstead. Soon he was writing Hassaurek, "Halstead thinks he pays me an extravagant price for my letters. I am offered the same money from other sources."[10] By May of that year he had decided to stay in journalism, and with Halstead, if he could work things right; he told Hassaurek, "Journalism is not only my forte—but there is money in it."[11] Halstead may have raised his pay; in July Piatt wrote, "Halstead . . . has always been very kind to me—pays me the highest price for these letters. . . . Still I would wish [him] to think them more valuable."[12]

Halstead and the *Cincinnati Commercial* gave priority to the news from Washington. A "special telegram to the Commercial" from Washington, written by Piatt, appeared weekly on the first page, and on page two a "Washington Letter" signed D. P. The "Letters" were sharp and critical but less so than his subsequent reports and comments from the national capital, in his own newspaper.

People began to take note of the man with the rare name; his reporting in the *Commercial* was being picked up by papers around the country. It was an age when newspapers were extremely important in informing the public and molding public opinion. In a true metropolis, political and social leaders might sway the populace with means other than the press, and a paper might count less—but no city in America was a metropolis like London or Paris. New York City was of course far larger than Washington and by 1870 had a population of a million.[13] This was sizable, but London had over three million. Moreover, New Yorkers made up little more than 3 percent of America's overall population, which was still three quarters rural. If rural, though, people were literate. In Piatt's Logan County, for example, the 1870 census reported that only 4 percent of those aged ten or more could not read.[14] And Americans in general had established the habit of reading their daily newspaper.[15]

Piatt was probably helped by having a name that few could forget—once they learned to spell it. The bearer of the name reported that during a vacation on Lake George in New York, he found that the village postmaster had failed to deliver to him eighteen letters, after reading his name as Pratt. When, Piatt said, he remonstrated, the postmaster replied, "Well, stranger, ef I had such an outlandish name as your'n I'd go back and be a baby, so as to be christened over, I would."[16]

Piatt returned to Ohio on a visit in October 1869. He hoped but failed to see Rutherford Hayes, now governor of Ohio, in Cincinnati. He had written the governor the previous December, to ask him to pardon a one-armed war veteran who had been sentenced to a year in prison "on the testimony of a drunken brute no decent man ought to believe."[17] When he missed seeing the governor in Cincinnati, he left him a note saying that he had wanted to tender his congratulations to "one of the two most fortunate political men in Ohio."[18] Hayes afterward wrote Piatt a friendly and also prescient letter: "I was sorry not to see you. I wanted to hear your talk . . . and as I am not likely to meet you often, I now want to know where you are to settle . . . that I can have the next best thing to your talk—your writings. Judging by our last conversation, for pecuniary and other reasons you prefer a position to being merely a disturbing element; but as I see it, the latter is your vocation—a vocation in which you can do great things."[19]

That same year Piatt, always an opponent of slavery although the grandson of a former Kentucky slave owner, visited Kentucky to speak at a Great Educational

Convention in Louisville that was chaired by the Reverend Henry J. Young, a prominent clergyman of the African Methodist Episcopal Church. There was at the time a massive movement in the North to help the South's former slaves, in good part by providing them an education. Thousands of Northern whites went south in what has been called "a dramatic moment of interracial fraternity."[20]

Other speakers at the interracial convention in Louisville included Martin R. Delaney, an African American graduate of Harvard who had served as the first black major in the Union army; John Gregg Fee, the son of a slave owner and the founder of interracial Berea College in Kentucky; and John Mercer Langston, an Oberlin graduate who was the first black lawyer in Ohio and first dean of the Howard University law school in Washington. The convention petitioned the Kentucky legislature "for the education of colored youth" and adopted resolutions setting forth the political grievances of African Americans and urging blacks "to cultivate habits of morality, industry and economy."[21]

Piatt maintained his interest in the condition of black Americans. Soon a few young black men were being nominated for West Point;[22] there were even African Americans in the U.S. Congress. However, Piatt wrote, "An American citizen of African descent can be crowded into the Senate, but then he boards at a colored hotel, and no Senator is bound to associate with him. And I can tell you that no Senator does."[23] Nor, he might have added, would he himself necessarily wish to do so. While Donn Piatt sympathized with the plight of black Americans, the majority of them remained poor and uneducated people.

Piatt had made clear in his 1865 speech in Dayton that he was no more ready to associate with black Americans in society than were other white Americans of his time. His interest in securing educational opportunities for the black youth of Kentucky went along with his continuing hope that Southern blacks would stay home rather than migrate to the North. Later, when an African American congressman, Robert Brown Elliott, spoke in favor of Senator Charles Sumner's bill to outlaw racial discrimination in public transportation, hotels, and schools, Piatt's paper would complain that Elliott wanted to "thrust the black upon the white."[24] (Horace Greeley, who before the war had been not just antislavery like Piatt but an abolitionist, seems to have felt still more strongly about black migration—and to have been prejudiced against black people. After his death he was reported to have written privately in 1870 to Josephine Griffing, a social worker helping freedmen in Washington, that African Americans were "an easy, worthless race, taking no thought of the morrow. . . . Your course aggravates their weakness. . . . Unless you change your course speedily and signally, the swarming of blacks to the District will increase, and the argument that slavery is their natural condition will be measurably strengthened.")[25]

Even if Piatt did not want to socialize with blacks, he wanted whites to realize that blacks were making progress, and he wanted to encourage the blacks who now made up a third of the population of the national capital. African Americans in Washington, unlike those in Ohio, had in 1867 gained the right to vote.[26] At an 1870 election rally in Washington, Piatt said, "To you, American citizens of African descent, I can say that I was your friend when you needed friends, and I seek to be your adviser now that you are clothed with the rights, privileges and duties of citizenship . . . having a right to speak in the streets and before the council chamber of our national capital. This city belongs to us all."[27]

A later Piatt article, entitled "Colored Men of Washington," gave sketches of a number of successful African Americans including Frederick Douglass, who was then editor and proprietor of the *New National Era;* Carter A. Stewart, a Washington businessman who "is in affluent circumstances, and is regarded as a cultivated man and a public-spirited citizen"; and John M. Langston, the Ohioan with whom Piatt had addressed the Louisville convention, who was now teaching law at Howard University and serving on the board of health of the District of Columbia.[28]

Some years after this, Piatt told a black church congregation in Washington that although African Americans were being denied the right to vote, "I have high hope of you. . . . The same sturdy patience that carried you through the long, sad period of unrequited toil, will serve you well in these later trials." He spoke to them mainly about education, and he said what might have been said a century later. There was a zeal then for schooling among African Americans. Piatt warned them that formal schooling was not enough; parents and churches had key roles to play, and "we measure our little ones for cells in the penitentiary when we neglect their moral training."

Piatt was never what today would be called politically correct, and one suspects some members of the Washington congregation felt he was talking down to them. This was the Fifteenth Street Presbyterian Church, and a number of members were prosperous merchants and artisans. Even before the war, the church had boasted a famous choir, cushions and carpets, gold-lettered pews, a marble-topped pulpit, and fine chandeliers.[29]

But Piatt did not stop with telling the congregation how to raise their children. He told them that the staying power of African Americans had been learned in slavery and that "slavery was your education, and therefore a blessing. . . . The master weakened, while the slave grew strong."[30] One can imagine stirring in the pews when he called slavery a blessing.

By 1871 Donn Piatt had become known across the country for his reporting out of Washington. Most, not all, comments about him were favorable. Typical was the response of *The Nation,* which in January 1871 styled him "the celebrated Washington correspondent of the *Cincinnati Commercial.*"[31] That March the editor of *The Galaxy,* a popular monthly, asked him to replace Mark Twain as a contributor of humorous pieces.

Twain was already well known for *The Innocents Abroad; Tom Sawyer* and *Huckleberry Finn* lay in the future. The author was distressed when both his little son and his father-in-law died, a friend died of typhoid in Twain's own bedroom, and his wife, Olivia, had a difficult childbirth and also came down with typhoid. His work for *The Galaxy* became, as Justin Kaplan puts it, a depressing chore; what he wrote was often not funny but bitter. Twain himself wrote ruefully, in his final contribution to *The Galaxy*, "I think some of the 'humor' I have written during this period could have been injected into a funeral sermon without disturbing the solemnity of the occasion."[32]

Enter Piatt, who had recently met the young Mark Twain at a dinner given in Twain's honor by Samuel S. Cox, once an Ohio editor and now a member of Congress from New York, at that most elegant Washington restaurant, Welcker's on Pennsylvania Avenue. While they were at dinner, Twain received a telegram informing him that Olivia was seriously ill, and he rushed off to take the next train home. A month later, when Olivia was out of danger, he finally wrote Cox to thank him for the dinner, adding that he had taken a strong liking to Donn Piatt.[33]

Piatt for his part had taken an equally strong liking to—or was it rather an interest in?—Mark Twain. Piatt sympathized with the younger writer's problems, yet he could not refrain from laughter when Twain tried to tell him his professional woes. After the Cox dinner he wrote a newspaper column that spoke of Twain with some slight mockery:

> This was my first meeting with Mark Twain. . . . He is not only careless about his clothes, but he is positively ignorant on the subject and labors under the impression that the garment that hangs so loosely upon his shoulders is a coat. . . .
>
> It is quite impossible for him to produce in his conversation a serious effect. The exceedingly droll quaintness of his solemn countenance, added to the drawl of his voice, makes one laugh when the speaker is really striving to be serious. . . .
>
> Unfortunately in the midst of the dinner he received a telegram telling him of the sickness of his wife, and he was forced to leave upon the next train. . . . I was anxious to know him personally. He and Bret Harte are the two men of all others one would go the greatest distance to look into and study.[34]

Mark Twain was apparently not offended by what Piatt had written about him and exchanged friendly letters with him, telling Piatt of his not altogether pleasant experiences with the proprietors of *The Galaxy*. They had paid him just three thousand dollars a year, and when he left, they owed him three months' pay. Piatt, perhaps helped by his new friend's advice, won a salary of five thousand dollars. He contributed several lighthearted pieces that added to his own growing reputation, and he asked Twain whether Twain could provide him with some material and whether Twain and his wife might join him and Ella that summer at Narragansett.[35]

Soon the *Brooklyn Eagle* was reporting that *The Galaxy* had survived the loss of Mark Twain very well. The paper complimented Piatt on bringing a number of other humorists into his new department in the magazine, the "Club Room," rather than doing all the writing himself, as Twain had done.[36]

It is not clear how long Piatt and Twain continued on close terms. The Piatts attended a dinner one evening at the New York home of Melville D. Landon, another well-known American humorist of the times, who wrote as "Eli Perkins." The other male guests at the dinner were Twain and David Ross Locke, who, writing as "Petroleum V. Nasby," had published a series of mocking letters during the Civil War that were favorite reading for Abraham Lincoln. After the last course, and after the ladies had retired, it was time for tall stories. Twain's contribution, Piatt later recalled, was a tale about a horse he had owned during his days in Nevada. The horse was so fast he had to be guided by electricity, since he ran faster than sound and commands would not reach him from behind.[37] Whether Piatt tried to outdo Twain he did not say.

Despite the comfortable income Piatt was making at *The Galaxy,* he soon left that magazine, and the *Cincinnati Commercial,* as well, for another enterprise, one that was to make him famous in America. Even if Murat Halstead paid him well for his weekly reports to the *Commercial,* Piatt was not satisfied with the pay. On the other hand, although Halstead often disagreed with the opinions Piatt expressed in his dispatches, he rarely edited what Piatt wrote.[38]

In Washington Piatt had soon made friends with George Alfred Townsend, who had been a correspondent for the *New York World,* covering the Civil War and then the brief Austro-Prussian war of 1866. Piatt wrote of Townsend, in one of his weekly reports for the *Cincinnati Commercial* at the beginning of 1870, that he was a man who had come out of the Civil War as "the most graphic and picturesque of correspondents," and who after coming to Washington "made a revelation and a revolution in the field of letters."[39] Townsend could not help liking a fellow who said things like that. He and Piatt agreed—we do not know which of them first raised the idea—that Washington needed a new paper, a weekly that was both political and had a literary tone. Money was needed, and Piatt was the one who found it. It appears that their financial backer was William S. Huntington of the First National Bank of Washington.[40]

Piatt soon left Halstead's employ, and his and Townsend's new paper, *The Capital,* first appeared in March 1871. They seem to have advertised their new paper widely. That June, for example, the Tioga County, Pennsylvania, *Agitator* carried a lengthy advertisement for the new paper, which was said to be "NOT A PAPER FOR THE OLD PARTY FOGIES! but adapted to the intellectual requirements of our period. . . . THE ORGAN OF THE BETTER POPULACE." Subscriptions were three dollars a year, to be paid in advance.[41]

When Piatt left the *Cincinnati Commercial,* one of his colleagues there drew a flattering—and perhaps not inaccurate—picture of him:

All men seem to know, or know of him. He has grown to be one of the ce-
lebrities of the land. Many fear or dislike him for what he has written, and many
love and respect the man for his inherent good qualities and genuine kindness
of nature. . . . Many who know him well—and among others George Alfred
Townsend—have told us that Piatt was one of the most kind and genial men
they had ever known—one of the most unselfish and generous—doing more
individual favors to poor devils who had no claim on him; securing by persever-
ing personal efforts more places for wounded and worthy soldiers than any man
in Washington. . . . Piatt is no Bohemian in any sense of the word; is not dependent upon his pen for support . . . and is in all senses an independent writer. . . .
Wrongs and frauds . . . receive no mercy at his hands. . . . The country owes him
a debt of gratitude.[42]

The partners decided to alternate as editors. Townsend took charge the first
month, in general avoiding attacks on agencies or individuals—although the paper's first issue attacked President Grant as ignorant, incapable, and jealous of
others.[43] That was what Piatt wanted: fiery stuff. He wrote an article attacking the
regular army. He thought West Point produced snobs rather than soldiers.

Criticism of the military academy and its graduates did not originate with Piatt; it had been frequently voiced during the late war by members of the Congressional Joint Committee on the Conduct of the War.[44] Townsend nevertheless
refused to print Piatt's article. They parted ways, amicably, it seems.[45] Townsend
left for California, and *The Capital* was Piatt's alone.[46] Later, Piatt would become
a wealthy man, but for now the new paper left him hard pressed financially, at a
time when he was also concerned about the management of his farmland and mill
back at Mac o check.[47]

The Capital was soon attracting attention and selling well. Four months after
its first appearance the paper reported, "THE CAPITAL has now by far the largest
circulation of any weekly published in the District. As this is a question affecting our advertising patrons only, we are prepared to prove our statement if any
such call upon us for a verification."[48] One or more of the daily Washington papers still outsold Piatt's weekly in sales, but among Washington weeklies he soon
outdistanced the competition. An 1872 directory showed *The Capital* claiming a
circulation of 12,000, while its nearest competitor, the *Sunday Morning Chronicle*,
claimed only 7,500.[49]

The Capital had begun as a Sunday paper, but in October 1871, as its sales outside as well as inside Washington increased, Piatt changed the publication schedule. Henceforth, the paper would go out on Saturday to subscribers outside the
capital, while an edition containing more local news would go to Washington
readers each Sunday. By the following year the paper's Baltimore business had

increased to the point that the paper opened an office in that city, with Eugene L. Didier as the Baltimore editor.[50] *The Capital* did not initially report circulation figures to its readers, but there is a casual mention in an issue of January 1873, a little less than two years from the paper's inception, that it had 30,000 subscribers and, it claimed, 100,000 readers.[51] Outside Washington, by early 1875 the paper was for sale at newsstands in a number of cities across the country, mainly in the East and Midwest. These included six locations in New York City and one as far west as San Francisco.[52]

Perhaps the claim of 30,000 subscribers had been exaggerated; it was not confirmed by an outside audit. On February 25, 1877, not quite six years after *The Capital* first appeared, the paper carried a sworn statement that 14,400 copies of the edition of February 18 had been run off. Fourteen thousand was less than mass circulation, even in those years—in New York City, Greeley's *Tribune* claimed a circulation of 150,000 for its weekly edition in 1872[53]—but the *North American Review,* perhaps the most influential journal in nineteenth-century America, had a circulation of less than 4,000.

Piatt's name was becoming known across the country, but not through what must have been relatively modest direct sales of his paper outside Washington. With increasing frequency his articles and editorials were quoted and reprinted, often within a day or two, in other papers and journals. The telegraph system had spread across the country—the transcontinental telegraph was completed in 1861, eight years before the transcontinental railroad—and newspapers in both small and large places made extensive use of pieces sent by wire.[54]

Beyond reports and editorials, the advertisements in *The Capital* were many, diverse, and no doubt profitable. They included offers for Wilstar's Balsam of Wild Cherry, the great remedy for consumption; bargains in men's clothing offered by Haber's, at 7th and D Streets; the marvelous Anti-Corrosive Pen; theatrical announcements; pleasant vacation resorts at Virginia's several springs or, for those staying in town, excursions down the Potomac River every summer Saturday on the splendid steamer *Georgianna;* and many attractive pieces of real estate. A beautiful country seat, thirty-five acres with a two-story mansion located just two miles from the Navy Yard, was offered for sale in 1872 for the low sum of $12,000, on easy terms. One could buy wooded lots of four to twelve acres along the famed and romantic Rock Creek, just ten minutes' drive from the city.[55]

Piatt enjoyed being his own boss. Now that he did not have to submit his reporting for approval by the editor of the *Cincinnati Commercial,* he could write,

MURAT HALSTEAD began his career as a great writer of fiction. The probabilities are he will end as he began.

MURAT HALSTEAD is said to be one of the most laborious men in the United States. He is in labor every twenty-four hours. But whether it is worth while to go to so much for so little, is a question of taste and parturition. . . .

The Cincinnati *Commercial* and New York *World* say that if we had less sense THE CAPITAL would be more successful. We never before so clearly understood the mysterious success of the *Commercial* and *World.* . . . [56]

The president of the United States, elected in November 1868 to succeed Andrew Johnson, was now U. S. Grant, Piatt's fellow Ohioan, who had led the Union army to victory in 1865. For Piatt, though, the greatest Union general had been not Grant but George H. Thomas, the "Rock of Chickamauga." Later—but only later—Piatt would write of Grant as the general who at the Wilderness had sacrificed to Lee much of "an army that he had not the ability to handle."[57] Grant was the general who at Shiloh could "expose his camp . . . to . . . horrible butchery while he remained drinking on a gunboat ten miles from the scene of disaster."[58] Piatt did not invent the story that Grant was drunk at Shiloh. Others, too, claimed that Grant drank at times—some said heavily—but there is no evidence that he did so at Shiloh.[59] No matter—Grant's alleged drinking was a theme that Piatt, once he took it up, would return to frequently.

The war was receding in people's memories, and the times were changing. The great general had changed, too. Grant was no longer the simple soldier who accepted Lee's surrender while wearing a dusty private's uniform. After the war he wore smart suits and, as one Grant biographer says, "the record shows twenty years of almost uninterrupted attention to the fancy folk on the right side of the tracks."[60]

It seems that most people initially assumed that, as Henry Adams put it, a general who had commanded half a million or a million men in the field must know how to administer a government.[61] But did he?

Before Grant's inauguration in March 1869, Piatt was cautiously optimistic about what Grant might do and be as president. He may well have wondered whether he might ask Grant to give him a post; perhaps he still had dreams of becoming minister to France. In any case, as a newsman he wanted a firsthand look at the man, and he did his best to find out Grant's plans. That January he reported in the Cincinnati *Commercial* that "the shrewder set" in Washington identified several persons sure to be named to Grant's cabinet, including Robert Schenck, who was to be the secretary of the navy.[62] That was not to be, but Grant would later give Schenck a diplomatic plum.

In February 1869, several weeks before Grant's inauguration, Piatt wrote in the *Commercial* that he must be the only man in Washington who had not met the president-elect. "I could," he wrote, "take my Congressman and tell him to introduce me, for my Congressman is bound to do whatever I order—or die. But I don't like the process; and yet I am curious to see what manner of man Providence has gotten up for us." Piatt then went to call on Mrs. Grant. He was pleased that when he left her at the end of his call, she had in a "gentle, thoughtful manner" called him "Colonel Piatt" and not Pratt or Platt as many others did. Therefore, he wrote, he had said to her, "You are a dear, good woman, and I hope your life may be as happy, as it is prosperous."[63] (Can one see in that "prosperous" that Piatt was already wondering about Grant's financial dealings?)

On March 3 Piatt boarded a horse car on F Street and was surprised to see "quietly seated in the corner our President elect." Piatt decided not to approach him. "Here's genuine democracy, thought I to myself, as I settled on the opposite seat and indulged in a healthy stare at the knobby, square head and solemn face before me. I was having an interview, and one about as satisfactory as anybody can have with this man, who smokes and says nothing." Another passenger was not so polite, Piatt said. A clergyman sat down next to Grant and began to importune him about something. Grant sat silent.

Finally, a few days after the inauguration, Piatt went to call on the new president, after someone who knew Grant "assured me that General Grant would take the visit kindly." There was also some matter that he wanted to raise with the president. Piatt went to the White House and was received by Frederick T. Dent, who had been Grant's roommate at West Point, whose sister Grant had married, who had been Grant's military secretary in the war—and who was now the senior White House usher. After a few minutes Dent ushered Piatt into Grant's office, where he saw the president seated at his desk "smoking his everlasting cigar, and listening to a gentleman far gone in years and adipose." Eventually, the old gentleman left—but Senator John Sherman of Ohio was there, ahead of Piatt, so Piatt sat and watched (but could not hear) the conversation between Grant and Sherman, which lasted a half hour. Sherman, Piatt could see, did almost all the talking. Finally, Piatt wrote,

I was introduced, and received the compliment of a quick glance that for the sixteenth part of a second lit up his eyes, and then passed out. For another sixteenth part of a second his hands lay passively in mine. I said:

"As I had no business with you, Mr. President, I was about leaving the city without even paying my respects, as I knew you were beset by good people having business."

"That is pleasant," he said, quietly.

"I fear," I continued, "that the pleasure will be short-lived, for I have found some business."

"That is not so pleasant," he said, and smiled.

"You will permit me to state it?"

"Certainly."

I then went into my little affair, that took about ten minutes of his time. Ending, I said:

"Goodbye, Mr. President. I hope you will have health and strength enough to reform our civil service, and get the revenues honestly collected and disbursed."

"I intend to try," he replied, "and if one set won't do it, I'll try another, and keep trying until I find honest and capable men."

I felt comfortable. I had called a quick look into his eyes, and had been honored with the longest speech he had uttered while I was in the room.

Now, if you ask me what I think of General Grant, I will tell you I do not know. I believe that he is honest, earnest, and in the great work he has before him, I hope, capable. He certainly walks out upon it alone. The old sort who gather about the President, are intimate with and influence him, are not about Grant. I do not feel the influence in the atmosphere. It may be all right, but I do not know. I only hope it is.[64]

What was Piatt's "little affair" that he raised with Grant? Did he perhaps ask to be considered for some government post, like minister to France?[65] If so—and an indication of this came later—he must soon have been rebuffed, because by the next month he was already poking fun at nepotism in the White House. He reported that there was a new arrival in Washington who was at first believed to be another Grant brother-in-law. He turned out to be only a forty-eighth cousin. He could not be made a postmaster, since he was illiterate; indications were that he would be given a diplomatic or consular appointment.[66]

Piatt's mockery, whatever his motives, proved prescient. The American diplomatic and consular spoils system was far from new, but there had been a movement toward reform of the system that, one experienced observer wrote, broke down under Grant.[67] The later judgment of State Department historians was that under Grant "the spoils system gained in influence. President Grant offered legations and consulates freely to relatives, friends, and partisans."[68] The recipients of diplomatic appointments included his brother-in-law M. J. Cramer, who became minister to Denmark, and his cousin Silas A. Hudson, sent as minister to Guatemala.

Particular damage seems to have been done by his first secretary of state, Elihu B. Washburne, who had absolutely no qualifications for the job. Years later Eugene Schuyler, a man the *New York Times* called not just the best but the *only* American diplomatist, wrote that, although Washburne had resigned after only twelve days in the job, he "did harm that it took his successor nearly eight years to remedy."[69] (Washburne then became minister to France—the post that perhaps Piatt had hoped for—where, after finally learning his job, he redeemed himself, turning in what has been called the best performance of any of Grant's appointees.)[70]

Piatt had initially been welcome not only in the Grant White House but at the homes of members of Grant's cabinet. He wrote a light piece for the *Cincinnati Commercial* describing how he and his friends "Jones" and "Robinson" had been among the many callers, on New Year's Day of 1870, at the homes of the secretaries of state, war, and treasury. To take them around, Robinson had hired an elegant coach with a driver and footman in livery. Piatt said, "I refused positively to enter the glassy varnished affair, with its coat of arms on the panels. It is against my principles to ride under livery . . . unpleasant to my Republican Democracy." The result was that they went calling in a carriage with worn-out horses and a shabby, perhaps drunken driver who looked still worse after he took a fall onto a muddy street.[71]

Even before starting *The Capital* in 1871, Piatt had decided to picture Grant to the public as an even greater failure as a president than he had been as a general. It was a view shared by many thinking Americans. Henry Adams, then a journalist in Washington, wrote that "Grant's administration outraged every rule of ordinary decency, but scores of promising men . . . were ruined in saying so."[72]

Piatt the journalist said so and was not ruined. He insisted that Grant was a heavy drinker and called him "His Inebriated Excellency." He claimed that the president could not be held responsible for what happened in his administration—because he was drunk.

The stories of Grant drinking in the White House cannot be confirmed, but Piatt believed them—or at least claimed to believe them. Conceivably, Murat Halstead encouraged him in this. Halstead was a close friend of General John A. McClernand, who had been Grant's subordinate until Grant removed him from command in 1863, and who had sent W. J. Kountz, commander of Grant's river steamboat fleet, to Lincoln with a secondhand report that Grant had been "Gloriously drunk."[73] Halstead himself had written a letter to Salmon Chase (and Chase had forwarded the letter to Lincoln) claiming that Grant "is a poor drunken imbecile . . . most of the time more than half drunk, and much of the time idiotically drunk."[74]

Even if the stories of Grant drinking were not true, major scandals began to come to light in his administration. At the top the scandals included the bribery of Vice President Schuyler Colfax and Secretary of War William W. Belknap (the only cabinet secretary ever impeached) in separate schemes, as well as the enlistment of another of Grant's brothers-in-law, Abel Corbin, by speculators Jim Fisk and Jay Gould in their attempt to corner the gold market, which ended in 1869 with "Black Friday."[75] Among occasional columns in *The Capital* was a "Court Journal," which reported the doings, which the editor found not just evil but laughable, of "His Excellency" and his coterie in the White House.

Piatt and *The Capital* were far from being the only critics of the president and his administration. Beyond allegations of Grant's drinking there were scurrilous stories in other papers—that during the war he had stolen silverware, that now he took a cut of the gains of corrupt officeholders.[76] There were also weightier attacks and criticisms, especially as evidence mounted of scandals in the administration. The *Brooklyn Eagle*, for example, reported that beyond the involvement of Grant's brother-in-law Corbin in Black Friday, Corbin had made a million dollars as a sleeping partner in the "Erie Ring," a group led by Fisk and Gould that bribed New York legislators to favor the Erie Railroad over the rival New York Central.[77]

Grant ignored such attacks. He and his people often snubbed the press and treated journalists shabbily. This did not always work. Sometimes for lack of accurate information the press reported cases of malfeasance that had not occurred.[78]

There was no outward indication that the president took any notice of Piatt's attacks on him until the end of 1870, when the White House decided to fight back. Grant's private secretary, Orville Babcock, wrote to Secretary of State Hamilton Fish on December 30, "I am informed that one Don Piat was once a secty of the Legation at Paris, and while there he did things not creditable to a gentleman. . . . I am also informed that he was an aspirant and perhaps an applicant for office at the commencement of the present administration. If you have any information in your department on either subject please have it hunted up. . . . Don Piat is of no especial account but. . . . If you can find any record of Don Piat considered of interest please let me have it as early as possible."[79]

Piatt would have exploded if he had known of Babcock's letter, but most probably he never did. In any case, whether because Grant had refused him a post or because Piatt simply disliked Grant, he was hitting the administration hard for alleged corruption. Corruption in America had begun long before Grant took office in Washington—at least as long ago as the Revolution—but the ethical climate had worsened during the recent war. As *Harper's* had written in April 1865, the new flow of paper money "brought everyone into Wall Street." The average price of shares had risen an unprecedented 300 percent between 1862 and 1864, and in a few weeks of 1863 the price of gold had shot up—due, it was commonly said, to the operations of a group of well-connected schemers known as the "Washington party."[80] Beyond this, there had been many cases throughout the war of contractors selling shoddy goods to the Union army, like the muskets that could not be fired at Bull Run. A former army quartermaster estimated that a good 20 percent of wartime expenditures had been "tainted with fraud."[81]

Years later it would be reported that there had even been a case of what today would be called insider trading, linked to the wartime White House. William Stoddard, the third of President Lincoln's three young private secretaries, had in 1862 apparently begun sending telegrams in cipher to a New York financier, reporting "information of a political, official and diplomatic character likely to affect gold, stocks, and other commodities."[82]

Was it not, in any case, time to take on President Grant with full force? Grant had installed in the White House a former lieutenant colonel, Adam Badeau, who had served him faithfully during the war as his military secretary and was now busy on a work glorifying Grant's wartime accomplishments. Badeau had already published in 1869 the first volume of what would eventually be a three-volume glorification of his commander and patron, *Military History of Ulysses S. Grant.*

Piatt saw another side to the Grant story waiting to be told. He found the Grant presidency reprehensible for a number of reasons. Beyond Grant's alleged drinking, and the gang of scoundrels that Piatt identified in and around the White House, there was what seemed to be an inability—or was it unwillingness?—of the chief executive to learn what was going on, to learn his job. As early as 1870

Piatt had written in one of his "Washington Letters" for the *Commercial,* "As His Excellency reads no papers, and permits no one to approach him who can or will tell the truth, he is forced to drive his unhappy executive skull against the stone wall of experience."[83]

Grant went, every summer of his presidency, to stay at Long Branch on the New Jersey shore, in a house provided to him without cost by three wealthy friends—newspaper publisher George W. Childs, industrialist George Pullman, and bank magnate Moses Taylor. In 1871, Grant left Washington for Long Branch for the summer early in June. He did not spend entire summers at the shore; he liked to travel around the country. Piatt wrote that this was the first president to "shrink his responsibilities . . . [by] running away regularly almost as soon as Congress adjourned. . . . Why, in the name of common sense, if General Grant considers the Presidency such a bore, does he intrigue so much for the succession? How much better it would be for him to drop politics. . . . He could get up a circus, and then he could travel all the summer and be attending to his business at the same time."[84]

To do Grant justice, he did make a kind of summer White House out of the Long Branch "cottage"—which had twenty-eight rooms—but then, as now, in a more electronic age, one can question whether America's chief executive can function effectively if he remains for an extended period far from the seat of government.[85] On the other hand, not much went on in Washington in hot summer. Congress was in recess. Foreign diplomats went off to the mountains and the seaside. Piatt himself took his wife to Narragansett.[86]

Piatt continued to find more reasons to hammer at the White House and its occupant. On October 21, 1871, *The Capital* published an editorial entitled "Our President," which made clear that Piatt thought it was not just a question of the president being surrounded by corrupt men; Grant himself was corrupt:

> We have been severely censured by some very sensible people for what they are pleased to call our continuous attacks upon General Grant, and no end of personal friends have asked us why, as if they thought some personal motive impelled us to the task. They cannot understand, it seems, that one might feel such a pride in the position of Chief Magistrate as to be indignant at its degradation. Nor is this feeling lessened by the fact that scarcely one among the more prominent supporters of this official but holds in his heart the same disgust. . . .
>
> If it were possible to overlook the many questionable acts that indicate a nature far from honest, to say the least, we might put up with the coarse brutality of a stupid man and endure four years more of this degradation. But the fact is no less apparent than appalling that our Chief Magistrate is nurturing about his high office a system of corruption that in time will make the New York Tammany ring respectable.

Piatt was far from being the only journalist or editor who was criticizing Grant and his people. For example, Piatt was able to cite Charles Dana's *New York Sun* as authority in reporting a series of transactions having to do with the house where General Sherman was living in Washington. The house had belonged to Grant when he was elected president, at which point, since he would be moving into the White House, he had sold the house to Washington's mayor, Sayles J. Bowen, for $40,000. After that, Grant had written to "a rich citizen of New York" to say that Sherman, the army's top commander, who was soon to move his headquarters from St. Louis to Washington, was too poor to afford the kind of house in Washington that the general of the army ought to have. The result was that a group of wealthy men had raised $100,000 for a house for Sherman, and then, said Piatt, quoting from the *Sun*, "General Grant *managed it so that out of this money thus collected at his own solicitation, $65,000 went into his own pocket to pay for the house he had just before sold to Mr. Owen for $40,000,* and thereupon Mr. A. T. Stewart, who had brought on the money and paid over to Grant the part of it which he chose to take for himself, was appointed by Grant *to the office of Secretary of the Treasury.*"[87]

Mayor Bowen, said Piatt, had been unhappy to lose his new house, but was assuaged when a number of patronage jobs that had been given to friends of the president were reassigned to friends of Bowen. And, Piatt concluded, "The case above is only one of many we could cite why an honest man, having a true love of country and pride in her institutions, cannot support General Grant for a second term."

The house in question was a large, four-story dwelling at 205 I Street, Northwest, that Grant acquired in October 1865. Grant's friend Abel Corbin, who married Grant's sister Virginia in 1869, had bought it for him. Grant paid nothing for it until the following year, when he was given a check for $105,000 (not $100,000, as Piatt said) by Daniel Butterfield, who had risen from sergeant to general in the Union army and had many friends in the New York financial world. The money had been raised on Wall Street as a testimonial to Grant's wartime service. Grant used a third of that testimonial to pay Corbin for the house, put $55,000 into government bonds, and took the rest in cash. A Grant biographer writes that the gift came at a time when Grant already seemed likely to become the next president: "As soon as wealth came his way, his good sense deserted him. . . . Grant was already, albeit unknowingly, shading the line between right and wrong. . . . Corbin and Butterfield were experienced operators from the dog-eat-dog financial world, and Grant should have been on guard."[88]

How many direct contacts Piatt had with members of Grant's administration is not clear. None, perhaps, from 1870 onward. However, shortly before his polite calls on Grant cabinet members on New Year's Day of 1870, he had in December 1869 met with Secretary of State Hamilton Fish, together with six other men, including his friend James A. Garfield, then a member of Congress from Ohio. The seven presented themselves as a committee representing western—meaning

largely midwestern—interests, and they wanted to ask Fish about relations with
Canada. It was a time when it seemed possible that Canadians might want to cut
their tie to Britain, that the United States might annex at least some Canadian
provinces.

Fish told his visitors that there seemed to be a growing feeling in Canada in
favor of annexation by the United States or else full Canadian independence. The
British, he was informed, might not oppose this. Piatt did not question the ac-
curacy of the secretary's information, but he told Fish that the western states preferred freer trade to annexation. Soon afterward it became clear that Fish was
not well informed on the annexation question. Most Canadians did not want
the neighboring republic to absorb them.[89] Piatt wrote in 1871 that Canadian
sentiment might be different had the United States not shut Canada out of U.S.
markets—but even so, as Canada's West became more populated, "the peculiar
conformation of the country, with a possible breadth suitable for cultivation of
only a hundred miles, will inevitably in time bring about its amalgamation with
the compact territory of the United States. . . . They will be then compelled to
seek absorption into our Union as the only means of affording them markets for
their industry."[90] (A reciprocity treaty in effect between 1854 and 1865 had given
duty-free access to the United States for Canadian coal, grain, and timber, but not
industrial products.)

But Canada really mattered little. As the decade progressed and memories of
the great war receded, an increasingly influential Donn Piatt could see far more
to criticize than to praise inside his own evolving country.

⊰ 6 ⊱

ALARMS AND EXCURSIONS

At *The Capital,* Piatt found he needed more help. He hired as his assistant editor—but with the full title of editor—a young journalist named Henry Reed, who had made a name for himself working on newspapers in Ohio and, more recently, Chicago. Piatt went on to acquire a range of good collaborators for his paper. Many were women. Women writers were not rare then in America, and there were even women editors and publishers.[1] One observer of the Americans reported that the number of women writers was "infinitely larger" than in Europe, and that women "form not only the larger part of the reading public, but an independent-minded part, not disposed to adopt the canons laid down by men."[2]

Sarah Bryan Piatt, his cousin's wife, contributed three dozen poems to *The Capital* over the course of some years.[3] Harriet Prescott Spofford wrote short stories. Austine Stead, writing as "Miss Grundy," reported on Washington's notables in her gossip columns, and her mother, who had written for the *Louisville Courier-Journal* under the pen name "Fay," occasionally stood in for her. Early in the paper's history Piatt published a story translated from German by "M.S." This turned out to be a young woman named Mary Safford, who in later years translated many volumes by German writers. A contributor to *The Capital* known as "Festus" turned out to be a young Ohioan named Mary S. Greene. She went back to the Midwest in 1873 to become the editor of the *Indianapolis Real Estate Gazette,*[4] but she continued to contribute to Piatt's paper.

Still another contributor was Helen H. Gardener, then in her twenties, who became a well-known freethinker and suffragist and, in 1920, the first woman member of the U.S. Civil Service Commission. It was not Gardener, though, but another writer who has not been identified who late in 1871 wrote for *The Capital* a long article on the eight hundred women employed in government departments. The article said that although a number of them held professional-level positions, many or most were paid less than men in equivalent positions.[5] One

wonders whether this writer may have been Mary Clemmer Ames, who in her
1874 book *Ten Years in Washington* gave concrete examples of this wage inequal-
ity, for example, in the Treasury Department, where women were paid only two-
thirds as much as men doing the same jobs.[6]

Among America's male writers, Mark Twain was rising fast. In 1873 he and his
friend Charles Dudley Warner collaborated on a novel that they decided to call
The Gilded Age. The authors hoped that the public and the critics would welcome
it as a major work. When it was published, Twain assumed that the often belligerent Piatt continued to reciprocate his friendly feelings. Piatt was one of two editors—the other was the editor of the *Baltimore Sun*—who, Twain instructed his
publisher, should be sent "very early copies."[7]

Two years earlier, in 1871, Piatt had published in *The Capital* a laudatory review of Mark Twain's new volume entitled *Mark Twain's Autobiography and First
Romance*. The review said, "By far the best humorist our country has produced
is the inimitable Mark Twain. His is genuine hearty humor. He asks no aids from
bad spelling or other tricks common to funny writers." (The reference, as readers
would have known, was to celebrated humorists like Lincoln's favorites, Artemus
Ward [Charles Farrar Browne] and Petroleum V. Nasby [David Ross Locke].)[8]

Now, though, Piatt changed his opinion about Mark Twain—or was it just a
question of *The Gilded Age?* Twain had worked hard and harmoniously with Warner on the book, but the result was less than harmonious. It was a pitiless yet
humorous attack on American scoundrels, and it remains important in American
literary history, but it has been described as "the most uneven of his novels . . . a
bewildering dissonance of moods and styles."[9] Even that admirer of Twain, Bernard DeVoto, wrote in *Mark Twain's America* that the story was cumbersome and
the plot absurd.[10] Piatt could see that, and he hated poor work. As a reviewer he
had what a colleague called an instinctive abhorrence of literary fault.[11]

One searches in vain in *The Capital* for any mention of *The Gilded Age* until a
short notice in August 1874 that "Mark Twain's forthcoming play, 'Colonel Sellers,'
is in a prologue and four acts, constructed from incidents in the Gilded Age."[12]

The play, centered around the chief character in the book, a scoundrel turned
Washington lobbyist named Sellers, opened on Broadway the following month.
Sellers was played by the well-known actor John T. Raymond. The original version of the play was not really Mark Twain's own work but that of G. B. Densmore,
a San Francisco drama critic, who had based it on Twain's and Warner's book.
Subsequently, though, as Twain told William Dean Howells, he took it over before it opened on Broadway and spent a month completely rewriting Densmore's
work.[13] The play initially got mixed reviews in the New York papers, but it continued to attract good audiences. Twain went on stage at the end of the hundredth
performance, was much applauded, and took full credit for what he called "this
play of mine."[14]

Piatt's paper took a dim view of Twain's play. *The Capital* reported from New York in November, "We had the pleasure of seeing and hearing this famous speculator. To say that we enjoyed it but feebly expresses our delight. It is a pity that the setting to this gem, the play itself, is not better. The heartiest laughs are over parts not meant to be laughed at."[15] Later the play was brought to Washington, and again "we" went to see it. Whoever the paper's previous reviewer had been, this one was clearly Piatt himself. He wrote, "For the first time we have something purely American that is purely good. The performance [by Raymond] is simply delicious, and in no place has it [been] or can it be so keenly appreciated as in Washington. . . . The character stands out from the play like a whale's back from a sea of dreary nothingness. It pains us to write this, but the setting of that one gem of a character is unworthy of our old friend Mark Twain."[16]

So far as known, Piatt and the old friend never met, or exchanged letters, after this. Twain, a sensitive and indeed thin-skinned man, must have felt that Piatt had treated him badly, both in ignoring the book and in the negative reviews of the play. Twain had also become an admirer of Grant and cannot have been pleased by Piatt's attacks on the President.[17]

It seems possible that in addition to finding imperfections in both novel and play, Piatt—who was also thin-skinned—had been upset by a passage in the novel. The book briefly introduces "a little newspaper editor" from a small town who goes to Washington, where "he was an important man, correspondent, and clerk of two house committees, a 'worker' in politics, and a confident critic of every woman and every man in Washington. He would be a consul no doubt by and by, at some foreign port, the language of which he was ignorant. . . . His easy familiarity with great men was beautiful to see . . . what a tremendous underground influence this little ignoramus had."[18] Did Piatt (who, like other journalists, at some point held a perhaps honorific but useful House clerkship)[19] see in the editor a disguised picture of himself?

One wonders, though, how much Piatt really cared about what Mark Twain thought or wrote. In the early 1870s Piatt was becoming nationally known for his straightforward, indeed slashing critiques.

John W. Forney, whom Lincoln had helped to become secretary of the Senate and who had also edited the *Washington Chronicle* during the war, published in 1873 a volume of *Anecdotes of Public Men*, in which he listed Piatt first among Washington correspondents and editors. Piatt, said Forney, was "the Edmond About of *The Capitol*."[20] That was high praise. Now that Emperor Napoleon III was gone, Edmond About, the French editor and publicist, had become a power in the Third Republic with his newspaper *Le XIXe Siècle*. What an American visitor wrote of About in 1874 might also have been said of Piatt: "He has received some pretty good knocks, and gives as good as he gets."[21]

In the early 1870s Donn Piatt was in his early fifties and was a physically attractive man. His friend Laura Ream, one of the first newspaperwomen in the Midwest

and later nationally known as a writer,[22] wrote fondly that Piatt "is scarcely of me-
dium height, but he has a good figure and remarkably fine carriage. . . . His head
is beautifully shaped . . . shaded by thick, brown hair. . . . The eyes are particularly
large and clear. . . . He has very remarkable conversational powers and is an eloquent
speaker. His voice is sweet and full and is rounded with a melancholy cadence or
'dying fall,' which makes it very effective."[23]

For some time the Piatts lived at the Arlington, a large hotel in Washington that,
like competitors such as Willards', the Ebbitt, and the National, had a number of
long-term boarders.[24] The Arlington was inhabited by enough interesting people
that news "from the Arlington" was for some time a regular feature of *The Capital.*

In 1871 the Piatts moved into a large house that they had bought from Alexander R. Shepherd, the head of public works in the District of Columbia, who privately was a large real estate investor.[25] The house had a double mansard roof and
was located at 601 18th Street, Northwest, on the corner of F Street. Here the Piatts
were just a block west of the White House grounds. Between the White House
and the block on which the Piatts' house stood, construction was progressing on
the great State, War & Navy Building.[26]

Piatt spent his Saturday evenings at his newspaper's offices on 10th Street,
Northwest. It would be two or three o'clock on a Sunday morning by the time the
new edition had gone to press and he could walk home. It was a good way to relax
after a long day. His route took him down to Pennsylvania Avenue, then west past
the great, darkened Treasury building and along the broad sidewalk of red Seneca
sandstone in front of the White House, where the exterior gas lights were kept
burning all night.

As Piatt passed the White House and was nearing home early on a Sunday
morning in late April, a policeman ran past him, presumably going after some
malefactor. Then a hack came by. The driver yelled at him—and Piatt realized that
there was a fire ahead. Could it be his house? He started running.

The fire had broken out in the basement of the house next to the Piatts'. This
house belonged to Alexander Shepherd, and he had rented it to J. N. Carpenter,
who together with his family had moved in only the previous day, after returning from service as fleet paymaster in the navy's Asiatic squadron.[27] By the time
Piatt arrived, the flames were mounting in the windless night, but a fire engine
was there and firemen were playing water on the Piatts' roof. The Carpenter family had escaped harm; Ella and the Piatts' servants were safe; a number of people
were carrying the Piatts' furnishings out to safety. The firemen saved the Piatt
house, but water sprayed by the engines did considerable damage to the house's
furnishings, which Piatt suddenly feared he had not insured. (He had.) It had
taken an hour for the engine to arrive, because there had been no policeman on
their quiet street to unlock and operate the nearby fire alarm box.

At least, Piatt wrote the following week in *The Capital,* the crowd that gathered was for the most part honest. Only a few things had been stolen, including

a pocketbook left under a pillow with a hundred dollars in it. "We can account for this," he wrote, "only on the fact that we had our calamity in the vacation of Congress, while not only the congressmen but most of the Executive were out of town."[28] Later, Piatt wrote that some unspecified papers of his had been lost in the fire.[29] One wonders whether his wartime diaries were among them.

After repairs had been made, the Piatts continued to live in the house until 1878. Then Donn if not his wife—who may have returned by then to Ohio, where a big building project was under way at Mac-o-cheek—moved to another hotel that took boarders, the Riggs House at 15th and G Streets, for the remainder of his time in Washington.[30]

In 1872 Piatt was distressed to hear that his nephew, Benjamin Piatt Runkle, a major in the regular army, had been court-martialed. When Runkle lost his mother, Donn's mother had taken him in and raised him. Donn, too, had shown him care and affection. Runkle had served gallantly in the Civil War. At Shiloh, as an officer of the Thirteenth Ohio, his jaw had been shattered, and he had been left for dead. Later, he had become, at only twenty-five, the colonel of the Forty-fifth Ohio. Most recently, he had been serving in Kentucky as a disbursing officer of the Bureau of Refugees, Freedmen, and Abandoned Lands. Questions were raised about his management of official funds; sizable amounts due to former slaves had been stolen. In the end he was tried for "conduct unbecoming an officer and a gentleman." The court sentenced him to be cashiered, to pay a fine of $7,500, and to serve four years in the penitentiary.

The case went to Grant's secretary of war, William W. Belknap, whose own impeachment came three years later. Piatt's friend, Congressman James A. Garfield, talked to Grant twice on behalf of Runkle, and in January 1873 the president remitted all of the sentence, except the finding that Runkle should be cashiered.[31] Runkle's, and Piatt's, position was that he was blameless, that he had had a number of subordinate officers who were assigned to his unit by the War Department, and that he was not responsible for their character nor aware of any illegal conduct on their part. In the coming years Piatt would work hard to have the sentence overturned. Grant's failure to remit the part of the sentence that ended his nephew's military career could only confirm Piatt in his dislike of Grant and his people.

By 1872 Piatt decided that Grant's presidency was turning imperial as well as corrupt. Nellie Grant, the president's sixteen-year-old daughter, went to Europe that spring, and in London she was presented to Queen Victoria. Piatt wanted his readers to know that "being President of the United States does not confer any recognized rank upon the family. . . . When, therefore, the secretary of our legation in London demanded an especial presentation for Miss Nellie because she was the daughter of an Administration, he committed a blunder so gross that it is an insult to an honest animal to call him an ass."[32]

Piatt continued to claim that Grant was drinking, heavily on occasion, in the White House. In May 1873, with the Grant presidency in its fifth year, *The Capital* was pleased to say that the president's health was good, despite recent reports that he might have Bright's disease. This, the paper explained, was a malady seated in the kidneys "and differs essentially from the bright disease, which fixes itself upon the brain—the symptoms of which were stated to be rubicundity of the countenance and an illumination of the nasal promontory."[33]

The next month the paper reported that the story was circulating in several different channels that Grant "is, to use the common phrase, drinking a good deal." However, said the paper virtuously, it did not believe the stories, and besides truth was not a simple thing; much depended on by whom and against whom it was narrated. Thus, said the paper,

> We no more credited the story related by Theodore Tilton of having seen Mr. Grant toddling along Pennsylvania avenue on a Sabbath day in a state of high intoxication than we credit the story told by Victoria Woodhull in which is intermixed this same Theodore Tilton. The relativeness of truth renders such discriminations necessary; and the requirements of good society are no less imperative. Does anyone suppose that the great David-Uriah scandal which, at a certain period, was so current among the gossips of Jerusalem, was in the slightest degree credited in the upper circles of that metropolis? Will anyone believe . . . that David was any other than the most proper man of the period?"[34]

(Tilton was the editor of *The Golden Age,* an independent weekly. Woodhull, great suffragist, was in 1872 the first woman to run for president, on the Equal Rights ticket.)

If Piatt did not see the president in the White House, he apparently saw him not infrequently on the street near the White House, when the editor was walking between home and *The Capital.* After reading a report by the proprietor of the *Louisville Courier-Journal* on a White House dinner, Piatt wrote, "Henry Watterson saw His Imperial Excellency between the sherry and champagne. We see him daily between the White House and the War Department, with the sherry and champagne in his executive countenance."[35] On another occasion, Piatt wrote that it was wrong to say Grant was a drinker; he just had "fits."[36]

If Piatt was not ruined by Grant and his people, he was threatened. One day in January 1874 Grant's son Frederick and brother-in-law James J. Casey barged into Piatt's home in Washington, armed with heavy sticks. Besides the continuing attacks on his father, Fred Grant presumably had in mind the nasty remarks that a correspondent of *The Capital* had written about his mother and sister, in a report of the Grants' New Year's reception at the White House—which, said the journalist, should not have been held at all, since Mrs. Grant's father had died just two weeks earlier. Afterward, the paper had received many letters from readers who thought *The Capital* had treated Mrs. Grant too harshly.

Piatt, who was out when Casey and Grant came calling, returned home after the visitors had left and found his wife understandably upset. He wrote in *The Capital* that it was "not customary in civilized communities to call one to a personal account in the presence of his family. . . . Hereafter whenever an aggrieved person attempts to call us to account in our house such person will be met by the police. There are no police, however, about our place of business, and we assure all such that an entrance will be unobstructed, whatever the exit may be."[37]

With this, said the *Atlanta Constitution,* ended "the farce of the presidential ruffians."[38] Not quite. Piatt learned that the White House had been trying to put the best face on the matter, and so the day after the comment in the *Constitution* Piatt published one more note in *The Capital:* "We abstain purposely from comment upon the indignity offered us personally and the attack on the press by two members of the President's family. We are willing the falsehoods telegraphed over the country by the sycophantic followers of the Administration shall go uncontradicted, for they carry the gist of the matter, which is that an independent, outspoken press is not to be tolerated in this Government reservation called the District of Columbia; where it is proposed that nothing shall prosper that lacks the sunlight of the royal countenance."[39]

The affair had in fact been good advertising for *The Capital,* even though Ella Piatt had been badly frightened. Piatt wrote Murat Halstead saying, "The stupid scoundrels in coming to my house as they did gave me a magnificent opening. . . . Fred Grant says that next time he will not make that mistake and I said in reply to his friend that I would pay the family a premium on my increased circulation if he would come to my office. It was an infernal outrage however and has had very sad consequences for me. Mrs Piatt was more injured by the fright than that of the fire—"[40]

Donn Piatt escaped injury, but on another occasion his assistant editor, Henry Reed, did not. *The Capital* reported that President Grant's brother-in-law, Judge Louis Dent—not the brother-in-law who had invaded the Piatt home—had used his relationship with the president to line his own pocket, taking money to arrange for a certain W. D. Farrand to be appointed consul at Callao in Peru. Other papers had made similar charges but not in such a caustic way, while Republican papers said the report was nothing but slander.[41] Dent was furious and went down to the offices of *The Capital.* Piatt was out of town, but Henry Reed was there. Dent walked up to Reed, called him a "God-damned scoundrel," and hit him repeatedly over the head with his heavy cane. Printers came running in from the composing room and pulled Dent off. Reed's head was cut and bruised. The paper's business manager, Frank Howe, told the men to hold Dent and called the police. Dent was fined a hundred dollars plus costs.[42]

There was also the case of Zachariah Chandler, the former senator from Michigan and one of the founders of the Republican Party. One historian ranked Chandler as one of the most influential of the men who "dominated" President Grant, indicating that this had something to do with the fact that Chandler "was always ready to smoke a cigar, take a drink, play a game of cards, or tell a good story."[43] There had long been reports that Chandler drank to excess,[44] and Piatt as well as others often ridiculed him as a drunk.[45]

Chandler stormed into the Washington office of the *New York Times* one spring day in 1875, armed with a large pistol and looking for "Dion Pott." The *Times* men asked if he meant Donn Piatt of *The Capital*. Yes, he said, "Dion Pott is my man—I am after him," adding, "I am going to kill off four or five of you." He finally calmed down and at the office door met his private secretary, whom he did not at first recognize, but who eventually talked him into returning home.[46]

From what Piatt wrote in *The Capital*, there would seem to have been a number of occasions when Chandler was unsure of what or who was around him. One night, Piatt said, he caught sight of Chandler on Pennsylvania Avenue:

> The distinguished senator . . . was tacking along, suffering from indigestion that had evidently flown to his legs. Suddenly he cried out, "Good night, fellers!" and rushed into the street.
>
> As there were no fellows near him we were impressed with the belief that the senator had gone crazy. . . . He hadn't gone mad, however, he had gone after a [street]car. He ran in the direction of one . . . and would have never reached it in this world had the car been in motion. But the one he was aiming at, having suffered a compound fracture of the off axle, had been run from the track and left there for repairs thereafter.
>
> The senator overtook the car; for a while we thought he was trying to head it off. He succeeded at last in reaching the rear end . . . and mounting the platform turned around and waved an adieu to the imaginary fellows on the sidewalk. He then staggered in and solemnly took his seat.[47]

Piatt wrote that he then, with what he called an abundance of benevolence, tried to explain to the senator that this streetcar was going nowhere. The senator told him to go away and not be a damned fool. Next day, said Piatt, the car was still there. Where the senator was, was not clear.

Chandler (whom Grant named secretary of the interior in October 1875) and Grant were not the only top federal officials whom Piatt accused of drunkenness. When, for example, John A. Logan was elected to the U.S. Senate from the state of Illinois for a second term, in 1879, *The Capital* decided to call him "The Hon. Demijohn A. Logan."[48] Piatt had another reason besides Logan's reported drinking to think ill of the man. At the end of 1864, after the Union army captured Atlanta and Sherman set off on his March to the Sea, Grant had been dissatisfied with Piatt's hero General George Thomas and sent Logan to replace him. (Grant had, however, countermanded the order when, at the battle of Nashville, Thomas crushed the Confederate forces under John Bell Hood.)

Years later an editor recalled that all of these incidents and alarms, coupled with what appeared on the pages of *The Capital,* made Piatt the best-known man in Washington after President Grant and another war hero, General William Tecumseh Sherman, whom Piatt liked as little as he liked Grant.[49]

Attacks on journalists in Washington were not rare occurrences. In February 1874 Piatt's old partner George Alfred Townsend, who had returned to Washington and was now "Gath," the well-known correspondent of the *Chicago Tribune,* was attacked, not physically but in print, in the rival *Chicago Times.* A *Times* correspondent, W. S. Walker, claimed that Gath was living in a house in Washington that had been given to him by the "District Ring" of corrupt local politicians. Townsend, in fact, lived in a rented house, and he was not about to let the slander go by. He called at the offices of the *Times,* where Walker told him that he had picked up his information at the offices of Townsend's own *Tribune.* The enraged Townsend shouted, "You lie, sir, you lie!" and began striking Walker over the head with his umbrella. Other staff members finally pulled Townsend away, but not before he had hit Walker a number of times, without causing him much injury.[50]

There were still other famous cases. Before the Civil War, Horace Greeley had been attacked at a Washington hotel by a member of Congress, Albert Rust. Not long afterward the owner of the *Washington Evening Star,* Douglas Wallach, was knocked down on a sidewalk by a former congressman known as "Extra Billy" Smith—but successfully defended himself by biting down on one of Smith's thumbs and keeping his hold.[51]

Aside from physical threats to Donn Piatt, there was at least one attempt by people around Grant to blacken his name through a leak to the press. Someone— perhaps Orville Babcock, who had been looking for dirt on Piatt—gave the *Washington Sunday Herald* the texts of a dozen documents about Piatt's departure from the Paris legation in 1855, including all the negative comments about Piatt that his old chief in Paris, John Mason, had sent to the State Department. Piatt was furious and asked Secretary of State Hamilton Fish how he came to permit such a violation of the rules. Even if it was Babcock who had given the texts to the paper, they must have come from someone in Fish's department. Babcock had asked Fish to supply whatever damaging material about Piatt he could. Fish had no doubt felt the need to try to comply with a request coming from the White House, though he had no love for Babcock. Fish had been angered and almost resigned his post when, unbeknownst to him, Grant in 1869 sent Babcock to the Dominican Republic, where he negotiated a treaty that—if approved—would have annexed the country to the United States.[52]

Piatt, whose paper sometimes called the secretary of state "the Honorable Fish," wrote later, "Hamilton Fish looks like a butler, but he feels like a gentleman, and when he told me that it was not his act, nor done with his knowledge, I accepted his statement, and began looking up the offender."[53] (Piatt wrote Fish twice about the leak of the dispatches from Paris. Fish replied that he knew nothing about the dispatches but had looked into the matter and had been assured that no copy had been made in the department within the past two years; however, he said he had also been told that there were "indications" that copies had been made at some earlier time.)[54]

Piatt identified the offender, he said, through a pretty young French woman who described herself as "ze demoiselle de compagnee" of the Russian minister's wife, and who was willing to provide information "for a leetle compensation." She told Piatt that his enemy in the State Department was J. C. Bancroft Davis—the assistant secretary of state, or deputy to Secretary Fish—and so, Piatt said, "I proceeded to make life a burthen to Bancroft." He also, for the first time, told in print how a succession of strokes had changed Mason from a kind and patient gentleman to a peevish and unreasonable type, who after Piatt's departure had accepted the lying account of Piatt given him by his private secretary, John B. Wilbor. And, since the press had been told how Mason had sent the State Department a bad report about Piatt, Piatt published the full text of the dispatch.[55]

One might wonder how much the young French woman really knew about the State Department. Quite a lot, apparently. A Washington insider, Benjamin Perley Poore, wrote that she had long spied on the Russian legation for the State Department and "was handsomely remunerated from the Secret Service Fund."[56]

Grant's secretary and old army comrade Babcock was later indicted for playing a part in the "Whisky Ring," a scheme whereby liquor dealers evaded taxes. He was found not guilty after Grant personally testified on his behalf. Bancroft Davis, on the other hand, went on to become the American minister to Germany. Was it Davis who had had copies made of the Paris dispatches? Davis had entered the State Department in March 1869. Two years and two months later, in May 1871, Fish assured Piatt that no copies had been made in the department—within the past two years.

One friend said Piatt had a private reason for despising an unidentified member of Grant's cabinet. One evening in Washington, the story went, Donn and Ella Piatt had gone to the theater, but arrived late. When they reached the row where their seats were, they had to make their way past others already seated, including the cabinet member and his wife. After Ella had passed, Piatt heard the wife make a remark about his wife being a cripple. And, said the friend, Piatt never forgot or forgave that.[57] It seems, though, that the friend had the story wrong. Piatt himself told of going alone to the theater one evening and seeing a young woman sitting near him with a face like an angel and a crutch at her feet. A prominent Washingtonian—but not a cabinet member—and his wife came in, and as they passed the girl, Piatt heard the wife say that people had no business bringing cripples to the theater. After that, Piatt said, he learned all he could about the distinguished couple and whenever possible reported unpleasant facts about them, reportedly causing them eventually to leave Washington.[58]

By this time many if not most literate Washingtonians sat down on Sunday with Piatt's paper, which—whatever its true circulation—now boasted that it had a larger circulation than all the other Sunday papers of Washington combined.[59] Papers across the country continued to replay Piatt's columns; Donn Piatt was now a national name.

Let us go back to 1872. Grant hoped he would be reelected that November, but the Republican Party had split into warring factions. As early as 1870 Piatt had written, "There is no more cohesion, beyond mere office holding and public plunder, in the Republican party than there is in a rope of sand."[60] Dissatisfaction within the party, and with the president, had reached the point by 1872 that a number of leading men, both Democrats and Republicans and including Donn Piatt, met together in Cincinnati in May at a "Liberal Republican Convention" in the hope of agreeing on a candidate to beat Grant. Henry Watterson, editor of the *Louisville Courier-Journal,* wondered whether Piatt's real purpose in coming had been "to make the most out of an occasion in which the bizarre was much in excess of the conventional."[61]

Perhaps it would be fairer to say that Piatt was trying to make sense out of a muddied political scene in America, and to decide what his and his country's best course might be. He himself had been a Democrat in his youth, had worked for the Free-Soil movement, and more recently had supported the Republican Party. Many other Americans had similar histories of moving from party to party over the years. Now, with Grant in the White House, Piatt could not abide the Republicans. That did not make him become a Democrat again. He had recently written in *The Capital,* "We would like to suggest to the Democratic party . . . that now is a very good time to put up the front shutters and decline business. . . . The old platforms are so decayed through exposure and worm-eaten through time that they will not serve any known purpose, while the speeches and past record are things the people do not care to preserve."

Nevertheless, he continued, "The Democratic party is immortal. It cannot die. It cannot commit suicide, nor can it retire from business, so long as an Irishman remains alive in the United States. . . . So long as ignorance exists the Democracy will exist, for it is ignorance in an organized condition."

But that was not all, he said:

No one can read correctly our past political record and not see that the Democratic party contains the governing element of the country. Made up of the masses, it has a capacity for drill and discipline no other organization ever even approached. . . . The Republican party is only an *ad interim* party, and sooner or later must give way to the governing element of all republics that exists in the democratic many. During the late war Democrats would not vote the Democratic tickets because of the disloyalty of the [Copperhead] leaders; and in the late elections thousands refused to sustain an organization responsible for the fearful stench of the New York [Tammany] ring. But the war will be forgotten, the ring will be killed, and the mass of free voters again swing into line and control the Government."[62]

The major national issue was, as it had been since the final defeat of the Confederacy, the Reconstruction of the South. Lincoln's assassination had made even moderate Northerners feel that the South must be treated severely. Lincoln's successor, Andrew Johnson, who came from a Southern state—Tennessee—and favored a lenient policy, had lacked the political skill and popular support necessary to contest the Radical Republicans, who wanted harsh Reconstruction measures and pushed them through Congress in 1866–68. In 1868 Johnson moved to dismiss the Radicals' ally Stanton as secretary of war, despite new legislation forbidding him to remove without Senate concurrence any official appointed by a past president. The House of Representatives impeached the president, and he escaped conviction in the Senate by only one vote. (Stanton soon resigned his position and resumed the practice of law.)

Piatt wrote that it was not Andrew Johnson but the whole Republican Party that had been on trial. Beyond that, the whole government was corrupt: "We have filled the offices with thieves and their pockets with stealings. . . . From the lowest official, up to Senators and Cabinet officers, the taint of corruption runs until the people, dazed and confused, confound the right and listen with indifference to the threats of exposure."[63]

It was a theme that Piatt would continue to play for many years.

When in 1868 Grant had been elected to his first term as president, he had had the Radicals' support, and it had been the new African American voters who gave him a majority of the popular vote—although he would have won the electoral vote without them.[64] The election did not give him a mandate for radical policy, but after the Ku Klux Klan had begun to spread its white-sheet terror through the South, the Congress in 1870 enacted the first of three Enforcement Acts aimed at the Klan. Grant's new attorney general, Amos T. Akerman, used the act to prosecute the Klan vigorously. Nevertheless, white Democrats in the South were beginning to gain control of state governments, and as memories of the war receded, many Northerners began to care less about Reconstruction. Many, including Piatt, believed that Southern governments run by a combination of white carpetbaggers and largely uneducated blacks had tipped the balance of government and discriminated unfairly against the white population of the South. By 1872 even the Radicals realized they must change direction. A sign of the times was the 1872 Amnesty Act, which restored voting rights to almost all former Confederates.

The Cincinnati convention resulted in the formation of a new Liberal Republican Party of the United States, which nominated Horace Greeley to run against

Grant in 1872. The Democratic Party subsequently added its own nomination of Greeley, rather than putting up a separate candidate.

Piatt had never thought that Horace Greeley would be an ideal president. Certainly, Greeley had never been a consummate politician, and people and papers had long made fun of his eccentric figure. *The Capital* was among these; it had recently recalled Greeley's incongruous appearance once at a ball in Washington "in his queer fitting clothes and smooth, innocent face, peering at the whirl about him through those never-to-be-forgotten spectacles."[65] Piatt, however, also defended Greeley as a far better man than Grant and "a shining mark in the American world of journalism."[66] One can argue whether Grant or Greeley was the better human—but as Greeley's most recent biographer says, he was "a great editor who wielded enormous moral power throughout the country."[67] Still, that did not mean he had the stuff to be a good chief executive.

Just after Greeley was nominated for the presidency, *The Capital* carried a column on its editor's recent dinner conversation with Jeremiah Black, who had been attorney general and secretary of state in the Buchanan administration and was now a prominent Washington lawyer:

> "Well, Judge, what do you think of our nomination at Cincinnati?"
>
> "Greeley? . . . Well, had you raked this world and the two adjacent you could not have found a fitter man to be a candidate, or a more unfit one to be President. . . . You recollect the story of the farmer who yoked up his hogs to plow. The farmer remarked subsequently that hogs were good to eat, but very trying when you attempted to plow with them. . . ."
>
> "You think he will be elected?"
>
> "It looks likely. . . . It is not easy to think of a man who ought not to beat General Grant. I say ought, for certainly no man can be found so little qualified for the place, who has committed such grave blunders, to use the mildest term, and whose shortcomings are so well known as Grant's."[68]

Black must have felt seriously embarrassed when he read Piatt's account of a private conversation, even if Piatt had reported correctly what he said—and even though many others felt the same about both Grant and Greeley. Black had no interest in making enemies of Grant and his administration. Later, he was to act as counsel for Grant's secretary of war, Belknap, in his impeachment trial. He was no doubt restraining himself when he wrote Piatt, "You are the greatest man alive when you express your own sentiments, but you miss it a little when you go for mine."[69]

Greeley campaigned hard for the presidency, from Maine to Texas, but he was the antithesis of a charismatic figure. Worse, perhaps, his image was hurt by reports that he had held stock in the Crédit Mobilier, a firm set up to act as the construction company for the proposed Union Pacific Railroad. Some claimed that he had received the stock in return for the favorable coverage that his paper had given to the rail project.

The Crédit Mobilier proved to be the great scandal of the age—and it was an age of many scandals. For years, beginning long before the Civil War, the federal government had seen the need for a transcontinental railroad. With the help of generous government subsidies the route was finally completed in 1869 when the Union Pacific met the Central Pacific at Promontory Point in Utah. It turned out that the subsidies for the Union Pacific had far outweighed the actual cost of construction, and that the men behind the Crédit Mobilier, including Oakes Ames, who was both a company director and an influential Republican member of Congress, had made huge profits, equivalent to several hundred million dollars of the early twenty-first century. Besides Greeley's involvement, a number of members of Congress were said to have been bribed by Ames with Crédit Mobilier stock, including a future president named Garfield.

As the 1872 election neared, Greeley's wife, Molly, long in poor health, fell more seriously ill. She died on October 30. The next week, Greeley lost the election to Grant, who gained 55.6 percent of the popular vote to Greeley's 43.8 percent and an overwhelming 286 out of 352 electoral votes. Three weeks later, discouraged and worn out at the age of sixty-one, Horace Greeley followed his wife to the grave. Meanwhile, it continued to be Donn Piatt and a few others who, Henry Watterson wrote, "divided the newspaper attention of the country."[70]

Piatt may never have met Greeley's great competitor in the New York newspaper world, James Gordon Bennett, founder and proprietor of the *New York Herald*. Whether he ever met him, he did not much like him. Bennett turned over control of the *Herald* to his son in 1866 and died in 1872, some months before Greeley. Piatt waited for some weeks after Bennett's death to print a long column that mainly quoted what other papers had said about him. What Piatt said in his own right about Bennett was cold in tone. Bennett, he said, was utterly devoted to his paper, and "had no prejudice one way or the other. He looked to his market. In the civil war he turned form the cause of slavery to that of emancipation in a single night, because the mob made a demonstration against his office, and so convinced him that public opinion had gone round. He thought that a newspaper should supply not the truth, but the facts, appearances of facts, rumors, scandals, plausible falsehoods, and opinions which the public liked to buy."

As 1872 ended and a new year came on, Piatt decided that *The Capital* should prepare something special for Grant's second inauguration, on March 4. Early that day, before the ceremonies at the Capitol, the paper put out an "extra" containing what appeared at first glance to be a real scoop: the text of the inaugural address that the president was about to give. The mocking piece claimed that Grant was going to say,

During the past four years I feel that I have done my duty. It is said that man acts best his part when he attends to his own affairs and lets those of others alone. I have, in most cases, made that my rule of conduct. I have taken good care of my own interests and let the country take care of its. . . . I feel a good deal indebted to the Republic—that is to say, the Republicans—for the honor of a second election. In consequence of the complicated manner in which I disposed of my dwelling in this city, I should, otherwise, have had no place of residence. . . . One of the most positive injunctions of the New Testament is to take care of one's own household; and . . . in this respect I have done my duty. . . . It is an agreeable task to a man of my feelings to acknowledge the receipt of articles of use or ornament presented to him as memorials of past or especially of future good offices. . . . My hopes for the future are, in every respect, as lively as my gratitude for the past.[71]

One cannot be sure whether Grant himself ever learned of this extra. After the inauguration, however, the Washington police took action to prevent any further sales. *The Capital* reported that "the newsboys were driven from the streets, and our sales stopped." Who had given orders to the police was not clear, but the paper assumed it was "the toadies and snobs about the President." (One can imagine Orville Babcock's hand in it.) Piatt or a colleague stopped a policeman "who gave as a reason for the arrest of one of our boys, that he was crying 'Extra Capital, attempted assassination of the President.'" This, the paper said, was a falsehood, but a better one than the denial that the White House had anything to do with the police action.[72]

Piatt's paper gave full coverage both to outrageous national scandals like that of the Crédit Mobilier and to lesser-known cases of what amounted—in his view—to bad or foolish behavior in high places. This included episodes in foreign affairs, notably some involving Cuba and Spain, then the owner of the island. Piatt the diplomat had carried to Washington in 1854 the report drafted by his senior colleagues at Ostend proposing that the United States acquire Cuba, by force if necessary. The threat of using force had been new, but every president from Thomas Jefferson onward, except for Abraham Lincoln, who was otherwise occupied, wanted to acquire Cuba for the United States.

In 1873 came a new crisis over Cuba. That October, a Spanish navy corvette intercepted a vessel called the *Virginius* that had been outfitted in the United States and was being used to run arms to insurgents in Cuba. More than forty of the crew were executed for piracy. Some, perhaps most, of them, had American citizenship. The American minister at Madrid, Daniel Sickles—the "American scoundrel" whom Piatt had last met at dinner before Sickles shot his wife's lover—threatened a break in relations.[73] The press in America reported that war with Spain might be imminent and victory would come quickly.

That press, that is, not including Donn Piatt's paper. This "on to Cuba" business reminded him, he said, of the heady days in the early summer of 1861 when Northern papers had said "on to Richmond," and it seemed the Union army would soon be there. Then had come the disaster of Bull Run and the end of such light talk. Piatt suggested Americans consider two facts.

First, although the United States had invested heavily over recent decades in coastal defense fortifications, it had never bothered to arm them properly. The result was that "Portland is in a defenseless condition. Boston is somewhat better off, but yet has nothing to protect her from iron-clads. . . . New York is in as bad, if not a worse, condition. Philadelphia is helpless, and we can follow down the coast to Galveston, Texas without an exception."

Second, Piatt warned, "Spain is second only to England in the number of her war vessels, the perfection of their model and build and weight of metal."[74]

War did not come with Spain in 1873, but one cannot say that Piatt's warning had much to do with that. It was not, of course, the end of the Cuba question. Nor was it the end of Piatt's concern about America's coastal fortifications. Congressman James A. Garfield recorded in his diary that in December 1874 he, Piatt, and General Stephen Vincent Benét, chief of the army's ordnance department, had a two-hour discussion over dinner about "the military armament of our fortifications." At a guess it was Benét, concerned about the sorry state of coastal defenses, who had briefed Piatt before his editorial appeared the previous year.[75]

Piatt found a second occasion to issue a warning about Cuba in early 1875. *The Capital* told its readers that after the recent midterm congressional elections, Grant's kitchen cabinet had told him that they saw just two ways to keep the Republican Party—which had lost votes in November—in power. One was to launch a vast program of internal improvements. The other was to get the people behind the administration by launching a war against some foreign power. Internal improvements—that is, public works—would require congressional support, and so, said *The Capital,* the administration had commissioned some trial editorials on the subject, and the response had not been favorable.

That left the question of bringing about a perhaps small but popular war. Grant, said the paper, had a message to the Congress prepared that in effect contained a declaration of war against Spain over the question of Cuba. But Secretary of State Hamilton Fish had heard of it and insisted the message be changed. This was done, and the earlier text that had been given to domestic newspapers recalled—but the Associated Press had cabled the earlier text to Europe, and that text could not be recalled. At the moment, official sources were saying that "our relations with Spain are not satisfactory." That seems a mild statement today, but many people then could remember Napoleon III's statement a few years earlier to the Austrian ambassador that French relations with Austria were not as good as he might wish—a statement taken rightly as a threat of war. Piatt's paper warned

Above left: Benjamin McCullough Piatt, father of Donn Piatt. (Piatt Castles) Above right: Elizabeth Barnett Piatt, mother of Donn Piatt. (Piatt Castles)

Mac-o-cheek, Donn Piatt's childhood home in Logan County. (Piatt Castles)

Left: Donn Piatt at age 15. The artist is probably John Peter Frankenstein. (Piatt Castles)
Center: Donn Piatt at 35. (Piatt Castles) Right: Donn Piatt, c. 1863. Carte de visite by
Mathew Brady. (Piatt Castles)

Left: Louise Kirby Piatt, Donn Piatt's first wife. (Piatt Castles) Center: Donn Piatt, Baltimore, c. 1863. (Piatt Castles) Right: Portrait of Piatt from Miller, *Donn Piatt* (1893).

Donn Piatt after the Civil War. (Brady-Handy Collection, Library of Congress)

Left: Newsboys delivering *The Capital* in the 1870s. From Miller, *Donn Piatt* (1893). Right: Piatt's study at Mac-O-Chee. (Piatt Castles)

Left: Ella Kirby Piatt, Donn Piatt's second wife. (Piatt Castles) Right: Ella Kirby Piatt, later in life. (Piatt Castles)

Above: Drawing of Mac-O-Chee, 1892. (Piatt Castles)

Mac-O-Chee today. (Piatt Castles)

Piatt tomb. (Piatt Castles)

Above left: Robert C. Schenck, Union major general, Member of Congress, U.S. envoy to Brazil and the United Kingdom, Piatt's friend and wartime commander. (Library of Congress) Above right: Helen Hamilton Gardener, Piatt contributor, and woman's suffrage leader. (Library of Congress)

Horace Greeley (seated, second from right) and staff of the New York *Tribune*. Charles A. Dana, later editor of the *New York Sun,* is standing, center; Henry J. Raymond, founder of the *New York Times,* is standing, right. (Library of Congress)

James A. Garfield, Piatt's friend, Member of Congress, and later President. (Brady-Handy Collection, Library of Congress)

Left: Clara Morris, leading actress, friend of Donn and Ella Piatt. (Library of Congress)
Right: Henry B. Banning, Member of Congress, Piatt's brother-in-law. (Brady-Handy Collection, Library of Congress)

Thomas Corwin, Governor of Ohio, Member of Congress, U.S. Secretary of the Treasury, envoy to Mexico, and Piatt's law teacher. (Library of Congress)

Left: Rutherford B. Hayes, Piatt's friend and later president, and Lucy Webb Hayes. (Library of Congress) Right, above: Edwin M. Stanton, U.S. Secretary of War and Piatt's friend and mentor. (Library of Congress) Right, below: John Y. Mason, Member of Congress, U.S. Secretary of the Navy and Attorney General, and Piatt's chief as U.S. envoy to France. (Library of Congress)

Michler Place, F Street Northwest at 18th Street, Washington, D.C., c. 1970. The house on the left belonged to Donn and Ella Piatt in the 1870s. (Library of Congress)

that the danger remained that Grant might launch a war, no matter what the secretary of state might want.

There had been a time, *The Capital* added, when a president guilty of such
conduct might be impeached, "But that day is past. Our Congress, in its majority,
is made up of hungry dependents on the President's will. Their master has yet two
years left him of power, and in that time, through the immense patronage of his
office, he can destroy politically any man who dares dispute his will."[76]

There have been other times both in America and abroad when leaders have
thought of launching a war for political advantage. America's war with Spain did
not eventuate in 1875; it came only in 1898, after the battleship *Maine* blew up in
Havana harbor—which many thought an inadequate reason to go to war. In 1898,
the American navy was already embarked on the major modernization and expansion program that would within a decade produce the "Great White Fleet." By
1898, in contrast, the Spanish navy—like the Spanish administration in Cuba—
was in bad shape.

Piatt was gone from the scene by then; would he have opposed the war? He
would presumably have been pleased that American victory came quickly. One
suspects, however, that like Mark Twain he would have expressed sharp criticism
of the American decision to hold on to the possessions it took from Spain, and of
the U.S. campaign against nationalists in the Philippines that led to the death of
four thousand American soldiers and at least a quarter million Filipinos.

In both 1873 and 1875, Piatt felt prosperous enough to take Ella on extended
trips to Europe, during which he sent half humorous contributions home to *The
Capital* that were drawn on by other papers across the country. (In August 1873,
for example, people in Davenport, Iowa, could read in their *Daily Gazette,* "Donn
Piatt describes the British House of Peers as 'a body of men exceedingly quiet and
unpretending in manner, not remarkably striking in countenance, and so badly
dressed that it seems an affectation.'")[77]

The 1873 trip seems to have been a pleasant one—except for the Atlantic crossing from New York to Londonderry in rough weather, aboard the fast, two-thou-
sand-ton steamship *Australia* of the Anchor Line. Ella and Donn took with them
one other lady, his sister Martha Piatt Worthington.

Piatt left Washington in June, when the capital was already sweltering in summer heat, and met the ladies in New York, where they spent a day and a half before
sailing. He called on Whitelaw Reid, with whom he had some business to transact.
Reid had taken over the *Tribune* after Horace Greeley's death and used it to further
his (Republican) political ambitions, while the paper's circulation declined.

No matter what business Piatt had with Reid, he had no great liking for him. In
a slightly mocking dispatch reporting the travelers' stay in New York, he described
going to see a foppish Reid at his sumptuous house, "where, in gorgeous dress-
ing gown and slippers, the great young man of the *Tribune* apologized for keeping

us waiting while he abluted. The room was artistically furnished. . . . Conspicuous was a delicate indelicate picture of Venus in a sea-shell. Venus on the half-shell was something we had not anticipated in the apartments of Whitelaw." Piatt remarked to Reid that he must work hard. "'Well, yes,' was the drawled reply. 'I am at the office until three in the morning; then I ride up to this place and sleep as I ride. I have a *coupé* waiting for me.'" Reid added that he simply could not ride the streetcars home, since after midnight the cars were full of "lost women, ruined men, thieves and cut-throats . . . that crowd goes for a gentleman and the police dare not interfere." As Piatt had told his readers more than once, he too came home from the office in the early morning, on foot; but Manhattan was admittedly a different place, "a city of roughs, financial blacklegs, thieves and swindlers."[78]

Besides himself, Piatt wrote, there was another gentleman in their party traveling to Europe. Piatt called him "Jones" in his dispatches to *The Capital.* Jones, he said, had been at sea all his life. "He is a great traveler; he has been to Coney Island and California. There is no part of Europe Jones has not visited. If he has not, he says he has, and that is just as good for conversation."[79] (Piatt had made mention of Jones earlier in his Washington reporting, but he may as easily have been a creation of the editor as a real man of the world.)

Reading Piatt's account of the voyage, one imagines he had in mind Mark Twain's first bestseller, *The Innocents Abroad,* which had come out four years earlier. Theirs was not to be as long a voyage as Twain's, but it could provide a tale worth telling. Poor Jones, Piatt wrote, was assigned a large stateroom, eight by six feet, together with a member of Congress, a professor, and a minister on his way to the Holy Land who was "addicted to a single-breasted coat and pious platitudes." People talked about fresh sea air, but, he said, "What with the oil devoted to machinery, the smell of ancient cooking and the exhalations from bilge-water, a steamer carries to and fro an atmosphere that gives one pleasing anticipations of sea-sickness and the punishment of the wicked in the world to come." The ship ran into unusually bad weather and huge waves. Some of the passengers feared the worst. Piatt counted a total of sixteen ministers of the gospel on board and said, "We never knew a set of men so averse to entering that other and better world about which they talk so much in this."

Eventually, the ship reached Londonderry. Piatt and party disembarked, had a pleasant trip through poor green Ireland, and went on to England. From London he reported on visiting Parliament and many other sights. The party walked from Westminster "to see in the sunlight of a rare summer's day the stream of carriages and horsemen pouring into Hyde Park. What a glittering, imposing procession." He wondered, though, whether the rich and powerful of England would stay on top when "the trades' union, the dreaded commune of suffering labor, are fiercely encroaching upon their privileges. If some day Hyde Park will look in vain for its lords and ladies, and if in one stormy revolution the glittering pageantry shall disappear . . . the event will be no new thing in the history of the human race."[80]

Piatt was thinking of France. Just two years earlier troops had put down the Paris Commune, and between ten thousand and fifty thousand people had been killed. England, though, was not France. The British Trade Union Congress was five years old, but membership was still small. The future would see bloody alter-cations between police and workers but nothing like the 1819 Peterloo Massacre in Manchester, in which eleven people had died. There would be bloodier confron-tations than that in America, and soon, and Piatt would witness the beginning of these at first hand; but there was to be nothing like a revolution in either country. There was more to the societal scene than what Piatt said. In England as in Amer-ica, poor envied rich, but there was mobility. Many poor people did not want to overthrow a system in which they might dream of rising high. More important, perhaps, was the extent to which the lives of rich and poor were kept separate in Victorian England and the fact that the rich were well policed and well armed."[81]

Piatt spent considerable time in London with his old commander, Robert Schenck, who was now the American minister and who had lately been criticized in the press for helping market in Britain the shares of an American mining com-pany while he was serving as the envoy to Britain. Piatt wrote that the criticism was unfair (and would write more about this, years later, as would others).

From England, Piatt and his fellow travelers crossed to Belgium. He did not want to see the site of the Battle of Waterloo, only the field of Gravelotte. There the French had been defeated by the Prussians, two years earlier, in the war foolishly begun by Napoleon III, whom Piatt had always thought incompetent or worse. From Gravelotte they went on to Germany and spent a number of days in the Rhineland. Their best excursion was to the picturesque ruins of the thirteenth-century castle of Ehrenfels. It was sunny and hot, and their climb from the Rhine up to the ruins left them tired and perspiring. The castle is only a hundred vertical yards above the river, but Piatt was not, it seems, in top shape. No one was at the castle. In a few minutes, though, they were pleased to see two women and three men mounting the path with baskets on their heads: the picnic lunch they had arranged for, with food and some welcome iced wine. (Piatt had eased up at least a little as regarded alcohol, since his youthful days at temperance meetings, but it appears that he never drank much.)

After the Piatts' return from their 1873 trip, Donn Piatt ran into Lew Wallace by chance one December evening on a street in Washington. During the war, it will be recalled, Wallace had been president of the commission investigating the conduct of General Don Carlos Buell as commander of the Army of the Ohio. Wallace had disliked what he saw as Piatt's efforts to pressure the commission to condemn Buell.

A decade later, Wallace's encounter with Piatt in Washington was a pleasant one. It came at a time when Wallace may have needed cheering up. He had recently published his first historical novel, *The Fair God,* which was set in Mexico at the time of the Spanish conquest under Cortés. He had begun to write the book years earlier, in 1849, shortly after his service as an officer in the Mexican War. The book was well received, but there was a charge, probably unfounded, of plagiarism. Someone claimed that Wallace had borrowed his theme and many of his ideas from an obscure, out-of-print romance called *Malmiztic the Toltec.*[82] (This was the only novel, published in 1851, by William Whiteman Fosdick of Cincinnati, the young man who had visited Donn and Louise Piatt at Mac-o-cheek and had written the popular song "Aura Lee.") Nor was Wallace doing well in politics. He had recently been a candidate for a seat in Congress, but he had lost the election. Many people remembered that Wallace, the youngest major general in the Union army, had been removed from command for poor leadership at Shiloh—and removed from command again after his defeat at Monocacy in 1864. Two weeks after the second occasion Grant had restored him to command, but stains remained on his reputation.

Piatt told Wallace when they met on the street that when he was recently in London, *The Fair God* had been selling very well. An English gentleman had told Piatt that it was not simply a good book, it was "the great American novel." It was encouraging news to Wallace, who was already planning a new book. His *Ben-Hur,* which was to appear seven years later, became America's best-selling novel until Margaret Mitchell's *Gone with the Wind* appeared in 1936.

After his encounter with Piatt, Wallace wrote his sister-in-law, "You can understand how very agreeable the colonel made himself. Upon coming down-street, I sent him a book with compliments, etc. That was day before yesterday. Next Sunday I suppose he will 'go for me' in the Capitol. Such is his way."[83] That may or may not have been Piatt's way. Nothing about Lew Wallace appeared in *The Capital.*

The Piatts vacationed in America in 1874, and decided to make another European trip in 1875. By that time Henry Reed had left *The Capital.* Piatt's new fellow editor was Ben G. Lovejoy, and the proprietor left the paper in his hands for almost four months.

This time the Piatts' traveling companion was to be their friend Clara Morris, the famous actress. Morris had married the previous year a well-to-do Long Islander, Frederick C. Harriott, but he did not go with them.[84] Before the travelers' departure from America in June, Piatt wrote in *The Capital,* "Ill-health in our family makes it necessary that we should be absent from Washington for the next ninety days."[85] The ill person seems to have been neither of the Piatts but Clara Morris. Piatt reported later that at Paris the doctors had treated her malady, which had been diagnosed as neuralgia, with "moxa." This, he explained, consisted of applying irons at white heat along each side of the spine. The treatment had been terribly painful, but it seemed to make her better.[86]

The long stay in Paris brought back to Donn and Ella many memories of months that they—and Louise—had spent there, two decades earlier. From there they and Clara went south, for a sojourn at Menton on the sunny Riviera. It appears that they also made their way over the border into Italy. Years later Piatt wrote that in Italy "I have not only seen temples to false gods despoiled to erect churches to the true God, but I have looked on great monuments of art despoiled to build hideous lodging-places for shopkeepers. It remained for us to mutilate the tombs of the deserving [presumably George H. Thomas] in order to set up memorials to others whose right to praiseworthy recognition is more than doubtful [Grant? Sherman?]."[87]

The travelers returned to England, and in London Piatt, the sometime littera-teur, paid a pleasant call on Charles Reade, whose masterful historical novel *The Cloister and the Hearth* had appeared in 1861. Since then Reade had written both novels and plays, some dealing with trade unions. He was a reformer, and his in-terests, Piatt found, were like his own. He told his readers that Reade was the best writer of English fiction.

Piatt also went to see another well-known writer living in London, his Ameri-can friend Moncure Daniel Conway, and wrote of him admiringly, too. Conway had been born to a slave-owning family in Virginia; when he was a young man, his cousin John Moncure Daniel—Piatt's diplomatic counterpart in Europe—had convinced him for a time that slavery was fully justified. Later Conway became an abolitionist Unitarian minister, and after the Civil War broke out he escorted his father's slaves from Washington through what was still slaveholding country—the state of Maryland—to freedom in Cincinnati. He and Piatt had first met in Cin-cinnati in 1863,[88] and Conway had gone to England later that year to argue the American abolitionist cause. He remained there and wrote major biographies of Thomas Carlyle and Thomas Paine.

In October 1875, after Ella and Clara had already returned home from Europe, Donn Piatt sailed from Liverpool for New York on the steamer *Celtic*. He shared a cabin with a stranger, an apparently wealthy businessman whose name was Al-exander Keith. This gentleman's cabin luggage included two large boxes. Before sailing Keith had tried to insure the boxes for twelve thousand pounds sterling, saying they contained gold dollars. He was denied insurance when he refused to open the boxes for inspection but nevertheless sailed, with his baggage.

Piatt found his cabin mate an agreeable man with a pleasant countenance. He was unaware—no one was aware—that Keith's large boxes contained explosives. Keith intended to debark at Queenstown (now Cork) in Ireland, after setting fuses to explode his boxes and destroy the ship after it sailed out into the Atlantic. Even if he would not be paid for the supposed loss of gold, he wanted to test his explo-sive mechanism.

The captain decided to head into the Atlantic without calling at Queenstown. The next port of call would be New York. Keith suddenly found he was going to have to defuse his devices if he was not to blow up with the ship. He got the purser to give him a separate cabin and managed to do the defusing out of sight of Piatt or others. After a thirteen-day voyage the *Celtic,* with Piatt and the passengers still unaware they had a would-be bomber in their midst, reached New York safely.

Piatt had clearly enjoyed the voyage. On learning from a fellow passenger that "a lady whom he had known in his early youth" was now living in Buffalo, he sat on deck and wrote her a long poem:

> So you're a mother!—matron sage!
> And I am growing old
> With all the faults of frosty age,
> So cynical and cold
> But oh! 'tis sweet to feel the bloom
> Brought out by merry chance,
> Of flowers that grow from out the tomb
> Of youthful, wild romance.[89]

That was very nice—but where was the still undiscovered bomber? Just two months later he repeated his scheme, intending to plant a bomb on a steamer sailing from Bremerhaven to New York. He would set the fuse and then debark at Southampton. But his bomb blew up as the baggage was being loaded onto the ship at Bremerhaven, causing a bloodbath; perhaps eighty people were killed. Keith, in his cabin, shot himself in the head and died five days later.

⦗ 7 ⦘

PRESIDENTIAL PRISONER,
PRESIDENTIAL FRIEND

President Grant finally found grounds for legal action against Donn Piatt in early 1877, when Grant's second, final term was ending. In the presidential election the previous November, the Republican candidate, Rutherford B. Hayes—governor of Ohio and Piatt's old comrade—had lost to his Democratic opponent, Governor Samuel J. Tilden of New York, in both the popular and, apparently, the electoral vote, even though Hayes had an excellent record as a three-term governor of Ohio. Tilden, a successful reformer and seemingly fit, was in fact sick and perhaps unable physically or psychologically to take on the burden of the presidency.[1] Piatt backed Tilden and on the eve of the election had written that his election was almost certain, adding that if Hayes should somehow win, he did not agree with some of his friends that the country would go straight to the devil.[2]

After the election a number of votes were thrown out as illegally or improperly cast. In the end twenty electoral votes remained in dispute, in three Southern states and Oregon. Unfortunately, as one historian puts it, the Constitution was "maddeningly ambiguous" on how to resolve such disputes.[3] On January 29, 1877, Congress passed a bill, which President Grant signed, deciding that the dispute should be resolved by a fifteen-person Electoral Commission composed of five members from each house of Congress and five justices of the Supreme Court. The commission awarded all twenty votes to Hayes, making him the winner by one vote.

Piatt had paid a friendly visit to his old friend Hayes, back in Ohio, in October 1876, just a month before the election. They were on opposite sides politically, but Piatt had long admired Hayes. Indeed, a Hayes campaign biography quoted approving things that Piatt (whom the biography called "a judge of ability, to say the least")[4] had written about the Republican candidate.

On his October visit, Piatt found Hayes "the same kind, genial gentleman" he had known earlier. Hayes introduced him to his wife, Lucy, whom Piatt had never met. She extended her hand to him and said that she had long known him by reputation, that her husband was a warm friend of his, and she was glad to meet him. Piatt wrote afterward, "I felt at that moment as if I could vote for Hayes. Nay, had she ordered, I would then and there incontinently have embraced old Chandler [Zachariah Chandler, the ex-senator who had gone gunning for Piatt]. This lady, I thought, has wit and tact, and ought to be mistress of the Executive Mansion."[5]

Piatt did not know, and Lucy Webb Hayes had perhaps forgotten, that in 1862, when it was rumored that Piatt was to be promoted to brigadier general, she had written her husband that Piatt's promotion would be "an outrage."[6]

Piatt changed his favorable opinion about Rutherford Hayes, and sharply, after the decision of the Electoral Commission. He saw the moves that produced Hayes's victory as corruption of the electoral process. It was not the kind of solution to the election dispute that he had hoped for. Two months earlier he had taken part in a dinner meeting with James A. Garfield and several other members of Congress in which, Garfield told his diary, "an attempt was made to find some common ground of action in the difficulties surrounding us."[7]

It was not, for Piatt, a question of the candidates' planned policies. Either a Hayes or a Tilden administration would bring an end to Reconstruction, which had—for a time—helped African Americans gain justice in the South. For his part, Hayes had promised that if elected he would withdraw the six thousand federal troops from the only two Southern states where they remained, Louisiana and South Carolina. They remained there after considerable violence in the South in the first postwar decade, including many lynchings of blacks and actions against white Republicans. In Louisiana, for example, the "Coushatta massacre" of six Republican officials and a number of freedmen in August 1874 had been followed in September by a coup d'etat in New Orleans that overthrew the state's Republican government with a loss of thirty-two lives.[8] Two years after that, though, Piatt agreed with many or most white Northerners, Republicans and Democrats, that it was time to end Reconstruction. That did not mean he could tolerate what had just happened in getting Hayes elected.

On February 18, 1877, Piatt published in *The Capital* an editorial entitled "Beginning of the End," which became an immediate sensation and was picked up by papers across the country.[9] To put it mildly, the editorial was inflammatory, and it attacked Piatt's friend Garfield as well as Hayes:

> The swift decay that in the last ten years has made our self-government a sham and a mockery, and in the executive and legislative branches shamed us before the world, has been slowly working its way through the judiciary, until now . . . it offends with its stench the nostrils of all honest citizens.
>
> . . . Through a dishonest returning board, made up of criminals who have escaped conviction and punishment under the protecting arm of a corrupt

government, enough votes are thrown out to render all their efforts vain and saddle upon them the old corruption and old horde for another term of years—perhaps forever.

From this an appeal was taken to five justices of the Supreme Court—for that, no more and no less, was the commission created. It was believed that by such process the question at issue . . . could be lifted from the political arena to a tribunal of high-toned, impartial judges, who would decide in accordance with law and justice.

To the amazement and disgust of all thoughtful minds, these justices divided, as the partisans had, on a political line, and three indecent old men joined with the enemies of the people in fixing corruption upon us, and destroying all confidence in the very foundation of our political structure, the ballot. . . .

. . . Their real brief is to be found in the utterance of one of their commission, James A. Garfield, who said boastingly: "You'll have to grin and bear it; we hold the cards and intend to play them."

. . . If the people tamely submit we may bid a long farewell to constitutional government. . . . If a man thus returned to power can ride in safety from the executive mansion to the Capitol to be inaugurated, we are fitted for the slavery that will follow the inauguration.

We do not believe the people of the United States are of this servile sort. We do not believe that they are prepared, without a blow, to part with their hard-earned, blood-stained possessions. Notice is now served on the citizens of Louisiana and South Carolina that they must care for themselves. How soon lamp-posts will bear fruit is for them to say.[10]

Many thought Piatt had gone too far. The *Boston Daily Globe* said he was in danger of going to jail "for Being an Ass."[11] Thomas Nast, the famous *Harper's Weekly* cartoonist, showed Piatt himself ready for a hangman's noose, adding a reference to his lobbying for a supposedly worthless formula to mothproof military uniforms.[12] Piatt had admitted the lobbying, however, and he later attacked the firm, whose crooked dealings he said he had not known of—more on that later.

Thomas Nast was much admired for his slashing portrayals of William "Boss" Tweed, who headed the corrupt Democratic machine, Tammany Hall, in New York City. Piatt agreed that Tweed was disgusting, but he liked Nast no better than Nast liked him. He had in words painted a not inaccurate picture of Nast several years earlier as a person "blind . . . to every outrage save those pointed at and paid for by his partisans."[13] Indeed, Thomas Nast had a favorite hero, Ulysses S. Grant, as well as favorite villains. A Nast biographer describes how he savagely caricatured leading senators "for their presumption in attacking the hero of the age."[14]

Early 1877 was without question a tense time in America. One veteran member of Congress recalled that after Hayes's victory was declared, there were frequent threats of a new civil war.[15] Grant quietly strengthened military forces in and around Washington.[16]

No doubt, Grant remembered that when he had first run for the presidency, in 1868, the Democratic candidate for vice president, Francis Blair Jr., had warned that Grant, if elected, would never leave the White House alive—a statement that sounded like a threat of assassination, though Blair said later it had been taken out of context. Beyond what Frank Blair had said, Grant had escaped two plots to kill him in late 1865, after the war ended, and he had received several direct assassination threats before the 1868 election.[17]

Some, not all, Americans were alarmed by what Piatt had written. The *New York Times* wrote that "some half-crazy person . . . might be excited by just such articles as that in the *Capital,* [and] undertake the dastardly deed of murder."[18] Ward Hill Lamon, Lincoln's comrade who had been away from Washington when Lincoln was assassinated—after failing to heed Lamon's warning not to go to theaters—wrote to the president-elect from West Virginia that he should beware. Piatt, Lamon said, "is one, who during his whole, civil, military and mixed editorial career has acted as a hardened criminal." Lamon warned that while Piatt, unlike John Wilkes Booth, might lack the courage to carry out an assassination, his "desperate Pals" might make an attempt.[19]

But there were yet others, in Washington and elsewhere, who thought such fears were exaggerated. That eminent Virginian Nathaniel Beverley Tucker—who had once been accused of participating in the plot to kill Abraham Lincoln—recalled how "we all sat around [Chamberlain's restaurant in Washington] laughing over the dead earnestness with which the people read the bloodthirsty lines which were published."[20] Murat Halstead wrote to the president-elect from Cincinnati, "I know you pay no attention to the twaddle about assassination. Donn Piatt will not hurt anyone."[21]

Piatt was not the only editor who called on the American people to protest in mass the election of Hayes. Piatt's friend Henry Watterson of the *Louisville Courier-Journal,* who thought Hayes's opponent Tilden the closest he ever saw to an ideal statesman, was incensed. After Watterson heard, on what he thought good authority, that Tilden had been told three times that he could have the presidency—for a price—he agreed to address a public meeting in Washington. There Watterson called for "a mass convention of at least 100,000 peaceful citizens," who would be exercising "the freeman's right of petition." That warranted a Nast cartoon in *Harper's Weekly* showing a ranting Watterson—while Murat Halstead, who supported Hayes, stands above, pouring water on Watterson's hot head.[22]

What apparently went unreported were comments made by young Joseph Pulitzer, soon to become famous with his *St. Louis Post-Dispatch,* who followed Watterson on the platform and said that the 100,000 ought to come fully armed and ready for business.[23]

Fiery remarks had also been made by Democrats elsewhere, notably in Ohio. James Steadman, a Civil War general, spoke in Toledo and offered to lead 100,000 men to Washington. In Columbus another former general, Thomas Ewing Jr., spoke pointedly of the need to resist tyranny, at a meeting that adopted a resolution saying that if Hayes should be installed as president, the action should be resisted by the people to the last extremity, even if that should mean a call to arms.[24] There were rumors that Tilden "minute men" were in fact enrolling in the North and that Southern rifle clubs planned to march on Washington to support Tilden.[25]

Grant did not allow copies of *The Capital* in his house, but when Secretary of State Hamilton Fish met with him there on the day after the anti-Hayes editorial appeared, Grant was well aware of what Piatt had written. Fish said he thought that Donn Piatt should be prosecuted. Grant immediately agreed. He sent for the attorney general, Alphonso Taft. The president told Taft to have a complaint made immediately against their fellow Ohioan and for Piatt to be arrested, with an indictment to follow as soon as possible.[26] Piatt was duly arrested and charged with inciting rebellion, insurrection, and riot. He was soon released, after paying bail in the amount of five thousand dollars.[27] He insisted that he had not called for assassination but rather for popular resistance, whatever that might mean.

President-elect Hayes seems not to have been overly worried about his safety. Perhaps he should have been. Even if Murat Halstead knew that Piatt would harm no one, who could tell what Piatt's editorial and other fiery statements might inspire some madman to do? A bullet was fired through Hayes's parlor window one evening in Columbus, when he was at dinner with his family in the adjoining room. The family was certainly concerned, even if he was not. His six-year-old son, Scott, must have been repeating what he had heard his elders say when he told his sister that their father had been elected president "and the Democrats will kill him."[28] Hayes's friends were equally concerned. They advised him that when it was time for him to travel to Washington, he should do so cautiously and, if possible, in secrecy. When the time came, the president of the Pennsylvania Railroad furnished two private rail cars, and Hayes reached Washington without incident.[29]

After Hayes was, also without incident, inaugurated in March 1877, he had his attorney general, Charles Devens, drop the charges against Piatt.[30] Jokes circulated, however, about "Rutherfraud" and "His Fraudulency,"[31] and *The Capital* put out an extra issue on Inauguration Day. As it had done for Grant's second inauguration four years earlier, the paper published a mock "inaugural address" by Hayes, in which the new president expressed "thanks to the Almighty for His divine intervention in our behalf." Piatt had Hayes say that his attention had been drawn to "certain turbulent spirits who threaten us with an armed resistance," including

Donn Piatt—but that "unless these gentlemen are more terrible in the next war than they were in the last we need not be disturbed in our dreams. [Loud laughter.]"[32]

In a more serious tone Piatt published an editorial blasting Hayes as a man "whose vulgar ambition makes him seize upon an office whose possession he can only disgrace with the fraud that brought him into it. . . . In the inauguration of Rutherford B. Hayes our Government is revolutionized. It passes from a republic to the lowest, vilest and meanest form of aristocracy possible to exist."[33]

Soon the situation changed abruptly. In May, just two months after the president's inauguration, an Illinois paper reported a rumor in Washington that "Donn Piatt has surrendered to the enemy. The rumor is that the haughty Donn has seen or been seen by the president and that as a result the heavy artillery of *The Capital* will be silent hereafter."[34] The following month the *Boston Daily Globe* reported, "President Hayes's latest and most astonishing convert is Donn Piatt and his Capital newspaper, which advised his assassination on Inauguration day. Piatt now wants Hayes's policy to have a fair trial."[35]

The reports were true. Was it perhaps the president who made the first move? Certainly Hayes, an able politician, believed in conciliation rather than confrontation in other, bigger fields. He was the first postwar president to bring into his cabinet a former Confederate officer—David M. Key, his postmaster general. Later, after Hayes toured Southern states, he was viewed there as a very apostle of reconciliation.[36]

Rapprochement continued between the president and the editor. In December 1877 Hayes invited Piatt to the celebration of his and his wife's silver wedding anniversary; Piatt wrote back to the president that he was sorry that his wife's health had made it impossible for them to attend.[37] Later, Piatt asked the president for patronage favors and invited him to the Piatt home—and Hayes once came.[38] Hayes never forgot their old camaraderie; years later he ended a personal letter, "Same as before"—adding that it was a phrase that Piatt had often used.[39]

Friendship did not mean that Donn Piatt would refrain from criticizing the Hayes administration. In late February 1878, when Hayes was nearing the end of his first year in the White House, *The Capital* asked in a headline, "What's Wrong with the Administration?"[40] We look in vain, the paper said, for the many reforms promised us at the time of the inauguration. The first of two intended major reforms was to have been the "pacification of the South"—that is, the end of Reconstruction—and that had been easily accomplished by withdrawing the federal troops that remained in just two states, Louisiana and South Carolina.[41]

The other major reform, the paper recalled, was to be reform of the civil service. Even before Hayes, as the paper did not need to remind people, there had been a growing movement to end, or at least reduce the dimensions of, the old spoils system. Civil service reform societies were formed in a number of cities. Alas, said *The Capital*, "not an inch has been gained. Indeed, if anything, we are in a worse condition than before." (Hayes did take limited steps forward as president, notably ousting the collector of the Port of New York, a firm believer in the spoils system, Chester A. Arthur. The Civil Service Reform Act, which put most federal jobs under a merit system, was enacted only in 1883—under President Chester A. Arthur.)

The central fact about this administration was, said *The Capital,* "President Hayes does not lack firmness but his firmness is not aggressive. It lacks that force which makes an opposition uneasy. He is too good. . . . [A] grim, ignorant devil, such as Grant, will count more in this wicked world of ours than the twelve apostles prepared for a meek, unresisting martyrdom."

There were also, it seems, limits as to how far Piatt wanted to be seen in society as a friend of this president whom he was continuing to criticize in his paper. In October 1878 Hayes gave a dinner at the White House for members of the Literary Club of Cincinnati who were living in Washington. Almost of all them were there through presidential appointments. Piatt the editor was not present. One source claims that he was "still bitter over the election [and] would not attend."[42] Perhaps he did not want to be seen publicly hobnobbing with Hayes—or with another fellow club member, Alphonso Taft, who as attorney general had lately had him arrested,

One of the first requests that Piatt made to Hayes as president was for help with the court-martial case of his nephew Benjamin Runkle. Whether Piatt was convinced that the charges against his nephew were false, we do not know. He wrote a confidential letter to Hayes in June 1877, saying, "He is a gallant, generous impulsive boy [Runkle was now almost forty] whose wound at Pittsburg Landing shattering his jaw has made insanity through indigestion[—]he cannot chew his food—a part of his life. This case is being prejudiced through a malign influence—at least I am led to believe this today. May I ask you in your grave duties to take his case yourself and consider it. I believe honestly that he has law and justice on his side."[43] Hayes did interest himself in the case, but it would be another decade before the verdict was fully overturned in the U.S. Supreme Court.

The February 1877 editorial against Hayes's assumption of office was not the last time Piatt suggested that the people might turn to the use of force. These were years when American manufacturing was booming. The value of American manufactured goods rose from less than two billion dollars on the eve of the Civil War to almost ten billion dollars in 1890.[44] Great fortunes were made—but workers were poor and overworked. It was not the society that Piatt had known as a young lawyer in Cincinnati, which had been a place of opportunity for all.

The fact that Piatt came from a well-to-do family did not make him like America's nouveaux riches. Louise Piatt had written, when they lived in Paris years earlier, of the rich Americans who wished they could buy a title of nobility. As the century progressed, an increasing number of matches were made between the daughters of rich Americans and the scions of European nobles. Piatt reported in August 1874, "One of those animated money chests . . . has lately sold his daughter to a nobleman. . . . He answers, if we recollect correctly, to the name of Jerome, and handicaps the poor girl with an immense fortune, that, in case of her death without issue, is to be the property of the noble purchaser."[45]

The father was Leonard Jerome, and he was known as the King of Wall Street. The *New York Times,* in which for a time he held a large share of the ownership, later called him one of the "most successful manipulators in Wall Street."[46] Four months before Piatt's article, Jerome's daughter Jennie had married Lord Randolph Churchill. She did not die without issue; in November she gave birth to a child whom the parents named Winston Spencer Churchill.

In American society the problem of poverty seemed intractable. During the depression of 1873 many and perhaps most employers in America had cut workers' pay, while the work week remained sixty hours or more. Many lost their jobs and became vagrants who roamed the country in search of work. The scene was as bad in Piatt's home state as it was elsewhere. A Cincinnati historian tells us, "Between dusk and dawn, Cincinnati's police stations were jammed with hundreds of homeless men and women who slept on the basement floor."[47]

Labor unrest in America, feeding on both poverty and injustice, continued and mounted as years passed. In 1876 the Molly Maguires tried to organize Pennsylvania miners, and ten of their leaders were hanged for murder and conspiracy. The year of 1877 was a year of railroad strikes—the most serious strikes yet seen in America.

Piatt took the Baltimore and Ohio Railroad for most of his trips between Washington and Ohio, and he liked to make fun of the line. It was forty miles from Washington to Baltimore, he wrote, and the B&O trains ran at reckless velocity: The management had brought the scheduled time down to three days and a half and were thinking of reducing it further.[48] In fact, trains were getting faster. By the 1870s, despite what Piatt wrote, B&O express trains took only an hour and a quarter from Washington to Baltimore. It took just twenty-two hours to cover the 570 miles from Washington to Cincinnati, and Piatt confirmed without mockery that the train was punctual "to the minute."[49] That was, nevertheless, a long trip, and even though he could travel in a modern Silver Palace Sleeping Car, trains then were not air conditioned and dust and cinders from the locomotives were a plague for passengers.[50]

On July 17, 1877, Piatt was on his way from Cincinnati back to Washington on the B&O. When the train reached Martinsburg, West Virginia, rail workers along that part of the line were on strike. They had gone on strike the previous day, a few hours after firemen had abandoned their engines down the line at Camden Junction, three miles from Baltimore.[51] It was the beginning of what became the Great Railroad Strike of 1877. The workers had struck after B&O management cut wages by 10 percent, as the Pennsylvania Railroad had also recently done. At Martinsburg the strikers were permitting passenger trains to pass through, but they stopped all freight traffic. (One imagines Piatt poking his head out of the window to see what was going on.)

The town's mayor asked for state militia. A contingent of the local Berkeley Light Guards was ordered to break up the group that was stopping trains. A striker was killed. John W. Garrett, the B&O president, asked President Hayes for federal troops, and three hundred soldiers arrived in Martinsburg the following day.[52]

When Piatt reached Washington, after considerable delay, he foresaw bigger trouble coming. He put out an extra edition of *The Capital* to report on the "mercenary soldiers" he had seen confronting an angry crowd at Martinsburg. The strike scene was a reflection, he wrote, of the avarice of monopolized wealth in America, an evil that was most powerful in the railroads and was ignoring the just rights of labor: "We rode through miles of gaunt, hungry, ragged forms in the mountains of Virginia, and we knew that the wages meant hunger, sickness, privations of all sorts; but a discharge meant death."[53]

Piatt wrote the pro-labor editor John Swinton that soon after reaching Washington he had gone to see President Hayes: "I begged that clear-headed and kind hearted official to keep his hands off. He told me in reply that while his sympathies were with the laborers, his duty was in the line of law and order, that while the Congress might legislate, and the Courts adjudicate, and had it in their hands to relieve the distress his sworn duty was simply to execute, and that he was bound to do."[54]

While Piatt thought he must appeal to Hayes, this was not a question of asking the president for just a small favor and Piatt cannot have been surprised when the president sent in federal troops. As he presumably knew, both Hayes and several members of his cabinet were close to top railroad executives. The latter included Thomas A. Scott, president of the Pennsylvania Railroad, as well as of the Texas & Pacific, who had helped secure the votes of Southern congressmen to elect Hayes and who had provided the private car that brought him to Washington for his inauguration.[55]

There was apprehension in Washington—might disorders spread to the capital? They did not, but in succeeding days in the East and the Midwest there came more strikes and bloody confrontations with militia and troops, mainly on the railroads, not just the Baltimore and Ohio but also the Pennsylvania and other lines. Eleven people were killed at Baltimore, twenty-six at Pittsburgh, as many as twenty at Chicago. By the time the strikes ended in August, as many as a hundred people were dead across the country and millions of dollars of property had been destroyed. America had never before seen such a conflict between owners and workers. It had, one observer recalled, "alarmed the respectable classes all over America."[56]

The Great Railroad Strike of 1877 convinced many workers that they needed better organization, but it would be a long time before America had effective large unions. The Noble Order of the Knights of Labor, founded in 1869, was rising in importance, but it was only in 1881 that Samuel Gompers brought together various trade unions into a federation that became the American Federation of Labor five years later.

Six months after the railroad strikes Piatt was invited to address a "workingmen's assembly" at Ford's Theater in Washington, where Lincoln had been shot in 1865. He told his audience, "Labor is slowly struggling up. It is only when the brawny hands of labor are on the neck of capital that concession is granted. Violence marks progress. Do not let us, my friends, be nice about using arms." He was no revolutionary, however, and no doubt preferred to avoid being charged again with inciting rebellion. He went on to say, "Violence may not be necessary, thank God; we have the ballot."[57]

In these years Piatt also published occasional song-poems backing the cause of labor, some of them in the paper put out by his friend John Swinton, a former editorial writer at the *New York Times* and *New York Sun*.[58] In 1884, when coal miners in Ohio's Hocking Valley went on strike after their wages were cut, Piatt visited the area, perhaps more to show his concern than to do reporting. His "Laborer's Hymn," published after his death, warns in a truculent way that while workers bear their burdens patiently, eventually

> The thunder's roll, the lightning glare,
> And storms come on amain.[59]

One author writes that Piatt took a nationalistic pride in American workers, seeing them as more advanced and independently minded than their oppressed, cowed European counterparts.[60] If so, the pride was limited. He seems to have been all in all disappointed by the working class. He reportedly once said, "While I have a kind feeling for the laborer, I do not respect him. He is as stupid, ignorant and vicious as the rest of us. The confounded fools, holding the power of reform in their hands, not only consent to oppression, but actually put and fasten the yoke upon their own necks."[61]

Whatever the limits were to his respect for American workers, his overall support for them did not sit well with many upper-class Americans who were frightened by the newly militant workers.[62] Piatt, as an independent editor, might say what he wanted, but it was a time when free speech could be limited elsewhere, including academia. The 1880s saw continuing growth in American reform movements, but liberal economists like Richard T. Ely and Henry Carter Adams suffered for their pro-labor views.[63]

Piatt's bitter critiques of domestic society did not lessen his interest in foreign affairs. His friend William Neely Thompson, who returned to the East after prospering as a merchant in California, later recalled how early in the Hayes administration Piatt helped improve American-Mexican relations. Three decades had passed since the Mexican War, but it was only one decade since the French had imposed Emperor Maximilian on the Mexicans. Grant, after defeating Lee at Appomattox, sent fifty thousand troops to the Rio Grande in 1865. Many in Washington called for a new war; there was an unfounded rumor that General Rosecrans planned to recruit twenty-five thousand men for a huge filibustering expedition to invade Mexico.[64]

Maximilian fell to a Mexican firing squad in 1867, but turbulence continued. Porfirio Díaz appointed himself president of Mexico in 1876 and was in charge in Mexico City by the time Hayes took office in Washington in March 1877. There were numerous problems between the two countries, not least the Mexican rustlers, who, according to congressional investigators in 1872, had reduced American cattle herds by two-thirds and cost cattlemen nearly $28 million.[65]

Díaz's new government sent José María de Zamacona, who knew the United States well, as its envoy to Washington to push for formal recognition of the Díaz government, which the United States had not agreed to. The Mexicans also hired several non-Mexicans to lobby in Washington, including Caleb Cushing, the former congressman and U.S. attorney general, who had just returned to Washington after serving as American minister to Spain, and a British resident of Mexico named William Pritchard, whom the American representative in Mexico called "an unprincipled scamp." The Mexicans paid Cushing two thousand dollars to lobby the Congress, but he accomplished little. Pritchard, on the other hand, got Dana of the *New York Sun* to agree to write pro-Mexico editorials.[66]

Piatt, according to his friend Thompson, at some point met Zamacona, who complained to him, "I am received in no gentleman's house. I am here in a false position, without a place in respectable society. Senator Matthews, who lives across the street from my house, has never called upon me."[67]

This was certainly disingenuous on the part of Zamacona. Whether or not gentlemen were receiving him, his agents were at work in Washington and rather than waiting on a visit from Matthews, he might more properly have offered to pay a call on Matthews—Stanley Matthews, Piatt's friend from Ohio.

In any case, Piatt decided to help. He got Matthews to call on Zamacona. Soon afterward, Thompson saw an acquaintance named Henry Banning, who was both Piatt's brother-in-law and the chairman of the military committee of the U.S. House of Representatives. Banning told Thompson that he feared the Hayes administration was bent on war with Mexico. Thompson told him he should talk with his brother-in-law, Piatt. The result was that Matthews, Piatt, and Zamacona had dinner at Welcker's, and later Zamacona reported to Mexico City that Banning was cordial and responsive to Mexican interests and had even invited him to appear before his committee.[68]

There was no war. Both houses of Congress pushed for normalization of relations with Mexico, and in March 1878 Washington extended formal recognition to the Díaz government. Within several years, American capital was flowing into Mexico. The Santa Fe and the Denver & Rio Grande railroads were both granted concessions to build rail lines from the U.S. border to Mexico City—and in 1880 former president Grant accepted an offer to become president of a line (never built) that was to run south from Mexico City toward Guatemala.[69]

In 1877 Piatt had several meetings with the famous Western writer Bret Harte, whom he had long wanted to meet and who had recently arrived in Washington from California. Piatt and Harte discussed the possibility of Harte joining the staff of *The Capital.* Harte wrote his wife in early July that he was about to sign a contract with Piatt "which will put $1000 in the Bank for me."[70] Later that month he wrote that Piatt was offering him three thousand dollars a year and a half interest in the newspaper.[71] Harte, as noted below, wrote a short novel to be serialized in the paper, but subsequently Piatt disappointed him by not hiring him, saying that some old debts against the paper had lately come up. Indeed, in October Harte wrote his wife that he understood Piatt's paper was bankrupt.

It is not clear that Piatt ever paid Bret Harte anything, nor is it clear that Piatt's paper was then having financial troubles, although financial management was not his strong point. He may, as one historian writes, have reneged on his agreement with Harte. If he did, he may have seen reason to do so. Harte had made clear to Piatt that he was not willing to take on the full risk of partnership, saying, "I only want to protect myself from any indebtedness of the Company over and above my Share in it, should we fail."[72]

Piatt may also have had doubts about Harte's personal financial situation. Harte was hard pressed financially, as we know from his letters to his wife. Mark Twain, who in 1877 collaborated with Harte on an unsuccessful play about a Chinese laundryman, *Ah Sin,* advanced large sums of money to Harte, and Harte did not repay him.[73] Soon Harte went abroad, appointed by President Hayes as American consul at Crefeld[74] in Germany.[75] One can imagine Piatt thinking that Harte was altogether a fine writer—but a poor businessman. Still, no evidence has been found that Piatt paid Harte what he undoubtedly owed him for the novel he commissioned.

Donn Piatt made no secret of his dislike for one of Washington's most famous citizens, his fellow Ohioan General William Tecumseh Sherman, older brother of Senator John Sherman. Piatt's dislike perhaps dated from a conversation he had had after the war with General John A. Logan (the same Logan whom Piatt would attack later as a drunken senator). Logan told Piatt that in June 1864 Sherman had launched his futile attack against Kenesaw Mountain in Georgia out of what amounted to envy. Before the battle, Logan said, Sherman had told other officers that while the nation's attention was focused on Grant and his Army of the Potomac, he was going to show people that his army could fight as well as Grant's did.[76]

Nor did Piatt think Sherman's famous March to the Sea had made strategic sense. It had left the Union vulnerable to a Confederate attack farther northwest, and in Piatt's view it was only the brilliance of his favorite general, George B. Thomas, that had prevented this. After Sherman had left Atlanta on his March,

Confederate General John B. Hood had invaded Tennessee and finally been defeated by Thomas at Nashville in December, just as Sherman was reaching the sea at Savannah. Piatt's negative view of Sherman's March was to be bolstered in several years by a famous European strategist.

Now, in March 1878, an article appeared in *The Capital* describing a pitiful figure who was to be seen on the streets of Washington. This was old Colonel Thomas Worthington, who as commander of an Ohio regiment before the battle of Shiloh (in April 1862) had tried, the paper said, to warn Generals Grant and Sherman of a dangerous weakness in the Union position. Worthington had found them "insolent and overbearing, deaf to all suggestions," and next morning a surprise Confederate attack had caused "the most frightful confusion and slaughter. . . . Grant and Sherman ought to have been court-martialed and shot. Instead of this, Colonel Tom Worthington was court-martialed and cashiered."[77]

Sherman, who hated journalists (other than his and Abraham Lincoln's good friend Henry Villard),[78] replied angrily that Worthington had been cashiered for habitual drunkenness. He said he had never known Piatt but understood he belonged to "that noble army of martyrs who suffered as provost marshals, judge advocates and sutlers at the rear."[79] Piatt then wrote that Sherman had forgotten that he, Piatt, had been at Sherman's elbow at First Bull Run—adding that he had been impressed by Sherman's courage there.[80]

What Piatt did not mention and Sherman perhaps did not know—he was a native of Ohio but had not lived in the state since his teens—was that the Piatt and Worthington families were closely connected by marriage. Piatt's sister Martha had lost her husband, N. C. Read, and later married James T. Worthington, the brother of Thomas Worthington, the colonel. (The Worthingtons were an eminent family in Ohio. The father of the two brothers, an elder Thomas Worthington, had been a governor of Ohio and a U.S. senator.)[81]

General Sherman's younger brother John had, as readers will recall, won out over Piatt's commander and friend, Robert Schenck, in 1866 for a seat in the U.S. Senate. Piatt said years later that on the eve of the vote for senator in the Ohio legislature, "All went merry as a marriage bell until the Hon. John appeared in the field, accompanied by his confidential and confidence man, Rush Sloan, and our majority melted away." Sloan, Piatt said, later told him that the financier Jay Cooke had provided thirty thousand dollars to buy votes for Sherman in the legislature.[82]

When Donn Piatt decided a man was bad, he usually kept him in his bad books. It was so with John Sherman. A number of times over the years Piatt told readers how interesting he found it that John Sherman, who had come to Washington with next to no money, was now, after years in the Senate on an annual salary of five thousand dollars, a millionaire. Indeed, a senator's salary was not enough for him even to meet his current expenses.[83] *The Capital* said flatly, "That John Sherman is a corrupt man no one knowing his career doubts for an instant."[84]

Piatt was not the only journalist to make such charges, but the senator had not become wealthy through corruption. Sherman himself insisted that he had been far from a poor man before coming to Washington in 1854. For several years he had been a lawyer in Mansfield, Ohio, where, he wrote in his 1895 memoir, he had made a number of real estate acquisitions.[85] How much this real estate was worth, and how much income he derived from it, Sherman did not say. However, Mansfield was a prosperous place located on three major railroads—and beyond real estate, Sherman invested in a Mansfield woodworking business and was involved in the lumber industry in Michigan.[86] If Piatt knew this, it did not matter to him. Sherman had, Piatt believed, defeated his friend Schenck for the Senate through bribery, and that made him an enemy for good.

Still another favorite target of *The Capital* was William McGarrahan, who had long laid claim to California lands with valuable mines. Although Piatt had not hired Bret Harte for a full-time position with his newspaper, he had, as noted, gotten Harte to write a short novel, *The Story of a Mine,* serialized in *The Capital* between July and October 1877 and published in book form that same year. The novel gave a fictionalized account of Piatt's view of McGarrahan's crooked dealings.[87]

Beyond fiction, McGarrahan's was in fact a long, tawdry story with links to both Congress and the Grant administration.[88] Grant's secretary of the interior, Jacob D. Cox, had resigned after McGarrahan unsuccessfully petitioned the Supreme Court for a writ of mandamus requiring the Interior Department to honor his claim[89] and Grant told Cox to leave the matter in the hands of Congress—which, as *The Nation* wrote angrily, had no jurisdiction.[90] Grant also ignored the negative opinion of his attorney general, Ebenezer R. Hoar, regarding McGarrahan's claim, and this is said to have been a factor in Hoar's own resignation at the end of 1870.[91]

McGarrahan unquestionably lobbied the Congress. Beyond that, *The Capital* reported, he was paying for members' support. And, said the paper, among the more pitiable aspects of the scene was the support that he was also getting from Montgomery Blair, once Lincoln's postmaster general and now "an aged lunatic." Blair, said the paper, had violently attacked his lifelong friend—who was also Piatt's friend—the eminent jurist Jeremiah Black, alleging that Black as attorney general had used public money to abuse poor McGarrahan.[92] (Piatt cannot have forgotten how Blair had worked against him with Lincoln in 1863, over the recruitment of slaves for the Union army. As for Jeremiah Black, who as noted had been unhappy with what Piatt wrote of him in 1872, one imagines that he did not mind Piatt defending him now.)

In February 1879 McGarrahan encountered Piatt in a Senate reception room in the Capitol, assaulted him without warning, and knocked him down. The blow itself did Piatt no harm, but he was badly bruised when he hit the marble wainscoting. The *Washington Post* reported, "Gossip at the Capitol yesterday revealed

PRESIDENTIAL PRISONER, PRESIDENTIAL FRIEND

the fact that the assault was premeditated, as a number of persons had been noti-
fied to be on or around the spot, as fun was likely to be had."[93]

The *New York Times,* no friend of Piatt, said that the assault came because Piatt
backed competitors of McGarrahan, the New Idria company—and indeed Piatt
was, as a lobbyist, in the pay of New Idria, a key fact that Piatt had left out of his
paper. Not only Piatt but former attorney general Black represented New Idria.
One may see conflicts of interest both in Piatt's dual role as lobbyist and journalist
and in Black's working on a case that had been before him at the Justice Department—where as attorney general he had found for New Idria.[94]

Piatt replied angrily to the *Times* that McGarrahan had turned to Congress for
help "after exhausting the courts with uniform decisions against him, running
from an alcalde up to the Supreme Court of the United States." Nevertheless, Piatt
said, House and Senate committees had found no merit in McGarrahan's claim,
although after bribing a member of the president's cabinet with worthless stock,
he had bought up a number of members of Congress in the same fashion.[95]

Some thought Piatt deserved the blows he had gotten from McGarrahan. His
fellow humorist Melville D. Landon used the assault to mock a Donn Piatt whom
he saw as less than blameless and overly quarrelsome. Landon's mythical "Eli Perkins" said he would never forget

> how Donn Pirate, a District of Columbia brigand, and I fell out and had a
> big fight. . . . I knew I had been whipped by Donn because I saw the marks on
> Donn's face and also talked with the doctor who sponged him off and put lini-
> ment on him. . . .
>
> . . . Donn had been saying how I had stolen some literary thunder out of his
> Capitol [*sic*]. I informed him politely how he had lied, and insinuated he was
> a d—f—, such as they have a good many of in the District of Columbia. This
> roused Donn's patriotism and yesterday he called at my rooms to thrash me . . .
>
> P.S. I send you my original poem by Artemus Ward and John Phoenix on
> my truthful and high-toned friend Donnel Pirate, the only licensed court-
> jester now living.[96]

There is, incidentally, no record of Piatt the aggressive editor ever engaging
in physical aggression after his assault on an Ohio editor as a young man. Twice,
at least, he was assaulted by others: by McGarrahan in 1879, and back in 1852 in
Cincinnati by A. W. Armstrong, who had recently served as the Hamilton County
auditor and who is said to have severely injured Piatt with a slung shot—a weight
tied to a cord—"in a personal encounter on Third Street."[97]

It was sometime in the 1870s that Piatt took on a part-time role as a Washington
lobbyist, and not just for New Idria. The work was to gain him a considerable

amount of both money and criticism in the years that he was directing *The Capital.* There is no indication that he had ever learned bookkeeping, as he would presumably have done if he had joined his father in the family's Ohio farming operations. He seems to have left his newspaper's finances to his staff, who may not have managed efficiently. (Miller says, "He was glad to be relieved of all details in financial matters, and relied implicitly upon . . . subordinates.")[98] In addition to the paper he had sizable personal expenses, inevitable if he was to find out what was going on in Washington by circulating in Washington society—as in any case he liked to do. The paper was a success, but he needed still more income. At least, he thought he did.

Lobbyists then as now were often vilified. Today, although a journalist would be condemned for lobbying, few condemn all lobbyists per se—yet even in Piatt's age at least one journalist, Piatt's old partner George A. Townsend, thought lobbying corrupt by definition.[99] Walt Whitman called lobbyists "crawling serpentine men."[100] John William De Forest, in three novels written in the Gilded Age, portrayed lobbyists as brutish, filthy, sickening, and clearly in league with the devil.[101] Indeed, there were lobbyists who employed bribery—and sex. That righteous clergyman James Dabney McCabe describes at length, in his 1873 work *Behind the Scenes in Washington*—which, since he was cautious as well as righteous, he wrote under a pseudonym—the wiles employed by "Mrs. Billpusher" and "Miss Memberhooker."[102]

A recent study of lobbying in Grant's time concludes, however, that all in all "lobbying's bad reputation is at least partly unearned."[103] Piatt's friend Ainsworth Spofford, the librarian of Congress, wrote that in fact "corruption is frequently wholly absent where the lobby is most industrious, numerous, persistent, and successful. . . . Bad legislation . . . is the fruit of ignorance, not of corruption."[104] Beyond the cases of bribery and corruption, lobbying was a necessary and legitimate part of the legislative process in a time when, in contrast to today's huge congressional staffs, members of Congress often had no staff at all unless they could hire a clerk out of their own pockets, and congressional salaries were very inadequate.[105] Members usually did their own research and wrote their own speeches.[106] Some lobbyists might bring them bribes, but others brought them reports and details of national problems that needed new legislation.

One writer concludes that although lobbyists in the Gilded Age were often viewed with disdain and sometimes accused of crime, they were badly needed for the efficient conduct of government business.[107] If so, that did not justify the lobbying being done by journalists like Piatt, on whom members of the public hoped they could rely for unbiased reporting about their government.

In addition to working for New Idria, for some months in the 1870s Piatt worked, as his opponents like Nast the cartoonist brought out, as a representative of the firm of Cowles & Brega. That company had long wanted to sell the War Department a product for mothproofing uniforms. There was a perceived need for this, because military warehouses contained hundreds of thousands of unused wool uniforms from Civil War days. Some argued that the economic thing to do was to discard the uniforms, since no major wars were in sight and moths had already done major damage to the stored stuff. The War Department decided on mothproofing, however, and began to ask Congress for appropriations for it. During the first half of the 1870s some $450,000 was appropriated—the equivalent of perhaps eleven million dollars in the early twenty-first century. A board set up by the quartermaster general found the Cowles & Brega formula the best among those of several contenders who were pushing their wares on the War Department. The firm was awarded a contract and was paid around $400,000 over the course of several years.[108] Some nevertheless questioned whether the process did all that was claimed for it—waterproofing and mildew control in addition to mothproofing.

Secretary of War William Belknap began to interest himself in the matter, at a time when the press was increasingly reporting that he himself was guilty of various kinds of malfeasance. In March 1876 Belknap resigned his post, but the House of Representatives nevertheless impeached him—not for involvement in mothproofing but for selling a job as trader at an army post in the West. He was tried and found guilty by the Senate in August.[109] Meanwhile, a House committee looked into the mothproofing business.

There were press reports that Donn Piatt was supposed to receive from Cowles & Brega 5 percent of the overall value of its government contract.[110] Piatt appeared before the House committee and confirmed that this was the case. In fact, he said, the company had confirmed orally to him that they would raise his compensation to 15 percent. His job had been to represent the company before the government, and it had needed him; he said, "They had no standing with the Government here except what I gave them." (He did not need to say that his friend James A. Garfield was chairman of the House appropriations committee.) The company's banker confirmed to the committee that between 1872 and 1874 Piatt had been paid a total of $22,934, half again as much as the salary of a member of Congress over a three-year period.

Piatt told the committee that he had worked for the company until 1874, when he learned that the company was paying him less than the agreed upon 15 percent. He had then asked the company's co-owner, George A. Cowles, for a complete written accounting. However, Piatt testified, "He told me that he could not render that because there had been an expense of money which he and Brega concluded to keep between themselves because it would not bear congressional investigation." Cowles did not elaborate on his statement, but it made Piatt recall an earlier occasion, when he had commented to Cowles that General Rufus Ingalls, who had originally opposed their process but later backed it, was a very useful friend. Cowles had then "made the remark casually that he was a very expensive one."

Piatt testified that he put this together with Cowles's remark about expense that could not be documented, sensed corruption, severed his connection with the company, and telegraphed Garfield to warn the War Department that no more funds should be expended.

Garfield's diary confirms that after Piatt wrote him, he wrote Secretary Belknap that he had heard that Cowles & Brega had paid money in order to secure the contract and that "if they had so said they ought not to receive any part of the appropriation made."[111] Both funding and mothproofing soon stopped, and the ultimate result was the House hearings.

In the hearings, the firm's co-owner, George W. Brega, gave another motive for Piatt's action. According to Brega, Piatt had threatened to go to Garfield if the firm did not pay him the additional amount agreed upon. There is no confirmation of this allegation. One may question whether Piatt, if simply acting from venality, would have taken action that might have led Brega to cut off the sizable amounts he was already being paid.

As for General Ingalls, he was a West Pointer with an excellent record who was now serving as a deputy quartermaster general. When he was called on to testify, he told the committee that the Cowles & Brega process was "really valuable"—and that he was innocent of any misconduct or wrongdoing.

The committee ended its hearing, and there seemed to be no consequence. However, there were continuing suggestions in the press that Piatt had acted not out of conviction but simply out of pique that he was not being paid enough. Then Piatt published a "manifesto" about Cowles & Brega in *The Capital*.[112] He wrote that while he had behaved properly as the company's agent in procuring the contract, he had ascertained recently that the company had bribed General Ingalls to help obtain War Department approval for their process—and that Cowles & Brega had also colluded with Ingalls to bribe General Randolph Marcy, who had sat with Ingalls on the commission looking at the mothproofing product and who was one of the army's four inspectors general. Piatt added, "I have the proofs that books were altered or destroyed for the purpose of concealing these fraudulent transactions, that witnesses were run away to Canada to escape appearance before the committee of investigation, and that the testimony of Messrs. Brega, Cowles and Ingalls is a tissue of falsehoods from beginning to end. All of which is respectfully submitted to the War Department and the grand jury for their judicial investigation."

There was still more to come. The *New York Times* reported that in addition to bribing Ingalls and Marcy, the company had paid a retainer to Marcy's father-in-law, General George B. McClellan, now retired but still influential.[113] Ingalls and Marcy requested a court of inquiry.[114] Neither officer was chastised, Piatt never produced his evidence, and the story died away. Ingalls ended his army career as the army's quartermaster general in 1883. Marcy retired as the top inspector general in 1881.

Piatt had broken no law in representing Cowles & Brega, but one can at a minimum accuse him of having a conflict of interest in working as both lobbyist and editor. Then came a case that raised new questions, about his ethics or, at a minimum, his good sense.

Piatt was reported in the press in 1874 to have served as one of several lobbyists for the Pacific Mail Steamship Company and to have received the not inconsiderable sum of five thousand dollars for his services.[115] The company received federal subsidies for carrying the mails to Asia. A congressional investigation indicated that a number of members of Congress had been bribed to support the subsidies. The subsidies were revoked at the beginning of 1875, but no one was ever indicted.

What had been Piatt's role? None, he told a hearing of the House Ways and Means Committee in January 1875. He was, he said, a personal friend of the company's chief lobbyist, Richard B. Irwin, and Irwin had lent him the five thousand dollars in 1872. The Capital was still a new venture, and, Piatt said, he was "in great distress for money." When he was asked whether the loan had any connection with the Pacific Mail subsidy, he replied, "None whatever; I opposed that measure from beginning to end." Nevertheless, he was asked, had he in any way sought to influence congressional action on the subsidy? "Yes," he answered, "I did all I could to defeat it."[116] Irwin in turn was asked by the committee to name the men who had assisted him in securing the subsidy. He named eighteen men, but not Piatt.[117]

Piatt said he needed money for his paper, as perhaps he did, but one must nevertheless ask why he turned for help to Irwin in particular. It is possible that he did so only after approaching others. There is no evidence that Irwin employed him to lobby the Congress—or to act as a channel for bribes to members of Congress—on behalf of Pacific Mail. One can argue that Piatt should have known that the loan would raise questions if it became known, but at the time he cannot have anticipated that it would be discussed in a congressional hearing.

Piatt was also criticized for his support of Alexander R. Shepherd, who ran the Board of Public Works of the District of Columbia government from 1871 to 1873. The two may have met soon after Piatt moved to Washington; they both spoke at a Washington election rally in May 1870,[118] and later the Piatts bought their Washington home from Shepherd.

There were charges of corruption against Shepherd as head of public works, and Piatt was called before a congressional committee in 1872 to explain his links with Shepherd, beginning with the house Shepherd had sold him at 18th and F Streets. He was asked whether improvements in the local streets had benefited him personally. Indeed, he said, they had; originally, his cellar had flooded in wet weather, but since the street level had been lowered, it stayed dry. What about certain advertising by the District government in The Capital? Piatt said he had been displeased to see it—it had been accepted not by him but by Henry Howe, who ran the financial side of the paper—but it had appeared. It had no effect on the editorial stance of *The Capital,* which "can tomorrow attack the government as bitterly as it pleases, if it sees cause, and it will, if it sees cause for it."[119]

Despite questions about Shepherd's probity, in 1873 President Grant appointed him the capital's territorial governor, replacing Henry D. Cooke, the first governor and brother of the financier Jay Cooke. The position of governor appointed by the president had been created by Congress, with Grant's support, to replace the three existing jurisdictions within the District of Columbia. A year later a congressional investigation found that the territorial government was bankrupt. There were indications of poor management and cronyism. Shepherd soon found himself out of a job, and the territorial government was changed to one headed by three commissioners, which remained in effect for the next century. Shepherd declared personal bankruptcy and later went to Mexico to seek his fortune in silver mining.

Whatever the form of the capital's government, it had long been evident that major efforts were needed to make Washington a better place. For the first several years after Piatt moved there, in 1868, the scene was in good part still one of muddy streets, open sewers, and wandering livestock. There were serious and influential people who wanted the capital removed to St. Louis. Piatt facetiously suggested that access roads to Washington be closed off before the centennial year of 1876, so that foreigners could not see what a miserable capital America had. In contrast, he found when he returned to Paris in 1875, after twenty years' absence, that the capital of France had become the most beautiful city in the world.

The changes in Paris were the work of Georges-Eugène Haussmann, whom Napoleon III had chosen in 1853 to modernize the city. In succeeding years, as prefect of the Seine, Haussmann created gardens and parks where there had been rundown old buildings, built new bridges and sewers and aqueducts, and ran broad boulevards through areas of twisting, narrow streets. He was widely praised, but he was also criticized for destroying much of the medieval city; Napoleon III fired him in 1870 because of his overspending—and in order to save the image of the emperor (who was nevertheless deposed six months later).

There were people in and outside Washington who saw an American counterpart to Haussmann in Alexander Shepherd.[120] Shepherd did not transform his city as much as Haussmann transformed Paris, and his purposes were somewhat different. Haussmann's grand avenues were designed in part so that rebels would find it difficult to build barricades as they had done in past, and artillery could more easily be used against them. Shepherd led in Washington what has been described by a recent historian as "a massive effort to grade and pave the streets, improve the parks, and install new lighting, water and sanitation systems. But by plunging forward with this effort without the expected level of financial support from Congress, he also left the city bankrupt."[121]

The scale of work in Washington was in any case impressive. In just over two years Shepherd's department built 120 miles of sewers, 30 miles of water mains, 39 miles of gas lines, and 208 miles of sidewalks, while also grading and paving

150 miles of the city's muddy and dusty streets. Tens of thousands of trees were planted. Two new markets and six new schools were built; until then, there had been only four public school buildings in the city.[122]

Thomas Nast, whose favorite target was Boss Tweed of New York, found a new city "boss" to attack in Shepherd, even though Nast, like Shepherd, was a longtime Grant supporter. Piatt, in contrast, had no hesitation about defending Shepherd, even as he despised Grant: "Half [Shepherd's] official life was passed under investigation. And yet his deadliest enemy in Washington will not assert that he is dishonest."[123]

Shepherd was never charged with any crime, but his reputation long remained tarnished. Not only had the improvements to Washington bankrupted the city, they had favored neighborhoods where Shepherd had personal interests and brought great profits to favored contractors. Piatt, however, wrote that Shepherd was maligned at least in part because he was not respectable, at least in the eyes of the people who called themselves the "old citizens"—old moneyed families of Washington like the Corcorans and Riggses.[124]

Some said that Piatt's support for Shepherd was not only wrong but might verge on the criminal. One of the less-remembered Roosevelts in public life, a Democratic congressman from New York named Robert B. Roosevelt, came back to the question of what Shepherd might be doing to sway Piatt, claiming in the House of Representatives that Piatt had received "plunder" from the government of the District of Columbia in the amount of $2,144.64.

Piatt replied that *The Capital* had earned exactly that sum from the District government, for advertising. He added, "We found that other papers in the city charged five and six thousand dollars for the same work, and denounced it in *The Capital* and before the committee as a swindle." The congressman, Piatt recalled, had in his speech quoted the famous statement that the mills of God ground slowly but exceedingly small. In fact, he wrote, "They reach even the Honorable Roosevelt"—who after one term in the House had recently failed of reelection—"and before the just indignation of his constituents he passes from the hopper to the bolting-cloth in such a minute particle that even the charitable shades of private life are not necessary to protect his obscurity."[125]

Piatt was never afraid of a fight, but in at least one case he decided it was time to end a quarrel. He had had major differences with Murat Halstead and had left Halstead's *Cincinnati Commercial* to found *The Capital*. Piatt was now a Democrat; Halstead had become a Republican. Nevertheless, over the years Halstead, like many other editors, often reprinted items from *The Capital*. In December 1878 Piatt, having heard that Halstead and his wife had suffered some unspecified affliction, wrote Halstead,

Although not on the best personal terms—Why I could never understand— I cannot refrain [from] thanking you for the generous space and treatment you give me in the *Commercial*.

I never realized how foolish our difference was until you and your dear wife's sad affliction awakened in me and Mrs. Piatt the deepest sympathy. I have gone through life carrying a like dead in my heart and I feel strongly impelled to tell you how sorry my wife and I were for you and yours.[126]

Among continuing national problems was the status of African Americans. With Reconstruction over, by the end of the 1870s their future seemed less bright. They were losing the vote, and coming decades would see harsh measures to enforce racial segregation. There were nevertheless still black members of the U.S. Congress, notably Blanche Kelso Bruce, senator from Mississippi, the son of a white Virginia plantation owner and a black house slave. In February 1879 *The Capital* described a piquant if not piteous moment in Washington society. Senator Bruce's wife, "a lady of education and culture, and, what is more, a woman of taste in the way of dress," went to the elegant Ebbitt House to return two calls made on her by white ladies who lived there. All would have gone well, said the paper, "But, unfortunately, she brought with her a friend, also of African descent, and the assembly was aghast at the invasion."

Then, said *The Capital,* a young woman named Wright, the daughter of a member of Congress and Democratic leader from Pennsylvania named Hendrick B. Wright, swept across the floor and held out her hand to Mrs. Bruce and her friend. "The move broke or melted the ice, and in a moment Mrs. Bruce and her friend were greeted and surrounded by the first ladies of Washington."[127]

What perhaps made it easier for the "first ladies" to greet Mrs. Bruce was that, as a recent author has suggested, she was not only tastefully dressed but lightskinned. She had been born Josephine Willson, daughter of a prosperous dentist in Cleveland, Ohio. She later became dean of women at Tuskegee Institute and played key roles in the Colored Woman's League and the National Association of Colored Women.[128]

One may doubt that any such scene as Mrs. Bruce's eventually warm reception at the Ebbitt House recurred in Washington in the course of the next century. Segregation became entrenched—and after Bruce left the Senate in 1881 there were no more black United States senators until Edward Brooke of Massachusetts was elected in 1966.

Piatt might be a Washington insider, but he did not feel committed to staying in Washington indefinitely. As early as 1876 he had talked of selling his paper and leaving town.[129] He loved Mac-o-cheek, and country life might be better for his infirm wife. Finally, in 1880, he turned the editorship of *The Capital* over to his thirty-three-year-old associate editor, Augustus C. Buell—while still retaining ownership of the paper—and he and Ella retired to Mac-o-cheek. It was not a sudden decision. By the summer of 1879, although the paper's masthead still showed Piatt as sole editor, there was already a "Review of the Week" that was signed by

Buell rather than Piatt, plus frequent reports from Buell in New York. Buell was a well-known Washington journalist who had written at various times for the *Cincinnati Enquirer, Detroit Free Press, New Orleans Democrat,* and *St. Louis Republican.* Like Piatt, he had incurred the wrath of former senator Chandler, who in 1874 had Buell arrested for criminal libel.[130] Chandler was no saint. Neither, it turned out, was Buell.

THE MAN IN HIS CASTLE

When Donn Piatt resigned his commission in the Union army in 1864, he and Louise planned a new house in the country at Mac-o-cheek. She died before it could be built. After the war ended and he married Ella, they built at Mac-o-cheek a modest-sized Swiss chalet on part of the two hundred or so acres that they now owned directly. Donn's brother Abram had already begun, in 1864, after his return from the army the previous year, to build at Mac-o-cheek a fine stone mansion for himself. Abram finished the house in 1871, named it Mac-A-Cheek, and moved into it together with the lady he had as a widower lately married, Eleanor Watts.

Donn and Ella decided that they too should have a grand house. In the 1870s they expanded their chalet into a stone chateau with twenty-eight rooms—only slightly smaller than Rutherford Hayes's brick mansion in Fremont, which Hayes was still enlarging. The Piatts' new construction did not destroy but redecorated the older part to match the new. Although the chateau was described as being in "the Flemish style," it seems more likely that (as an Ohio history claimed)[1] the inspiration was some castle on the Rhine, a river much traveled by American visitors, including Donn and Ella.

Donn and Ella's new country seat, which would become known as Mac-O-Chee, was in good part built by Donn's nephew William McCoy Piatt—whose name is still on the facade in stone—but the original architect was the Austrian-born John L. Smithmeyer, who together with his partner in Washington, D.C., Paul J. Pelz, was becoming perhaps the most prestigious architect in America. Piatt's friend Ainsworth Rand Spofford, who had been the librarian of Congress since 1864, had long dreamed of a great new building to house the Library, and in 1873 Smithmeyer's and Pelz's neoclassical design, later modified to include neo-Baroque features, won the architectural competition for the new building.[2] Smithmeyer and Pelz also designed the central, tall stone building of Georgetown University in Washington, now known as Healy Hall, which was begun in 1877.

Donn and Ella's Ohio chateau was completed in 1879. It cost, the papers said, $85,000 to build—the equivalent of two and a half million dollars or more in the early twenty-first century. The Piatt chateau is much smaller than either the Library of Congress or the Georgetown University building, but its two towers, one with an elevation of eighty feet, and massive limestone walls make it a smaller cousin of the latter (which still dominates the Georgetown skyline and is said to have cost over $300,000 to build). The interior of the Piatts' house features high ceilings with frescoes by the French artist Oliver Frey,[3] as well as fine carvings and parqueted oak and walnut floors. It was altogether a costly place, but the Piatts were wealthy now.

It is difficult to analyze Donn Piatt's finances. In addition to what he made from lobbying, it appears that *The Capital* eventually became a very profitable enterprise. Even if there was no longer an incumbent President Grant to attack and Piatt had achieved a different relationship with President Hayes, in the late 1870s people across the country still wanted to know what Donn Piatt had to say, and people in Washington and elsewhere were buying his paper. In August 1878 the editor apologized for not having met the demand for copies for three straight weekends; the Christmas 1878 issue ran to twelve pages. A journalist who interviewed Piatt some years later wrote, "It is said that he realized $50,000 in two years from it."[4] (The value of the dollar then was perhaps twenty-five times what it is today.) He also derived a certain amount of income from the farming operations at Mac-o-cheek.

On the other hand, he had apparently taken losses in the stock market and in real estate. He wrote in 1875 that "since the Chicago fire [of 1871], followed so closely by the failure of Jay Cooke & Co., we have found it necessary to economize in a way that really at times makes us ashamed of ourself."[5] All in all, Piatt's biographer Miller claims that Piatt left Washington poorer than when he had arrived there, perhaps because of his poor financial management.[6]

Whatever the Piatts' financial situation may have been in the 1870s, things changed decidedly for the better. Timothy Kirby, Piatt's father-in-law, died at the age of eighty in Cincinnati in January 1876 and left a large estate, valued at between two and three million dollars. Ella, who already had at least some money of her own, was one of the chief beneficiaries of the estate, along with her two brothers; her sister, Julia, who was the wife of Congressman Henry Banning; and three others.[7] Perhaps it was because of the prospect of the Kirby inheritance coming to his wife that, as noted, Piatt had thought in 1876 of selling his interest in the Washington paper (but in the end stayed with it for four more years).

The inheritance was not disbursed without problems. In 1878 Kirby's four children went to court to contest a provision of his will that left one-sixth of his estate to three children who were supposedly his illegitimate offspring. The legitimate children charged that old Mr. Kirby had been duped by three designing women with whom he was infatuated, including a certain Mary Ann Francis, who had served several jail terms for drunkenness and disorderly conduct. Supposedly, she had procured the three children from a hospital and other places. The three children lost out on the inheritance. The *New York Times,* never a friend of Donn Piatt, reported from Cincinnati that people criticized the legitimate heirs for blackening their father's memory.[8]

Whatever "people" may have said, the Cincinnati newspapers reported at length the frank testimony given at the trial by both Donn Piatt and Henry Banning. Piatt and Banning agreed that old Kirby's behavior had become increasingly irrational, and each had a number of examples to offer. Once, Banning said, when some boys were playing ball outside, Kirby had started screaming, grabbed a pistol, and said he would shoot "those d—n scoundrels." Banning had physically restrained him, and Kirby had then struck Banning, his son-in-law. Kirby, always a foreign-trade protectionist, had decided that any imports from Europe were immoral and would fly into a rage at Piatt, his other son-in-law, for supporting free trade, although Banning thought Kirby liked Piatt better than he did his own sons. Banning said Kirby had once accused Piatt in all seriousness of going to England in order to take British gold for his free-trade views. Piatt testified that he thought the change in Kirby had begun after the death of his beloved daughter, Piatt's first wife, Louise.

Piatt's testimony also revealed details about the health problems of his second wife. He said nothing about Ella having been involved in a train accident en route to her mother's funeral in 1866, a dozen years ago. He said, rather, that she had had a "horrible attack" on the day of her mother's funeral. For two years she could not walk or speak. He had taken her to New York for treatment, and she had improved. A dozen years later, though, she still walked with a limp and could not use her right arm. "She now talks very well to me and the family, yet the moment she is addressed by a stranger she seems to lose the power of utterance completely." She was, Piatt said, a very brave woman. When their house in Washington had caught fire "she attended to the carrying out of the furniture, and when I got there she was seated on the other side of the street in an arm-chair, apparently as calm as if nothing had happened, but the next day she broke down and almost died."[9]

Is it possible that Ella's problems derived from not just the railroad accident but also, perhaps, a stroke she suffered later? What is clear is that she was to some extent disabled and that her husband took good and loving care of her until his death.

Donn and Ella's Mac-O-Chee was just across the little Ohio valley from Abram's and Eleanor's equally grand Mac-A-Cheek. The two brothers had been close since childhood; they felt closer now as age came slowly upon them. Abram had long been involved in managing his sizable farming, animal raising, and milling interests. In addition, like his brother he interested himself in politics and in writing. He liked to write poetry, he contributed articles to the *North American*

THE MAN IN HIS CASTLE

Review, and, as mentioned earlier, for a time both before and after the war he put out a local paper that was read across Ohio, the *Mac-a-cheek Press.* The paper included among its contributors Donn Piatt, as well as their cousin and his wife, John J. Piatt and Sarah Bryan Piatt, who were both making names for themselves as American poets.

Abram had dreams of a political career but never won an election. He ran unsuccessfully for lieutenant governor of Ohio in 1872, and then for governor as the candidate of the short-lived Greenback Party, which aimed at expansion of the currency to end farmers' woes and in 1877 had a short-lived success, winning fourteen seats in the U.S. House of Representatives.

Donn Piatt backed his brother in his search for office, but that did not make him a Greenback. In 1879 Donn made a speech at Worthington, Ohio, in which he fiercely attacked a former Democrat who had been the Greenbacks' recent candidate for vice president, Ohio politician Samuel Fenton Cary. One paper called it "the loudest blast given on the stump since the days of John Randolph." Piatt was merciless with Cary, saying, "His very existence is a casualty. He never was designed for any known purpose." Cary reminded Piatt of the piglet in a oversized litter that could not find a teat on the mother sow, and so sucked on the mother's tail. "He has fastened on the tail end of the old Democratic swine, and there he squeals and sucks and sucks and squeals until Providence shall remove him to another and better world."[10]

During the dozen years that Donn Piatt spent mainly in Washington, from 1868 to 1880, he employed his nephew Billy—Abram's son William McCoy Piatt— to manage his portion of the family's large acreage at Mac-o-cheek, which then amounted to around seventy acres and a mill. Later, as noted, Billy would help Donn build his big chateau. During Piatt's Washington years his relationship with his nephew was a troubled one. Donn had made clear to Billy that he wanted to hear from him at least once a week,[11] but Billy wrote less often. Perhaps Billy was not exerting himself overmuch on his uncle's behalf, but he was also involved in running his father's much larger farming and milling enterprise at Mac-o-cheek.

By 1869 Donn was sending exhortatory letters to his nephew, saying that he had treated him as affectionately as if Billy were his son, and reminding him that he was to receive half the profits from farm and mill—if there were profits. This would depend on Billy's work; in Donn's opinion a man should be out of bed by six in the morning, and livestock should be cared for before breakfast.[12]

It was not just laziness or having other work to do. Billy drank, and after promising to stop he relapsed. Donn wrote to express his concern, but exhortations did not help. In August 1878, on a visit to Mac-o-cheek Piatt heard that Billy and another of his nephews, Ben Runkle, had been arrested in Bellefontaine for drunken and disorderly conduct. He wrote Billy, "I asked you to guard Ben Runkle and this conduct is the answer to my request."[13] The following year, Piatt wrote his nephew in all frankness, "When you are sober you are a kind hearted gentleman. When you are drunk you are a brute." It was not impossible, Donn told him, to stop drinking; his cousins Ben Piatt and Ben Runkle had both done so.[14] (One begins to wonder whether there was more to the court-martial case of Benjamin Runkle than meets the eye.)

We know less about the relationship between Donn and his nephew after Donn and Ella retired to Mac-o-cheek, since the exchange of letters ceased. In any case, Donn was now on the ground and able to oversee directly his property, which had grown to around two hundred acres through purchases from his brother Abram.

By 1880 Piatt's visits to Washington were ever more infrequent, although he was still listed as editor on the masthead of *The Capital*. In February 1880 Augustus Buell printed in the paper a letter Piatt had sent from Mac-o-cheek:

> My Dear B.: I have been expecting to reach Washington every week for three months past. But man never is, but always to be, blessed. . . .
>
> The winter here has been what they call an open winter. I have most earnestly wished it were closed for repairs.[15]

So it was that Piatt was not present for the inauguration of a new president of the United States, yet another friend and fellow Ohioan: James A. Garfield. The two men may have first met in 1863, when Piatt went to Washington as a Union officer and found lodgings in the same establishment as Garfield, who had just resigned his army commission in order to take, at Abraham Lincoln's urging, a seat in Congress. (Biographer Miller says that Piatt and Garfield had met long before the war, adding that then and later they were "intimate as brothers.")[16] After the war Piatt and Garfield continued their friendship. Clara Morris wrote that "as Colonel Piatt was an Ohio man, it seemed perfectly natural that he should find a boon companion and close friend in that other Ohioan, the big, gentle Garfield."[17]

When Garfield became the Republican candidate for the presidency in 1880, there were numerous allegations that he was tied to major scandals, notably the Crédit Mobilier affair in 1873. At that time Garfield had been an influential member of Congress. He was said to have accepted ten shares of Crédit Mobilier stock at a deep discount, as well as a "loan" of three hundred dollars. Other members of Congress had been bribed with shares of the stock, with Congressman Oakes Ames directing the company's bribery efforts in the House.

Garfield testified before a congressional committee that he had been offered the stock but had turned it down. He admitted accepting the loan but said that he had repaid it and it had not influenced his actions in the House of Representatives.

Piatt, whom the press called "one of Garfield's most intimate friends,"[18] professed to be convinced that his friend was innocent of wrongdoing. He had said so as early as July 1873 in a letter to another friend, Friedrich Hassaurek, the Cincinnati editor and sometime diplomat.[19] Piatt had at the same time worked privately with Garfield to help defend him against the charges made in the press.[20]

In 1880 a Garfield campaign biography, strongly denying Garfield's involvement in the Crédit Mobilier affair, in support quoted Piatt as someone who had gone deeply into the matter. However, even if Piatt thought Garfield innocent, what he had written was less than a strong defense of the man: "General Garfield, personally considered, is singularly pure. . . . Garfield's purity . . . gives him a perilous confidence in men, and has gotten him into trouble." Garfield, Piatt said, "does not know one man from another, so far as the inner workings of that mysterious machine called man, is concerned. . . . The sweetness of his nature is something amazing. He cannot be made to think any one means him ill."[21]

Piatt's qualified support for Garfield cannot have surprised him. If Piatt had helped Garfield in the Crédit Mobilier case, he had also said critical things about him in *The Capital* that, like the passage quoted above, touched not only on Garfield's actions but on his character.[22] Garfield did not react in public—he needed Piatt's help—but he wrote of Piatt in his diary, "He is a strange man, develops a strong and firm friendship mingled with a recklessness about his friends that is sometimes amazing."[23] (Other friends, too, found defects in Garfield's character, but unlike Piatt they did not speak of them during his lifetime.)[24]

By the time Garfield entered the White House, his friendship with Piatt had cooled. It may be germane to add that the year before he was elected president, Garfield and Henry Banning—not just Piatt's brother-in-law but his good friend—had exchanged angry words in the House of Representatives over the question of election fraud in Ohio.[25]

One Garfield biographer calls his involvement in the Crédit Mobilier case "complex and ambiguous" and notes that while in Congress Garfield accepted five thousand dollars from another company involved in a scandal. The latter case dated to 1872, when Garfield, who was then the chairman of the House Appropriations Committee, accepted five thousand dollars from the DeGolyer & McLellan company, which was seeking a federal contract to pave Washington streets with their patented system of "ironized" wooden blocks. DeGolyer had originally hired Richard Parsons, another member of Congress from Ohio who was also an attorney, to act as the attorney in presenting the company's case before the Board of Public Works for the District of Columbia. When Parsons was called out of town, he asked Garfield to finish up the case, and Garfield did so.

Later, when it was reported that Chairman Garfield had been bribed, he insisted that he simply acted as a lawyer for the company and had been paid a legitimate fee. But, although he claimed that he worked hard on the case, his surviving case file is described as remarkably thin.

Even at the time, most people thought Garfield had put up a pretty thin defense. Various witnesses subsequently testified that the money had been paid in order to win the chairman's support. If that was true, it worked; Garfield's committee approved the contract. The matter would not go away. When in 1878 the *Washington Post* resurrected the scandal, Piatt sprang to Garfield's defense. His acceptance of the legal fee, Piatt said, had been perfectly proper, and indeed it had not been an excessive amount. Piatt went on to say, "Garfield is a poor man—and he does not drink, nor gamble, nor run after strange women, to account for his poverty. . . . He has held positions in which, had he been dishonest, he could have winked himself into millions. And had he done so he would not now be open to attack."[26]

Despite the doubts about Garfield's probity, he was nominated for president at the 1880 Republican national convention, defeating U. S. Grant, who, although he did not actively seek a third term, would clearly have been willing to return to the White House if nominated. (Jesse Grant quotes his father as saying, "It must be as the people determine.")[27] That November, Garfield was elected president of the United States, defeating the Democratic candidate, another former Union general, Winfield Scott Hancock.

Piatt then took the extraordinary step of publishing what the *New York Sun* termed an "astonishing statement of Col. DONN PIATT in regard to his intimate friend the president elect of the United States," namely, that when Garfield was under attack over the Crédit Mobilier scandal, he had for a time contemplated suicide. The paper wrote, "If it was his friend DONN PIATT who persuaded him of the folly and wickedness of the plan, then GARFIELD owes PIATT one of the greatest debts which one man can owe another."[28]

If Piatt's account was true, it was hardly something that the president-elect could comment on. Indeed, it was a good thing for Garfield that the story had not come out before the election.

Piatt wrote an open letter to Garfield just after his election in which he did not repeat the suicide story but, as the *Boston Globe* put it, talked to the president-elect like a brother.[29] He viewed Garfield as a man who, like Rutherford Hayes, was not as sternly aggressive as he should be in pursuing the right course:

> Now that this senseless political row is over, and you are the president-elect, I venture, before you are buried in that mansion, through the thick walls and plate glass of which no word of truth ever reaches the incumbent, to write you a few words in the same intimate and friendly spirit that marked our intercourse when we both occupied a cheap boarding house, when I earned my fortune on the slender nib of a pen as a newspaper correspondent and you sought to support yourself and family on the meagre pay of a congressman. I go back to the time when you gladly accepted my aid and sympathy in your troubles and my heartfelt congratulations on your triumphs, and I yours. I feel more anxiety about you, my friend, now that you are fortunate than in the darkest

hours of your life, when life itself seemed so horrible that an escape from it was a temptation.

Piatt went on to say that not only was Garfield no politician, he was hated by politicians. He warned Garfield darkly that there were certain persons "who are bent on changing the form of our self-government. They seek to make the presidency a life tenure. . . . You know the man [presumably Grant, who was interested in a third term] who is to serve their purpose in the treasonable scheme they base upon his military record and supposed popularity." He ended his letter by saying, "You are not a great man. You read in your library of heroic achievements; your soul swells over the poetic expression, you are full of thought and impulse, and all ends in a support of men you despise and a party with which you have nothing in common."

Piatt also wrote a private letter to Garfield in which he did not repeat his criticisms but offered congratulations on his election—adding, however, "My anxiety to see you elected was only equaled, in intensity, by my disgust at the success of your party."[30] That seems to have been the last communication between the two men.

In early June 1881 Piatt returned home from a trip and learned from Ella that former president Hayes had done him the honor of coming to Mac-O-Chee to see him. Piatt wrote Hayes, "This has been my confounded luck through life. When the sky rains quails I have an umbrella instead of a frying pan." He was, he said, particularly sorry to miss seeing Hayes because he wanted to ask Hayes to help his cousin John James Piatt, "the poet who is dying by inches in the Cincinnati post office." The poet was hoping to be given a post abroad as consul; Hayes while president had given literary men like James Russell Lowell and Bret Harte posts abroad,[31] "and Garfield ought to be influenced by your example. Cant you help me. I know you will if you can."[32]

Donn Piatt may not have known that Abraham Lincoln, who would do nothing at all for him, had a month before his assassination asked Secretary of State Seward if he could arrange for Piatt the poet to get one of "those moderate sized consulates which facilitate artists a little in their profession."[33] After Lincoln died, it seems, this went nowhere. Several years later, though, in 1871, J. J. Piatt had been appointed the librarian of the House of Representatives. For a time life seemed good for him. Mary Clemmer Ames, perspicacious journalist, wrote in 1874 that among the notables like Walt Whitman whom one could see strolling on Pennsylvania Avenue was "John James Piatt, now Librarian of the House of Representatives, with his blonde hair and blue-eyed wife, who is quite as much a poet as he is."[34]

The next year, though, J. J. Piatt lost his job on Capitol Hill. Now in 1881 he was about to be fired from his low-level clerkship in the Cincinnati post office. He went to work on his own to seek support in high places. He got up a petition to the president on his behalf, which was signed by Thomas Bailey Aldrich,

Oliver Wendell Holmes, William Dean Howells, Henry Wadsworth Longfellow, John Greenleaf Whittier, and other famous men.[35] Perhaps no other American had secured such strong support for a presidential appointment—with the exception of the poet's cousin Donn Piatt, when Donn had sought a diplomatic post a quarter-century earlier. But would the petition get J. J. Piatt a post?

Soon there was no need for Donn Piatt to think about people using Garfield as their instrument—or about Garfield giving his cousin an appointment. The president was shot by an unbalanced office seeker in July 1881, just four months into his term of office, and died two months later. The country was horrified; and, among other and greater consequences, for the moment J. J. Piatt was without a paying job.

That same year D. Appleton & Company in New York published the memoirs of former Confederate president Jefferson Davis, a two-volume work entitled *The Rise and Fall of the Confederate Government*. The book was sold largely by subscription, and during the years after its appearance it did not sell well. Davis began to sense a northern conspiracy to keep down sales. If there was a conspiracy (but there was not), it was certainly a broad one. Northern newspapers on the whole ignored the work; a few magazines reviewed it, but grudgingly, as a Davis biographer puts it. The tepid reception of his book was just one more of many disappointments Davis faced in the postwar decades.[36] What made it worse for him was that in contrast, the memoirs of U. S. Grant, published soon after Grant's death in 1885, sold extremely well.

Appleton said that if President Davis had doubts about the company's efforts and good faith, he should ask someone to investigate. Davis called on the well-known Donn Piatt for help. Appleton asked another publisher, George Haven Putnam, president of the firm G.P. Putnam's Sons, to represent it.

Why did Jefferson Davis turn to Donn Piatt?[37] Did he still remember the younger diplomat who had called on the secretary of war more than three decades earlier? After the war Piatt had written about Davis, as he did about many others, in a mocking way. Piatt had said that he would be happy if the pious Davis could work his way to heaven—but that quite aside from his feelings toward Northerners, "J.D. has such bitter personal prejudices that were he to meet some of his old Southern friends 'loafing about the throne,' we fear there would be a disturbance and somebody would be hoisted over the battlements . . . or the late president would gather up his celestial robes and march out with a dignity that would fill St. Peter with amazement."[38]

What perhaps counted most for Davis was that Piatt had befriended a well-known former Confederate whom Davis respected: Lucius Quintus Cincinnatus Lamar of Mississippi. In 1874, with the war receding into the past, Lamar was elected to the U.S. House of Representatives and in 1877 to the U.S. Senate. In 1879, when Piatt's frequent target Zachariah Chandler reentered the Senate, his first speech was a diatribe against the South and against Jefferson Davis, and Lamar rose to defend his former president. There were many issues on which Piatt and Lamar had different views, but they could agree that Chandler was a scoundrel. They also agreed on the need for national unity, which had been the theme of Lamar's moving speech in Congress after the death of Senator Charles Sumner, known as one of the South's great enemies.[39] Lamar was attacked afterward as having been unfit to make the speech; Piatt strongly defended him. Privately, Piatt told a visitor that, although Lamar was a quiet, even shy, man who disliked meeting strangers, "He calls me friend, and treats me as one."[40] It seems quite possible that Lamar told the disappointed Davis that Piatt was a man to be trusted.

After George Putnam reviewed the Davis memoirs for Appleton, he decided that the former leader of the Confederacy had missed his chance to write a noteworthy history. Putnam's conclusion was that Davis had produced a thousand pages of personal views and a "specious defence" of his actions.

Piatt, who had long felt that authors were ill treated by both publishers and legislators, initially sent Davis what the latter must have found an encouraging letter, saying that "the treatment of authors by publishers, in the United States, is simply infamous."[41] Piatt later told Davis that he had consulted both a prominent publisher, Robert J. Belford, and his friend George Hoadly, recently governor of Ohio and now a lawyer in New York.[42] Both Belford and Hoadly had thought Davis had a good case; Piatt opined that Appleton probably owed Davis a good forty thousand dollars. He also sought help for Davis from Walter George Smith, a Philadelphia lawyer known for having provided legal help with the memoirs of U. S. Grant. (Smith's father—a Union general in the war—had been Piatt's friend in prewar Ohio, and his mother was a Piatt cousin.)[43] Davis's heart must have leaped when Piatt wrote that he ought to get forty thousand dollars; he was very short of money.[44]

In the end—wrote Putnam years later, long after both Davis and Piatt had died—Piatt had not disagreed with Putnam; he had told Putnam that frankly Davis was old and confused. According to Putnam, "Piatt was very gentlemanly about the whole business and the matter was, of course, easily made straight with the Appletons."[45] What Appleton may have eventually paid is not known; nothing, it seems, before Davis died. A summary made after his death, apparently by lawyer Smith, indicated that the publishers owed Davis's estate $8,544 plus interest.[46]

After Jefferson Davis died, his widow wrote in his defense that the form of his book reflected the fact that he had lost all his papers and, lacking documentation, had to draw heavily on his memories. While writing the book, he had also been crushed by the death of their last surviving son, at twenty-one, of yellow fever. That was not the full story. There had been a long delay in producing a manuscript, and when Appleton finally saw the first two chapters, the company decided that without fundamental changes the work would fail. They stepped in directly, sending a staff member, W. J. Tenney, to Davis's Mississippi home, where, as a Davis biographer put it, it was Tenney who finally "set about making a book."[47]

There is nothing to indicate that Piatt ever read the Davis memoirs. Even if he knew that it was not a good book, he seems to have been motivated to help the old ex-president not only because of his grudge against publishers but because of a liking and respect for Davis that is surprising to find in a Union veteran who strongly opposed slavery.

Two days after Davis died, in December 1889, Piatt sat down at Mac-o-cheek and wrote his widow Varina Davis that he had hoped to invite Davis to Mac-o-cheek so "that he might enjoy . . . the reward found in a just recognition of his noble career, and heroic character." Piatt thought that "the blinding mists born of sectional prejudice, and bloody war" were now melting away and Northerners were beginning to see "the high qualities of this great, and good, man, who had calmly accepted the consequences of a terrible strife he did not originate, and remained the one advocate of a cause he inherited, that was rendered odious by defeat."[48]

A letter of condolence is not, in general, a place to discuss past differences with the deceased. If, however, this letter had been published, some would no doubt have commented that Piatt ignored the fact that Davis ended his "noble career" by leading a war to defend human slavery. But Piatt's was a private letter to a grieving widow, and there is not even a copy in Piatt's archives. Piatt had enemies with whom he could never make peace, but like many other Northerners he saw the need for reconciliation between North and South. His biographer Miller wrote, dramatically but presumably on the basis of what Piatt's widow told him, that Piatt wanted "to make of the union of blood a union of love."[49]

As Piatt sat in his den in the countryside, he continued to write letters, poetry, and prose. He had also for years liked writing plays, but that proved one of his least successful endeavors. Only one of his several works for the theater, *The Royal Favorite,* was ever produced. The play opened on October 4, 1879, not on Broadway but in Brooklyn, on the inauguration night of the elegant, eighteen-hundred-seat Brooklyn Theater, which had been rebuilt after a disastrous fire. Piatt's friend Clara Morris, known as the most famous if not necessarily the best actress in America, played the lead role. Donn Piatt, too, was famous, if not as a playwright, and the house was packed. Many local notables attended, including Brooklyn's mayor, James Howell.[50]

Piatt wrote his play in blank verse, and it was long—five acts long. He may have written it expressly as a vehicle for Clara Morris; he had written a play for her several years earlier that never got produced.[51] The new play was based on the story of Jane Shore, the mistress of King Edward IV in the 1470s, and Clara played Jane. Piatt had no doubt come on Jane Shore during the reading he had done as a boy at Mac-o-cheek. Sir Thomas More had written that she was fair and lovely, merry and intelligent.[52] She had been persecuted after Edward's death by Richard III, adding to the possibilities for a good drama. (An earlier drama, *The Tragedy of Jane Shore,* written in 1714 in England, had been performed occasionally in America with some success.)[53]

The day after the 1879 opening, the *Brooklyn Eagle* wrote that there were some brilliant passages in Piatt's play. It praised Morris's acting, adding that one must make some allowances for the first performance of a new play in a new theater, and said, "everybody seemed to be perfectly satisfied." The *New York Times,* however, said flatly that the opening night had been "a very dismal affair." The fault lay in part outside the play. The theater's management had hurried to get the theater opened; there had not been enough rehearsals, and the backstage crew had not fully learned its job. At one point in the first act the poor star had to yell at them to stop hammering. The *Times* said, "Of her acting it is impossible, perhaps, to write with absolute justice at this time, for her attention last evening was occupied principally with a continual racket behind the scenes." Still the paper reported that Morris as Jane Shore was less than inspiring.[54] The *Chicago Tribune* said briefly and scoffingly that Piatt's play was "a dramatization of the Greenback platform in Ohio."[55] The play soon closed and was not revived.

Piatt had first met Clara Morris in Columbus just after the war, when he was a member of the Ohio legislature. One day he saw a teenage girl in the visitors' gallery, acting as nursemaid to two small children. He spoke to her and learned that she was also a ballet dancer; the next time he met her was years later, after seeing her name on a New York playbill.[56] She became a frequent guest of the Piatts in Washington. When she was there, she liked to go horseback riding with Donn—as infirm Ella could not do.

Was Piatt ever more than a good friend and admirer of Morris? She saw him often. In 1875 Clara, then an attractive woman in her mid-twenties, had accompanied Donn and Ella on their trip to Europe—without her new husband, Frederick Harriott. Clara's marriage was not happy. Although Harriott came from a prosperous family, Clara supported him; she complained in her diary about his expenses. Within several years she learned that he had taken a mistress.[57] One should perhaps not make too much of Clara traveling to Europe with the Piatts; on another occasion she visited Europe with other friends, the well-known comedian James Lewis and his wife.

But back to Jane Shore. Thomas More tells us that although she was married, "she not very fervently loved for whom she never longed. Which was haply the thing that the more easily made her incline unto the king's appetite when he required her."[58] Jane and Edward, Donn and Clara?

In January 1882 Oscar Wilde arrived in New York to begin his famous American lecture tour, and Morris was the American actress he most wanted to meet. Soon he did so at a reception in Manhattan. When he then saw her perform in New York, he decided she was the greatest actress he had ever seen. He tried to get her to star in his first, forthcoming play about Russian revolutionaries, called *Vera, or The Nihilists.*[59] When Wilde visited Cincinnati later in his tour, Piatt went to see him at his hotel, "laden with a message from a fair lady in the East to this lover of the lily, all about a remarkable play that he has written." Morris had decided not to appear in the play, which had its premiere in New York in 1883 and closed after a week. It has seldom been revived, though not for lack of melodramatic content. Vera, a young Russian barmaid, joins the nihilists and is assigned to kill Tsar Alexis. She had known Alexis when, as tsarevich, he had in disguise joined the nihilists, and she had fallen in love with him. In the end she cannot carry out her task—she learns that the tsar loves her, too—and she kills herself.

Gilbert and Sullivan had portrayed Wilde as the foppish poet and esthete Reginald Bunthorne in their comic opera *Patience,* which had been a great success in London the previous year. Their producer, Richard D'Oyly Carte, was paying for Wilde's American tour for publicity purposes, and Wilde was doing his best to portray himself as a Bunthorne.

Piatt found Wilde standing by the fire in his room at that grand Cincinnati hotel, the Burnett House. He saw a tall young man (Wilde was twenty-eight) with a vacant face, "flanked on either side by a youthful [John] Bull. At least, if they were not Bulls they were good imitations of the chromo sort now so common to our Eastern cities."[60]

After delivering his message from Clara Morris, Piatt said, he told Wilde that he sympathized with him "in your missionary efforts to teach us the beautiful. But I fear you will find the American people very much like St. Paul in one respect."

> "Haw is that?" he asked; not quite so broad, but quite out of our vernacular.
> "Much learning makes them mad, and they are mad at you."
> "Naw, reely, that is rawther good, you knaw," and he laughed. The two Bulls evidently thought I was quoting scripture, and they took it as festive people do toasts to the dead, in silence and standing.

Piatt said that he then suggested it might be useful if Wilde visited Mac-o-cheek, where he could give him a few hours of instruction in stump oratory. Wilde wanted to hear more about that. Well, said Piatt, stump oratory meant setting aside your manuscript and talking as if you were thinking on your legs. "Hair parted in the middle [as Wilde's was] is a national crime, to be punished with death. The only approach to knee-breeches [which Wilde wore] that will be tolerated is pantaloons stuffed in the top of your boots. With these few simple rules, and with an allusion at intervals to the fact that we are the greatest and only free people on the face of the earth, I think a lecture on the beautiful could be made very acceptable."

> Where was Mac-o-cheek? asked Wilde. Near Columbus, Piatt said.
> "Ah! yes; Co-lum-bus—principal town of Ohio."
> "I beg your pardon—the most unprincipled. The legislature meets there."
> "Naw reely, you do say some odd things; very odd, you knaw."

Piatt thought he "detected a very shadowy 'h' in that odd." A lower-class accent? "The horrible suggestion . . . sent me to the door, and I took my leave."

Wilde may not have advanced his image as a genuinely foppish esthete through this meeting with Piatt, which, to be sure, Wilde had not sought. Piatt told his readers, "Personally Oscar Wilde is a great, lubberly, unpleasant boy, and leaves one in doubt whether he is in earnest and a fool, or whether he is playing a part for the sake of the notoriety and the cash."[61] Later, in 1888, when Wilde's sexual affairs with men were still little known, Piatt was to write in a volume of published stories of a "square-shouldered, good looking young man . . . [who] would have won the heart of Oscar Wilde."[62]

As a young man in Ohio, Piatt had tried his hand at writing, among other things, popular songs. His play for Clara Morris had been a flop, but in 1883, in his early sixties, he tried again, writing a comic opera called *Keno* with music by the young German-born composer Bruno Oscar Klein. It was never performed in a theater, but Piatt was pleased with the work and a published version appeared, one suspects at the author's expense. As the *Salt Lake Herald* said, it "abounds in political hits."[63] The *Cleveland Herald* called it "strikingly Piattic . . . more vinegar than honey—that is, more of caustic wit than good-natured humor."[64] In the opera a crooked senator named Pilaster secures an appropriation of two million dollars for a supposedly extinct Indian tribe, the Omahogs, planning to divert the funds to his own use, but then finds that the tribe really exists. In the end Keno, the Omahog chief, and the senator are to split the appropriated funds between them.

There is no indication that Piatt in his late middle age—old age, most people would have said then—was seriously disappointed by his lack of success in writing for the theater. It was not a field in which he expected to get rich; he probably felt some satisfaction in demonstrating that this was one more endeavor in which he was competent though far from great. This is not to say that he did not care what others thought about his writing. There is a story that he had written a play sometime in the 1850s and had challenged a Cincinnati critic to a duel for writing a devastating review.[65] He could sometimes laugh at himself, but he did not like others to do so. His father had nicknamed him Big Fire with reason. Jeremiah Black reportedly once said that his friends Donn Piatt and James A. Garfield were much alike, in that each had the horns of a bull and the thin skin of a rabbit.[66]

Piatt's formal education had ended in his teens after he threw a professor out of a window. In 1882 he was pleased to be offered an honorary doctorate of laws by the University of Notre Dame, which invited him to speak on the occasion. He hastened to respond that he would be there on June 20, "the Lord and the locomotive permitting," and would speak on a novel subject: education.[67] The Lord did not interfere, the trains ran, and Piatt got his degree and made his remarks. Unfortunately, we lack the text of what may have been an interesting talk; one newspaper reported that "he lectured to the young ladies of the institution on the subject of 'corsets.'"[68]

U. S. Grant, smoker of many cigars, died of throat cancer in July 1885. He had suffered financial ruin after leaving the presidency but later had seen the way to provide a sound future for his wife through the generous contract Mark Twain offered him for his war memoirs. Grant completed the memoirs just four days before he died and was praised after his death for the grit and courage he had shown up to the end. That was very well, but Donn Piatt did not believe the story of Grant's final days should erase his overall record. Piatt sat down in his study and wrote long pages condemning a man whom he had consistently viewed as a bad general and a worse president. This time, what he wrote remained unpublished.[69]

Piatt had also written privately to former president Hayes the year before, to contrast Hayes's administration with that of a corrupt and hard-drinking Grant: "We who lived in Washington and saw the administration taken in off the street drunk and the White-house a crib for stolen goods know how the atmosphere changed in thirty days after your inauguration and not only honor and honesty reinstated but decency made familiar to the government. I want a favorable chance to say these things, and I am a disinterested witness, for, you remember, I wanted to kill you, and all the scoundrels of the country have been in sorrow, since, that I did not. I dont want to boast but when I say any thing I have listeners."[70]

Hayes must have been pleased to hear that Piatt said positive things about his administration to others as well. A mutual friend of Hayes and Piatt wrote the former president that when she had recently visited Mac-O-Chee, Piatt had told her and other guests that the Hayes administration had brought about a decided change in atmosphere within its first sixty (not thirty) days in office; it had been the purest administration the country had ever seen.[71] Certainly Hayes had gained nothing financially from the presidency, nor had he needed to. He was very well to do, having inherited the fortune of his uncle and foster father, Sardis Birchard. He had also made sizable profits from investments in land in Minnesota and West Virginia.[72]

Toward the end of 1885, Piatt met another president with whom he had relatively little fault to find: Grover Cleveland. Piatt told a reporter that when he called on the president, he found him—in contrast to the other presidents he had known—"sitting in the White House with the same easy, natural air that he [had when he] sat in the sheriff's office in Buffalo."

Cleveland, a Democrat, had first been elected to public office in 1870 as sheriff of Erie County. He had become mayor of Buffalo in 1881 and governor of New York in 1882, and he was elected president in 1884. Piatt found that Cleveland had both an intellectual cast and a piercing eye. Still, he said, there was "an immense deal of organized rascality surging in and out of the White House," and he was sorry to see that Cleveland tended to overestimate the men with whom he came in contact.[73]

Two years later, visiting Washington, Piatt told another reporter that he thought the whole country viewed the president as "an honest, honorable, able man" and he hoped Cleveland would be reelected in 1888. (Cleveland lost to Benjamin Harrison in 1888 but was again elected president in 1892.)

Piatt added that he had voted for Cleveland in 1884, and, somewhat surprisingly for this most political of men, he said that this was the first time he had voted in many years. But he no longer wanted to be seen as a party man. His interviewer wrote, "He regards the Democratic party as the organized ignorance of the country and the Republican party as the organized rascality."[74]

Grover Cleveland was the first president to reward Donn Piatt with a political appointment since, decades earlier, Franklin Pierce had made him secretary of legation at Paris. Cleveland made him postmaster of Mac-o-cheek, Ohio, at a salary of forty dollars a year. Piatt wrote to a friend,

> It was greatness thrust upon me, as a practical joke. The patrons of the office do not find it so funny now. I have moved the office to my house and taken down the old sign from my gate, which was "No admission on business," and in its place hung up a tin horn, with directions which read, "Any one having business with this postoffice will blow the horn and give the P.M. time to obtain his dogs." I have to guard against county commissioners, lightning-rod men, book agents and other nuisances, two huge mastiffs, one St. Bernard and a bull-dog of amazing pertinacity of purpose.[75]

The new government official took it on himself to send to Adlai E. Stevenson, the first assistant postmaster general, detailed proposals on how the postal service might be improved. Stevenson replied that in the absence of Postmaster General William Vilas all of the department's business was hanging over him, and so, he said, "I cannot at this moment undertake to discuss the abstract questions involved in your letter." Stevenson added that he would however be happy to do so in person, later, and he hoped to have the pleasure of seeing the postmaster of Mac-o-cheek in the near future.[76] (Stevenson had conceivably told Piatt he was open to ideas, and since his appointment the postmaster had already paid at least one call on the first assistant postmaster general.)[77]

Piatt seems to have approached President Cleveland on occasion on behalf of other friends. In 1885 Cleveland made Piatt's friend Lucius Lamar his secretary of the interior, and in 1887 he nominated Lamar for the Supreme Court. It was reportedly Piatt who more than any other had pushed for Lamar's appointment to the latter post—as he had earlier pushed for his fellow Ohioan Stanley Matthews's appointment to it.[78]

Piatt's support for Matthews was no doubt useful, but it was perhaps not crucial. Matthews was first nominated to the Supreme Court in 1881 by Hayes—who had been his college roommate—just before Hayes left the White House, but the Senate did not act on the nomination. Piatt's support may have been more important when, later in 1881, Matthews was renominated by the new president, James Garfield. Matthews joined the Court after the Senate confirmed him in a close vote, 24–23.

In May 1887 Piatt received good news about his nephew Ben Runkle. Former president Hayes had, over some years, done what he could to overturn the court-martial verdict against Runkle. While in the White House, Hayes had reviewed the case and in August 1877 ordered Runkle's return to the army, but the court of claims had thereafter, in 1884, decided that the president had no right to do that. Piatt wrote Hayes that he had told the lawyers to appeal to the U.S. Supreme Court.[79] In May 1887, the Supreme Court found for Runkle, saying that the findings of the court-martial had never been approved by President Grant, as they should have been, while President Hayes's action had been proper. All this had taken fifteen years.[80] Piatt happily wrote Hayes, "'Truth crushed to earth will rise again'—she gets up slowly, some what stunned, and some times soiled by the earth—but the old lady gets up, and has her second wind to the confusion of her enemies."[81] (No doubt coincidentally, the chief justice whose Court had found for Runkle was an Ohioan, Morrison R. Waite.)

A visitor to Mac-o-cheek in the autumn of 1886 wrote afterward in the *Indianapolis News* that she found it noteworthy that despite all "the versatile and brilliant" things Piatt had written, he had never published a book.[82] It was not for want of trying. Two years earlier, he had written Rutherford Hayes, "I have by me nearly ready for publication a book to be called 'Twelve years in the Reporter gallery at Washington,' which I think will take, because I have aimed to make it amusing. There are some matters connected with your administration I would like to have you tell me of—if you like—of course without the use, in any way, of your name. What do you think of it?"[83]

Did Hayes think ill of it? We know only that the book never appeared.

Piatt had also written a novel about Washington called *A Romance of the Secret Service,* but that never found a publisher, either, although Piatt wrote to his former partner George Alfred Townsend that the book was "rather a good thing."[84] Later, Piatt ended his long and mainly friendly relationship with Townsend. He took umbrage at something that Townsend had written, and wrote him, "It is hard to say which is the more exasperating, your infernal egotism or your ludicrous assumption of superiority." An equally angry Townsend returned the letter to Piatt, and it was found in his papers after his death.[85]

In 1887 Piatt published his first book and most important single work, *Memories of the Men Who Saved the Union,* which gave frank but positive portraits of Lincoln, Stanton, Chase, Seward, and George H. Thomas. The book was put together from Piatt's previous articles on these leaders in the *North American Review.* The *Westminster Review* praised it as "the record of great geniuses, told by a genius."[86] It sold well, and a second edition appeared in three months. It was a frank work; Piatt pulled no punches. Although he himself had taken an active part in the Civil War, he wrote, "I found myself, through my temperament, more of a looker-on than a participant. I had, instinctively, a horror of war. The cruel brutality sickened me and, so wiping out all ambition in that line, left only a sense of duty to hold me to the service. This enabled me to look at men and events from the stand-point of an observer . . . my position enabled me to coolly measure all that has a right to history."[87]

Piatt described rather bluntly what he had sought to do in the book, in a letter he sent that July to Sir Charles Dilke, enclosing a copy of his work. Dilke, whom Piatt had apparently met in London in 1873, had been spoken of until recently as a future British prime minister. His career crashed after he was accused of adultery—with a girl whose mother turned out to be his mistress. Perhaps Piatt thought Dilke needed cheering up. In addition, he had probably started thinking how he could use Dilke's story in other writing, although he did not say so in this letter. He wrote Dilke, "I undertook the thankless task of rescuing the statesmen and truly great of our late civil war from the mass of political fanaticism that makes heroes of the 'brainless bullet-heads' as Hawthorne called the accidental, and incompetent leaders of the late conflict."[88]

The first question Piatt wanted to address in his book was the character of Abraham Lincoln. Lincoln's comrade Ward Hill Lamon once said that the apotheosis and deification of the martyred president had begun soon after his death. Lamon had in mind people like Joseph H. Barrett, who had written an 1860 campaign biography with Lincoln's blessing, but in his revision, published soon after the president's assassination, made Lincoln, who was in no way an orthodox Christian, into a kind of Christian saint: "Who . . . can point to any man . . . as a truer example of the Christian character as set forth in the Sermon on the Mount? . . . Few, very few, in this world, have ever more truly *lived* the life of purity, of charity, of universal good-will, of gentle forgiveness."[89]

Piatt was no friend of Ward Lamon, but he resembled Lamon in his unwillingness to play any part in deifying Lincoln—or in paving over the defects of other Union leaders. He had written years earlier, "I do not indulge in hero-worship. All my heroes died young, and after death I worship no man save the saints. Nine hundred and ninety-nine saints are enough to keep one man busy."[90] He wrote now, in *Memories of the Men Who Saved the Union*, in a slightly different vein: "Pure hero worship is healthy. It stimulates the young to deeds of heroism, stirs the old to unselfish efforts, and gives the masses models of manhood that tend to lift humanity above the common-place meanness of ordinary life. . . . [But] to have such hero-worship healthy it must be true."[91]

Piatt went on to attack fanaticism, which many people saw as evidence of belief but was, in fact, he wrote, "a frenzied assertion of what one wants to believe, but is conscious that it cannot be sustained by reason. . . . This holds good of fanaticism in all faiths. We see it illustrated in the men and matters made prominent by the late war. Hence to question the greatness of Lincoln is to excite pity or contempt, to doubt that of Grant is to run the chance of being knocked down. . . . This is shameful. . . . In this broad land of ours there is space for many monuments. Grant should have all that to which he is entitled." But not more.

Piatt wrote in his new book that, although Lincoln was the grandest figure in American history, he had also been a man who, while disliking slavery, was descended from poor whites of a slave state and inherited "the contempt, if not the hatred, held by that class for the negro."[92] Piatt said Lincoln had been a skeptic with a low, if good-natured, view of human nature, and it was this that had initially blinded him to the South and made him doubt that men would get up and fight for an ideal. But, said Piatt, he had also been strong. A more delicate and sympathetic man, like Chase or Seward, would have broken down in the presidency, but "Lincoln had none of this. He faced and lived through the awful responsibility of the situation with the high courage and comfort that came of indifference." As Lincoln had said to Piatt and Robert Schenck one day in the darkest period of the war, despite the nation's worries he still "ate his rations and slept well."[93]

Lincoln had also, Piatt wrote, commanded respect from others. When he was young, his companions respected him because "they felt of his muscle and his readiness in its use." His fellow lawyers had respected him for his ready wit. But there was much more to Lincoln than that. "Through one of those freaks of nature that produce a Shakespeare at long intervals, a giant had been born to the poor whites of Kentucky, and the sense of superiority possessed President Lincoln at all times." Men like Chase and Stanton, "great as they were, felt their inferiority to their master." Piatt added that he had only seen Lincoln angry once, when Lincoln cursed him in 1863 for ordering enlistment of slaves in Maryland, "and I had no wish to see a second exhibition of his wrath."[94]

As for Grant, Piatt wrote that, unlike Lincoln, he had been an execrable president, but as a general he had been a brave man who would fight—as testified to, Piatt added bitterly, by the many Union dead he had sacrificed. All in all, Grant was "a man whose operations in the field will not bear inspection, and whose Civil Service and financial operations can be condoned only on the ground of his miraculous ignorance and stupidity."[95]

Piatt made clear his admiration for Chase, Stanton, and Seward. It was also clear to him, though, that during the war the last two "were drunk with the lust of power. They fairly rioted in its enjoyment."[96] He added that Stanton too often let his personal prejudices sway him: "Stanton used the fearful power of the Government to crush those he hated, while he sought, through the same means, to elevate those he loved." Piatt thought that Stanton's treatment of General Rosecrans, which had come after Rosecrans had unintentionally slighted him; he had been cruel and indeed infamous. The secretary of war had also felt a great contempt for Grant, stemming from his travel to Louisville to consult Grant when the Union forces at Chattanooga were apparently facing either starvation or surrender. Grant, said Piatt, failed to show up for the meeting with Stanton. "At last, long after midnight, the General was found in a place, and under circumstances, not necessary to relate to those who knew the habits of this renowned warrior."[97] Still, Stanton could pardon Grant's drinking and other faults, because, as he always said, "This man will fight." (Grant's own account of the meeting with Stanton is utterly different. He wrote in his memoirs that he and his wife and Stanton had traveled together by train from Indianapolis to Louisville, where he and the secretary continued their discussion.)[98]

Piatt's portrait of Stanton was of a man who could be both sad and hard. Before the war he had once found his friend in a Washington hotel room convulsed in tears, thinking of his late wife. But there had been moments during the war when Stanton had reminded Piatt both rudely and sarcastically that the secretary of war and the mid-grade army officer were no longer equals. Piatt could understand this, but he did not forget it.

Piatt had long had negative views about the United States Military Academy, "that teaches everything but patriotism and the art of war."[99] To some extent his views stemmed from West Pointers' opposition to Stanton, as well as their criticism of Schenck, when the war began. In 1861, Piatt wrote now, although half of the West Pointers had remained faithful to the Union, even the faithful ones secretly despised abolitionists. "West Point," he wrote, "is more of a social feature than a military school, and as reformers are not fashionable, seldom, if ever, even respectable, the cadet had a horror of the howling Abolitionist. These are unpleasant things to say now, but I am giving Stanton's views at the time, and the views shared by his eminent [civilian] associates."[100]

Piatt's own view of Stanton was more positive than the view that many others held of the man in the decades after the Civil War; it was less positive than that of many writers today. Generals Grant, Sherman, and McClellan all expressed strong criticisms of the great war minister. The year before Piatt's book appeared, the *Brooklyn Eagle* wrote that among Stanton's few defenders "is a stranded Bohemian named Don Piatt, whose reputation in this age is what the reputation of Ananias is in every age, and who is to be left out of every account of any serious consideration of the subject."[101]

After the war Piatt had shared materials from his collection on Salmon Chase with Chase's first biographer, Robert Warden, who together with Piatt had read law at Mac-o-cheek decades earlier.[102] Chase had invited Warden to move into his Washington home and shared with him his personal letters and diaries;[103] but apparently there were items lacking that Piatt could and did provide to Warden, whose biography of Chase appeared in 1874. Now, in 1887, it was Piatt's turn to picture Chase. He wrote in *Memories of the Men Who Saved the Union* that Chase

had an elemental fault: He lacked an understanding of human nature. Nevertheless, he had been an eminent secretary of the treasury; and it was greatly to his
credit that he had opposed the arbitrary wartime arrests and "irresponsible military rule" that Seward and Stanton had initiated with Lincoln's agreement.[104]

Early in the war Chase had been Stanton's most intimate companion.[105] After
the war, Stanton had severed their personal relationship.[106] By now, though, both
friendships and rivalries were finished. Seward, Stanton, and Chase were all, like
Lincoln, in their graves.

General George B. McClellan, who had died three years earlier, also figured in
Piatt's book. For a time during the war, McClellan had been spoken of as a "young
Napoleon." Piatt said he had been an imitation Napoleon, for whom he felt sorry:
"He had the egotism of a weak character, that he and his friends mistook for the
confidence of genius. This made him arrogant on parade and timid in the pres-
ence of a grave responsibility."[107]

As for General William T. Sherman, whom Piatt had long despised, he was still
alive, living a comfortable life in New York City and much in demand as a speaker.
Piatt had always thought Sherman's March to the Sea had been unwise and im-
prudent, since it had left open the possibility of a Confederate attack northward
toward the Ohio Valley—a possibility that Confederate General John B. Hood
had seized on, until his defeat by General George H. Thomas.

Now Piatt found new authority to bolster his criticism of Sherman. He reported
in an appendix to his book that the elder Helmuth von Moltke, the longtime chief
of staff of the Prussian army, who planned and led Prussia's successful wars against
Austria in 1866 and France in 1870–71, had told an unnamed American officer that
Sherman's march had been successful "because no enemy was in the way to make it
perilous. Having no objective point, in a military sense, to make such a movement
advisable . . . it was by the merest accident that the enemy did not regain through
that movement of the United States Army all that had been secured through years
of campaigning and hard fighting."[108] Who was the American officer to whom Marshal von Moltke said this? At a guess, it could have been Piatt's friend General Stephen Vincent Benét, who had gone to Europe the previous August.[109]

Piatt had long made clear his admiration for George H. Thomas. His chapter
on Thomas in *Memories of the Men Who Saved the Union* paints an appealing portrait of the "Rock of Chickamauga." Thomas, who unlike many Civil War veterans
never published memoirs of his own, was a native of Southampton County in Virginia, as was John Y. Mason, Piatt's chief at the legation in Paris. It was Mason who
had recommended Thomas for admission to West Point, and Thomas was the first
man from Southampton to graduate from the academy.[110] When the Civil War
began, Thomas, like Robert E. Lee and other army officers from Virginia, had to
decide between North and South. Piatt wrote that Thomas for a moment "paused
in painful anxiety between his duty and his inclination."[111] Unlike Lee and most

of the other Virginians, Thomas opted to serve the Union, though it cost him the affection of most of his family.

Piatt said he had first met Thomas in person when, as advocate general of the commission investigating Buell's command of the Army of the Ohio, he had summoned Thomas to appear before the commission. He had been impressed by Thomas's "cool, quiet, incisive statement." After the war ended, Piatt, wanting to get to know Thomas better, went with James Garfield to call on him one day at Washington, where Thomas was awaiting word on a new assignment. This must have been in 1869, when Thomas finally left his wartime command in Tennessee and was offered by President Johnson a promotion to lieutenant general, with the prospect of replacing Grant as general-in-chief. Thomas declined the promotion, not wanting to be a party to politics, and was then sent to command the Division of the Pacific at San Francisco, where he died of a stroke the following year.

Piatt recalled in his new book that he and Garfield had found the Rock of Chickamauga a modest and simple man in private conversation. Thomas had spoken with them frankly, but they had found him shy and diffident when it came to the question of his own merits. In his 1887 work, Piatt did his best to bring out Thomas's merits and virtues, while urging less adulation of Sherman and Grant. Grant had wanted to remove Thomas from command at Nashville because he was slow to attack Hood, and even after the war both Grant and Sherman had written slightingly of Thomas as having been "slow." Unlike Thomas, Piatt said, Sherman was in no way shy: "The war was fought from beginning to end by this wonderful man, if we are to believe his own story, while all the credit he cannot take to himself by reason of absence or other slight obstacle he graciously gives to Grant."[112]

Piatt made his first and only visit to the battlefield at Chickamauga in the spring of 1889, after his book had come out. He traveled from Cincinnati to Chattanooga in a special railway car attached to the end of a southbound express. The car's passengers were a group of former officers, both Union and Confederate, the most senior of them General Rosecrans. Rosecrans was returning to Chickamauga for the first time since he had been relieved—unjustly, Piatt thought—of his command after the battle, in which Rosecrans had been Thomas's superior officer. The purpose of the trip was to rough out the boundaries of a national park proposed for the battleground. The other veteran officers in the party included two of Piatt's close collaborators, Henry Boynton and Henry Cist, and his brother Abram. They were joined at Lexington, Kentucky, by Cassius M. Clay, the great abolitionist who during the war had served as minister to Russia. Clay had brought along a copy of his memoirs, which he soon began reading to his fellow passengers.

Piatt liked Clay, but this was not a day to hear about Russia. As the train headed south, he left the party of aging men, to go stand out on the rear platform. The express had left the bluegrass country, he wrote, and began "to climb mountains, skim along the edge of precipices, cross on dizzy bridges above streams where beetling crags drop shadows on water far below. . . . When from this one glides down to the valley of the Tennessee no words can tell of the beauty of the silent but swift river with its islands and banks of thick foliage. . . . I stood entranced upon the platform . . . taking the world of living into my world of dreams."[113] Piatt had not quite reached the summit of society, but he had known many of those who stood on top. Now he, unlike most of them, was still on earth, savoring life at seventy, traveling through flowering spring in the South.

Piatt had asked Jefferson Davis if he would like, health permitting, to come meet the group of officers at Chickamauga. If so, Piatt wrote, he would be happy to provide Mr. Davis transportation—adding that for some of the "old fellows" it might be the next to last trip, before they went on to God's "silent camping ground."[114] Davis did not go to Chickamauga; he was nearing eighty and not well and would go on his own final trip just eight months later.

What Piatt did not say in his book about major wartime leaders was that none of them had inevitably been destined to rise so high or to stay on top. People have long suggested that Lincoln might not have become president in 1860 if the Republican nominating convention had not been held in his home state; he was far behind Seward on the first ballot for the nomination. And if the war had not turned in the Union's favor in 1864, he would probably not have been reelected that year. As for that great grim war minister, Edwin Stanton, Lincoln had promoted him not knowing that Stanton had drafted a message for his chief, Secretary of War Cameron, to which Lincoln had taken strong exception. But even before entering the War Department, Stanton might well have taken, and remained in throughout the war, a far less important post, that of district attorney of Washington—if U.S. Attorney General Edward Bates had not felt he could work better with some subordinate other than Stanton.[115]

Donn Piatt never discussed in print, or so far as known in private writing, how he compared himself—if indeed he did compare himself—to the famous Americans who for so long occupied his attention. Was there some envy behind his slashing attacks on, as well as praise for, men who had become generals and national leaders? It may be so—we cannot tell—but all in all we can see in Piatt a man satisfied in himself if not in his world.

One wonders whether Piatt was amused or angry when the North American Review turned the tables on him in a review of his new book. He had denounced the fanaticism that made gods of plain men—but, said the review, Piatt had done the same thing in singling out just five Union leaders: "To eulogize these five as the men who saved the Union . . . is to invite the suggestion, not simply of hero-worship, but of idolatry." Still, said the reviewer, "in spite of his prejudices, Donn Piatt's work is always brilliant and captivating."[116]

In 1888 Piatt published his second book, a volume of fictional stories, The Lone Grave of the Shenandoah and Other Tales. Like Memories of the Men Who Saved *the Union,* it sold well.[117] The book included a note by the publisher that said, "The *Westminster Review,* which is the ablest of the great Reviews of Europe, says . . . that it is the best-written and most delightful work by an American that has reached London in half a century." The book included tales from the Civil War, including the title story about a Union lieutenant killed by a sniper and a Southern girl who built him a marble monument, and also stories from more recent years of Americans ground down by injustice.

Piatt's foreword urged copyright legislation that would better protect authors. He had been working for this, he said, but Congress listened only to "the publishers who have grown fat from theft."[118] It was a bitter subject, and Piatt was not the only complainant. E. P. Roe, America's best-selling novelist, said Congress "libeled and slandered the American people by acting as if their constituents . . . chuckled over pennies saved when buying pirated books."[119] Edward Eggleston, author of the best-selling *Hoosier Schoolmaster,* wrote that English publishers complained about unauthorized reprints of their books in America "while they themselves pounced upon every line of American production that promised some shillings of profit."[120] An international copyright convention had been signed in 1886, but the United States had not adhered to it.

In 1888 the *North American Review* published a volume put together by the magazine's editor, Allen Thorndike Rice, of reminiscences of Lincoln written by a number of "distinguished men of his time," including Donn Piatt and Walt Whitman. What Piatt thought of Whitman's contribution we do not know, but Whitman did not like Piatt's understated praise for the poet's great hero. Horace Traubel recalled that after Whitman read Piatt's contribution to the book, he said to Traubel, "He makes me think of a sloop, a yacht, without an anchor, that would forever keep on going like hell. . . . He is a fiery cuss who burns but does not shine."[121] Many Americans would have agreed—but people did like to read what the fiery cuss wrote. (Piatt's view of Whitman was that he had "no more poetry in him than in a board fence.)[122]

In November 1888 the *Washington Post* published a wide-ranging interview with Piatt, giving his overall views on the country, somber rather than fiery. Subsequently, Piatt wrote the paper that he had not made himself perfectly clear to the reporter, who had asked him inter alia about the current relationship between North and South. What Piatt had wanted above all to say was that the American republic was now threatened by two grave dangers. One was the corrupt use of money in elections. The other was the continuing strife between the two sections of the country. Piatt thought that with Reconstruction over and Southern blacks suffering increasing discrimination, in the North there was even more animosity toward Southern whites and feelings in favor of blacks than there had been in 1861. But he did not think he needed to dwell on these problems: "They are patent to the world, and a source of alarm to all true patriots."[123]

❧ 9 ❧

EAST AGAIN, AND HOME TO STAY

In that same year of 1888, Piatt left Ohio and moved to New York City for the second time in his life to become at the age of sixty-nine the editor of the new *Belford's Magazine*. It was a coup for the magazine's well-known publisher, Robert Belford. The *Springfield Register* said that the magazine "had been wise enough to select the keenest and most slashing writer at its command, Col. Donn Piatt, to edit it and to contribute."[1] Piatt's friend Gertrude Garrison, in a dispatch written for papers across the country, wondered why Piatt, a man of means as well as a versatile genius, had agreed to "give up his beloved leisure and once more take the public in hand. . . . Presumably it was the love of expressing himself, which writers never entirely lose."[2]

At sixty-nine Piatt was an old man to be still working. The hero of Edward Bellamy's utopian novel *Looking Backward,* published that January, opines, "At forty-five . . . a man still has ten years of good manual labor in him, and twice ten years of good intellectual service."[3] At that, Bellamy was exaggerating. More than half of American men died before they reached sixty.[4]

Robert Belford had visited Piatt at Mac-o-cheek the previous August, to discuss the idea of starting a new liberal review that would advocate good government—including free trade—and would also publish lighter matter for family reading.[5] Piatt met with Belford again in May 1888, in Washington, just as the magazine was being launched. Piatt told reporters that the new magazine would be backed by a syndicate of wealthy and prominent gentlemen who had guaranteed a circulation of 75,000 for at least the first six months.[6] Whether or not this was the case, Belford did arrange to provide 70,000 copies of the magazine to the Democratic Party's national committee. The longtime chairman of the committee, William H. Barnum, was about to be succeeded by Calvin Stewart Brice, a fellow Ohioan, who like Piatt had been a lawyer and a Union lieutenant colonel. Piatt found the two reluctant to take and distribute the copies. Barnum called the magazine a "nauseous pill" and said that he really sympathized with those who supported high tariffs—that is, the Republicans. In fact, both Barnum and Brice were protectionists and far from President Cleveland's, or Donn Piatt's, views on trade.

Piatt went to the attorney general, August H. Garland, sometime before the presidential election that November, to ask him to tell President Cleveland that he was being betrayed by his own party's national committee. Cleveland, Piatt learned, reacted by saying that even if Piatt's charge was true (and in effect it was), it was the party that had chosen Barnum and Brice and he had no right to interfere.[7] Perhaps Cleveland should have interfered; in the November election he lost the White House to Benjamin Harrison.

At the beginning of January 1889 editor Piatt sent a letter to that world-famous author Mark Twain. The text of the letter was typed and presumably was sent to a number of other persons, as well. It asked the recipient if he would provide information about his favorite works of prose fiction and said, "By complying with this request, you will entertain the public, so much interested in your own efforts." Piatt signed the letter, "Donn Piatt, Ed Belford." It is addressed, also in his own hand, to "Mr Saml Clemmens." Did Piatt not know how to spell Clemens correctly? In any case the once promising friendship between the two writers was long finished. Mark Twain wrote, "No answer," on the envelope, perhaps after a moment of anger.[8]

Certainly Twain had not forgotten Piatt, and certainly Twain could be vengeful. Years earlier he had decided to take revenge on another editor, Whitelaw Reid of the *Tribune,* after Reid refused to let the well-known journalist Edward House review *The Gilded Age* for the paper and later published pieces critical of Twain. The revenge was to come in the form of a biography of Reid that Twain never completed. In 1880, Twain attended a testimonial dinner for U. S. Grant and found that Reid, who in the past had openly opposed Grant, was the introductory speaker. Twain went home and thought again of his planned revenge on Reid—and of Piatt, who had sharply changed for the better his view of another president, Rutherford Hayes. Twain wrote in his notebook, "Donn Piatt [. . . .] G.A. Townsend [. . . .] Changing policy of Tribune frequently [. . . .] Get Nast to illustrate."[9] (Nast had no more love for Whitelaw Reid than he did for Donn Piatt.) But Twain had other things to do; *Life on the Mississippi* and *Huckleberry Finn* lay not far ahead, and Piatt may have well dropped out of his mind—until he got that form letter.

Piatt did not really need anything from Mark Twain for *Belford's.* His contributors included a wide range of well-known names like Henry George, Joaquin Miller, James Whitcomb Riley, and Henry Watterson. *Belford's* was serious reading and not designed as a humor magazine. One issue, though, carried a story, "About Dead-Shot Dan," by the well-known actor William J. Florence that another magazine called "as humorous and unique as anything Mark Twain ever did."[10]

Piatt also accepted the work of a number of lesser-known figures. One of these was Hamlin Garland, whose first major work, *Main-Travelled Roads,* was to appear in 1891, and who soon became famous for his realistic descriptions of the bitterness in American frontier life. In July 1888 *Belford's* published a Garland story called "A Common Case," a piteous account of the death of a farmer's wife after a poor and joyless life in the Midwest. That same summer Garland made a trip back to his Midwest homeland, which he called the Middle Border. He returned to Boston still more angry and bitter over the sad plight of his relatives and other pioneers. His father had farmed good land in Wisconsin before the Civil War. What had impelled him to keep moving farther west, ending in drought-struck Dakota? After his summer trip Garland wrote a tragic tale about a midwestern farmer that he called "John Boyle's Conclusion" and submitted it without success to several magazines. Piatt accepted it for *Belford's* but perhaps in the end decided he did not need more grimness from Garland. The article was not published until 1959.[11]

Another of Piatt's contributors was Alice Chenoweth Day, who wrote as Helen Hamilton Gardener. She was born in 1853, and, after making a name as a writer, freethinker, and suffragist, she eventually became, in 1920, the first woman member of the U.S. Civil Service Commission. She once recalled that she had written her first piece of fiction for Piatt, and he had quickly sent back a telegram saying it was tiptop and she should send another. It was, she said, "a kind and hearty way for an old editor to receive the first venture in fiction of a new and unknown writer. It helped me wonderfully and I have always appreciated it."[12]

Piatt gave a different account, one that was no less flattering to Gardener but lacked a telegram. He recalled that on a perfect June day, sitting in his office in great Manhattan and dreaming of "the shady glens, and green, willow-fringed meadows of the Mak-o-chee," he suddenly saw before him a graceful and indeed beautiful woman, who announced herself as Helen Gardener and offered him some sketches for publication in *Belford's*. He said he read the sketches, was charmed by them, and printed them in the magazine.[13] Both his and her accounts of this first meeting omit the fact that Gardener was, if new to fiction, not an unpublished writer. Her book *Men, Women, and Gods, and Other Lectures*—which lambasted Christian men for using the Bible to keep down women—had been published four years earlier, in 1885. When she met Piatt, she had recently presented to the first meeting of the International Council of Women a paper refuting the contention of some male physicians that women's brains were structurally different from men's.[14]

Piatt's contributor Henry George had become famous after publication in 1879 of his work *Progress and Poverty,* which sold three million copies and made him universally known for his proposal to abolish all taxation except a single tax on land values. Like Hamlin Garland, who supported him, George found in mid-America not an "agrarian utopia in the garden of the world" but a land where poor farmers were oppressed not just by climate but by land speculators and railroad monopolists.[15] In 1886 George ran for mayor of New York City; he lost to Abram Hewitt, the Democratic candidate, but far outdistanced the third candidate, young Theodore Roosevelt. George's popularity continued. If Piatt had been the third-most famous man in Washington after Grant and Sherman, Henry George was said to have become the third-most famous man in America, after Mark Twain and Thomas Edison. A number of Single Tax Clubs were founded, including one in Manhattan, which offered George a dinner in 1888 when he returned from a trip abroad. Among the speakers was his admirer Donn Piatt.[16]

Still another contributor to *Belford's* was an old collaborator from the days of *The Capital,* a New Yorker named J. S. Moore. Moore had lived and worked as a merchant in many countries, including England, India, South Africa, and Australia, and had also spent years in the New York Customs House. His great cause was tariff reform, and he was the most influential journalist in that field. Before writing for *Belford's* he had made many contributions to *The Capital,* writing under the pseudonym of The Parsee Merchant, not just on tariffs but on the New York business scene.[17]

Piatt asked Rutherford Hayes to contribute to *Belford's.* The former president had taken an active interest in prison reform since leaving the White House in 1881, and in August 1888 Piatt wrote him to solicit a Hayes article on the subject, saying, "I can promise a wide circulation—we sold nearly 80000 copies of our July number—and you will not only help in a good cause but greatly benefit."[18] For whatever reason, Hayes did not write the article Piatt wanted.

James Whitcomb Riley was both a contributor and a friend. Riley liked to visit Mac-o-cheek. He had spent what was perhaps a long stay there during the summer of 1884,[19] and besides his work for *Belford's* he wrote a poem of four fourteen-line stanzas that praised Piatt's home and its owner:[20]

> Donn Piatt of Mac-o-chee—
> Not the one of history,
> Who with flaming tongue and pen
> Scathes the vanities of men. . . .
> Give the simple man to me,
> Donn Piatt of Mac-o-chee. . . .
> Lolling in an easy chair
> On the terrace while he told
> Reminiscences of old—
> Letting my cigar die out,
> Hearing poems talked about,
> And entranced to hear him say
> Gentle things of Thackeray,
> Dickens, Hawthorne and the rest,
> Known to him as host and guest—
> Known to him as he to me,
> Donn Piatt of Mac-o-chee.

The Hoosier poet's famous ditty "When the frost is on the punkin and the fodder's in the shock" was said to have been inspired by the view from Mac-o-cheek.[21] That seems unlikely—but perhaps Donn Piatt provided more direct inspiration. Piatt had written a poem, widely reprinted, that Riley's poem closely echoed:

> I heard the bob-white whistle in the dewy breath of morn:
> The bloom was on the alder and the tassel on the corn.[22]

Years later Julius Chambers, a noted journalist and editor who as a boy had befriended Piatt in Ohio, wrote that he had been told by a friend of Riley that Riley's poem "was written as a parody on the late Colonel Donn Piatt's famous verses."[23] If so, there is no indication that Piatt took offense. Did he say to himself, Imitation is the most sincere form of flattery?

In any case Piatt's friendship with Riley did not keep him from criticizing frankly what Riley wrote. When the poet published a volume of prose pieces entitled *The Boss Girl,* Piatt wrote him that while the title story was as good as anything by Charles Dickens, the rest was disappointing.[24]

In 1888 Richard Watson Gilder, the editor of *Century* magazine, founded in New York a Fellowcraft Club of artists and writers. The editor of *Belford's* was quick to join. The following March the *New York Times* reported that Piatt had just addressed the club's monthly dinner, along with those well-known naturalists John Burroughs and Theodore Roosevelt and, in addition, George Kennan, whose articles in *Century* were exposing the horrors of the czar's Siberian prisons.[25]

There was no city like New York, and the editor of *Belford's* had a big job, but a year was enough. In the summer of 1889 Piatt moved back to Ohio for good. He turned seventy years old that June, and he was having continuing problems with his health.[26] That was not, however, why he left the magazine, he told Jefferson Davis.[27] There was "an organized band of ruffians at New York" that held a monopoly of distribution for all American periodicals through newsstands and vendors on trains. *Belford's,* however, depended mainly on subscriptions that went out through the mail. All had worked well, Piatt wrote, as long as Don M. Dickinson had been the postmaster general. Now that he had resigned, the monopoly had turned on *Belford's,* and it had been a fatal blow. The monopoly, or near monopoly, was the American News Company, which besides newsstands and sales on trains handled—or wanted to handle—magazine distribution by mail.[28]

Nor was that all. In the middle of the circulation crisis, Piatt wrote Davis, he had received "a severe criticism from the house of B.C. [Belford, Clarke] & Co. at Chicago on my style of editing. I responded promptly with a resignation, which will appear in the July number." It appears that Piatt's recent decision to join the Catholic Church, of which more later, played a part in all this. According to the archbishop of Cincinnati, after Piatt had written editorials in the magazine favorable to public support for Catholic schools—editorials that were "brief but forcible—as all his writings are"—the Protestant "School Book Interest" induced the news agency to refuse to circulate the magazine; as a consequence Piatt resigned as editor.[29]

Even if this was the immediate reason for his resignation, his health may well have played a part. In February of the previous year he had fallen seriously ill while staying at Chamberlain's Hotel in Washington, and the illness had lasted for weeks. A *Washington Post* reporter who talked with him in May 1888 described him as "spare of frame, gray of whiskers, hawkeyed and eagle-headed, slowly shaking off the thralldom of illness."[30]

Despite his condition, Piatt had gone to Capitol Hill on April 9 to testify before the Senate Committee on Post Roads and Post Routes, together with his old friend Ainsworth Rand Spofford, the librarian of Congress. The two witnesses both urged passage of a bill to prohibit transmission of cheap literature—dime novels and pirated reprints—by mail at the current rate of just one cent a pound. Piatt cited three reasons for action: Postmasters (of which he was one) were complaining of being overburdened; authors and honest publishers complained that cheap rates for such junk mail amounted to unjust discrimination; and—perhaps he was exaggerating a little here—the conscience of the country was outraged.[31]

Piatt had been having at least occasional problems with his health for years before his 1888 illness in Washington. In 1867 concern over his health had led him to write his first will. In 1872 he fell from a buggy and hurt his left arm and shoulder, and as a result, he told his readers two years later, rheumatism had set in. In 1884 he broke the same arm in a fall on a hotel stairway in Toledo, where he had gone to help the reelection campaign—which proved unsuccessful—of a Democratic member of Congress, Frank Hurd.[32] He must have had other problems, as well. In 1885, he wrote from Mac-o-cheek to his younger friend Nathaniel Wright Lord, who headed the Department of Mining and Metallurgy at Ohio State University, "While as well as usual in feeling and appearance my Doctors here after a solemn diagnosis told me I was as good as dead. I took this to be fact until I hit Doctor Murphy at Cincinnati and he restored confidence."[33]

A Philadelphia paper reported that the main reason Piatt left the magazine was not business problems; his health was wrecked. A Cincinnati paper responded that if the reporter had accompanied Piatt on his recent week-long visit to the Chattanooga battlefield, "he would have concluded that the Colonel was about the brightest mental and the most vigorous physical wreck he had seen in a long time."[34]

For whatever reason, it was a good time for Piatt to leave Manhattan. The proprietors of *Belford's*—Belford, Clarke & Company—were having severe financial problems, presumably related to the circulation crisis. That October the creditors closed in, and the company was reorganized.[35]

It appears likely that Piatt was no longer taking any regular physical exercise. Ten or fifteen years earlier, in Washington, he had still liked to ride horseback. The

capital then was not a city of autocars but of horse cars—and cavaliers. Of a visit
to the Piatts there, Clara Morris recalled,

> With my host and some of his friends I enjoyed many delightful and some
> rather exciting rides—especially that wild rush to escape arrest at the hands of
> the police, I, as a stranger, having tangled my horse all up in the red tape so
> plentiful at that time in the park at the Soldiers' Home. Mr. Henry Watterson
> suggested that we run for it. We did, and the policeman proved he was better
> mounted than we had believed. We escaped, but at the same time we had a race
> well worth remembering. One day as Colonel Piatt was about to lift me from
> my horse, he noticed a gentleman was leaving his door, and called out as his
> face lit up with pleasure: "Oh, I say, old fellow, go back! go back! We'll be there
> in one second! I want to see you!" And as I slipped from the saddle, he added
> to me: "There's the man I particularly wish you to know."[36]

The man was James Garfield, who, like Morris, enjoyed riding with his friend
Piatt. His diary for the 1870s records a two-hour ride with Piatt one day across
Rock Creek Park, followed by a long talk at Garfield's home on "political and liter-
ary questions"—and then another two-hour ride with Piatt the following day, plus
two other occasions when Garfield planned to combine riding with dinner at the
Piatts'.[37]

Piatt was good company for many, not just for Garfield and Morris and not just
on horseback. He was fun to be with. His friends—and they were numerous—
talked of his "endless powers of entertainment."[38]

Even though Piatt at seventy had physical complaints, now that he was back in
Ohio, he was writing perhaps as much as he had done in earlier years. He did not
need *Belford's Magazine* in order to appear in print. He was turning out frequent
articles for a new syndicate, the American Press Association, that were published
in newspapers across the country.[39] In addition, he had begun working on a biography of the Civil War general George H. Thomas.

Meanwhile, he had been involved in a recent literary sensation, the seven "Letters to Prominent Persons" that appeared in the *North American Review* between
January 1886 and January 1889 under the name of "Arthur Richmond." The letters—they were really long essays—had been addressed to several notable Americans, including Secretary of State Thomas Bayard, the author James Russell Lowell, and President Grover Cleveland.

The first of the letters had savaged Bayard, and "Arthur Richmond" was also vicious in what he wrote about President Cleveland. The letter in the *Review* for the
December 1886 issue said that until the Democratic Party had seized on Cleveland as a candidate, his life had been "one continuous negation." During the Civil
War, said the writer, Cleveland had been a young man in his twenties, but none of

his associates could recall him ever uttering a single word of interest in the country's welfare—and he had dodged military service by buying a substitute. Until he had been nominated for the presidency, there was no record of his ever saying a word on any question of national policy. Both as a statesman and as a patriot, "Richmond" concluded, Cleveland's record was pitiful.

The same issue of the *North American Review* carried Piatt's article on Salmon P. Chase, which he was soon to use for his book *Memories of the Men Who Saved the Union*. Did Piatt know what the *Review* was saying about President Cleveland in the same issue? The following month's *Review* contained a note from Piatt expressing outrage over the "Richmond" piece on Cleveland. It was, he said, an unjustified and vituperative assault. The president was admittedly not a great man and he made no pretensions to statesmanship; but, Piatt wrote emphatically, he was honest, unpretending, and able, and he was giving the country a clean administration.[40]

Three years later, in 1889, it transpired that Piatt himself had been one of what he called "that syndicate of blackguards" who under the name of Arthur Richmond had written the series of letters.[41] Which one, or ones, had he written? The first letter, savaging Secretary Bayard, was written by William Henry Hurlbert. Another of the "blackguards" was the essayist Mary Abigail Dodge, who wrote as "Gail Hamilton." There were reports that Julian Hawthorne, a prolific author and the son of Nathaniel Hawthorne, was a contributor; Hawthorne denied that he had been involved.

Piatt enjoyed notoriety, but it strains credibility to think he could have written the attack on Grover Cleveland—whom he seems honestly to have admired—and then attacked his own anonymous work the following month. The former president does not seem to have believed that Piatt authored the attack; he wrote Piatt two friendly notes the following year.[42]

One might have guessed that Piatt wrote the letter addressed to James Russell Lowell. He had reason to be jealous of Lowell, who had a bigger name than he did in the literary world and had surpassed him in diplomacy by gaining the top American diplomatic post, minister to the United Kingdom.

In fact, though, Piatt's "Richmond" letter was the one that attacked Samuel J. Randall, a Pennsylvania Democrat who was speaker of the House in 1876–81 and remained a member of the House until his death in 1890.[43] Randall had been spoken of as a possible candidate for the presidency, but "Arthur Richmond" saw him as unworthy, as "coarse, ignorant, cunning, and conceited . . . the embodiment of the popular politician."[44] Piatt may have chosen Randall as a target in part because Randall was a protectionist, while Piatt always championed the cause of free trade. The letter makes clear, however, that his main reason for attacking the man was that Randall had been speaker at the time of the 1876 presidential election. Although Randall was a Democrat, he had, said "Richmond," played a principal role in the decision to give the election to the Republican candidate, Hayes. "Richmond" wrote that "at your suggestion probably, certainly through your consent, a bargain was made with the defeated party which, ignoring the voice of the people, inaugurated as President the candidate of the minority."[45] If true, that was not quite fair; Randall seems to have done his best to prevent Hayes's inauguration, even urging legislation that would have made Hamilton Fish the president ad interim until a new national election could be held.[46]

When the 1880s ended, Piatt was contributing to a number of publications, perhaps mainly through the syndicate. These publications included the *Brooklyn Standard-Union,* then edited by Murat Halstead. Two decades earlier, Halstead had given Piatt free rein in what he wrote. Later they had quarreled, then made peace. In 1890, Piatt was incensed when Halstead cut out of one of his articles for the *Standard-Union* the statement that future historians "would laugh at Sherman's 'March to the Sea' as a crazy retreat saved only by Thomas' superb campaigning." This was Piatt's central criticism of Sherman as a general—though not the only reason he disliked the man—and he had written critically about the March to the Sea, at some length, in *Memories of the Men Who Saved the Union.* Piatt wrote to Halstead, perhaps for the last time,

> You have undoubted right to say, what shall, what shall not, appear in your paper. I have never questioned this. But, such authority gives you no right to treat, even the humblest contributor, with discourtesy. For my part I don't propose to submit to it. My opinions are my opinions, with the name attached. If you dont like them, you are at liberty to return them. . . . I had means, you did not avail yourself of during the war [Halstead, as noted earlier, had not done military service], of knowing on the field, and in the camp, precisely what we lack. You would be astonished at your own ignorance.[47]

(Halstead had been named U.S. minister to Germany the previous year, but the Senate had rejected the nomination because of what the *New York Times* called his "scathing editorials" charging that some senators had bought their seats.[48] What would the Senate have done if Donn Piatt had ever been named to head a diplomatic mission?)

At Mac-o-cheek Piatt was now spending much of his time on his biography of General Thomas. He worked in his study or "den," a second-story room with a large bay window opening on the peaceful stream valley below. His main library was downstairs, but the walls of the den were lined with elegant carved bookcases filled with both old books of his and recent reference works.[49]

Piatt now had a collaborator, General Henry M. Cist of Cincinnati. Cist was a brevet brigadier general. He had ended the war in 1865 as only a major, but after leaving the army, he received during 1866 successive brevet promotions to lieutenant colonel, to colonel, and finally to brigadier general. Piatt, it may be recalled, had been offered in 1866 a brevet promotion to brigadier general from his final wartime rank of lieutenant colonel but had turned it down as a farce and a mockery. What he thought of Cist's three quick postbellum promotions we do not know.

What presumably counted most for Piatt was Cist's service on the staff of General Thomas in the Army of the Cumberland and the fact that Cist had published a detailed history, *The Army of the Cumberland*, several years earlier. Cist, like Piatt, was a great admirer of Thomas. Cist wrote in his 1882 history, "There is nothing finer in history than Thomas at Chickamauga . . . the hardest fought and the bloodiest battle of the Rebellion."[50] (With a total of nearly 35,000 casualties on the two sides, it was in fact the second bloodiest; the casualties at Gettysburg, two months earlier, had totaled 51,000.)

Cist was more than just a literary collaborator. Since 1888, as a Cincinnati lawyer, he had managed Donn's and Ella's considerable real estate interests in that city. The couple was deriving a net income of several hundred dollars a month from Cincinnati rental properties—perhaps eighty thousand a year in today's dollars—and Cist was also arranging to sell properties for them. The correspondence between Cist and the Piatts indicates that Donn did well to leave business details in the hands of others. ("My dear Donn: Your letter of the 7th duly at hand. You did not sell the Asch property, you sold the Dierkes property just below the Asch property.")[51]

As Piatt and Cist worked on the biography of Thomas, Piatt found confirmation from a perhaps unlikely source, Jefferson Davis, for his belief that Thomas's feats at Chickamauga and thereafter had been all important. Speaking to the twenty-fifth reunion of the Army of the Cumberland in 1890, Piatt said that the old Confederate president had written him shortly before his death the previous December "that Chattanooga the granite gateway of the South was the Key to the situation, that their only comfort at Richmond was that our Government did not seem to know what to do with it, after securing possession. And Jeff Davis was right. But Chattanooga was nearly lost to us, when Sherman moved off to the support of the Sea, leaving no one at the front but George H. Thomas."[52]

While Piatt saw great virtue in Thomas, he perceived obvious faults in other commanders at Chickamauga and the subsequent battles around Chattanooga. Both Grant and Sherman had made mistakes there, as had the impulsive Rosecrans. Grant had forgiven Sherman his missteps, while taking a negative view of Thomas as too slow generally and too quick to argue, an opinion Grant would continue to hold.[53] Rosecrans's chief of staff, Garfield, was seen by his colleagues as a man for whom loyalty to his superior commander fell second to his ambition.[54] Worse, Secretary Stanton's observer in the field, Charles A. Dana (later of the *New York Sun*), had sent hysterical reports from Chattanooga to his chief—and was soon rewarded by being named assistant secretary, Stanton's deputy. In contrast, Piatt saw Thomas as methodical rather than slow, loyal rather than ambitious.[55] When in March 1864 Grant was made general-in-chief of all the Union armies, it was his friend Sherman who replaced him in the West, rather than Thomas, who was senior to Sherman in rank. For Piatt this was "the nakedest favoritism that ever disgraced a service."[56]

While Piatt worked on his Thomas biography, his cousin and friend John James Piatt, and John's wife, Sarah Bryan Piatt, were continuing to publish their poetry.[57] They had now been happily abroad for some years. J. J. Piatt had finally gotten the post he wanted. President Chester A. Arthur named him American consul at Cork in June 1882, and the couple went to Ireland for what turned out to be a stay of eleven years. The poet may never have known that Donn had written to the University of Notre Dame in January 1882 to ask that his cousin be considered for the position of professor of belles-lettres.[58] (One may wonder whether this was somehow linked to the university's subsequent decision to honor Donn Piatt with an honorary degree.)

Piatt's old comrade and commander Robert Schenck died in 1890. Piatt paid tribute to him in a long article in *Belford's Magazine.* He described Schenck as a man who, after he had been "crowded out" of Lincoln's cabinet, had enjoyed a brilliant career in the army and in politics.[59] He had been ridiculed without mercy, Piatt said, after his regiment was ambushed at the beginning of the war, but he had clamped his jaws, said nothing, and gone on to gallant service. Later he had met "the same sort of adverse combination" as a diplomat. Piatt had written in 1869 that he was sure that President Grant would choose Schenck for his cabinet. Grant had not done so. Instead, the following year Grant made him the American minister to the United Kingdom. He had done that, Piatt said, after Schenck, on a trip to Paris, had seen a woman's hat so beautiful that he bought it and brought it home for the wife of the president—and the president returned the small favor by naming Schenck to America's most prestigious diplomatic post.[60]

The new "adverse combination" that Piatt mentioned began soon after Schenck reached London. The British press began to criticize the American envoy for allowing his name to appear as a director of the Emma Silver Mining Company of Utah in advertisements for the sale of company shares in Britain. Secretary of State Fish asked him to resign his directorship in the company. Schenck did so, but then publicly endorsed the mine—whose shares became worthless after a cave-in in Utah. Fish let him stay on in London, but his name became a byword in Europe. It was all unfair, Piatt said; Schenck was the soul of honor. He added that some of the vilest abuse had come from Americans living in England, including Moncure D. Conway, Piatt's old abolitionist friend, whom Piatt had last seen in London and whom he now mocked as an "evangelical teacher of evolution."

What Piatt did not mention was that beyond the abuse, a congressional investigation had brought out the undoubted fact that Schenck had been able to dispose of his company holdings at a high price. He had returned to the United States in 1876 in disgrace—and resumed the profitable practice of law in Washington.[61]

Although Piatt did not criticize his old chief for his wrongdoing, he did criticize the overall quality of American diplomats in one of the articles he wrote for the American Press Association in June 1890:

> The so-called diplomatic agents sent abroad are really nothing but clerks. . . . We could put up with this sort of flummery were it not that we get laughed at. . . . We reserve these places as rewards for political services, and the men selected are not only ignorant of the European diplomacy, but the history and nature of their own government. They cannot speak the diplomatic language; they generally cannot speak their own correctly. . . . If our so-called diplomatic agents were sensible men, and able to appreciate the situation, we might at least escape the ridicule that is now heaped upon us.[62]

Piatt was now into his eighth decade. He was still going strong, but as he increasingly felt age come upon him, he thought more about faith and religion. Despite his Catholic mother's influence when he was young, he had turned away from Catholicism as an adult. For a time he had interested himself in spiritualism, like many of his contemporaries.[63] After the Civil War he had attended several seances at a doctor's home in Cincinnati, where a woman named Mary Hollis claimed to be calling up the spirits of a number of deceased persons, including Piatt's first wife, Louise. Piatt, it was alleged, took a deep interest in the proceedings, but in fact he seems to have been less than fully convinced that Hollis was contacting the realm of spirits.[64]

The Capital was a Sunday paper, and for several years Piatt included in each issue a column he called "Sunday Meditations." They were fervent Christian homilies, not very remarkable but perhaps more thoughtful than many sermons that Washingtonians might hear in church. The "Meditations" did not have a sectarian bent, but eventually Piatt decided that it was Catholicism that met his spiritual needs and, like his mother and father decades earlier, formally joined the Catholic Church. Just when this happened is not clear. The archbishop of Cincinnati, William Henry Elder, wrote in 1889 that Piatt had been a "practical Catholic" for the last two or three years.[65] That November, Piatt was a delegate from Ohio to the landmark Catholic Congress held in Baltimore and on Elder's recommendation was elected one of the vice presidents of the congress, although there was already one vice president from the Cincinnati archdiocese.[66]

In a sense, Piatt's entry into the church was not surprising. He had had in part a Catholic education; his marriage to Louise had taken place in the Catholic cathedral of Cincinnati, and the same priest, Father Edward Purcell, had married him and Ella. For many years, however, Miller tells us, he had been "an unbeliever in the tenets of any church" and had resisted occasional attempts by Father Charles I. White, the pastor of St. Matthew's Catholic Church in Washington, to bring him back into the fold.[67]

Piatt had also once contributed to a Methodist magazine, and he had attended Methodist services—although he liked to poke fun at the pastor of the Metropolitan Methodist Church in Washington, the Reverend Dr. John P. Newman. Newman was not his real target, though. The target was Newman's parishioner Ulysses S. Grant, whom Piatt mocked for his attempts to appear pious. Piatt wrote that he doubted that the president would get to heaven through his churchgoing.

Later Donn and Ella began attending services at St. Matthew's on a regular basis, though on occasion he also mocked Father White. When rumor spread that the pope was to name an American cardinal, Piatt wrote that White had hurried to get his head measured for a cardinal's red galero.[68] In the end, when it was time to be fully serious, Piatt decided that he was definitely a Catholic.[69]

Piatt had been working for a long time on what would be a religious novel. Press reports said he had already decided on the title: *The Reverend Melancthon Poundex.* Poundex was not a new Piatt creation. Back in 1874 *The Capital* had carried chapters from an unpublished work by "Jones" that featured a Poundex: *The Minister's Wooing, after Harriet Beecher Stowe.*[70]

Piatt said that his novel would take a position directly opposite to that expressed in *Robert Elsmere.*[71] This was a best-selling recent novel by the British writer Mrs. Humphry Ward (Mary Augusta Arnold), whose central character is a clergyman who leaves the Anglican Church and starts a new Unitarian-like sect. Piatt's novel, which appeared in full only after his death, portrays a Catholic monsignor named Edward Carroll, who remains in the Catholic Church, goes through a terrible financial crisis, and is seen to be a far better and more saintly man than the Protestant Poundex.[72] Poundex commits adultery, and reviewers were reminded of a famous scandal in the 1870s, when the Reverend Henry Ward Beecher, brother of Harriet Beecher Stowe and America's greatest preacher, was reported to have had an affair with Elizabeth Tilton, the wife of his best friend.

If Poundex looked like Beecher, Carroll was widely reported to be based on Father Purcell, the priest who had married Donn and Louise and then Donn and Ella.

Like Monsignor Carroll, Father Purcell had seen his reputation ruined—as well as that of his brother, John Baptist Purcell, the archbishop of Cincinnati—by the financial disaster that the priest brought on the archdiocese by mismanagement of its finances.[73] The problems had first come to light at the end of 1878, and by the following year it transpired that the debts amounted to four million dollars, a huge sum. The archbishop offered his resignation to Pope Pius IX but was told that the pope thought it "inopportune to accept it at present."

This was widely seen as Vatican sarcasm. During the 1870 Vatican Council, Archbishop Purcell had been one of a number of Catholic bishops who initially opposed the doctrine of papal infallibility—saying it was "inopportune" to decide on that now.[74] Purcell, like all but one American bishop, eventually voted for infallibility, but he died in 1883 with the financial crisis of his archdiocese still unresolved.[75]

In January 1891 Piatt finally made clear the strength of his Catholicism in an article entitled "A Roman Catholic's View," which appeared in *The Arena*, a Boston monthly magazine. He wrote, "From whence my religion came, and how, and whether sensible or not—I only know that it is here, and that it is true. The sense of dependence, the longing for aid, the hope of something yet to come, purer and better, are born in us. The recognition of God is a part of humanity. . . . It is the Christ that is in us which is making Christianity conquer the world, and gives my church its immortality."[76]

No matter that his faith was finally strong, we are left wondering, when we read one of Piatt's many "maxims, opinions, reflections and sentiments," whether this faith derived from a search for truth or from his admitted need for a kind of protection: "Let one turn over a flat stone in a meadow on a sunlit day and note how the insects will flee and worms writhe, to realize the pitiable plight of humanity when the vaunted reason of man pulls down the shelter of a creed."[77]

For a decade after he left Washington in 1880 Piatt retained an interest in *The Capital*, while Augustus Buell continued as the paper's editor. Piatt's biographer Miller reports, "He continued . . . to hold his stock in the paper until an offer came so advantageous, that he could not refuse, and in February 1890, he signed over his entire interest to A.C. Buell."[78]

As mentioned earlier, Buell had once been sued for criminal libel by former Senator Zachariah Chandler, before Buell joined Piatt on *The Capital*. From what we have seen of Chandler, Buell's attacks on him may have been accurate. Some of Buell's later work is more questionable. In 1882, after Piatt had retired to Mac-o-cheek, Buell was not only running *The Capital* but also editing a Washington daily called the *Critic*. He alleged in the *Critic* that several other well-known journalists had been involved in the infamous Whisky Ring scandal several years earlier, but when called in by a congressional committee, he backed off from his allegations.

That same year Buell was called into court in connection with the still larger Star Route scandal. In 1880 the second assistant postmaster general, Thomas J. Brady, and six other men, including a former U.S. senator, were indicted by a federal grand jury for conspiring to defraud the government of almost five million dollars in connection with contracts to carry the mail in western states along what were known as star routes. The trial went on for almost three years. When Buell went to court in 1882, he testified that he had first met Brady in February 1880, at which point Buell was not only managing *The Capital* but was a clerk on a congressional committee. The *New York Times* reported that Buell "said he had purchased his controlling interest in the Capital from Donn Piatt in March, 1880, for $10,000, Gen. Brady furnishing the money." Buell had, he said, been running the paper even before that time; "Col. Piatt was away, and he was only a voluntary contributor, not receiving any salary."[79] The Star Route trial ended in 1883, and Brady and all but one of the defendants were acquitted. There had been intense public interest in the case, and afterward many people remembered Buell's name unfavorably.

Some time after this, Buell decided to become a historian. In 1900 he published a two-volume work, *John Paul Jones: Founder of the American Navy*. The work quoted a list of "Qualifications of a Naval Officer," which, Buell said, Jones had drawn up. For decades these qualifications were memorized by all midshipmen at the Naval Academy—and then in 1986 naval historian James C. Bradford proved that Buell had fabricated them. Indeed, it has been clear for several decades that Buell fabricated much of what he wrote, not just in his biography of John Paul Jones but also in works he published on Andrew Jackson, Sir William Johnson, and the Civil War.[80]

What does all this imply for Buell's veracity as a journalist, as well as his ethics overall? Was he a fabricator before he turned to writing biography, during his years at *The Capital*? If he was, did Piatt know it? What did Piatt think, when he learned—as he must have done, not later than 1882—that Buell had bought control of his paper in 1880 with funds from one of the principals in the largest scandal of the day? Although Miller says Piatt "continued to hold his stock in the paper" until 1890, it would seem that this was at most a minor interest. Nevertheless, why did Piatt not sever relations with the unsavory Buell before 1890? Documentation seems lacking. The present writer can only raise these questions and leave them to others to answer.

In the spring of 1891 the press reported that Piatt was planning to launch yet a new publication, a magazine, of which he would be editor-in-chief, and that he had already secured financial backing and found a staff of skilled writers.[81] But no magazine appeared.

There was also a report in the *New York World* that early in the summer of 1891 Robert Belford, who had continued to publish *Belford's Magazine* despite financial problems, received an offer from John W. Young, a businessman who was one of the sons of Mormon leader Brigham Young, to invest forty thousand dollars in the magazine on the condition that Donn Piatt would return to his old position as managing editor. The *World* understood that the money had been put up but that Belford had backed out of the deal at the last minute, fearing that Piatt was scheming to wrest control of the magazine from him.[82] At this point the firm's creditors had closed in, and the magazine ceased publication. Belford himself wrote to the paper to insist that it had been wrong in reporting that Piatt wanted "to ruin the magazine."[83]

But even if Young had wanted Piatt to take over *Belford's Magazine* again, either to run it or to ruin it, Donn Piatt had no thought now of leaving peaceful Mac-O-Chee to live and work again in great New York. It appears from a handwritten note among his papers that he did consider briefly, but dismissed, the possibility of working as an editor of some publication from Mac-O-Chee or even from Europe. His thoughts were already turning in other directions, at least on the summer day at Mac-O-Chee when he sat down and wrote a sad poem beginning,

> Why should I shrink from thy dark presence, Death,
> So near me now while fleeting years are brief;
> Soon thy chill touch will be my sole relief
> From racking pains, dimmed eyes and gasping breath.[84]

That was private, not public, sadness; the poem was never published. What he wanted to tell the public was that, since people could not make themselves over and be young and enthusiastic again, "We must fold our arms and go over our Niagara with dignity."[85] But he was not quite ready for that.

In August 1891 newspapers across the country reported that while Piatt was working on his Thomas biography, he had come on proof that James Garfield, the assassinated president, had as a Union officer during the Civil War betrayed his commander, General William S. Rosecrans. Garfield had reportedly written to Treasury Secretary Chase to try to bring down Rosecrans, and this supposedly kept reinforcements from being sent to Rosecrans, the result being the difficult battle of Chattanooga. Rosecrans told the press that he had no certain knowledge of the particular letter cited by Piatt, but "that treacherous letters from Garfield were written to Chase is a certain fact . . . the army of the Cumberland was put in deadly peril."[86]

Piatt said that his discovery of the letter that Garfield had written to Chase (which was apparently in the possession of Chase's daughter, Kate Chase Sprague)[87] had caused him a sorrow deeper than what he had felt when Garfield was shot. He said that he and Garfield had long been as intimate as brothers— certainly they were friends, but this was an exaggeration, from all available evidence—and that during the Crédit Mobilier scandal, Piatt said, "I believe I saved him from suicide by bringing him in contact with the late Dr. Garnot, of Washington, who prescribed good old rye whisky."[88] Piatt did not mention that he had more recently written a long poem lamenting Garfield's death.[89] But his feelings for Garfield could not keep him, he said, from telling the truth about him. (The author has found no evidence that Garfield ever contemplated suicide, although his diary makes clear that he was depressed by the attacks against him over the Crédit Mobilier. By the spring of 1873, Garfield could write, "My soul is emerging from the shadows which the late winter of outrage has thrown upon me.")[90]

Although Piatt had come on an unpublished Garfield letter, it was not the first such letter from Garfield to Chase. Shortly after Garfield's assassination, a similar letter had been made public by J. W. Schuckers, Chase's former secretary.[91] Now, though, a quarter century after the war and years after Garfield's death, neither the general public nor most newspapers wanted to see the reputation of the murdered president undermined again. Piatt was widely attacked for making public what he had found, even if it was true. The *St. Paul Pioneer Press* called him "a mischief maker," the *New York Recorder* said he was simply "rehearsing old stories," and the *Chicago Herald* said that if Garfield had criticized his commander sharply, during the war others under stress had done the same thing.[92]

Piatt's revelation of the Garfield letter was just one more case of his telling hard things about popular people, from presidents on down. He was not, however, always interested in denigrating others. In an 1884 article he had told the story of a conversation with Allan Pinkerton, the famous chief of Union spies during the war, and Colonel Thomas Key, who had been chief of staff to General George B. McClellan. Pinkerton told the others a story so incredible—about what, we do not know—that after he left, Piatt asked Key whether he thought "the famous detective . . . would palm off a dime novel on us as a true occurrence." Key replied that Pinkerton's facts were stranger than fiction. Piatt left it at that, so that his article if anything enhanced Pinkerton's reputation—a reputation that has suffered a little in more recent years.[93]

As August neared its end in Ohio, in the year 1891, Ohio farmers were preparing for the harvest. There would be a full moon soon—the harvest moon. A group of young ladies and gentlemen in Urbana decided to plan a carriage ride through the countryside in the moonlight, which would end with a surprise visit to Colonel and Mrs. Piatt at Mac-O-Chee. Without telling the Piatts beforehand, they would drive up in their carriages and then a caterer would arrive with supper for all. An orchestra was engaged, and there would be dancing.

The party that drove to Mac-O-Chee in the warm moonlit night numbered three dozen young people. When they got there, the Piatts said they were indeed surprised, and also very pleased, to see them. The refreshments arrived, but for some reason the orchestra did not. Fortunately, the Piatts knew of a self-taught violinist who lived not far from them. He was called in, and he played, as one of the party wrote later to a Cincinnati newspaper, "the old dancing tunes of our fathers and mothers—'Money Musk,' the 'Twin Sisters' and the 'Virginia Reel.'"

Finally, as the moon was going down after midnight, the party left.[94] One imagines Donn and Ella as they got ready for bed that night, thinking back a half century and reminiscing about the years when they, too, had been young. Did Donn also think of Louise, so lovely and so soon lost?

Some weeks after the harvest moon party, one pleasant day in late September, M. P. Nolan, an old friend of Donn Piatt—the two had first met in 1845—visited the Piatts at Mac-O-Chee. Nolan was impressed by Ella, who made the house "radiant" with her friendly way and entertaining conversation. But it was Donn's devotion to his wife that most impressed him: "He seemed to live for her. She was his world, the past was hers, and there was no future for him without her form therein."[95]

Two decades earlier, Piatt had published a story about a Virginia gentleman who after a wild youth was now a "quiet, pious, benevolent old man, so devoted to his invalid wife."[96] Piatt was not quiet, even now, and many people would not call him benevolent; but the rest of it fit.

He was staying as busy as ever with his writing, though his peers were fast passing from the scene. In March 1891 he published a lengthy reminiscence of a recently deceased friend, Washington McLean, owner of the *Cincinnati Enquirer* and *Washington Post,* in his old magazine, *Belford's.*[97] He was also contributing regular articles to the *Cleveland Plain Dealer*—sixteen in the course of a year. He wrote in the *Cleveland Plain Dealer* in September 1891, "There are quite a number of like surprises in store for the blessed American people, who will have to, in toto, readjust their admiration for heroes under epaulettes who will appear as heroes of bloody disaster. However, I have had my share of the business."[98]

In fact, though, he had still not quite finished with the Garfield business. In October he wrote an article for the *Plain Dealer* that began by looking forward to the November elections. He attacked Senator John Sherman, this time for his defense of high tariffs—and then he returned once more to his revelation, a decade after Garfield's assassination, that Garfield had betrayed his wartime commander. It was simply a question, Piatt said, of telling the truth: "When the Credit Mobilier scandal was developed I was a newspaper man at Washington intimate with Garfield, and knowing him to be innocent of any wrong doing I hastened to his defense. It was like calling up hogs in a hurricane. I stood alone in the peltings of the pitiless blast. . . . Now the same press that howled him down while living howl me down for daring to tell the truth about him dead. What is there in death that sanctifies wrong and leaves records so distorted that they cease to be history?"[99]

It was a fair question, but not one to which he would provide an answer. At the end of October 1891 Piatt took the train to Cincinnati. His main purpose was to give the evening's address at the anniversary dinner of the Cincinnati Literary Club, of which he had been a member for almost forty years. He had been sorry to miss the previous year's dinner and had written a long letter beforehand to the club president to make his excuses. He could not come, he said, because he had to get Mac-O-Chee in shape for the winter; after being in hot water all his life, he was now having to wait for workmen to install a new hot water heater. He added, "My heart is with you. . . . The pleasantest memories of my life are twined about our Literary Society. I never knew an association that had in it so much kindly feeling. . . . I intend when I reach that broad gate kept by Saint Peter to show the Saint my certificate of membership of the Cincinnati Literary Society and I expect him to fling open the gate and cry out 'come in old fellow and tell us about the Mac-o-chee post office. How did you leave the dogs?' I shall expect to find the Literary reorganized in Heaven, sitting on reserved seats of damp clouds."[100]

At the 1891 anniversary dinner Piatt sat next to his old friend Patrick Mallon, with whom he had successfully defended the Fenians in that filibuster case in Cincinnati, thirty-five years earlier.[101] When Piatt rose to speak, he told the members that his doctor had told him to stay home. He seemed well, and he looked considerably younger than his years, but it was no secret that he had health problems.[102] Several papers had reported that the previous year he had traveled to New York, where he was late in meeting an unnamed friend for dinner one evening. (The friend was

Julius Chambers, recently managing editor of the *New York Herald*.)[103] When he finally arrived at the restaurant, he said that he had made a mistake in trying to walk there; he had an incurable malady. It was one that had baffled doctors for six thousand years. What was it? asked the friend. Old age, said Piatt.

Piatt explained to the Literary Club members, "I am suffering from a complication of chronic complaints and a violent attack of the McKinley bill"—and added that he would be missing from the next year's meeting.

The members may have wondered just what he was saying about himself, but they knew a lot about McKinley, another Ohioan, a recent member of the House of Representatives and a Republican. Like Donn Piatt, William McKinley had enlisted in the Union army as a private, and for a time he had been a commissary sergeant in the regiment commanded by a future president—another future president—Rutherford B. Hayes. McKinley had ended the war as a captain and afterward, unlike Lt. Col. Piatt, had accepted a retroactive brevet promotion, to major.[104]

In 1890, McKinley, who had served in Congress for some years and now chaired the House Ways and Means Committee, pushed through a high-tariff bill that to Piatt's disgust became law, helped by widespread worry over the balance of trade turning against the United States. The McKinley Tariff produced a steep and unpopular rise in consumer prices, and angry Ohio voters ousted McKinley from his seat in Congress. Undaunted, he contested the incumbent governor of Ohio, Piatt's friend and fellow Democrat James E. Campbell, for the governorship in the fall of 1891. Piatt liked McKinley no better than he had liked Grant; he called him a solemn charlatan, a small Napoleon. Several months before going to Cincinnati for the Literary Club meeting he had written, "It is not that personally Bill McKinley meets with much opposition, but he makes one of a class singularly obnoxious to the majority. This class is composed of eminently respectable men, pious bankers, brokers and merchants who solemnly say on all occasions, 'In the name of God amen, let us rob someone.'"[105]

Piatt spoke for some time to the Literary Club, and the members applauded him warmly. The meeting lasted until after midnight. When he reached his hotel, he was very tired and supposed he would feel ill in the morning—but after rising, he wrote Ella, he felt unusually well.[106]

He had some appointment that day in Cincinnati and so spent one more night in the city and then took the train home to West Liberty. It was the beginning of November, and the weather was unusually cold for the season. The train's steam heating system was not working. He caught a chill. When he came home, he told his wife he was not feeling well. The following day he felt better and went out driving. The day after that, he took to his bed. What had seemed just a cold turned to pneumonia, and he went downhill.

Donn Piatt died at the age of seventy-two, at Mac-O-Chee, on November 12,

1891. He was buried on November 15 beside his first wife, Louise, in the fine tomb he had built for her.

Some years earlier Piatt had written to his longtime acquaintance John Hay, Lincoln's secretary and later assistant secretary of state, "You have not only genius but what is better you have friends. I have not. One mourning coach will carry all of my funeral procession when I try the golden stair."[107]

He was quite wrong. The *San Francisco Examiner* reported, "Thousands thronged to the family mansion to get one last glimpse of his features and to do him honor and reverence. . . . Then followed the last sad rites, and the funeral procession formed, more than a mile in length."[108] Obituaries appeared in small and large newspapers across the country. The *Daily Leader* of Davenport, Iowa, said that this was a man whose selection of words was perfect and style charming and who could put more dynamite into a sentence than any other man of his time. In Oshkosh, Wisconsin, the *Daily Northwestern* wrote that Piatt had been born independent; that he had remained sturdily independent through all his eventful life. The *Bismarck Daily Tribune* in North Dakota said that for twenty years he had been the "stormy petrel" of American literature and politics. The *Washington Post* expressed the hope that he now slept well, saying that he had been a man of genius, relentless in his criticism of public men and once "perhaps more widely read than any man in the country as the master of journalistic excoriation." The *Post* added, "Beneath the trenchant and bellicose garb that he wore to the outside world . . . Donn Piatt harbored many kindly traits of character and a fundamental sense of human justice." The *New York Times* ran a polite obituary, which, as had happened in the *Times* before by chance or by design, misspelled his first name. It acknowledged, however, that "the almost interminable line of carriages that followed the hearse to the grave told of the esteem in which he was held."[109]

Ohio's outgoing governor, James Campbell, was one of Piatt's ten pallbearers. Campbell had just lost the governorship to McKinley, although, Piatt had said in his last *Plain Dealer* article, it was a fight between an admirable eagle and a snapping turtle. Perhaps McKinley felt relieved that he would no longer be subject to attacks by the man of Mac-O-Chee. As for Campbell, he had lost a friend, one who might well have helped him—if somehow Piatt had lived, if somehow Campbell had only defeated McKinley—to succeed Grover Cleveland as president of the United States in 1897.[110] But Piatt died, after living longer and doing more than most men of his time, and history took a different turn.

LOOKING BACK AT DONN PIATT

Two years after Piatt's death his first biography appeared. It was written by another of his pallbearers, Charles Grant Miller, a man in his late twenties who for the past year or more had worked as Piatt's private secretary at Mac-o-cheek. Miller was a journalist who would eventually become editor-in-chief of the *Cleveland Plain Dealer*. The biography he wrote, financed by Donn's widow, Ella, was described later as fulsome but accurate.[1] In fact, it painted Piatt's virtues and mentioned only the faults that Piatt himself had admitted. Before Miller's own death in 1928 he was to become something of a superpatriot if not a chauvinist. He wrote a series of articles for the Hearst press that one historian called unscrupulous anti-British propaganda.[2] He also became a fierce critic of what he considered unpatriotic histories of the United States; he once called Columbia University a "font of treasonable history."[3] One wonders whether he would eventually have discerned treason in the attacks that Piatt had made on so many national heroes.

In 1893, too, Ella arranged for publication of Donn's novel about the Reverend Mr. Poundex, which he had finished before his death but set aside to work on the Thomas biography. Far more important than the novel was the appearance that same year of the biography. Ella had arranged for the last three chapters to be written by Henry V. Boynton, who had spent his youth in Ohio and perhaps had met Piatt there, and who had been Piatt's friend and fellow journalist in Washington after the war. As early as the end of 1869 Piatt had written, in his weekly Washington Letter for the *Cincinnati Commercial*, of his "active young friend General Boynton" and his "facile and sensational pen."[4]

Boynton, like Piatt, thought highly of General Thomas, and Boynton had served under Thomas at Chattanooga. Like Piatt, Boynton had ended the war as a lieutenant colonel and, like Piatt's other collaborator, Henry Cist, after the war had become a brevet brigadier general. The year the biography of Thomas appeared, Boynton was finally awarded the Congressional Medal of Honor for his bravery at Missionary Ridge thirty years earlier. Over the postwar decades he had become one of Washington's most reputable newspaper writers.

Henry Cist had already ended his association with the Piatts. In 1892, the year after Donn Piatt died, he went to Germany for a long stay, suffering from some malady and taking the waters at Wiesbaden. He was worried that with Piatt gone, he would be identified as Piatt's main collaborator on the Thomas biography and would become the target of angry reactions to the book's criticisms of Grant and other heroes. He wrote Ella from Wiesbaden that under a contract he had made with Donn, he had the right to review the manuscript before it was published. However, he produced no such contract.

Ella consulted a friend in West Liberty, William H. West, who, though he had lost his sight and lived in a small town now, had been Ohio's attorney general and a member of the state supreme court. (This was the same West who in 1860 had taken away Piatt's seat at the Republican convention that nominated Lincoln for the presidency.) West assured Ella that as Donn's heir she held all rights to the manuscript, but that it would nevertheless be prudent to get Cist to relinquish any right he might conceivably have in the publication, for a reasonable compensation. Boynton agreed with West. In the end Ella paid Cist two thousand dollars. He duly signed away his rights—and asked her to send him two copies of the book when it was published.[5]

The book got generally good reviews, but some complained that Piatt had continued to take a contrarian line. Those who had read his *Memories of the Men Who Saved the Union* were not surprised by the new book's praise of Thomas, but few agreed with the authors that Thomas had been the Union's greatest general. Nor did many agree with Piatt and Boynton—who was to become the first official historian of a new Chickamauga and Chattanooga National Military Park—that the much admired William Tecumseh Sherman deserved serious criticism either for the mistakes he had made in the battles in eastern Tennessee or for his March to the Sea. Most reviewers also disagreed with Piatt's assertion that Lincoln had looked down on black Americans.

Murat Halstead attacked the book more strongly than most. Although Piatt and Boynton, said the non-veteran Halstead, had both "won distinction, and served creditably in the military forces," their book was a work not of history but of controversy. Piatt, in particular, "was constitutionally inaccurate. He had no use for arms of precision, but always fought with rockets." Grant and Sherman had admittedly made mistakes, but the authors had criticized them unfairly, "smearing on the blood with a broom."[6]

Someone with the initials of Henry V. Boynton responded fiercely in the *New York Tribune* that Halstead was no one to talk about criticizing wartime leaders. In 1861, said H. V. B., Halstead had written in an editorial that Sherman was "stark mad." In 1863, after the battle of Shiloh, Halstead had written, "Our Army of the Mississippi is being wasted by the foolish, drunken, stupid Grant. He can't organize, or control, or fight an army. . . . I know he is an ass." H. V. B. also quoted from a letter that Halstead had at some point written about Lincoln to Treasury Secretary Chase: "The President's weak puling humanitarianism is death and hell to the army. . . . There are persons who would feel it was doing God service to kill him, if it were not feared that [Vice President] Hamlin is a bigger fool than he is."[7]

After Donn's death at least one more notable visitor came to visit the Piatts: Ohio Governor James M. Cox, who is seen in a 1917 photograph standing with several Piatts on the front terrace at Mac-A-Cheek, as he was touring the state to advocate American involvement in the World War. (One might imagine Donn Piatt putting hard questions to him about that.) Three years later Cox became the Democratic candidate for president of the United States. Like his predecessor James Campbell, who had lost the governorship to William McKinley, Cox was defeated by another Ohioan, Warren G. Harding, although Cox had an able younger running mate named Franklin D. Roosevelt.

When Donn Piatt died at the age of seventy-two, Ella was just fifty-three. After some time she moved out of the great chateau that she and Donn had built. In succeeding years she built four houses in the neighborhood, a large Italianate house near Mac-O-Chee and three places in West Liberty. During her moves, unfortunately, some of Donn's papers were mislaid and probably lost.[8]

Ella, a modern woman, bought the second Locomobile in Logan County. She lived in prosperity for three decades after Donn's death, despite her infirmity, and after paying for the education of several nieces and nephews, she died in 1920 at the age of eighty-two. The *Atlanta Constitution* said that Donn's devotion to Ella had formed one of the brightest pages in his career, that "for thirty years he was lover, husband, and friend—all and everything to this stricken woman."[9]

Abram Sanders Piatt also outlived Donn by many years, dying in 1908 shortly before his eighty-seventh birthday. He was survived by his second wife, the former Eleanor Watts. His loss, like that of his older brother, was widely lamented in Ohio.

The two poets John James and Sarah Bryan Piatt eventually returned to America from their years in Ireland. Decades after both had died, she would be recognized as one of America's foremost female poets.[10] Their son Arthur Donn Piatt remained in Ireland, served as American vice consul at Dublin, and married the daughter of the Celtic scholar George Sigerson.

Arthur Piatt's son, another Donn Piatt, was educated in a nationalist school founded by Padraic Pearse, later executed by the British as a leader of the 1916 Easter Rising. This Donn Piatt became a left-wing scholar who played a part in the Celtic revival in newly independent Ireland and wrote a history of the Irish language.[11] Irish was losing out to English, but, wrote the young socialist Piatt, the language would be out of danger "the day the most English thing in Ireland goes, the social system of the English."[12] Earlier he had written, "The person who sets out to be a writer in Ireland must have leave to examine and tell the naked truth. Let him not avoid the ugly thing, if it is necessary to examine it."[13] His older namesake, who had always been proud of his own frankness and had defended Irish patriots in the Cincinnati filibuster trial, would have been pleased that the spirit of Big Fire lived on in this Irish cousin.

Among those who remembered Donn Piatt were the much maligned Mormons. The *Deseret News* wrote, "The Saints have reason to retain a warm place for him in their memories, as he many times wrote in their defense when they were the objects of attack from almost every other quarter."[14] Piatt had written in his time, "The polygamy of Utah is doing no harm to the United States. . . . The difference between the Mormons and the Christian statesmen is that the Mormons marry their mistresses, the congressmen don't."[15] Was polygamy worse than adultery? The Mormons were, he had to say, fanatics, but "they turned the desert into a garden, and flourished in spite of Yankee Philistines and grasshoppers."[16] Piatt liked to be what today is called a contrarian, but his relatively positive view of the Mormons may have derived at least in part from his apparent friendship, referred to earlier, with John W. Young, the son of one of Brigham Young's several dozen wives. He had also been on friendly terms with the Mormon leader George Quayle Cannon, a longtime member of the church's First Presidency, editor of the *Deseret News,* and the Utah Territory's delegate in Congress from 1873 to 1881. Beyond that, Piatt, as a young Cincinnati lawyer, may have once helped defend the church's future prophet, Brigham Young.[17]

Years after Donn Piatt died, Clara Morris invited to lunch one day the Episcopal bishop of New York, Henry C. Potter. The bishop was struck by a painting on her wall that was signed by George P. A. Healy, famous for his portraits of American and European statesmen.[18] This picture, she told the bishop, had been painted in Paris, long ago. It was "the portrait of the truest, most unselfish friend I ever had . . . Donn Piatt." The bishop thought the name was "curiously familiar." Who was this Piatt?

> "Well," Morris remembered saying, "he had been many things. A lawyer, a farmer, a politician, a soldier, and last an editor."
> "Ah!" cried the Bishop sharply, "Washington! His was a Washington paper. I have him now. A wit, a man of most cynical, biting humor."

Morris wrote that she answered the bishop, trying hard to keep the quaver out of her voice, "Yes, that was the mask that hid a knightly honor and a woman's tenderness of heart. If he faced the world with a clenched hand it was because the world had been very hard to him."[19]

The world had not really been that hard to Donn Piatt; in a sense it was he who had been hard to the world. Perhaps, though, Morris was recalling what he had told her. We do not know whether it was he—or conceivably Ella after he died—who gave Morris what was probably the most important portrait ever done of him.

It was Horace who wrote, "*Non omnis moriar.*" Piatt, too, must have hoped that he would not wholly die. Nor did he, not wholly. By the end of the nineteenth century reminiscences of Donn Piatt were far less frequent in the press, but mentions of the man continued to appear in both city and small-town newspapers. The *Washington Post* wrote in 1900 that he had been "known and loved and hated, all the way from the Atlantic to the Pacific."[20] In 1902, to cite one of a number of examples from small-town papers, one could read in an Iowa newspaper a letter from Washington recalling how once "his weekly paper teemed with columns of wit and wisdom, all of it emblazoned and more or less embittered with sarcasm of the most biting character."[21] Two years later the *Washington Post* again wrote of Piatt, as a man who, while amiable, "drove the stiletto into the vitals of his enemies."[22] In 1903 a retrospective work on Washington journalists thought Piatt "might be regarded as the central figure of the reconstruction period among Washington newspaper editors."[23]

By the 1920s Piatt was practically forgotten, but, as Americans began to buy more automobiles, occasional articles began to appear in Midwest newspapers that urged a visit to Mac-O-Chee as part of a driving trip through Ohio. In 1931 a paper in Fitchburg, Massachusetts, carried a report by Paul Jacob that he had recently been in the romantic spot where James Whitcomb Riley had written "When the frost is on the punkin"—the tower room in Donn Piatt's mansion. The house was empty now, Jacob reported, and the property no longer belonged to the family—"What is the future of this great pile, built to withstand the centuries? No one knows."[24]

Recent years have brought publication of a compendium entitled *The Wit and Wisdom of Donn Piatt,* and several of Piatt's works are now available in reprint.[25] Altogether, though, little has been said of Piatt for decades.[26] The same can be said for other journalists of his time who had a national following, like Halstead, Townsend, and Boynton and, say, Samuel Bowles of the *Springfield (Massachusetts) Tribune* and Horace White of the *Chicago Tribune.*[27] But our focus is on Donn Piatt, who was once perhaps the most famous—or infamous—of them.

In attempting an overall judgment of the man today, we get quickly to the question of his probity and objectivity. As Mark Wahlgren Summers has written, in Piatt's time "Objective reporting appeared never."[28] How much objectivity do we find now? Some contemporary historians call objectivity at best an ideal, a noble dream. Beyond the question of objectivity, Summers calls Piatt a corrupt personality because he "refused to remain as an observer. He was a political participant."[29]

Piatt, indeed, took sides politically. He did not hesitate to work as a lobbyist while remaining an influential editor—and we must wonder why later he let a man like Augustus Buell take over his paper—but it is too much to say he was corrupt. He should not have mixed lobbying with journalism, even if he did so when standards of conduct for journalists were still in the process of becoming established. It was after—soon after—his lobbying concluded that a Standing Committee of Correspondents in Washington finally drew up, in 1879, a list of rules about lobbying that was later endorsed by Congress.[30] That left much more to do. By the late nineteenth century, when Piatt had retired from the editorial scene, editors aimed to rid their news columns of partisan bias, leaving political opinion to the columnists.[31] Still, it was not until 1908 that the world's first school of journalism opened at the University of Missouri and began to teach the ethics of journalism to young aspirants. That did nothing for major publishers like Robert R. McCormick of the *Chicago Tribune,* whose prejudices and bias informed his paper until his death in 1955. As his biographer writes, the *Tribune* "became a megaphone to amplify the publisher's caprices."[32]

One can fault Piatt for other things than mixing lobbying with journalism. His acts, not least those as Schenck's chief of staff in Baltimore, sometimes amounted to insubordination. The letters he wrote to newspapers in wartime, when he was serving as a Union officer, were certainly out of line. Beyond insubordination, his editorial calling on citizens to prevent Hayes's inauguration in 1877 can indeed be viewed as a call to riot and rebellion. Beyond all this, Piatt's editorial attacks were not just fierce but sometimes vicious.

Still, it is his lobbying while he was an influential editor for which he deserves most criticism. Though he never praised lobbyists, he acknowledged their main role in Washington life and saw the associated evils. The king of the lobbyists during his years in the capital was Samuel Ward, brother of Julia Ward Howe and friend of Henry Wadsworth Longfellow. Piatt said there were two invitations in Washington that were never declined. One was from the president. The other was from Sam Ward. It was not good etiquette to decline the first, and it was not good sense to decline the last.[33]

Piatt denied having lobbied for the Pacific Mail Corporation. Ward, on the other hand, not only lobbied on behalf of Pacific Mail but in 1875 entertained the Ways and Means Committee of the House of Representatives with a long and humorous account of his lobbying.[34] Leaders on both sides of the Atlantic liked Ward. When U. S. Grant embarked on a trip around the world in 1877, after leaving the White House, he called on Umberto I in Rome and was amazed when the king's first question was about his "dear friend, Sam Ward of New York."[35]

Donn Piatt did not offer his writing to his readers on the basis that it was objective or unbiased or, still less, scientific. Indeed, he said, "Intellectual training makes men timid, for the more we know the less satisfied we are with our knowledge." He did not want people to view him as timid, any more than he wanted them to focus on the dimple in his chin that, Clara Morris once said, led him to grow his fine beard. He wanted people to believe that nothing would keep him from saying what he thought—no matter what others thought—about a country that was rich in politicians but "singularly barren in statesmen," where the two political parties differed only in name and in who held office, and where only five million people in a population of fifty million did any reading "and not more than one million read intelligently."[36]

That Piatt injected his biases and beliefs into the newspaper he owned was not a remarkable thing for his time. His contemporary, but not his friend, Henry J. Raymond, founder of the *New York Times* and its proprietor until his death, was at the same time a leading figure in the Republican Party. It was a time when, as a recent article in the *Wall Street Journal* says, "Newspaper publishers scoffed at the idea that they should hide their political prejudices under a cloak of objectivity."[37] Raymond, writes the *Journal*, decided at one point that the *Times* should try to be more impartial; he announced, "We shall make it a point to get into a passion as rarely as possible." If in fact he and his colleagues tried to be dispassionate, they seldom if ever spoke positively of Donn Piatt, either in Raymond's lifetime or later. Nor did Piatt like the *Times* or its politics.

Piatt's friend Henry Watterson, like Raymond, served in Congress while maintaining his position as editor of his influential Louisville paper. Horace Greeley served in Congress while remaining editor of his *Tribune*. Piatt was never offered the chance to run for Congress in his Washington years, but if the offer had been made, it would not have been on moral grounds that he rejected it.

There is no reason to whitewash Piatt. During his years at *The Capital* he was at times in the pay of people who were much in the news, people who could profit from his favorable coverage of them. He considered himself an honest man, however. He said flatly, "Fraud degrades." He always insisted that he steered clear of scandal. Perhaps he was not in the middle of any scandal, but he was not uninvolved in some cases that became scandals—and who could trust his views on the mothproofing affair when he was paid so richly by the mothproofing makers?

Piatt was accused in his time of near criminal activity in supporting Alexander Shepherd, who was himself accused of malfeasance in his work to improve the city of Washington. In recent years, however, Shepherd has been described as an unjustly maligned civic leader and an urban visionary. His statue, which had been removed from its pedestal in front of the District of Columbia government building in Washington, was returned to the site in 2005. When Washington's mayor Anthony A. Williams completed his term of office in 2006, he was given a small statue of Shepherd as what the *Washington Post* called "an icon to remember the District."[38] The full story of Shepherd remains to be told, but Piatt supported him, not to pave over the man's faults, but because Shepherd paved the streets and planted the trees and built the sewers that made Washington, if not another Paris, a far better city than it had been.

It is not to justify Piatt to say that other journalists of the time certainly engaged in more questionable activities than he did. Perhaps the worst offender was

Uriah Painter of the *Philadelphia Inquirer.* Painter was the first reporter to smell out the Crédit Mobilier scandal, but his acceptance of fees, as a historian of the time has written, "strained the definitions of legitimate journalism."[39] He could be bought either to help his clients or to attack their enemies—or both.[40]

Painter's sins are documented, but few historians have written of Abraham Lincoln's young secretary William Stoddard, whom the president liked well, twice sent on special missions, and later named federal marshal of Arkansas. During his three years in the White House, Stoddard, as noted earlier, engaged in what might be called insider trading. He also contributed 120 weekly dispatches to the *New York Examiner,* under the pseudonym of "Illinois," that amount to a running apologia for the Lincoln administration in both dark and hopeful wartime days.[41] Stoddard's columns were a kind of propaganda that we have seen at times coming from later presidential administrations, but a kind antithetical to ethical journalism in any age. His actions did not escape the attention of Donn Piatt, who said Stoddard's cipher messages conveying sensitive government information to a friend on Wall Street had made him "a buzzard in the eagle's nest."[42]

While Piatt always defended his own actions, he found the scandalous behavior of others a good subject for fiction, as well as for journalism. His play *Life in the Lobby,* published in 1875 but never performed on stage, describes how a congressman and a "Christian statesman" misuse millions of dollars that ex-slaves have deposited in the Freedman's Bank. It was a dramatized version of a real scandal. The bank had collapsed in 1874, leaving stranded most of its 61,000 mainly African American depositors. (One depositor was Piatt, who had opened an account there for *The Capital* after the bank gave him some advertising.)[43] W. E. B. Du Bois wrote, "Not even ten additional years of slavery could have done as much to throttle the thrift of the freedmen as the mismanagement and bankruptcy of the savings bank chartered by the nation for their especial end."[44]

If the bank had continued to operate, it could have helped develop a large class of middle-class black Americans. It had, however, been used to help finance the building boom in white areas of Washington. The power behind the bank was Henry D. Cooke, brother of Jay Cooke, who made a great success of selling U.S. Treasury bonds to finance wartime Union operations. It was Jay Cooke who, Piatt believed, spent thirty thousand dollars to get John Sherman elected to the Senate instead of Robert Schenck. More recently, Jay Cooke's financial dealings had helped to precipitate the nationwide Panic of 1873. But the Cookes, like the statesman in Piatt's play, were known for their Christian piety.

One must conclude that Donn Piatt, despite his faults, did years of useful service to the American republic. He was a national gadfly, mocking powerful men and digging into evils in high places. He was a muckraker a quarter century before Upton Sinclair, Lincoln Steffens, and Ida Tarbell were given that name for blasting abuses and corruption in America.

If Piatt had his faults and blind side, so did the muckrakers of the twentieth century. In 1926, two years after Fascist thugs murdered the leader of the Italian Socialists and Benito Mussolini cracked down on opposition to his regime, Ida Tarbell came home from Italy to praise Mussolini's "admirable social experiment."[45] Lincoln Steffens visited the Soviet Union in 1921, the year the first Soviet death camp was set up, and on his return told financier Bernard Baruch, "I have been over into the future, and it works."[46] In 1937, with Stalin's horrendous purges well under way, Upton Sinclair noted that Ralph Waldo Emerson had urged people to hitch their wagon to a star, "and just now the Soviet star seems to be the biggest and brightest star in the whole sky."[47]

Piatt often mocked others. He could also make fun of himself. Once, he said, when his brother-in-law, Henry Banning, was running for Congress, he had offered Banning "the use of his fraternal voice on the stump." Banning arranged for Piatt to make twenty appearances. The first of them, Piatt found, was to be the day after the election.[48]

One can only wonder how many of the stories Piatt told amounted to tall tales. Some were certainly outrageous. One tale he told was how as a young lawyer he had taken on the defense of a man indicted for arson. He won the case, but his client had no money to pay him. Then, Piatt said, "the demon of humor betrayed me." He told his client that across the street from his lodging was a black church that was holding a revival. The late-night shouting kept him from sleeping. If his client would just burn down the church, Piatt would feel fully paid for his services in defending him. The next night the church burned. A week later, Piatt said, he received a letter from the client, who was in St. Louis on his way west and who wrote to express the hope that Piatt was satisfied with the results—adding that he was "a man of honor, who never failed to repay an obligation."[49]

Piatt was always, from boyhood onward, fearless and frank. He liked to say that the man who had no enemies had no following—and that "entrenched wrong finds its most powerful defense in its respectability." He wrote with what was sometimes not just a barbed but a vicious pen. He was an activist to his end; he wrote, "We should never do nothing. It is better to wear out than to rust."[50] He wondered whether he himself had done great things and decided that a man's greatness could be measured by his enemy. We were all born, he said, to have a giant to kill, and when a man selected his giant, he instinctively took one who would give him some chance of success.

Piatt chose his giants rather well. He was no less on the mark in his criticism of America's great and mighty than were the muckrakers who followed him or, say, H. L. Mencken, the "sage of Baltimore," who snarled at blacks, Jews, and Asians as well as American presidents, and who once called the Declaration of Independence a piece of platitudinous poetry.[51]

Mencken and the muckrakers are still a live memory to American readers,[52] but time has been unkind to the memory of that complex and accomplished American, Donn Piatt. We do well to take a new look at him. We need not admire Piatt or condone his work, but what he did, what he said about famous figures and major events, can help provide a fuller view of our nation's past. If we do not know our past, as Arthur Schlesinger Jr.—somewhat echoing George Santayana— warned us before his death, we will be disabled in dealing with both our present and our future.[53]

One wishes that more survived of Piatt. What, in particular, happened to the diaries that he kept, other than the two little books that survive from his youth? Were they among the papers lost in the fire in his Washington house—or did someone deliberately burn them, angry at his frank description of Lincoln—or will they someday turn up?

The Piatt Castles, the grand houses that Donn and Abram built, still stand in the quiet and lovely countryside of western Ohio. Donn's house, now called Mac-O-Chee, was sold out of the family after Ella's death, but Abram's descendants held on to his house, Mac-A-Cheek. A Piatt family partnership bought back Mac-O-Chee in 1956, and today both of the houses and about 80 acres of the original 1,700 acres bought by Benjamin Piatt in 1828 are Piatt property. For the Piatts this is still "home," but the two houses are open to the public as a museum that interprets two centuries of Ohio land and Ohio people.[54] The surrounding country is for the most part still unspoiled farmland.

Go there, stand under the trees. Look at the two mansions, the little cemetery, and the hills and quiet stream, and imagine old days there. Imagine if you can the day in 1778 when the Shawnees captured Simon Kenton; the day in 1861 when William Dean Howells watched Donn Piatt's recruits training to be Union cavalrymen; the many days when an aged Piatt sat in his study, looking out over the countryside as he wrote to castigate evils he had seen in his long life—evils that did not end with him.

NOTES

Introduction

1. Charles W. Calhoun, "The Political Culture: Public Life and the Conduct of Politics," in *The Gilded Age: Perspectives on the Origins of Modern America,* ed. Charles W. Calhoun (Lanham, Md.: Rowman & Littlefield, 2007), 239–40.

2. Rutherford B. Hayes to Donn Piatt, November 7, 1869. Charles Richard Williams, ed., *Diary and Letters of Rutherford B. Hayes* (Columbus: Ohio State Archaeological and Historical Society, 1922), 2:69.

3. In 1906 President Theodore Roosevelt used the label for writers such as Lincoln Steffens, Upton Sinclair, and Ida Tarbell, who were exposing corruption in America. He took the term from the muck-raker in John Bunyan's *Pilgrim's Progress,* who looked only downward, raking up straw and dust, but would have seen a celestial crown if he had looked up. That was not Piatt, however, who, although he attacked those he viewed as corrupt, could also write inspirational fiction and, in his later years, Christian homilies.

4. *The Capital* (Washington, D.C.), January 23, 1873, 1.

5. There are thirty-one references to Piatt, many of them describing horseback rides, dinners, and other meetings, in Garfield's diary. See Harry James Brown and Frederick D. Williams, eds., *The Diary of James A. Garfield* (Lansing: Michigan State University Press, 1967–81).

6. James Bryce, *The American Commonwealth* (London: Macmillan, 1890), 2:660.

7. Robert C. Schenck to his daughter Sally, November 23, 1860, quoted in Lloyd Ostendorf, *Mr. Lincoln Came to Dayton* (Dayton, Ohio: Otterbein Press, 1959), 35–36.

8. Until now the only biography of Piatt has been Charles Grant Miller, *Donn Piatt: His Work and His Ways* (Cincinnati: Robert Clarke, 1893).

1. Big Fire and His Family

1. There were several Roosevelts named Nicholas. This one was a great-great-uncle of President Theodore Roosevelt.

2. The line of descent from René to Donn Piatt, worked out by Piatt family researchers, is summarized at http://www.angelfire.com/ar/pyeatt. There is more than one spelling of the name. Some Piatts pronounce the name "Pie-att," but at the Piatt Castles it is pronounced "Pee-att."

3. Jacob Piatt made a sworn declaration of his service in the Revolution on August 4, 1832, when he was eighty-five, in order to gain pension benefits under recent legislation. The text of his declaration can be viewed at http://persi.heritagequestonline.com/hqoweb/library/do/revwar/results/image?urn=urn%3Aproquest%3AUS%3Brevwar%3B50725%3B3 8150%3B1%3B&offset=0.

4. Miller, *Donn Piatt*, 12. Hannah Cook McCullough Piatt was said by Miller to have been a descendant of Captain Cook, the explorer, but she was born two years before he married, and in any case it is believed that he left no direct descendants.

5. The stories are "Hetty" and "Old Shack," in Donn Piatt, *The Lone Grave of the Shenandoah, and Other Tales* (Charleston, S.C.: BiblioBazaar, n.d.; reprint of 1888 edition).

6. Donn Piatt, *Poems and Plays* (Cincinnati: Robert Clarke & Co., 1893), 34–35.

7. Caroline Piatt Morris and Elizabeth McCullough Smith, *A Memorial Biography of Benjamin M. Piatt and Elizabeth, His Wife* (Washington, D.C.: Gray & Clarkson, Printers, 1887), 21. The biography was written by the Piatts' granddaughters, cousins of Donn Piatt. There are copies in the Piatt Castle archives [hereafter Castle archives], West Liberty, Ohio, and the library of the Ohio Historical Society at Columbus.

8. Morris and Smith, *Memorial Biography*, 33.

9. Piatt had been appointed attorney general by Governor Ninian Edwards on October 28, 1810. Clarence Edwin Carter, ed., *The Territorial Papers of the United States*, vol. 17, *The Territory of Illinois 1814–1818* (Washington, D.C.: Government Printing Office, 1950), 634–35, 646–47.

10. Miller, *Donn Piatt*, 22.

11. "Cincinnati's First Banker," clipping from unidentified newspaper, series I, box 1, Castle archives.

12. Henry B. Peetor, "Cincinnati's First Banker," *Cincinnati Enquirer*, n.d., quoted in Morris and Smith, *Memorial Biography*, 24–27. A letterbook of John Piatt, with copies of wartime correspondence with Major General William Henry Harrison and Secretary of War John Armstrong Jr. about purveying rations, is in the Manuscript Division of the Library of Congress.

13. *The Literary Club of Cincinnati 1849–1949: Centennial Book* (Cincinnati: Roessler Brothers Printers, 1949), 14.

14. Mrs. Trollope, *Domestic Manners of the Americans* (London: Whittaker, Treacher, & Co., 1832), 46–89.

15. Captain Basil Hall, *Travels in North America* (Edinburgh: Cadell and Co., 1829), 3:388.

16. Morris and Smith, *Memorial Biography*, 21.

17. Information from Family Farm Project brochure, Piatt Castles, 2007.

18. David M. Lucas, "Our Grandmother of the Shawnee: Messages of a Female Deity," http://132.235.101.197/folknography/publications/Our%20Grandmother.pdf. See also Noel Schutz Jr., "The Study of Shawnee Myth in an Ethnographic and Ethnohistorical Perspective" (PhD dissertation, Indiana University, 1975), 398–422; and R. Douglas Hurt, *The Ohio Frontier: Crucible of the Old Northwest, 1720–1830* (Bloomington: Indiana University Press, 1996), 10–12.

19. R. W. McFarland, "Simon Kenton," *Ohio History* 13, no. 1 (January 1904): 11–12.

20. Hurt, *Ohio Frontier,* 73–75.

21. Donn Piatt, "Some Memories of Mac-o-chee," clipping from Urbana, Ohio, newspaper [name not shown], December 21, 1889, Castle archives.

22. Simon Kenton got his revenge; he and a Kentucky settler named Daniel Boone were officers in the expedition. Joshua Antrim, *The History of Champaign and Logan Counties, from Their First Settlement* (Bellefontaine, Ohio: Western Pioneer Association, 1872), 181–84.

23. Perrin, William Henry, and J. H. Battle, *History of Logan County and Ohio* (Chicago: O.L. Baskin & Co., 1880), 169.

24. *National Intelligencer,* November 5, 1834. Summary in Joan M. Dixon, *National Intelligencer Newspaper Abstracts, 1834–1855* (Bowie, Md.: Heritage Books, 2000), 222.

25. Information kindly provided by James White from Family Farm project, Piatt Castles, 2007.

26. Miller, *Donn Piatt,* 34.

27. Carl Wittke, ed., *History of the State of Ohio,* vol. 3, Francis P. Weisenburger, *The Passing of the Frontier 1825–1850* (Columbus: Ohio State Archaeological and Historical Society, 1941), 37.

28. Piatt, Donn, *Sunday Meditations and Selected Prose Sketches* (Cincinnati: Robert Clarke & Co., 1893), 223–24.

29. Morris and Smith, *Memorial Biography,* 46. *Walk-in-the-Water* was the first steamboat on Lake Erie, built in 1818 and supposedly given that name by Native Americans. There was reportedly a Delaware chief named Big Fire who lived in Indiana and was a friend of the whites until his village was destroyed in the War of 1812. "Documentary: Indian Towns in Marion County," *Indiana Magazine of History* 1, no. 1 (January-March 1905): 15–16.

30. One of Donn Piatt's nephews, who bore the same name, said nine years after his uncle's death that it was his uncle himself who had changed his name to Donn after quarreling with the Dunns ("Career of Donn Piatt," *Washington Post,* November 18, 1900, 7). However, a report cited in the *Piatt Family Newsletter,* kindly brought to the author's attention by Laverne Ingram Piatt, says that it was Benjamin Piatt who changed his son's name after quarreling with the Dunns when the boy was very young. (The source cited in the newsletter is N. Louise Dodge, *The Tribe of Jacob,* 3rd ed. [Springfield, Mo.: Young-Stone Printing Co., 1934], 112–13.) It may be relevant that Donn Piatt wrote at the back of his diary for 1843, "Dann Piatt/Dunn Piatt."

31. Henry Nash Smith, *Virgin Land: The American West as Symbol and Myth* (New York: Vintage Books, 1950), 11.

32. The original Piatt house was occupied after the deaths of Benjamin and Elizabeth Piatt by descendants and was also occupied at times by tenants and laborers. In the 1970s the building was reconstructed and became a gift shop. It is now a private home.

33. Elizabeth B. Smith, "Some Remarkable Kentucky Converts," *Catholic World* 59, no. 351 (June 1894): 385.

34. Miller, *Donn Piatt,* 90.

35. Donn Piatt, "Richard Realf," *The Current* (Chicago), April 24, 1866; clipping in Castle archives.

36. Piatt family lore says that when the coast was clear for refugee slaves, Donn's mother would plant a flag in the cast-iron hand of a hitching post at the roadside—and remove it when Donn's father was home.

37. Miller, *Donn Piatt*, 43, 47–48.

38. Smith, "Some Remarkable Kentucky Converts," 386.

39. Miller, *Donn Piatt*, 33.

40. Ibid., 42.

41. Ibid., 46–47.

42. Ibid., 47.

43. David Lowenthal, "'Flesh warm & nobly human!': The impassioned purity of Hiram Powers" (paper presented at the conference "Hiram Powers e Firenze," Gabinetto Vieusseux, Florence, Italy, September 20, 2005).

44. Miller, *Donn Piatt*, 47–48.

45. Margaret C. DePalma, *Dialogue on the Frontier* (Kent, Ohio: Kent State University Press, 2004), 127.

46. Miller, *Donn Piatt*, 45–46.

47. Ibid., 50.

48. Papers of Donn Piatt and Ella Piatt, series IV, box 4, Castle archives.

49. William Blackstone, *Commentaries on the Laws of England* (Oxford: Clarendon Press, 1765), 1:36.

50. Morris and Smith, *Memorial Biography*, 93, quoting Judge Robert B. Warden in *Cincinnati, Past and Present*.

51. Miller, *Donn Piatt*, 51.

52. Diary of Donn Piatt, April 22, 1840, Castle archives.

53. Ibid., April 23, 1840; he is quoting from a 1793 poem by Robert Burns.

54. Morris and Smith, *Memorial Biography*, 70–71.

55. Walter A. McDougall, *Throes of Democracy* (New York: HarperCollins, 2008), 99.

56. Diary, March 6, 1840.

57. Ibid., March 9, 1840.

58. "The 'Sponsible Editor," *The Capital*, September 24, 1871, 2.

59. A printing press reportedly used by the young Franklin in London in 1726 is in the collections of the Smithsonian Institution.

60. Diary, July 20, 1840.

61. Some of Piatt's fights may not have had to do with politics. His diary for January 1, 1840, reports, " . . . off to a country dance in the evening—wound up with a fight. Home tired and sleepy. Washed my teeth and in bed at half past six."

62. Miller, *Donn Piatt*, 64–67.

63. Ibid., 57.

64. Ibid., 43–45; see also Keren Jane Gaumer, "Mac-o-chee Valley," *Ohio History* 26, no. 4 (October 1917): 466.

65. Clay is said—not by Donn Piatt—to have once been a guest at Mac-o-cheek (Gaumer, "Mac-o-chee Valley," 464).

66. Miller, *Donn Piatt*, 71, quoting from an 1841 diary that has not been found.

67. Christopher Leahy, "Torn Between Family and Politics: John Tyler's Struggle for Balance," *Virginia Magazine of History and Biography* 114, no. 3 (2006): 324–25.

68. Miller, *Donn Piatt*, 72.

69. Ibid., 75. Miss Woodbury made enough of an impression on Piatt that he mentioned her almost half a century later in *The Lone Grave of the Shenandoah and Other Tales*. At a guess, she was Mary Elizabeth Woodbury, the twenty-year-old daughter of Senator Levi Woodbury and the future wife of Montgomery Blair, a man whom Piatt grew to despise.

70. Ibid., 73. Piatt did not give the first name of "Miss Tyler," but Elizabeth was the only one of the president's three daughters who was then unmarried and in Washington.

71. Ibid., 74.

72. "John Marshall by Hiram Powers (1805–1873)," U.S. Senate website, http://www.senate.gov/artandhistory/art/artifact/Sculpture_21_00014.htm. See also Hiram Powers to George Perkins Marsh, December 31, 1857, George Perkins Marsh Collection, University of Vermont Library, Burlington, Vt.

2. Writer, Envoy, Lawyer, Voice

1. Gaumer, "Mac-o-chee Valley," 466.

2. Charles Dickens, *American Notes for General Circulation* (New York: D. Appleton & Co., 1868), 69.

3. In 1830, alcoholic consumption in America had reached an astonishingly high peak of 7.1 gallons per capita yearly. By 1840 this had dropped sharply to 3.1 gallons, but in 1842 a young Illinois lawyer named Lincoln could still lament that everyone had a relative who was a drunkard (Roy P. Basler, ed., *Collected Works of Abraham Lincoln* [New Brunswick, New Jersey: Rutgers University Press, 1990], 1:278). By 1850 annual consumption was down to 2.1 gallons, roughly what it has been in recent years. Franklin E. Zimring and Gordon Hawkins, *The Search for Rational Drug Control* (New York: Cambridge University Press, 1992), 54.

4. Diary, August 16, 1843.

5. Arthur M. Schlesinger Jr., *The Age of Jackson* (Boston: Little, Brown, 1953), 187.

6. "Birney withdrew from the firm this morning. D. Piatt atty. at Law." Diary, October 9, 1843.

7. For a biographical sketch of the younger James Birney see Allen Johnson, ed., *Dictionary of American Biography* (New York: Charles Scribner's Sons, 1964), 1:290.

8. Miller, *Donn Piatt*, 90.

9. In the library at the Piatt Castles is a book (*Abrégé du Voyage du Jeune Anacharsis en Grece*) awarded to her at the school on July 14, 1843, for "1st Class. Excellence."

10. Henry Howe, *Historical Collections of Ohio* (Cincinnati: C.J. Krehbiel & Co., 1908), 2:116.

11. "The Sage of Mac-o-chee," *Cincinnati Commercial Gazette,* November 13, 1891, no page; clipping in Castle archives.

12. Column by "Bell Smith" (Louise Kirby Piatt) in unnamed newspaper, September 2, 1848; Clippings scrapbook, Castle archives.

13. Piatt wrote to his new friend Salmon P. Chase on July 27, 1848, that "Louise sends her love and also the card of Master Mac-a-chee Piatt to Mrs. Chase," Salmon P. Chase Papers, Library of Congress.

14. Miller, *Donn Piatt*, 89.

15. Two songs published in the 1840s with lyrics by Piatt, "By Fair Ohio's Waters" and "We May Not Meet Again," are in the American Sheet Music collection of the Library of Congress. There is no reason to believe that Piatt found lyric writing profitable, or that he spent much time at it.

16. Miller, *Donn Piatt*, 89, says they were "constant contributors" to the four papers. A number of newspaper columns by Louise are in a scrapbook labeled "SCRAPS," Castle archives.

17. McDougall, *Throes of Democracy*, 15.

18. Frederick J. Blue, *Salmon P. Chase: A Life in Politics* (Kent, Ohio: Kent State University Press, 1987), 29.

19. Miller, *Donn Piatt*, 90–91. Birney had the year wrong. Piatt's diary for 1843 shows that he spent the nights of July 31 and August 1 helping to defend Burnett's house. It does not record blows inflicted.

20. William Birney, *James G. Birney and His Times: The Genesis of the Republican Party with Some Account of Abolition Movements in the South before 1828* (New York: D. Appleton and Company, 1890), 251.

21. *Journal of the House of Representatives,* February 20, 1846, http://loc.gov/cgi-bin/ampage?collId=llhj&fileName=041/llhj041.db&recNum439.

22. Steven J. Ross, "We Who Built the Queen City," *Queen City Heritage* 47, no. 1 (Summer 1989): 13–14.

23. James S. Buckingham, *The Eastern and Western States of America* (London: Fisher, Son, & Co., 1842), 2:382.

24. Miller, *Donn Piatt*, 88, gives a list of visitors.

25. Joan Steele, *Captain Mayne Reid* (Boston: Twayne Publishers, 1978), 23. *The Rifle Rangers* was published in London in 1850.

26. Donn Piatt, "Memories of Eminent Authors," quoted in Elizabeth Reid and Charles H. Coe, *Captain Mayne Reid: His Life and Adventures* (London: Greening & Co., 1900), 83.

27. John Niven, "Introduction," in *The Salmon P. Chase Papers,* ed. John Niven, 1:xviii–xxi (Kent, Ohio: Kent State University Press, 1993).

28. Virginia Tatnall Peacock, *Famous American Belles of the Nineteenth Century* (Philadelphia: J.P. Lippincott Company, 1901), 220.

29. "The Free Territory Convention of Ohio," *National Era* 11, no. 78 (June 29, 1848): 103.

30. Donn Piatt, *Memories of the Men Who Saved the Union* (New York: Belford, Clarke & Company, 1887), 100.

31. For a brief summary of Chase's political evolution see http://en.wikipedia.org/wiki/Salmon_P._Chase.

32. Robert Bruce Warden, *An Account of the Private Life and Public Services of Salmon Portland Chase* (Cincinnati: Wilstach, Baldwin & Co., 1874), 328. See also Niven, *Salmon P. Chase Papers,* 1:198.

33. John Niven, *Salmon P. Chase: A Biography* (New York: Oxford University Press, 1995), 118–123. Also see "Black Laws of 1807," Ohio History Central: An Online Encyclopedia of Ohio History, http://www.ohiohistorycentral.org/entry.php?rec=1505.

34. Warden, *An Account,* 659.

35. Piatt, *Men Who Saved the Union,* 50.

36. Carl Sandburg, *Abraham Lincoln: The War Years* (New York: Harcourt, Brace & Company, 1939), 1:445.

37. One might wonder whether Stanton had gone to Zanesfield, the town near Mac-o-cheek, rather than across the state to Zanesville, but Piatt said it was Zanesville in *Memories of the Men Who Saved the Union,* 54.

38. Benjamin Thomas and Harold M. Hyman, *Stanton: The Life and Times of Lincoln's Secretary of War* (New York: Knopf, 1962), 41.

39. Blue, *Salmon P. Chase,* 67.

40. Information from the 1850 census and other sources, reproduced in "They Lived Long on the Land," Family Farm Project brochure, Piatt Castles, 2007.

41. Miller, *Donn Piatt,* 93.

42. Ibid., 94.

43. Ibid., 95.

44. Eslie Asbury, "Rutherford B. Hayes and the Literary Club," *Queen City Heritage* (Spring 1989): 34.

45. Watt P. Marchman, "Rutherford B. Hayes, Attorney at Law," *Ohio History 77,* no. 1, 2, 3 (Summer 1968): 23–25.

46. Philip Weeks, *Buckeye Presidents: Ohioans in the White House* (Kent, Ohio: Kent State University Press, 2003), 92.

47. Gertrude Garrison, "Our New York Letter. As to Donn Piatt and His Life Work," *Hornellsville Weekly Tribune* (Hornellsville, New York), June 22, 1888, 7. Garrison was associate editor of the *New York Sun* and a novelist. If Piatt and Hawthorne remained friends, it was at a distance. After their initial meeting it seems unlikely they ever met again, although Piatt was in Paris for part of the time Hawthorne served at Liverpool, and they may have been in Washington at the same time in 1862.

48. Coffin's work in bringing over three thousand slaves to freedom over three decades is described in Fergus M. Bordewich, *Bound for Canaan* (New York: Amistad, 2005).

49. R. A. M., "A Reminiscence of the Slavery Era," *Boston Traveller,* December 5, 1891; clipping in Castle archives. R. A. M. does not name the little college in Northwood where he said he studied, but Geneva Hall was founded in Northwood in 1848, was later renamed Geneva College, and moved to Beaver Falls, Pennsylvania, its present location, in 1880.

50. Piatt, "Old Shack," in *The Lone Grave of the Shenandoah,* 81–82.

51. For example, most British ambassadors to the United States have been members of the British diplomatic service; the last one who was not (Peter Jay) left Washington in 1979. In contrast, since 1785 there has been only one American ambassador to the United Kingdom (Raymond Seitz, 1991–94) who was a career officer. As of the end of 2011, every major American embassy except those in Baghdad, Brasilia, Cairo, Jakarta, and Kabul was in the hands of a political appointee, while all the foreign ambassadors to the United States from major countries were career officers. For a current list of American ambassadors see http://history.state.gov/departmenthistory/people/chiefsofmission. For a list from 1778 to 1990—which identifies individuals as career or non-career—see *Principal Officers of the Department of State and United States Chiefs of Mission 1778–1990* (Washington, D.C.: Department of State, Office of the Historian, 1991).

52. Wood to Marcy, November 19, 1853, Marcy Papers, Library of Congress.

53. The recommendations and the Giffin letter are in Records Relating to Appointments & Commissions 1853–59, Department of State, Records Group (hereafter RG) 59, Microfilm Publication (hereafter M) 967, roll 35, National Archives & Records Administration, College Park, Maryland (hereafter NARA). Also included is an undated list of recommendations for Piatt received in the State Department, including one from "Hon. Stephen A. Douglass." There is, however, no letter from Senator Douglas in the file.

54. "Foreigners—Two Views," *National Era* 9, no. 432 (April 12, 1855): 58.

55. O'Sullivan was a reformer who stood for American military intervention abroad in support of democratic movements—and who was to support the Confederacy in the Civil War. Before the 1852 election, his *Democratic Review* had urged election of a president aged around thirty-five, the minimum age under the Constitution. After Pierce was elected, the journal did a flip-flop, saying he would be only forty-nine when inaugurated.

It was O'Sullivan who invented the term "manifest destiny." Peter Bridges, *Pen of Fire: John Moncure Daniel* (Kent, Ohio: Kent State University Press, 2002), 29–30, 63–64, 74.

56. Thomas Keneally, *American Scoundrel: The Life of the Notorious Civil War General Dan Sickles* (New York: Nan A. Talese / Doubleday, 2002), 20, 31–32; John W. Forney, *Anecdotes of Public Men* (New York: Harper & Brothers, 1873), 318.

57. Letter from Louise to her father, February 1853, quoted in Miller, *Donn Piatt,* 100.

58. Although the Piatts reached Europe safely, sea voyages then were not without danger. A year after their crossing, the ship they had taken, the *Franklin,* was wrecked off the coast of Long Island, fortunately without loss of life.

59. Letter from Louise to her father, August 4, 1853, quoted in Miller, *Donn Piatt,* 101–103.

60. Bridges, *Pen of Fire,* 115–16, n250.

61. "Romance of a Countess," *Indiana Progress* (Indiana, Penn.), October 17, 1878, 2.

62. Louise Kirby Piatt, *Bell Smith Abroad* (New York: J.C. Derby, 1855). See also "A Charming Volume," *National Era* 9, no. 437 (May 17, 1855): 79. Before going to France "Bell Smith" had contributed a number of pieces to the *Louisville Journal* on life in Cincinnati that were reprinted in the *Cincinnati Commercial;* clippings are in a scrapbook entitled "SCRAPS," Castle archives.

63. Miller, *Donn Piatt,* 107, says Piatt "wrote constantly for the American and English press" in his first year in France. The author has not been able to confirm this. Some of Piatt's articles may have been published anonymously.

64. Abram wrote the president on March 29, 1854, that Donn was still waiting for his commission, "having gone to France prematurely on your kind and generous assurance . . ." (Records Relating to Appointments & Commissions 1853–59, RG 59, M 967, roll 35, NARA).

65. Paris dispatches to secretary of state, no. 1, January 28, 1854, and no. 30, August 7, 1854, Letterbook A, Mason Family Papers, 1825–1902, Virginia Historical Society, Richmond (hereafter VHS).

66. The only full biography of Daniel is Bridges, *Pen of Fire.*

67. Daniel W. Crofts, *Old Southampton: Politics and Society in a Virginia County, 1834–1869* (Charlottesville: University Press of Virginia, 1992), 34–35.

68. Piatt, "Cuba and the Ostend Manifesto," *Harper's New Monthly Magazine* 40, no. 240 (May 1870): 901.

69. Paris dispatches to secretary of state, no. 36, October 25, 1854, and no. 37, October 30, 1854, RG 59, M 34, roll 9, NARA; copies also in Letterbook A, Mason Family Papers, VHS.

70. For a summary of events relating to Cuba; the Ostend Manifesto; and related matters, including Piatt's travels to London—he went to see Soulé twice—see Samuel Flagg Bemis, ed., *The American Secretaries of State and Their Diplomacy* (New York: Knopf, 1928), 6.183–216.

71. For Paris legation reporting on France and the Crimean War, see Letterbooks A and B, Mason Family Papers, VHS.

72. "Four Days Later from Europe," *National Era* 8, no. 413 (November 30, 1854): 191.

73. Piatt reported to Mason on his meetings in Washington in two letters, both dated November 27, 1854, Mason Family Papers, section 24, VHS.

74. The legation informed the foreign minister, Count Alexandre Walewski, of Mason's illness on January 16, 1855. Mason wrote the minister in a note of May 16, 1855, that he had returned to work, his health restored. Letterbook B, Mason Family Papers, VHS.

75. Piatt to Marcy, January 18, 1855, RG 59, M 34, roll 40, NARA.

76. Letters written by Mason after his return to work are in a miniscule, quavering hand with many words crossed out and rewritten; Mason Family Papers, section 24, VHS.

77. Piatt left Paris on October 16, 1855; Paris dispatch to secretary of state, no. 79, October 18, 1855, Letterbook C, Mason Family Papers, VHS.

78. Folder "October and November 1855, Correspondence with and concerning Donn Piatt," RG 84, Department of State, Records of Foreign Service Posts, France 1853–59, vol. 0660, NARA.

79. "Americans Abroad," *National Era* 9, no. 465 (November 29, 1855): 189.

80. Piatt to Daniel, October 17, 1855, quoted in Bridges, *Pen of Fire,* 109.

81. Bridges, *Pen of Fire,* 92–94, 104–6, 108–9; Miller, *Donn Piatt,* 121–22.

82. Letter from Justice Peter Vivian Daniel, Washington, D.C., to John Moncure Daniel, Turin, July 30, 1857, quoted in Bridges, *Pen of Fire,* 130.

83. Crofts, *Old Southampton,* 23–25.

84. Donn Piatt to Robert C. Schenck, December 6, 1860, Abraham Lincoln Papers, Library of Congress.

85. Piatt, *Bell Smith Abroad,* 323–26.

86. A silver loving cup presented to the Piatts by grateful Americans in Paris still forms part of the collection of the Piatt Castles in Ohio.

87. "Memories of Greeley," *The Capital,* May 12, 1872, 2.

88. Glyndon G. Van Deusen, *Horace Greeley, Nineteenth-Century Crusader* (Philadelphia: University of Pennsylvania Press, 1953), 196.

89. "Memories of Greeley."

90. Horace Greeley, *Recollections of a Busy Life* (New York: Arno Press, 1970; reprint of 1868 edition), 333–35. Andrew Dickson White (later president of Cornell University and three times an ambassador) recalled how after Greeley's release he went to Madame Busque's restaurant, much frequented by Americans, and wanted to order green beans: "Addressing one of the serving-maids, he said 'Flawronce, donney moy—donney moy—' and then, unable to remember the word, he impatiently screamed out in a high treble, thrusting out his plate at the same time, '*beans.*' The crowd of us burst into laughter; whereupon Donn Piatt, then secretary of the legation at Paris . . . said 'Why, Greeley, you don't improve a bit; you knew beans yesterday'" (Andrew Dickson White, "Russia in War-Time," *Century Illustrated Magazine* 58, no. 4 (August 1904): 602).

91. "Dick Tinto" (Frank Boott Goodrich), "Parisian Gossip," *New York Daily Times,* November 1, 1855, 2.

92. Greeley to Piatt, October 18, 1855, Department of Rare Books and Special Collections, Rush Rhees Library, University of Rochester, Rochester, New York. Greeley's wife had suffered miscarriages and the loss of an older son and was in poor health. She did not take ship with Piatt but stayed on in Europe for some months.

93. Donn Piatt, "Souvenir of Imperial Sovereigns," *The Galaxy* 11, no. 2 (February 1871): 241–46. Mason also appears in Donn Piatt, "Our Presentation at Court," *Harper's New Monthly Magazine* 38, no. 226 (March 1869): 495–98, and Piatt, "Cuba and the Ostend Manifesto," 898–901.

94. Donn Piatt, "My Diplomacy at Paris," *The Capital,* December 8, 1878, 6.

95. In the Civil War the younger Wise became a Confederate officer and was killed at the battle of Roanoke Island. "War Notes," *Virginia Magazine of History and Biography* 27, no. 1 (January 1919): 78.

96. "Americans Abroad," *New York Times,* November 19, 1855, 1. Piatt had induced Fleischmann and another American friend to start an English-language newspaper in Paris called *The American.* The paper apparently ceased publication soon after Piatt left France, perhaps because of competition from a better-known English-language paper, *Galignani's Messenger,* a sort of *International Herald Tribune* of its day. *Galignani's* had been publishing for decades and was widely read by Americans across the Continent for its news from America (Miller, *Donn Piatt,* 120–21; Bridges, *Pen of Fire,* 87).

97. Piatt's letter to the *Times* was reprinted in the *National Era* 9, no. 465 (November 29, 1855): 189.

98. Piatt, *Men Who Saved the Union,* 54–55.

99. Gordon N. Ray, ed., *The Letters and Private Papers of William Makepeace Thackeray* (Cambridge, Mass.: Harvard University Press, 1946), 3:594, n85.

100. Gaumer, "Mac-o-chee Valley," 468.

101. Bridges, *Pen of Fire,* 56.

102. McDougall, *Throes of Democracy,* 344.

103. See Robert E. May, *Manifest Destiny's Underworld: Filibustering in Antebellum America* (Chapel Hill: University of North Carolina Press, 2002). Filibustering by Americans went on for a long time. As late as 1898 Stephen Crane wrote of "the filibustering industry, flourishing now in the United States" (Crane, "Flanagan and His Short Filibustering Adventure," *The Open Boat and Other Stories* [London: William Heinemann, 1898], 132).

104. Charles Theodore Greve, *Centennial History of Cincinnati and Representative Citizens* (Chicago: Biographical Publishing Company, 1904), 1:735. For the judge's finding that the defendants should be discharged, see Circuit Court of the United States, February Term, 1856, *United States v. Samuel Lumsden et al.,* in *Reports of Cases Argued and Determined in the Federal Courts Held in Ohio* (Norwalk, Ohio: Laning Printing Company, 1900), 3:344–59. The author is indebted to Charles E. Kallendorf of the Hamilton County Law Library, Cincinnati, for locating this volume.

105. The name Republican dates from a rally held in Jackson, Michigan, in July 1854. (Among the organizers at Jackson was Zachariah Chandler, who was to become a U.S. senator and later a favorite target of Donn Piatt.)

106. William E. Gienapp, *The Origins of the Republican Party 1852–1856* (New York: Oxford University Press, 1987), 308.

107. Buchanan to Pierce, April 7, 1854, in James Bassett Moore, ed., *The Works of James Buchanan* (Philadelphia: J.P. Lippincott, 1909), 9:176.

108. Payment was approved by a private Act of March 2, 1857 (George Minot and George P. Sawyer, eds., *Statutes at Large and Treaties of the United States of America from December 3, 1855, to March 3, 1859* [Boston: Little, Brown, 1859], 11.507).

109. Piatt to James A. Pike, September 13, 1857 (Pike, *First Blows of the Civil War* [New York: American News Company, 1879], 376).

110. Stanley Harrold, *Gamaliel Bailey and Antislavery Union* (Kent, Ohio: Kent State University Press, 1986), 190, 209–10.

111. Most American cities had volunteer firemen, a system dating to the company Benjamin Franklin founded in Philadelphia in 1736. By the mid-1800s, though, many volunteer companies were composed of ruffians who fought one another and blackmailed citizens for higher rates. Jacob Wykoff Piatt, member of the city council, proposed a paid department to replace the volunteers and was shouted down by a mob in the council chambers.

Later a larger mob gathered at his house and threatened to hang him. Eventually, Wykoff's proposal won out; soon all major cities had professional firemen. Years later Donn Piatt told the story for Wykoff's descendants in "The Paid Fire Department," dated October 1886, in Morris and Smith, *Memorial Biography,* 85–89.

112. Miller, *Donn Piatt,* 123–24.

113. For a list of more than fifty poems Sarah Bryan contributed to the *Journal* before she married, see Larry R. Michaels, ed., *That New World: Selected Poems of Sarah Piatt, 1861–1911* (Toledo, Ohio: Bihl House Publishing, 1999), 247–51.

114. Burlingame became famous in the following decade as the American envoy to China—and, later, China's envoy to the major powers.

115. As a Union general at the battle of Gettysburg in 1863, Sickles endangered the Union's left flank by bringing his forces too far forward from Cemetery Ridge. Later, though, he was viewed by many as a hero, after losing his leg in the battle. While serving as American envoy to Spain after the war, he notably carried on an affair with the former Queen of Spain, Isabella II—but in Paris, not Madrid (Keneally, *American Scoundrel*).

116. Donn Piatt, "Washington Letter. Anson Burlingame," *Cincinnati Commercial,* March 1, 1870, 8.

117. "Dreadful Tragedy," *New York Times,* February 28, 1859, 1.

118. "Mr. Donn Piatt," *National Era* 13, no. 646 (May 19, 1859): 79, reprinted by Mac-a-Cheek Press.

119. *Literary Club of Cincinnati,* 56.

120. By the time the club reached its centennial year, in 1949, its members had included two American presidents, two chief justices, seven cabinet members, four ambassadors, and twenty members of Congress (*Literary Club of Cincinnati,* 31).

121. Later that year Spofford left journalism for good, initially in order to become the chief assistant to the librarian of Congress, John G. Stephenson. Three years later Stephenson resigned, and Spofford began to direct the affairs of the Library of Congress. Over the next three decades, with support from Hayes after he became president, Spofford built a small congressional research library into the great library of today. See John Y. Cole, *Ainsworth Spofford: Bookman and Librarian* (Littleton, Colo.: Libraries Unlimited, 1975). Cole, director of the Center for the Book in the Library of Congress, has published many works on Spofford and the library. For Cole and a listing of his works, see *Historical Essays in Honor of John Y. Cole,* ed. Mary Niles Maack (Washington, D.C.: Library of Congress, 2011), 170–97.

122. Piatt, *Men Who Saved the Union,* 133–71. Piatt's claim to intimacy with Seward does not seem to be confirmed by existing evidence, although they met at least several times and the University of Rochester library contains a friendly letter Piatt wrote Seward on June 4, 1856.

123. Alan Nevins and Henry Steele Commager, with Jeffrey Brandon Morris, *A Pocket History of the United States* (New York: Pocket Books, 1992), 208.

124. Piatt, "Richard Realf." For a recent fictionalized version of Realf's life, see George Rathmell, *A Passport to Hell: The Mystery of Richard Realf* (Lincoln, Neb.: Authors Choice Press, 2002); see also "Richard Realf: Memories of a True Poet and Selections from His Poems. George Newell Lovejoy in the Baldwin's Monthly," *Washington Post,* August 10, 1884, 6. Richard J. Hinton, Union officer and biographer of John Brown, claimed that rather than Piatt helping Realf, Realf lent Piatt $600; this seems very unlikely. See memoir by Hinton in Richard Realf, *Poems of Richard Realf* (New York: Funk & Ingalls, 1898), xlvii–liii. Realf

went on from West Liberty to Columbus, where he met a young writer named William Dean Howells, who decades later remembered him as well dressed and "a charming youth . . . girlishly beautiful" (Howells, *Years of My Youth* [New York: Harper & Brothers, 1916], 191). Realf, born into a poor family in England in 1834, became a Union officer in the Civil War. He was a talented poet but a failure financially; he killed himself in California in 1878.

125. After the Civil War, West served as Ohio attorney general and then as a justice on the Ohio state supreme court.

126. *Providence Journal,* no date, quoted in the *National Era* 13, no. 640 (April 7, 1859): 54.

127. "A correspondent of the *Press,*" quoted in Miller, *Donn Piatt,* 135.

128. "The Gentle, the Polished, and the Humane," *New-York Daily Tribune,* August 18, 1860, 6.

129. "Young Men's Republican Union," *New-York Daily Tribune,* August 29, 1860, 5.

130. Schenck to Lincoln, August 16 and August 18, 1860, Abraham Lincoln Papers, Library of Congress, Series 1, General Correspondence 1833–1916; Lincoln to Schenck, August 23, 1860, in Roy P. Basler, ed., *The Collected Works of Abraham Lincoln* (New Brunswick, N.J.: Rutgers University Press, 1953), 4:99–100.

131. Morris and Smith, *Memorial Biography,* 8.

132. Lincoln and Herndon to Zopher Case, clerk of the U.S. circuit court, Carlyle, Illinois, December 29, 1859 (Basler, *Collected Works,* 3:513).

133. Clare Dowler, "John James Piatt, Representative Figure of a Momentous Period," *Ohio History* 45, no. 1 (January 1936): 7.

134. Miller, *Donn Piatt,* 135.

135. "The Campaign in Egypt," *Chicago Daily Tribune,* November 2, 1860, 2.

136. "Personal," *New-York Daily Tribune,* September 29, 1860, 5.

137. Donn Piatt, "Robert Cummins Schenck," *Belford's Magazine* (June 1890), 46.

138. "Appointments of Hon. R. C. Schenck and Donn Piatt," *Chicago Press and Tribune,* October 8, 1860, 1.

139. Piatt, *Men Who Saved the Union,* 29.

140. John Sherman, *Recollections of Forty Years in the House, Senate and Cabinet* (Chicago: Werner Company, 1896), 215.

141. Ida M. Tarbell, *The Life of Abraham Lincoln* (New York: Macmillan Company, 1928), 1:418.

142. Basler, *Collected Works,* 4:136.

143. Donn Piatt, "Mrs. Lincoln and Pension," *Cincinnati Commercial,* May 9, 1870, no page; clipping in volume titled "Correspondence," Castle archives.

144. "The Urbana Citizen," *Mac-a-cheek Press,* April 20, 1861, 4.

145. Piatt, in Allen Thorndike Rice, ed., *Reminiscences of Abraham Lincoln by Distinguished Men of His Time* (New York: North American Review, 1888), 479.

146. Piatt, *Men Who Saved the Union,* 29.

147. Ibid., 30.

148. Miller, *Donn Piatt,* 140.

149. Ward Hill Lamon, *Life of Abraham Lincoln* (Lincoln: University of Nebraska Press, 1999; reprint of 1872 edition), 457.

150. Carl Sandburg, *Abraham Lincoln: The Prairie Years* (New York: Harcourt, Brace & Company, 1926), 2:411.

151. "Lincoln at Home," *Mac-a-cheek Press,* November 17, 1860, 4 (article written by "A friend lately on a visit to Springfield," undoubtedly Donn Piatt).

152. Villard dispatch dated November 25, 1860, quoted in Harold G. and Oswald Garrison Villard, eds., *Lincoln on the Eve of '61: A Journalist's story by Henry Villard* (New York: Knopf, 1941), 85.

153. "So Ho! Don!" *Vanity Fair,* December 8, 1860, 289.

154. Robert C. Schenck, Tremont House, Chicago, to "My dear Sally," November 23, 1860, quoted in Ostendorf, *Mr. Lincoln Came to Dayton.* Ostendorf noted that the letter was then in the "Schenck papers, owned by R. C. Schenck, Dayton."

155. Piatt, *Men Who Saved the Union,* 33–34.

156. "Hon. Donn Piatt and the President Elect," *Mac-a-cheek Press,* December 22, 1860, 4.

157. "The Incoming Administration: The Cabinet of Mr. Lincoln Completed," *New York Herald,* March 3, 1861, no page, http://www.accessible.com/accessible/text/civilwar/00000006/00000631.htm.

158. William O. Stoddard Jr., ed., *Lincoln's Third Secretary: The Memoirs of William O. Stoddard* (New York: Exposition Press, 1955), 7–10.

159. At least, the *Mac-a-cheek Press* for December 22, 1860, said there was such a rumor.

160. "A Lincoln man," Cincinnati, to Hon. Abraham Lincoln, November 23, 1860, Abraham Lincoln Papers, Library of Congress. Image at http://memory.loc.gov/mss/mal/mal1/046/0461000/001.gif.

161. Robert C. Schenck, Newark, Ohio, to Hon. Abraham Lincoln, Springfield, December 10, 1860, Abraham Lincoln Papers, Library of Congress. Image at http://memory.loc.gov/mss/mal/mal1/049/0496500/001.gif.

162. Lamon, *Life of Abraham Lincoln,* 459.

3. A Soldier in the Great War

1. Quoted in Lamon, *Abraham Lincoln,* 509.

2. Greeley, quoted in Ray Allen Billington, *American History Before 1877* (Lanham, Md.: Littlefield Adams, 1981), 215.

3. Susan Goodman and Carl Dawson. *William Dean Howells: A Writer's Life* (Berkeley: University of California Press, 2005), 48.

4. Francis P. Weisenburger, "Lincoln and His Ohio Friends," *Ohio History* 68, no. 3 (July 1959): 242–45.

5. *Mac-a-cheek Press,* April 20, 1861, 4.

6. Miller, *Donn Piatt,* 141.

7. Ibid., 143.

8. Howells, *New York World,* May 15, 1861, quoted in Thomas Wortham, ed., *The Early Prose Writings of William Dean Howells* (Athens: Ohio University Press 1990), 315.

9. A. Sanders Piatt to Lincoln, March 28, 1861, RG 59, M 650, roll 39, NARA.

10. Robert P. Kennedy, *The Historical Review of Logan County, Ohio* (Chicago: S.J. Clarke, 1903), 267.

11. Fred B. Joyner, "Robert Cumming Schenck, First Citizen and Statesman of the Miami Valley," *Ohio History* 58, no. 3 (July 1949): 293.

12. Schenck to Lincoln, May 17, 1861, Abraham Lincoln Papers, Library of Congress, series 1, General Correspondence, 1833–1916. Lincoln's original offer to Schenck is reported by several sources; see, for example, Peter Bridges, "Lawyer, Ex-Judge Answer the Call," *Washington Times,* April 6, 2007, 8.

13. "Gen. Schenck's Defense," *New York Times,* June 30, 1861, 3.

14. Fred B. Joyner, "William Cortenus Schenck, Pioneer and Statesman of Ohio," *Ohio History* 47, no. 4 (October 1938): 363–71. The brother of Robert C. Schenck, James Findlay Schenck, served as a navy officer from 1825 to 1869 and retired as a rear admiral.

15. Herbert H. Harwood Jr., *Rails to the Blue Ridge: The Washington and Old Dominion Railroad 1847–1968* (Fairfax Station: Northern Virginia Regional Park Authority, 2000), 16–17. Even though the war was just beginning, anti-Union sentiment ran high in northern Virginia. The bodies of the ten Ohio soldiers lay in the sun for some days, scorned by the villagers. Finally, a local man, worried about disease, dug a large hole and buried them. That evening he heard that a posse was coming after him as a Union sympathizer, and he fled Virginia until war's end (Colonel [ret.] G. H. Dimon Jr., USAF, who was told the story when he lived in Vienna, 1968–71, by a woman whose ancestor had buried the soldiers; communications to the author dated July 24 and July 30, 2007).

16. "Brig.-Gen. Schenck," *New York Times,* June 19, 1861, 1. See also Bridges, "Lawyer, Ex-Judge Answer the Call."

17. R. B. Hayes, Up Gauley River, Camp Sewell, to S. Birchard, October 3, 1861, in *Diary and Letters of Rutherford Birchard Hayes,* 2:106–7.

18. Sherman to Ellen Ewing Sherman, July 28, 1861, in Brooks D. Simpson and Jean V. Berlin, eds., *Sherman's Civil War: Selected Correspondence of William T. Sherman 1860–1865* (Chapel Hill: University of North Carolina Press, 1999), 124.

19. "A Lesson from Bull Run," *New York Times,* August 14, 1861, 2.

20. "What the London Times Correspondent Saw at Charleston," *New York Times,* May 28, 1861, 2. William Howard Russell, *My Diary North and South* (Boston: T.O.H.P. Burnham, 1863), 391, 404.

21. Miller, *Donn Piatt,* 150–51.

22. Ibid., 153.

23. Erasmus Darwin Keyes, *Fifty Years' Observation of Men and Events, Civil and Military* (New York: Charles Scribner's Sons, 1884), 435.

24. Piatt, quoted in Donald Grant Mitchell, *Daniel Tyler: A Memorial Volume Containing His Autobiography and War Record, Some Account of His Later Years, with Various Reminiscences and the Tributes of Friends* (New Haven, Conn.: Privately printed, 1883), 72–73; text at http://persi.heritagequestonline.com/hqoweb/library/do/books/results/imag e?urn=urn%3Aproquest%3AUS%3Bglhbooks%3BGenealogy-glh35550174%3B-1%3B-1%3B.

25. "Mr. Russell and the London Times on the Bull Run Panic," *New York Times,* August 21, 1861, 4.

26. Margaret Leech, *Reveille in Washington* (New York: Carroll & Graf, 1991; reprint of 1941 edition), 126.

27. Bruce Tap, *Over Lincoln's Shoulder: The Committee on the Conduct of the War* (Lawrence: University of Kansas Press, 1998), 28–29.

28. Piatt, address to 25th Reunion of the Army of the Cumberland, Toledo, Ohio, manuscript copy, no date, Box 5, file 8, series IV, manuscripts, subseries I, Castle archives.

29. Mitchell, *Daniel Tyler,* 73–74.

30. Leech, *Reveille in Washington,* 288.

31. Mary Todd Lincoln to Elizabeth Todd Grimsley, September 29, 1861, in Justin G. Turner and Linda Levitt Turner, eds., *Mary Todd Lincoln: Her Life and Letters* (New York: Knopf, 1972), 106.

32. Jean H. Baker, *Mary Todd Lincoln* (New York: Norton, 1987), 187.

33. Cox, an Ohioan, was later governor of Ohio and U.S. secretary of the interior.

34. Jacob D. Cox, "McClellan in West Virginia," in *Battles and Leaders of the Civil War,* ed. Robert Underwood Johnson and Clarence Clough Buel, 1:145 (Edison, N.J.: Castle, 2004; reprint of 1887–88 edition).

35. C. H. Ambler, "General R.E. Lee's Northwest Virginia Campaign," *West Virginia History* 5, no. 2 (January 1944): 101–15.

36. Letter in *New York Tribune,* December 30, 1861, signed Donn Piatt, no page; clipping in Castle archives.

37. Miller, *Donn Piatt,* 151–62.

38. Bridges, *Pen of Fire,* 180.

39. Piatt, Washington, D.C., to Schenck, January 19, 1862, Robert C. Schenck Collection, Miami University Archives, Oxford, Ohio.

40. Copy, not in Piatt's hand, of Piatt letter to John Swinton, April 13, 1886, series IV, box 6, Castle archives.

41. Piatt, Willard's Hotel, Washington, D.C., to Schenck, February 13, 1862, series IV, box 6, Castle archives.

42. Piatt, Washington, D.C., to Schenck, February 4, 1862, series IV, box 6, Castle archives.

43. Ibid., February 17, 1862.

44. Ibid., February 18, 1862.

45. Miller, *Donn Piatt,* 152.

46. James M. McPherson, *Tried by War: Abraham Lincoln as Commander in Chief* (New York: Penguin Press, 2008), 102.

47. George B. McClellan, *McClellan's Own Story: The War for the Union* (New York: Charles L. Webster, 1887), 149–50.

48. Donn Piatt, "Memoirs and Memories of John Charles Fremont, Part II," handwritten manuscript, series IV, subseries I, box 5, Castle archives. Miller presumably used this manuscript, dated 1886, for his slightly different account of the Stanton-Piatt meetings in *Donn Piatt,* 155–56.

49. Leech, *Reveille in Washington,* 190.

50. John Pope, "The Second Battle of Bull Run," in Johnson and Buel, *Battles and Leaders of the Civil War,* 2:487.

51. Hunter was to serve in 1865 as president of the military commission that tried the eight persons accused of conspiring to kill President Lincoln.

52. Miller, *Donn Piatt,* 158.

53. Wallace to his wife, December 14, 1862, quoted in Stephen D. Engle, *Don Carlos Buell: Most Promising of All* (Chapel Hill: University of North Carolina Press, 1999), 325.

54. Lew Wallace, *An Autobiography* (New York: Harper & Brothers, 1906), 2:643.

55. Henry M. Cist, *The Army of the Cumberland* (New York: Charles Scribner's Sons, 1882), 76.

56. Engle, *Don Carlos Buell,* 92–93, 281.

57. Gerald J. Prokopowicz, *All for the Regiment: The Army of the Ohio, 1861–1862* (Chapel Hill: University of North Carolina Press, 2001), 186.

58. Engle, *Don Carlos Buell,* 201.

59. Kenneth M. Stampp, *Indiana Politics During the Civil War* (Indianapolis: Indiana Historical Bureau, 1949), 158–59.

60. Miller, *Donn Piatt,* 159–60.

61. Engle, *Don Carlos Buell,* 287.

62. Piatt, quoted in Mitchell, *Daniel Tyler,* 75.

63. Holt, a Republican lawyer from Kentucky, had been postmaster general and secretary of war in the Buchanan administration. In 1865 he was the presiding judge in the trial of the eight persons accused of having conspired, together with John Wilkes Booth, to kill President Lincoln.

64. Piatt, Cincinnati, to Holt, March 26, 1863, Joseph Holt Papers, Library of Congress.

65. Noah Brooks, journalist and friend of Lincoln, told the president "that Halleck was disliked because many people supposed that he was too timid and hesitating in his military conduct" in Brooks, *Washington in Lincoln's Time* (New York: Rinehart & Company, 1958; reprint of 1895 edition), 131.

66. Piatt, quoted in Mitchell, *Daniel Tyler,* 76.

67. Wallace gives the text of the Opinion in his *Autobiography,* 2:646–52. The full record of the commission's proceedings is in chapter 28, "Findings of the 'Buell Commission' and Accompanying Documents," *Official Records of the Union and Confederate Armies, Additions and Corrections to Series I, Volume XVI* (Washington, D.C.: Government Printing Office, 1902). 6–726.

68. Piatt, *Men Who Saved the Union,* 38–39.

69. Mitchell, *Daniel Tyler,* 73–74.

70. Piatt, *Men Who Saved the Union,* 37–39. Another, similar account by Piatt of the encounter with Lincoln is in Mitchell, *Daniel Tyler,* 78.

71. Presumably, Dr. John A. Murphy, a longtime Cincinnati physician whom Piatt described as "my very clever physician and friend," Piatt, *Sunday Meditations,* 182.

72. Louise Piatt, Baltimore, to Ella Piatt, May 29 [1863], series IV, Castle archives.

73. Donn Piatt, Baltimore, to Louise Piatt, September 8, 1863, series IV, Castle archives.

74. *Official Records of the War of the Rebellion* (Washington, D.C.: Government Printing Office, 1889; hereafter *O.R.*), series 1, vol. 27 (part 2), 124–25.

75. Robert C. Schenck, "Notes on the Battle of McDowell," in Johnson and Buel, *Battles and Leaders of the Civil War,* 2:298.

76. Piatt to Schenck, June 13, 1863, *O.R.*, series 1, vol. 27 (part 3), 128.

77. Lincoln to Schenck, June 14, 1863, in Basler, *Collected Works,* 6:274.

78. Schenck to John L. Chapman, mayor of Baltimore, June 20, 1863; Schenck to Henry B. Judd, June 26, 1863; Schenck to Commodore Dornin, Commanding Naval Station, Baltimore, June 28, 1863. Letterbook, vol. 1 (January 2, 1863-February 29, 1864), Middle Department & 8th Army Corps, RG 393, part I, NARA.

79. McPherson, *Tried by War,* 3–4.

80. Miller, *Donn Piatt,* 172–74.

81. "Indorsement," signed A. Lincoln, October 27, 1863, *O.R.*, series 1, vol. 27 (part 2), 197.

82. Robert J. Brugger, *Maryland: A Middle Temperament, 1634–1890* (Baltimore: Johns Hopkins Press, 1988), 293.

83. Piatt, "Baltimore During the War," *Cincinnati Commercial,* July 4, 1870, no page; clipping in Castle archives.

84. Miller, *Donn Piatt,* 163.

85. McPherson, *Tried by War,* 68.

86. Sandburg, *The Prairie Years,* 282.

87. Sarah-Eva Carlson, "Lincoln and the McCormick-Manny Case," *Illinois History*

48, no. 2 (February 1995): 30–31. For a somewhat different account see that of Ward Hill Lamon in Dorothy Lamon Teillard, ed., *Recollections of Abraham Lincoln* (Lincoln: University of Nebraska Press, 1994; revision of 1895 edition), 236–37.

88. Schenck to Lincoln, June 30, 1863, Abraham Lincoln Papers, Library of Congress; see also Ira Berlin, ed., *Freedom: A Documentary History of Emancipation 1861–1867,* series 1, vol. 2, *The Wartime Genesis of Free Labor* (New York: Cambridge University Press, 1993), 486.

89. Lincoln to Schenck, July 4, 1863, in Basler, *Collected Works,* 6:317.

90. Stanton, to Colonel Birney, Fortress Monroe, July 5, 1863, Microfilm publication 473, roll 83, NARA; Birney, to Stanton, July 5, 1863, M473, roll 110, NARA.

91. Niven, *Chase Papers,* 490–91.

92. Letter to the editor from A. W. W., *Christian Recorder,* July 25, 1863, no page, http://www.accessible.com/accessible/text/freedom/00000587/00058723.htm.

93. Piatt said this at an 1870 election rally in the District of Columbia; clipping from *Washington Evening Star,* May 25, 1870, kindly provided to author by John P. Richardson.

94. Robert I. Cottom Jr. and Mary Ellen Hayward, *Maryland in the Civil War: A House Divided* (Baltimore: Maryland Historical Society, 1994), 83. For Birney's life and career see "Birney, William" in *Dictionary of American Biography,* ed. Allen Johnson (New York: Charles Scribner's Sons, 1964), 1:294.

95. W. H. Chesebrough, AAG, to Col. Wm. Birney, September 2, 1863, forwarding September 2 message from C. W. Foster, AAG, War Department, to Schenck, Letterbook, vol. 1 (January 2, 1863-February 29, 1864), Middle Department & 8th Army Corps, RG 393, part I, NARA.

96. Ira Berlin, ed., *Freedom: A Documentary History of Emancipation 1861–1867,* series 2, *The Black Military Experience* (New York: Cambridge University Press, 1982), 184–85.

97. Lincoln to "Col. Birney, Baltimore, Md.," October 3, 1863; Birney to Lincoln, same date, in Basler, *Collected Works,* 6:495.

98. Piatt, *Men Who Saved the Union,* 43–46.

99. Charles L. Wagandt, "The Army versus Maryland Slavery, 1862–1864," *Civil War History* 10 (1964): 144; see also Henry Howe, *Historical Collections of Ohio* (Columbus, Ohio: Henry Howe & Son, 1891), 112 *et seq.*

100. Paul M. Angle, *The Lincoln Reader* (Rutgers, N.J.: Rutgers University Press, 1947), 411.

101. "The Election in Maryland—Emancipation Accepted," *New York Times,* November 6, 1863, 4.

102. Sandburg, *The War Years,* 2:21–22.

103. David Donald, ed., *Inside Lincoln's Cabinet: The Civil War Diaries of Salmon P. Chase* (New York: Longmans, Green, 1954), 232.

104. Piatt published several accounts of his encounter with a furious president. That which got widest circulation was probably in his contribution to Rice, *Reminiscences of Abraham Lincoln,* 494–97; see also "Piatt, Donn," in *Dictionary of American Biography,* ed. Dumas Malone (New York: Charles Scribner's Sons, 1962), 8:556.

105. Doris Kearns Goodwin, *Team of Rivals: The Political Genius of Abraham Lincoln* (New York: Simon & Schuster, 2005), 602.

106. Ward Hill Lamon interview with William H. Herndon, c. 1865–66, in Douglas L. Wilson and Rodney O. Davis, eds., *Herndon's Informants: Letters, Interviews and Statements about Abraham Lincoln* (Urbana: University of Illinois Press, 1998), 466.

107. Sally Denton, *Passion and Principle* (New York: Bloomsbury USA, 2007), 318–21.

108. Piatt, Baltimore, to Hon. E. M. Stanton, July 23, 1863, M-473, roll 110, NARA; Stanton, to Piatt, July 24, 1863, M473, roll 83, NARA.

109. Piatt telegram to Capt. Robert N. Scott, Judge Advocate, August 13, 1863, press copies of telegrams sent July 1863-August 1866 from Middle Department, RG 393, Part I, N. 2334, NARA.

110. Piatt wrote to Schenck from the Middle Department headquarters on December 11, 1863, for reasons that are not clear, "I find by reference to yours and Captain Scott's telegrams that you left Boston about the 27th of August. You were in N.Y. on the 28th in Phil. on the 30th in Balt. on the 31st and in Washington on the 1st of September," Robert C. Schenck Collection, Miami University Archives, Oxford, Ohio.

111. Hay diary, October 21, 1863, in Hay, John, *Letters of John Hay and Extracts from Diary* (New York: Gordian Press, 1969; reprint of volume printed but not published in 1908), 111–12.

112. Jeremiah S. Black to William H. Herndon, August 18, 1873, Herndon-Weik Collection of Lincolniana, Manuscript Divison, Library of Congress.

113. Harold R. Manakee, *Maryland in the Civil War* (Baltimore: Maryland Historical Society, 1961), 125–26.

114. Gabor Boritt, *The Gettysburg Gospel: The Lincoln Speech That Nobody Knows* (New York: Simon & Schuster, 2006), 62.

115. *National Intelligencer,* November 21, 1863, no page; summary in Joan M. Dixon, *National Intelligencer Newspaper Abstracts, Special Edition: The Civil War Years* (Bowie, Md.: Heritage Books, 2000), 2:82.

116. Perrin, William Henry, and J. H. Battle, *History of Logan County and Ohio* (Chicago: O.L. Baskin & Co., 1880), 584.

117. Lucy Hayes, Cincinnati, to Rutherford B. Hayes, March 13, 1862, Civil War Letters of Lucy Webb Hayes, Rutherford B. Hayes Presidential Center, Fremont, Ohio.

118. Telegram from William Cannon and N. B. Smithers, Bridgeville, Del., to His Excellency Abraham Lincoln, November 10, 1863, Abraham Lincoln Papers, Library of Congress.

119. Gerald S. Henig, *Henry Winter Davis* (New York: Twayne Publishers, 1973), 196, quoting letter from Davis to Samuel F. Du Pont, January 16, 1864. There are other accounts that do not cite sources, e.g., Miller, *Donn Piatt,* 46.

120. Charles C. Fulton to Lincoln, December 15, 1863. Abraham Lincoln Papers, Library of Congress.

121. T. Harry Williams, *The Union Restored,* vol. 6, *Life History of the United States* (New York: Time-Life Books, 1974), 11.

122. Donn Piatt, "Bull Run," *Cincinnati Commercial,* July 20, 1870, no page; clipping in Castle archives.

123. The resignation was effective July 2, 1864 (Thomas H. S. Hamersly, ed., *Complete Regular Army Register of the United States Army for One Hundred Years (1779 to 1879) together with a Register of All Appointments by the President of the United States in the Volunteer Service during the Rebellion* [Washington, D.C.: T.H.S. Hamersly, 1880], 85).

124. Donn Piatt, Cincinnati, to John Anthony, Wakefield, June 18, 1864, box 4, file 4, series IV, Castle archives.

125. Obituary, *New York Times,* October 7, 1864, 2.

126. "Louise Kirby Piatt," *New York Times,* October 7, 1864, 2.

127. Greeley, New York, to Piatt, Cincinnati, October 19, 1864, Department of Rare Books and Special Collections, Rush Rhees Library, University of Rochester, Rochester, N.Y.

4. What to Do in Peacetime?

1. Piatt's telegram has not been found, but the letter (which refers to his telegram) that he wrote Stanton from Cincinnati, April 18, 1865, is in the Edwin M. Stanton Papers, Manuscript Division, Library of Congress.

2. "Colonel Donn Piatt on the Hon. E.M. Stanton. From a Speech at the Soldiers' Welcome, at Salem Grove, Logan County, Ohio," *Mac-a-cheek Press,* October 6, 1865, 6; text is also in *Extract from a speech of Colonel Donn Piatt, on the Hon. E.M. Stanton* (Washington: L. Towers, Printer, 1865?).

3. Mark E. Neely Jr., *The Fate of Liberty: Abraham Lincoln and Civil Liberties* (New York: Oxford University Press, 1991), 19–23, 115, 233–34.

4. Charles H. Coleman, "Three Vallandigham Letters, 1865," *Ohio History* 43, no. 4 (October 1934): 461–64.

5. "Colonel Donn Piatt on Clement L. Vallandigham [From a speech delivered in Dayton, October 9, 1865]," *Mac-a-cheek Press,* October 13, 1865, 13.

6. Dan Reigle of the *Ohio Civil War Genealogy Journal* has kindly brought to the author's attention the figure of 35,475 (11,588 killed or mortally wounded and 23,887 deaths from all other causes, mainly disease) cited in an 1889 work by William F. Fox. Mr. Reigle notes that totaling the losses reported for individual army units produces contradictory figures.

7. Advertisement for Davison & Woodward. *Mac-a-cheek Press,* August 10, 1866, 352.

8. The Miller company continued to manufacture hearses and ambulances until some years after World War II.

9. K. Todd McCormick, "A Brief History of Logan County, Ohio"; text at http://www.co.logan.oh.us/museum/Logan_County_History/body_logan_county_history.html.

10. "Communications," *The Republican* (Bellefontaine, Ohio), September 1, 1865, no page; clipping in Logan County Historical Society.

11. Rebecca Strange Edwards, *New Spirits: Americans in the Gilded Age* (New York: Oxford University Press, 2006), 31.

12. Miller, *Donn Piatt,* 180.

13. Ibid., 199–200.

14. "Tecumseh," in *The Wit and Wisdom of Donn Piatt,* ed. Angela J. Warye (Dayton, Ohio: Westindorf Printing, 2000), no page.

15. Howe, *Historical Collections of Ohio,* 114.

16. William Gillette, *Retreat from Reconstruction, 1869–1879* (Baton Rouge: Louisiana State University Press, 1979), 7–9.

17. Miller, *Donn Piatt,* 209.

18. Piatt, Columbus, to Schenck, January 26 and February 28, 1866, Robert C. Schenck Collection, Miami University Archives, Oxford, Ohio. Steedman never made it as far as the cabinet; his reward came when Johnson made him collector of internal revenue at New Orleans.

19. Certificate of Marriage, July 12, 1866, box 4, file 16, series IV, Castle archives.

20. Will, box 4, file 19, series IV, Castle archives.

21. Dodge to "your Honor," June 25, 1869, Mary Abigail Dodge Papers, Manuscript Division, Library of Congress.

22. "A Sensational Suit," *Chicago Daily Tribune,* September 13, 1885, 3.

23. Joseph Cookman Nate, *The History of Sigma Chi Fraternity, 1855–1925* (Chicago: Sigma Chi Fraternity, 1925), 3.

24. "A Chapter in Donn's Life," *New York Times,* September 14, 1885, 1; "From Ohio's Metropolis," *Chicago Daily Tribune,* September 20, 1885, 1.

25. Some of the affidavits by Donn Piatt, Nellie Piatt, and others are in the Castle archives. Other affidavits are in the records of the Logan County Court of Common Pleas, Cases #3076 and #4370, which are held by the Logan County Genealogical Society in Bellefontaine. These records do not show what decision the court reached in either case, but they include a notarized extract showing that the Ohio Supreme Court dismissed Case #3076 in 1890 "for failure to file printed record." The author would like to express his thanks to Kristina Eleyet, president of the Genealogical Society, for her help in locating the surviving documents.

26. Celia Logan, *Her Strange Fate,* published in 1888 by Piatt's favorite publisher, Belford, Clarke, & Company in Cincinnati.

27. Miller, *Donn Piatt,* 175–77.

28. Piatt was about to turn forty-seven.

29. Piatt, Mac-a-cheek, to Stanton, May 17, 1866, Edwin M. Stanton Papers, Manuscript Division, Library of Congress.

30. Donn Piatt, "Our Fever for Titles" in Piatt, *Sunday Meditations and Selected Prose Sketches* (Cincinnati: Robert Clarke & Co., 1893), 290.

31. Robert D. Sawrey, *Dubious Victory: The Reconstruction Debate in Ohio* (Lexington: University Press of Kentucky, 1992), 111.

32. Piatt, quoted in J. Q. Howard, *The Life, Public Services and Select Speeches of Rutherford B. Hayes* (Cincinnati: Robert Clarke & Co., 1876), 66.

33. Daniel R. Porter, "Governor Rutherford B. Hayes," *Ohio History* 77, no. 1–3 (Winter, Spring, Summer 1968): 62.

34. Alan Lewis, "Dr. Taylor's Improved Movement Cure Institute," http:www.oocities.com/unclesamsfarm/drtaylor.htm.

35. Miller, *Donn Piatt,* 211.

36. Donn Piatt to William Piatt, August 22, 1870, series IV, box 4, Castle archives.

37. Miller, *Donn Piatt,* 212.

38. Ibid., 212–13.

39. Miller claimed that Piatt was the first to use the word *crank* to describe an odd person. A later author said that this was a story "which one would like to be able to believe" (George H. McKnight, *English Words and Their Background* [New York: B. Appleton, 1923], 349–50). In fact, the usage predated Piatt; the definition appears in an 1833 dictionary.

40. Frederick A. P. Barnard and Arnold Guyot, eds., *Johnson's New Universal Cyclopaedia* (New York: Alvin J. Johnson & Son, 1878), 1246, said that Piatt "was engaged in starting the New York Sun." Not so; the *Sun* started in 1833, when Piatt was fourteen.

41. Frank W. Scott, "Newspapers since 1860," in *Cambridge History of American Literature,* ed. William Peterfield Trent, John Erskine, Stuart P. Sherman, and Carl Van Doren, 2:324 (New York: G.P. Putnam's Sons, 1921).

5. Piatt to the Capital

1. Louise Piatt, *Bell Smith Abroad*, 119.

2. Jack Beatty, *Age of Betrayal: The Triumph of Money in America, 1865–1900* (New York: Knopf, 2007), 58–60.

3. Edwards, *New Spirits*, 18–19.

4. Lewis O. Saum, *The Popular Mood of America, 1860–1890* (Lincoln: University of Nebraska Press, 1990), 195.

5. Bryce, *American Commonwealth*, 2:70.

6. Halstead was thirty-four when conscription of men aged eighteen to thirty-five began in 1863. Although his biographer Donald Curl does not discuss the matter in *Murat Halstead and the Cincinnati Commercial* (Boca Raton: University Presses of Florida, 1980), perhaps he paid for a substitute to serve in his place, as was often done.

7. Frank W. Scott, "Newspapers Since 1860," *The Cambridge History of American Literature*, ed. William Peterfield Trent et al. (New York: G.P. Putnam's Sons, 1921), 3:324.

8. Mark W. Summers, *The Press Gang* (Chapel Hill: University of North Carolina Press, 1994), 83.

9. Piatt, New York, to Friedrich Hassaurek, January 3, 1868, Ohio Historical Society.

10. Piatt to Hassaurek, January 23, 1868, Ohio Historical Society.

11. Piatt to Hassaurek, May 12, 1868, Ohio Historical Society.

12. Piatt to Hassaurek, July 2, 1868, Ohio Historical Society.

13. In 1870 New York City—including Brooklyn, still separate politically—had 1,338,391 people.

14. *Ninth Census*, vol. 1, *The Statistics of the Population of the United States* (Washington, D.C.: Government Printing Office, 1872), 425.

15. Bryce, *American Commonwealth*, 2:270.

16. "'Donn Piatt and the Postmaster.' (Correspondence of the Cincinnati Commercial.)," *Washington Evening Star*, October 8, 1870, 2.

17. Piatt, Washington, to Hayes, December 16, 1868, Rutherford B. Hayes Presidential Library, Fremont, Ohio (hereafter Hayes Library).

18. Piatt to Hayes, dated "Oct. 1869," Hayes Library.

19. Rutherford B. Hayes, Cincinnati, to Donn Piatt, November 7, 1869, Williams, *Diary and Letters*, 2:69.

20. Edward J. Blum, *Reforging the White Republic: Race, Religion, and American Nationalism, 1865–1898* (Baton Rouge: Louisiana State University Press, 2005), 52.

21. "A Letter from Louisville, Ky," *Christian Recorder* (Philadelphia), July 31, 1869, http://www.accessible.com/accessible/text/freedom/00000872/00087256.htm. Langston was later the first African American member of Congress from Virginia and served as American minister to Haiti in 1877–85.

22. The first black cadet entered West Point in 1870.

23. Donn Piatt, "The Nigger in the West Point Wood Pile," *Cincinnati Commercial*, July 8, 1870, 4.

24. "The Black Member and His Speech," *The Capital*, January 11, 1874, 1.

25. "Notes from Washington. Another Letter of Horace Greeley of Interest to Colored Men," *New York Times*, October 25, 1872, 1.

26. Congressional legislation granting blacks the right to vote in the District of Co-

lumbia had been vetoed by President Johnson, but the veto had been overriden (James H. Whyte, *The Uncivil War: Washington During the Reconstruction, 1865–1878* [New York: Twayne Publishers, 1958], 54–57).

27. *Washington Evening Star,* May 25, 1870, 3.

28. "Colored Men of Washington," *The Capital,* April 16, 1871, 4.

29. Leech, *Reveille in Washington,* 237.

30. "Education. (From the lecture of Donn Piatt at the Fifteenth-street church, colored.)," *The Capital,* December 22, 1878, 2. Summers, *Press Gang,* 351, n33, claims that Piatt was voicing "nostalgic views toward slavery."

31. *The Nation* 12, no. 289 (January 12, 1871): no page; quotation at www.nationarchive.com/Summaries/v012i0289_07.htm.

32. Mark Twain, "Memoranda," *Galaxy* 11, no. 4 (April 1871): 615.

33. Victor Fischer, Michael B. Frank, and Lin Salamo, eds., *Mark Twain's Letters* (Berkeley: University of California Press, 1995), 4:346–47.

34. Donn Piatt, *Cincinnati Commercial,* February 11, 1871, 2.

35. Piatt to "My dear fellow," March 28, 1871, Mark Twain Papers, Bancroft Library, University of California, Berkeley.

36. "More from Want of Thought Than from Want of Feeling" and "The Galaxy for May," *Brooklyn Eagle,* April 28, 1871, 2.

37. Melville D. Landon, *Wise, Witty, Eloquent Kings of the Platform and Pulpit* (Chicago: F.C. Smedley, 1891), 507–9.

38. Donald Curl, *Murat Halstead and the Cincinnati Commercial* (Boca Raton: University Presses of Florida, 1980), 45.

39. D. P., "Washington Letter," *Cincinnati Commercial,* February 2, 1870, 2.

40. Miller, *Donn Piatt,* 226, quotes Townsend as saying Piatt told him he had found the money to start the paper; the backer is not named. Miller also says that Frank H. Gassaway was connected with *The Capital* from the start, and that he was at that time "the private secretary of the late William S. Huntington, who was the president of the First National Bank of Washington, and who aided financially the paper" (p. 232).

41. "A Weekly Newspaper in the Right Spot," *Tioga County Agitator,* June 21, 1871, 3, http://digitalnewspapers.libraries.psu.edu.

42. "Washington Letters," *Cincinnati Commercial,* February 9, 1871, 2, quoted in Fischer and Frank, *Mark Twain's Letters,* 4:347, n2.

43. "Grant and Sumner," *The Capital,* March 12, 1871, 2.

44. Tap, *Over Lincoln's Shoulder,* 46–47.

45. On November 10, 1872, *The Capital* began serialization of *Married Abroad, An American Romance of the Quartier Latin,* by George Alfred Townsend.

46. Miller, *Donn Piatt,* 225–27.

47. Donn Piatt, Washington, to William McCoy Piatt, August 10, 1871 ("I propose to pay your uncle Jake but since I went into the paper I have not had the money. I am sorry for him and will pay him soon as I can."), box 4, file 7, series IV, Castle archives.

48. "Notice," *The Capital,* July 16, 1871, 2.

49. *George P. Rowell & Co's American Newspaper Directory* (New York: George P. Rowell, 1872), 23.

50. "Announcement," *The Capital,* November 16, 1872, 2.

51. "That Duel," *The Capital,* January 12, 1873, 2.

52. *The Capital*, March 28, 1875, 1.

53. *George P. Rowell & Co's American Newspaper Directory*, 118.

54. By 1882 the Associated Press wire service provided small town newspapers in the Midwest with as much as 80 to 100 percent of their news copy (Paul Starr, *The Creation of the Media* [New York: Basic Books, 2004], 184).

55. *The Capital*, April 21, 1872, 3.

56. "Personal Notes," *The Capital*, April 2, 1871, 2.

57. Piatt, *Men Who Saved the Union*, 284.

58. Ibid., 296.

59. E. B. Long has written that he is convinced Grant was doing "some drinking . . . not an unusual custom among soldiers" before he resigned from the army in 1854 (Long, "Ulysses S. Grant for Today," in *Ulysses S. Grant: Essays and Documents*, ed. David L. Wilson and John Y. Simon [Carbondale: Southern Illinois University Press, 1981], 11). Elsewhere, John Y. Simon dismisses as "irrelevant" the "speculation that Grant drank himself out of the army" (Simon, "Forging a Commander: Ulysses S. Grant Enters the Civil War, in *New Perspectives on the Civil War*, ed. John Y. Simon and Michael E. Stevens [Madison, Wis.: Madison House, 1998], 53). For a detailed consideration of claims about Grant drinking during the Civil War, see Brooks D. Simpson, "Introduction to the Bison Books Edition," *Three Years with Grant As Recalled by War Correspondent Sylvanus Cadwallader*, ed. Benjamin P. Thomas (Lincoln: University of Nebraska Press, 1996), v–xv. There are few reports of Grant drinking in later life.

60. William S. McFeely, *Grant: A Biography* (New York: Norton, 1981), 244.

61. Ernest Samuels, ed., *The Education of Henry Adams* (Boston: Houghton Mifflin, 1974), 260.

62. "Washington Letter" dated January 9, 1869, *Cincinnati Commercial*, date of publication uncertain; clipping in Castle archives.

63. "Washington Letter" dated February 14,1869, date of publication uncertain.

64. "Washington Letter" dated April 1, 1869, date of publication uncertain.

65. At a guess, if Piatt asked Grant for a post it was that of minister to France. When he was in the Paris legation in 1855 he had written Secretary of State Marcy to suggest he be named minister when and if the incumbent, John Y. Mason, resigned. Lincoln had received a report in 1860 that Piatt was telling people he was going to become minister to France. However, by the time Piatt called on Grant, presumably toward the end of March 1869, Elihu B. Washburne was on his way to become the minister to France after resigning on March 16 as secretary of state. Some other appointments as chiefs of U.S. diplomatic missions in Europe remained to be made but were quickly being filled. See *Principal Officers of the Department of State*.

66. "Washington Letter" dated April 9, 1869.

67. Albert Rhodes, "Our Diplomates and Consuls," *Scribner's Monthly* 13, no. 2 (December 1876): 172.

68. William Barnes and John Heath Morgan, *The Foreign Service of the United States: Origins, Development, and Functions* (Washington, D.C.: Historical Office, Department of State, 1961), 134. Nor was it only in the diplomatic field that Grant was accused of nepotism. Senator Charles Sumner claimed in 1872 that altogether there were at least "thirteen relations of the President billeted on the country" (Sumner speech in the U.S. Senate, May 31, 1872, quoted in Louis Arthur Coolidge, *The Life of Ulysses S. Grant* [Boston: Houghton Mifflin, 1922], 391–92).

69. Eugene Schuyler, *American Diplomacy and the Furtherance of Commerce* (New York: Charles Scribner's Sons, 1886), 8.

70. Barnes and Morgan, *Foreign Service,* 135.

71. A correspondent reported seeing Piatt at a White House reception in the spring of 1870 in the company of George Alfred Townsend and editor and author Benjamin Perley Poore ("A Reception at the White House," *Harper's Bazaar* 3, no. 20 [May 14, 1870]: 313). His calls, on New Year's Day 1870, together with his friends "Jones" and "Robinson," on three members of Grant's cabinet are reported in "Washington Letters," *Cincinnati Commercial,* January 2, 1870, 2.

72. Samuels, *Education of Henry Adams,* 280.

73. The report by Kountz is enclosed with McClernand to Lincoln, March 15, 1863, Abraham Lincoln Papers, Library of Congress. For Halstead's friendship with McClernand, see Victor Hicken, *Illinois in the Civil War* (Urbana: University of Illinois Press, 1991), 162–65. In 1874 Kountz may have sought Piatt's editorial help in a business dispute; see "A Pittsburg Libel Suit," *New York Times,* March 10, 1874, 5.

74. Halstead to Chase, April 1, 1863; Chase to Lincoln, April 4, 1863, Abraham Lincoln Papers, Library of Congress.

75. For a summary of major scandals in the Grant administration, see http://www.u-s-history.com/pages/h234.html.

76. Summers, *Press Gang,* 175.

77. "The New York Times Trundling Its Tub," *Brooklyn Eagle,* September 26, 1870, 2.

78. Summers, *Press Gang,* 176–82.

79. O. E. Babcock, Executive Mansion, to Fish, Confidential, December 30, 1870, Hamilton Fish Papers, General Correspondence 1804–1894, Manuscript Division, Library of Congress.

80. "Wall Street in War Time," *Harper's New Monthly Magazine* 30, no. 179 (April 1865): 615–16.

81. Beatty, *Age of Betrayal,* 55–56.

82. Clinton Rice in 1877, quoted in the introduction by Michael Burlingame in William O. Stoddard, *Inside the White House in War Time* (Lincoln: University of Nebraska Press, 2000; reprint, with addition of "White House Sketches," of 1890 edition), xvi.

83. Donn Piatt, "King Log," *Cincinnati Commercial,* March 11, 1870, no page; clipping in Castle archives.

84. "The Perambulating President," *The Capital,* June 11, 1871, 1.

85. Grant's Long Beach residence was not the first "summer White House." Earlier, Washington had summered at Mount Vernon and Buchanan at Bedford Springs, Pennsylvania. The president with the most such retreats seems to have been Coolidge, who summered in various places, including the State Game Lodge in Custer State Park, South Dakota.

86. We find, for example, "Dion Piatt, of Washington" listed among sojourners at Narragansett in July 1871 ("Newport," *New York Times,* July 28, 1871, 2).

87. Emphasis is in the original. Stewart, a millionaire merchant, never took office because of a 1789 law that prohibited the appointment as Treasury head of anyone engaged in trade or commerce.

88. Jean Edward Smith, *Grant* (New York: Simon & Schuster, 2001), 419–20, 462–63.

89. Allan Nevins, *Hamilton Fish: The Inner History of the Grant Administration* (New York: Frederick Ungar, 1957), 1:299–300.

90. "Canadian Annexation," *The Capital,* September 3, 1871, 2.

6. Alarms and Excursions

1. Frederic Hudson, *Journalism in the United States, from 1690 to 1872* (New York: Harper & Brothers, 1873), 498–99.

2. Bryce, *American Commonwealth,* 2:612–13. Curiously, a number of recent works ignore the importance of American women writers in the Gilded Age. See, for example, Angela Marie Howard, "Women and Gender," in *Encyclopedia of the Gilded Age and Progressive Era,* ed. John D. Buenker and Joseph Buenker (Armonk, N.Y.: Sharpe Reference, 2005), 1:51–60.

3. Sarah's contributions are listed in Michaels, *That New World,* 251–53.

4. *The Capital,* August 3, 1873, 2.

5. H. M. B., "Women as Government Clerks: Their Work and Their Pay—Fair Play," *The Capital,* November 4, 1871, 1.

6. Mary Clemmer Ames, *Ten Years in Washington* (Hartford, Conn.: A.D. Worthington, 1874), 353–64.

7. Lin Salamo and Harriet Elinor Smith, eds., *Mark Twain's Letters* (Berkeley: University of California Press, 1997), 5:461–62.

8. "The New Authors," *The Capital,* March 26, 1871, 4.

9. "Mark Twain," *Cambridge History of English and American Literature* (electronic edition; New York: www.bartleby.com, 2000), vol. 17, part 2, no page, http://www.bartelby.net/227/0116.html.

10. Bernard DeVoto, *Mark Twain's America* (Cambridge, Mass.: Houghton Mifflin, 1932), 285.

11. A. C. Buell, quoted in Miller, *Donn Piatt,* 288.

12. "Green-Room Gossip: Items," *The Capital,* August 16, 1874, 2.

13. Albert Bigelow Paine, *Mark Twain: A Biography,* vol. 1, part 2, chapter 95, no page, www.gutenberg.org/etext/2984.

14. "The One Hundredth Representation of 'The Gilded Age,'" *New York Times,* December 24, 1874, 4.

15. "Green-Room Gossip," *The Capital,* November 15, 1874, 1.

16. "Green-Room Gossip," *The Capital,* February 7, 1875, 7.

17. See Mark Perry, *Grant and Twain: The Story of a Friendship That Changed America* (New York: Random House, 2004), *passim.*

18. Mark Twain and Charles Dudley Warner, *The Gilded Age* (New York: Oxford University Press, 1996; reprint of 1873 edition), 398–99.

19. Another journalist who held a congressional clerkship was Benjamin Perly Poore (Summers, *Press Gang,* 121). In addition, some members of Congress had relatives who were journalists (Margaret Susan Thompson, *The "Spider Web": Congress and Lobbying in the Age of Grant* [Ithaca, N.Y.: Cornell University Press, 1985], 161).

20. Forney, *Anecdotes,* 244.

21. Albert Rhodes, "Edmond About at Home," *Galaxy* 18, no. 2 (August 1874): 256.

22. Ream was a member of the editorial staff of the *Indianapolis Sentinel* and Indianapolis correspondent for the *Ohio Gazette* of Cincinnati.

23. Ream, quoted in Miller, *Donn Piatt,* 220–21.

24. "The Cost of Living: Washington as a Residence Compared with Other Cities," *Washington Post,* December 24, 1877, 1.

25. Piatt told a congressional committee in 1872 that, in fact, the house "was purchased by my wife of Mr. Shepherd out of her own property, and paid for by her at what was considered, at the time, the full value of the property, $11,900" (*Investigation into the Affairs of the District of Columbia,* 42nd Congress, 2nd Session [1872], Report No. 72 [Washington, D.C.: Government Printing Office, 1872], 317).

26. The building, completed in 1888, was nearly demolished in 1957. It now houses various Executive Branch offices. The Piatts' house was replaced years ago by a modern office building, which retains a little of the house's facade. A fine relic of the era remains just across 18th Street from where the Piatts lived: the red brick mansion built in 1825 by Tench Ringgold, U.S. marshal for the District of Columbia. Ringgold's mansion, later owned by Congressman Robert Low Bacon, is now the headquarters of DACOR (Diplomatic and Consular Officers, Retired) and is known as DACOR Bacon House. It was the home, when the Piatts lived nearby, of the widow of William Thomas Carroll, clerk of the Supreme Court from 1827 until his death in 1863. See William D. Calderhead, "Curator's Corner: Intertwined Histories of the Supreme Court of the United States and DACOR Bacon House," *DACOR Bulletin* 58, no. 2 (February 2007).

27. Shepherd himself lived in a mansion he had built the previous year on the corner of Connecticut Avenue and K Street (Whyte, *Uncivil War,* 143).

28. "Losses by Fire," *New York Times,* April 28, 1873, 1; Piatt's account is "A Fire and Its Lesson," *The Capital,* May 4, 1873, 2.

29. Donald Grant Mitchell, *Daniel Tyler: A Memorial Volume Containing His Autobiography and War Record, Some Account of His Later Years, with Various Reminiscences and the Tributes of Friends* (New Haven, Conn.: Privately printed, 1883), 71.

30. The annual *Boyd's Directory of the District of Columbia* shows Donn Piatt residing at 601 18th Street from 1873 through 1878, and then at the Riggs House. Just when the Piatts moved into the house is not clear, but they were there by sometime in 1871; *The Capital* for December 31, 1871, said that Ella would receive callers there on New Year's Day.

31. Brown and Williams, *Diary of James A. Garfield,* 2:135, 139.

32. "Our Yankee Doodle Princess in Europe," *The Capital,* May 18, 1872, 3. One doubts anyone would have written such an article in recent years, when members of presidential families are often given special treatment. The author recalls the visit to Florence, some years ago, by President Richard Nixon's daughter and her husband. The American consul general, a distinguished senior officer, was told flatly that he must get out of his pleasant home on the Arno, so that the young couple could stay there. So far as known, this was never reported in the press. One imagines that if the visit had occurred in Piatt's time, he would have both learned of it and commented on it.

33. *The Capital,* May 11, 1873, 1.

34. "Why Is This Thus?" *The Capital,* June 8, 1873, 1.

35. *The Capital,* May 24, 1874, 2.

36. Allegations about Grant's drinking were, of course, made by others besides Piatt, and they continued for years. For example, after Grant had left the White House and was on a world tour, the *Washington Post* reported, "Grant's ability to drink in every language, is of great assistance to him all over Europe" ("Personal," *Washington Post,* January 8, 1878, 2).

37. "A Card," *The Capital,* January 18, 1874, 2.

38. "The Crown Prince and Donn Piatt," *Atlanta Constitution,* January 17, 1874, 2. The visit by Casey and young Grant was widely reported. See, for example, "Fred. Grant after Donn

Piatt with a Club," *Georgia Weekly Telegraph and Georgia Journal & Messenger,* January 20, 1874, 1. Miller, *Donn Piatt,* 263, thought that the visitors had been Frederick Grant and the president's son-in-law, Frederick Dent. One may wonder whether Casey and Grant would have assaulted Piatt if he had been home—but he was not. Benson Bobrick nevertheless says that Piatt was "almost killed" (Bobrick, *Master of War: The Life of General George H. Thomas* [New York: Simon & Schuster, 2009], 339).

39. "To Our Friends, the Public," *The Capital,* January 18, 1874, 2.

40. Piatt to M. H., "Washington Jany 23 73," Hayes Library. (Piatt was apparently not yet used to writing "1874.")

41. See, for example, "Wholesale Slander Manufactory," *New York Times,* July 17, 1872, 4. After Farrand left Callao, a U.S. Treasury investigator reported that his local reputation was bad and that he had left Peru before he was to be tried there on financial charges (*Reports of De B. Randolph Keim, Agent of the United States, etc., to the Secretary of the Treasury relating to the Condition of the Consulates of the United States* [Washington, D.C.: Government Printing Office, 1871], 111, 118). The American minister to Peru, Alvin P. Hovey, reported to the State Department that the charges against Farrand related to shares of stock issued by a Peruvian tramway company of which Farrand had been president before he became consul (Dispatch No. 243 from Hovey to Secretary of State Fish, September 18, 1870, *Papers relating to the Foreign Relations of the United States* [Washington, D.C.: Government Printing Office, 1870], 510).

42. "Card from Henry Reed," *The Capital,* September 8, 1872, 2; see also "Washington Notes," *New York Times,* September 3, 1872, 1. President Grant's younger son Jesse, in his memoir of his father published only in 1925, got the story wrong, saying that it was his late brother Fred who had gone to the office of *The Capital* and that it was Piatt himself who had been thrashed (Jessie R. Grant, *In the Days of My Father General Grant* [New York: Harper & Brothers, 1925], 198–99).

43. Wilmer C. Harris, *Public Life of Zachariah Chandler, 1851–1875* (Ann Arbor: Michigan Historical Commission, 1917), 116.

44. Harris, *Public Life,* 106.

45. Others, however, might write about Chandler with a lighter touch: "While John Sherman goes on the stump in Ohio, boasting of our splendid wheat crop . . . Mr. Z. Chandler . . . declares that rye is good enough for him" ("Personal," *Washington Post,* October 8, 1879, 2).

46. "Zach Chandler: His Raid on Newspaper Row and Donn Piatt," *Atlanta Constitution,* May 2, 1875, 3.

47. "Capital Grins: Senatorial Adventure," *The Capital,* June 8, 1872, 2.

48. "Minor Notes," *The Capital,* January 26, 1879, 4.

49. "The Death of Donn Piatt," Editorial Department, *Belford's Monthly and Democratic Review* 8, no. 43 (December 1891): 495.

50. "Newspaper Row," *Chicago Tribune,* March 4, 1874, 1.

51. Benjamin Perley Poore, *Perley's Reminiscences of Sixty Years in the National Metropolis* (Philadelphia: Hubbard Brothers, 1886), 1:455, 466.

52. For Fish's reaction on learning of Babcock's trip, see Jacob D. Cox, "How Judge Hoar Ceased to be Attorney-General," *Atlantic Monthly* 76, no. 454 (August 1895): 166–67.

53. "Washington Diplomatic Life" *Budget* (Troy, N.Y.), June 5, 1887; clipping in Castle archives.

54. Piatt to Fish, April 29, 1871; Fish to Piatt, May 1 and May 8, 1871, Hamilton Fish Pa-

pers, Library of Congress. Fish's letter of May 8 refers to a letter from Piatt dated May 3 that has not been found.

55. Piatt, "My Diplomacy at Paris," *The Capital*, December 8, 1878, 6.

56. Poore, *Perley's Reminiscences*, 2:277–78.

57. Frank T. Howe, "Donn Piatt As He Was," *Toledo Blade*, November 21, 1891, no page; clipping in Castle archives.

58. Miller, *Donn Piatt*, 246–47.

59. *The Capital*, March 3, 1878, 4.

60. Piatt in the *Cincinnati Commercial*, June 9, 1870, quoted in Sean Dennis Cashman, *America in the Gilded Age* (New York: New York University Press, 1993), 247.

61. Henry Watterson, *"Marse Henry,"* An Autobiography (New York: George H. Doran, 1919), 1:252.

62. "Political," *The Capital*, October 15, 1871, 2.

63. Piatt, quoted in "The Most Corrupt Party That Ever Existed," *Observer* (Erie, Pa.), June 11, 1868, 1, http://digitalnewspapers.libraries.psu.edu.

64. Gillette, *Retreat from Reconstruction*, 16.

65. "Our New York Letter," *The Capital*, July 28, 1872, 2.

66. "Horace on the Track," *The Capital*, July 2, 1871, 2.

67. Robert C. Williams, *Horace Greeley: Champion of American Freedom* (New York: New York University Press, 2006), 300.

68. "Hon. Jere. S. Black Interviewed," *The Capital*, May 18, 1872, 3.

69. Black to Piatt, June 4, 1872; image of letter, offered for sale in October 2005, at http://www.railsplitter.com/sale10/autographs.html.

70. Watterson, *"Marse Henry,"* 2:227.

71. "The Inaugural Address of March 4th, 1873," *The Capital*, March 9, 1873, 1.

72. "Suppressing 'The Capital,'" *The Capital*, March 16, 1873, 2.

73. Peter Bridges, "An Appreciation of Alvey Adee," *Diplomacy & Statecraft* 10, no. 1 (March 1999): 34.

74. "On to Cuba," *The Capital*, November 23, 1873, 1.

75. Brown and Williams, *Diary of James A. Garfield*, 2:401. General Benét, the grandfather of the poet, was deeply concerned about modernizing coastal fortifications (see Daniel R. Beaver, "The U.S. War Department in the Gaslight Era: Stephen Vincent Benét at the Ordnance Department, 1870–91," *Journal of Military History* 68, no. 1 [January 2004], 105–32).

76. "Our Foreign War," *The Capital*, January 24, 1875, 4.

77. "New and Notes," *Daily Gazette* (Davenport, Iowa), August 24, 1873, 1.

78. "Editorial Correspondence: D.P. Abroad," *The Capital*, July 13, 1873, 2.

79. Ibid.

80. "Editorial Correspondence: D.P. Abroad," *The Capital*, August 17, 1873, 2.

81. A. N. Wilson, *The Victorians* (London: Arrow Books, 2003), 383.

82. Wallace's autobiography misspells the name of the work as *Malmistic*.

83. Wallace, *Autobiography*, 2:891–92. Although *Ben-Hur* was Wallace's greatest success, *The Fair God* also sold well over the years: 145,750 copies between 1873 and 1905.

84. Harriott was a member of the firm of Harriott & Sons, wholesale flour merchants in New York, and a nephew of a mayor of New York, William F. Havemeyer ("Marriage of Clara Morris," *Brooklyn Eagle*, December 1, 1874, 4).

85. "A Brief Respite," *The Capital*, June 13, 1875, 4.

86. Moxibustion, using moxa, the herb better known as mugwort, and the application of heat, is a form of medical therapy long used in Asia. The French doctors seem to have used a harsh variant of it on poor Clara.

87. Piatt, *Men Who Saved the Union,* xiv.

88. "Editorial Correspondence: D.P. Abroad," *The Capital,* September 28, 1873, 2.

89. Ann Larabee, *The Dynamite Fiend* (New York: Palgrave Macmillan, 2005), 126–33. Larabee says she has "taken very few liberties with the historical record" (p. 201). Be that as it may, she makes factual mistakes, saying inter alia that Donn Piatt had been ambassador to France. Piatt's poem to his old friend—and the poem she wrote in response—appeared in "Donn Piatt's Versatility," *Buffalo Times,* December 10, 1891, no page; clipping in Castle archives.

7. Presidential Prisoner, Presidential Friend

1. Gillette, *Retreat from Reconstruction,* 303, 306.

2. "The Election," *The Capital,* November 5, 1876, 1.

3. Eric Foner, *Reconstruction* (New York: History Book Club, 2005), 576.

4. Howard, *Life, Public Services and Select Speeches,* 66.

5. "Donn Piatt and Governor and Mrs. Hayes," *Boston Daily Globe,* October 2, 1876, 2.

6. Lucy Webb Hayes to Rutherford B. Hayes, March 13, 1862, Lucy Webb Hayes Correspondence, Rutherford B. Hayes Presidential Center, Fremont, Ohio.

7. Brown and Williams, *Diary of James A. Garfield,* 3:400.

8. Gillette, *Retreat from Reconstruction,* 118.

9. Some papers reprinted the full editorial, e.g. *The Daily Tribune* (Denver), February 24, 1877, 4.

10. *The Capital,* February 14, 1877; quoted in Miller, *Donn Piatt,* 270.

11. "The Nation's Business," *Boston Daily Globe,* February 20, 1877, 1.

12. Nast's cartoon in *Harper's Weekly* for March 17, 1877, is reproduced in Summers, *Press Gang,* 136.

13. "Donn Piatt on Nast," *Chicago Daily Tribune,* December 5, 1873, 8.

14. Morton Keller, *The Art and Politics of Thomas Nast* (New York: Oxford University Press, 1968), 45. Nast had an able if lesser known opponent in cartoon art and politics, Joseph Keppler. See Richard Samuel West, *The Political Cartoons of Joseph Keppler* (Champaign: University of Illinois Press, 1988).

15. George F. Hoar, *Autobiography of Seventy Years* (New York: Charles Scribner's Sons, 1903), 1:369.

16. James G. Blaine, *Twenty Years of Congress: From Lincoln to Garfield* (Norwich, Conn.: Henry Bill, 1886), 2:582.

17. Smith, *Grant,* 461.

18. "Donn Piatt's Infamy," *New York Times,* February 20, 1877, 1.

19. Lamon to Hayes, February 21, 1877, Hayes Library.

20. Clipping from *Brooklyn Times,* datelined Washington, D.C., July 28, year not given, in clippings scrapbook, Castle archives.

21. Halstead to Hayes, February 21, 1877, Hayes Library.

22. The cartoon, in *Harper's Weekly* for February 3, 1877, is reproduced in Summers, *Press Gang,* 305.

23. Watterson, *"Marse Henry,"* 1:280, 302–4.

24. Harry Barnard, *Rutherford B. Hayes and His America* (New York: Russell & Russell, 1967), 341–42.

25. Coolidge, *Life of Ulysses S. Grant,* 509.

26. Diary of Hamilton Fish, February 18, 1877, quoted in *The Papers of Ulysses S. Grant,* ed. John Y. Simon, 28:121 (Carbondale: Southern Illinois University Press, 2005).

27. "From the Capital," *Boston Daily Globe,* February 22, 1877, 1.

28. Stefan Lorant, *The Glorious Burden* (Lenox, Mass.: Authors Edition, 1976), 341.

29. Ellis Paxson Oberholtzer, *A History of the United States Since the Civil War* (New York: Macmillan, 1926), 3:317.

30. A number of newspapers reported that on April 7, 1877, the district attorney for the District of Columbia entered a nolle prosequi in the case, with the approval of the U.S. attorney general.

31. Hugh Brogan, *The Penguin History of the Unites States of America* (London: Penguin Books, 1985), 381.

32. "The Inaugural Address," *The Capital,* March 5, 1877, 1.

33. "What We Are to Grin and Bear," *The Capital,* March 5, 1877, 4.

34. *Edwardsville Intelligencer,* May 9, 1877, 1.

35. "Slings and Arrows," *Boston Daily Globe,* June 19, 1877, 4.

36. Charles W. Calhoun, *Conceiving a New Republic: The Republican Party and the Southern Question, 1869–1900* (Lawrence: University Press of Kansas, 2006), 99, 138, 147, 158.

37. Piatt to Hayes, January 3, 1878, Hayes Library. The *Washington Post* reported, however, that Piatt was among the guests ("White House Silver," *Washington Post,* January 1, 1878, 1).

38. Piatt to Hayes, November 9, 1882, Hayes Library.

39. Williams, *Diary and Letters,* 4:268.

40. "What's Wrong with the Administration?" *The Capital,* February 24, 1878, 4.

41. A few federal soldiers remained in the South, but they would no longer play a political role; Foner, *Reconstruction,* 582.

42. Asbury, "Rutherford B. Hayes and the Literary Club," 36.

43. Piatt, Washington, D.C., to Hayes, June 3, 1877, Hayes Library.

44. "Manufactures," *Census Reports,* vol. 7, *Twelfth Census of the United States, Taken in 1900* (Washington, D.C.: Government Printing Office, 1902), xlvii.

45. "Summer Notes," *The Capital,* August 30, 1874, 2.

46. "Leonard W. Jerome Dead," *New York Times,* March 5, 1891, 8.

47. Ross, "We Who Built the Queen City," 22.

48. "Mr. Dodd on the Baltimore and Ohio," *The Capital,* April 21, 1872, 2.

49. "Letter from D.P.," *The Capital,* September 29, 1872, 2.

50. Piatt claimed he had a solution—an invention he never patented—in which a hood over the engine's smokestack connected with a pipe running along the tops of the cars, to convey the smoke to the rear. Undated memorandum, series IV, box 6, Castle archives.

51. Philip S. Foner, *The Great Labor Uprising of 1877* (New York: Monad Press, 1977), 33–35.

52. John F. Stover, *History of the Baltimore and Ohio Railroad* (West Lafayette, Ind.: Purdue University Press, 1987), 136–38.

53. "Extra! The Death Struggle," *The Capital,* July 23, 1877, 1.

54. Piatt, Mac-o-cheek, to "My Dear John Swinton," April 13, 1886, series IV, box 6, file 17, Castle archives.

55. Foner, *Great Labor Uprising*, 15, 40–41. For an account of Tom Scott's career see Beatty, *Age of Betrayal*, 232–68.

56. Bryce, *American Commonwealth*, 2:390.

57. "'Violence Marks Progress.' The Speech of Col. Donn Piatt Before His Fellow-Laborers," *Washington Post*, February 6, 1878.

58. Clark D. Halker, *For Democracy, Workers, and God* (Urbana: University of Illinois Press, 1991), 63. For an obituary of Swinton, see "John Swinton Dead," *New York Times*, December 16, 1901, 9.

59. Piatt, *Poems and Plays*, 32–33.

60. Leon Fink, *Workingmen's Democracy* (Urbana: University of Illinois Press, 1983), 5.

61. Piatt, quoted in Mark Wahlgren Summers, *Party Games* (Chapel Hill: University of North Carolina Press, 2004), 175.

62. Edwards, *New Spirits*, 216.

63. Douglas Charles Rossinow, *Visions of Progress* (Philadelphia: University of Pennsylvania Press, 2008), 13–14; Ruth C. Crocker, "Cultural and Intellectual Life in the Gilded Age," in *The Gilded Age: Perspectives on the Origins of Modern America*, ed. Charles W. Calhoun, 222 (Lanham, Md.: Rowman & Littlefield, 2007).

64. "Filibusters Denounced," *New York Times*, May 12, 1865, 1.

65. David M. Pletcher, "Mexico Opens the Door to American Capital, 1877–1880," *The Americas* 16, no. 1 (July 1959): 1. From other sources it appears that the figure of two-thirds was exaggerated.

66. Pletcher, "Mexico Opens the Door," 4; see also William E. Gibbs, "Diaz' Executive Agents and United States Foreign Policy," *Journal of Interamerican Studies and World Affairs* 20, no. 2 (May 1978): 171–73.

67. Miller, *Donn Piatt*, 276–77.

68. Gibbs, "Diaz' Executive Agents," 177.

69. Pletcher, "Mexico Opens the Door," 12.

70. Harte, Georgetown, to "My dear Nan," July 8, 1877, quoted in Bradford A. Booth, "Unpublished Letters of Bret Harte," *American Literature* 16, no. 2 (May 1944): 135–36.

71. Harte to Anna Harte, July 27, 1877, quoted in Axel Nissen, *Bret Harte, Prince and Pauper* (Jackson: University of Mississippi Press, 2000), 158.

72. Harte to Piatt, August 20, 1877, Hayes Library.

73. Albert Bigelow Paine, ed., *Mark Twain's Letters* (New York: Gabriel Wells, 1923), 1:293.

74. Now Krefeld, in the Rhineland.

75. Geoffrey Bret Harte, ed., *The Letters of Bret Harte* (Boston: Houghton Mifflin, 1926), 55–63. The editor, who was Bret Harte's grandson and was working two decades after his grandfather's death, makes some mistakes in his account of Harte and Piatt, saying, for example, that the editor of "The Capitol" was John J. Piatt rather than Donn Piatt.

76. Lloyd Lewis, *Sherman: Fighting Prophet* (New York: Harcourt, Brace, 1932), 375.

77. "A National Disgrace," *The Capital*, March 24, 1878, 4.

78. See wartime letters from Sherman in John F. Marszalek, *Sherman: A Soldier's Passion for Order* (New York: Free Press, 1993), 184.

79. "Sherman to the Front," *Washington Post*, March 29, 1878, 1.

80. "Donn Piatt Pitches In," *Washington Post*, March 30, 1878, 1.

81. See, for example, "Morrow Resident Worthington Got W.T. Sherman's Attention," in Dallas Bogan, *Warren County Local History*, USGenWeb Project, http://www.rootsweb.

com/~ohwarren/Bogan/bogan198.htm; see also James D. Brewer, *Tom Worthington's Civil War* (Jefferson, N.C.: McFarland, 2001). One might wonder why Sherman the well-connected Ohioan did not know of Piatt's family connection with Worthington. However, Sherman left Ohio at sixteen for West Point and never lived in the state again.

82. Clipping from *Chattanooga Times,* May 1, 1889, reprinting letter from Piatt in *Cleveland Plain Dealer,* n.d., in Clippings scrapbook, Castle archives.

83. David J. Rothman wrote in *Politics and Power: The United States Senate 1869–1901* (Cambridge, Mass.: Harvard University Press, 1966), 139, "Members' $5,000 salaries could not cover living, transportation, and entertainment expenses."

84. "The Danger from Banks," *The Capital,* December 29, 1878, 4.

85. Sherman, *Recollections of Forty Years.*

86. "John Sherman," *Ohio History Central,* Ohio Historical Society, http:www.ohiohistorycentral.org/entry.php?rec=338.

87. Summers, *Press Gang,* 124, calls the Harte work *Romance of a Mine,* but it was *The Story of a Mine* and was serialized in *The Capital.* Summers says that Piatt "having promised Harte a generous sum to write the serial, welshed on the deal" (p. 125).

88. See the account in Mark Wahlgren Summers, *The Era of Good Stealings* (New York: Oxford University Press, 1993), 194–97.

89. *The Secretary v. McGarrahan,* 76 U.S. 298, 19 L.Ed. 579, 9 Wall. 298, U.S. Supreme Court, December Term, 1869.

90. "The 'Examination' in Reply to Mr. Cox," *The Nation* 11, no. 281 (November 17, 1870): 324.

91. Mary L. Hinsdale, *A History of the President's Cabinet* (Ann Arbor, Mich.: George Wahr, 1911), 211–12.

92. "Montgomery Blair," *The Capital,* February 2, 1879, 4. Piatt wrote that he introduced himself to Black at a dinner in Washington in 1870, saying that he had often heard their late mutual friend, Edwin Stanton, speak of Black (*Weekly Arizona Miner* [Prescott], May 21, 1870, no page; reprinted from the *Cincinnati Commercial*).

93. "McGarrahan's Stuffed Club," *Washington Post,* February 28, 1879, 1.

94. See "McGarrahan on the Stand," *New York Times,* March 17, 1878, 1.

95. "A Fight in the Capitol," *New York Times,* February 27, 1879, 1; "Letters to the Editor," *New York Times,* March 7, 1879, 2. See also Gustavus Myers, *History of the Great American Fortunes* (Chicago: C. Kerr, 1911), 3:319–23.

96. Melville D. Landon, *Eli Perkins: Wit, Humor and Pathos* (Chicago: Belford, Clarke, 1884), 131–34.

97. *Cleveland Herald,* August 7, 1852, 2.

98. Miller, *Donn Piatt,* 278.

99. Donald A. Ritchie, *Press Gallery: Congress and the Washington Correspondents* (Cambridge, Mass.: Harvard University Press, 1991), 100.

100. Whitman, 1856, quoted in Thompson, *"Spider Web,"* 54.

101. Thompson, *"Spider Web,"* 57.

102. Edward Winslow Martin [James Dabney McCabe], *Behind the Scenes in Washington* (New York: Continental Publishing, 1873), 215–47.

103. Thompson, *"Spider Web,"* 20.

104. Spofford, quoted in Thompson, *"Spider Web,"* 68.

105. By the year 2008 almost 6,700 people were employed by the Senate and around

10,700 by the House (Ida A. Brudnick, "CRS Report for Congress: The Congressional Research Service and the American Legislative Process" [Washington, D.C.: Congressional Research Service, March 19, 2008], 2).

106. Calhoun, "The Political Culture," 249–50.

107. Thompson, "*Spider Web*," 276.

108. The fullest account of the mothproofing affair is found in "Testimony Regarding the Contracts with Cowles & Brega for the Extermination of Moths in Army Clothing," Report of the Committee on Expenditures in the War Department, 44th Congress, 1st Session, House of Representatives, Report No. 799, August 5, 1876, 415–66. Piatt's testimony is quoted from that report.

109. For a full summary of Belknap's impeachment and trial, see Asher C. Hinds, *Hinds' Precedents of the House of Representatives of the United States* (Washington, D.C.: Government Printing Office, 1907), 3:902–47.

110. "Moths: A Remedy Worse Than the Disease," *The Chicago Tribune,* April 20, 1876, 1.

111. Brown and Williams, *Diary of James A. Garfield,* 3:276.

112. *The Capital,* September 30, 1877, 1. Piatt's manifesto was reprinted in many other papers.

113. "Moths in the Army," *New York Times,* October 2, 1877, 4.

114. "Notes from the Capital," *New York Times,* October 5, 1877, 5.

115. "Lobby Money Abandoned," *Washington Post,* June 24, 1879, 2.

116. "Donn Piatt and the Pacific Mail," *The Capital,* January 24, 1875, 6.

117. "China Mail Service," Report of the Committee on Ways and Means, 43rd Congress, 2nd Session, House of Representatives, Report No. 268, February 27, 1875; see especially 354–55, 383–85, 410–19, and 461–62.

118. As John P. Richardson has kindly brought to the author's attention, the *Washington Evening Star* reported on May 25, 1870, the speeches given by Piatt and Shepherd the previous evening.

119. *Investigation into the Affairs of the District of Columbia,* 42nd Congress, 2nd session (1872), Report No. 72 (Washington, D.C.: Government Printing Office, 1872), 317.

120. Alan Lessoff, *The Nation and Its City* (Baltimore: Johns Hopkins University Press, 1994), 68. Lessoff concludes, in a 2003 review of *Historical Dictionary of Washington, D.C.,* published on Humanities and Social Sciences Net, http://www.h-net.org/reviews/showrev.php?id=7722, "Only the most hostile critics charged Shepherd with malfeasance for direct personal gain; his agreed-upon misdeeds were reckless finance, high-handed administration, and the funneling of contracts to political and personal allies."

121. "Rimensnyder Asks for New Respect for Washington's 'Boss' Shepherd," summary of Overbeck History Lecture by Nelson Rimensnyder, November 9, 2005, sponsored by Capitol Hill Community Foundation, http://www.capitolhillhistory.org/lectures/html.

122. Lessoff, *Nation and Its City,* 72.

123. "Personal Notes," *The Capital,* June 28, 1874, 2.

124. William Wilson Corcoran and George Washington Riggs formed the Washington banking house of Corcoran and Riggs in 1836. The art gallery Corcoran built on Pennsylvania Avenue is now the Smithsonian's Renwick Gallery; his name is borne by today's Corcoran Gallery of Art. Riggs chaired the committee that pushed for an investigation of Shepherd and his Board of Public Works; the Riggs National Bank survived until 2005, when it merged with PNC Financial Services after corporate scandals.

125. *The Capital,* February 23, 1873, 2. Roosevelt, an uncle of President Theodore Roosevelt, spent one additional year in a federal post, as American minister to the Netherlands in 1888–1889. He was also a member of the Committee of Seventy, which broke the notorious Tweed Ring; a Brooklyn Bridge commissioner; and a conservation activist. See Douglas Brinkley, *Wilderness Warrior: Theodore Roosevelt and the Crusade for America* (New York: HarperCollins, 2009), 77–86.

126. Piatt to Halstead, December 10, 1878, Hayes Library. Typescript; notation says original is in "Murat Halstead Collection (Mrs. Henley)."

127. "The Color Line," *The Capital,* February 23, 1879, 2.

128. The story of Blanche and Josephine Bruce is told in Lawrence Otis Graham, *The Senator and the Socialite* (New York: HarperCollins, 2006).

129. Piatt to Orville Babcock, October 7, 1876, Hayes Library.

130. "Arrest for Criminal Libel," *New York Times,* April 4, 1874, 1; see also Miller, *Donn Piatt,* 287.

8. The Man in His Castle

1. Henry Howe, *Historical Collections of Ohio* (Norwalk, Ohio: Laning Printing, 1896), 2:115.

2. This central building of the Library of Congress, now known as the Jefferson Building, was not completed until 1897, some years after Smithmeyer and Pelz had been dismissed as the architects; see Mathilde V. Rovelstad, "The Library of Congress, a 19th-Century Neo-Baroque Monument," *Libri* 49 (1999): 243–54.

3. Not to be confused with the comic strip artist Oliver Frey, born in 1948.

4. Gertrude Garrison, "Our New York Letter: As to Donn Piatt and His Life Work," *Hornellsville Weekly Tribune,* Hornellsville, N.Y., June 22, 1888.

5. "Editorial Notes Abroad," *The Capital,* August 8, 1875, 2.

6. Miller, *Donn Piatt,* 266, 278.

7. Kennedy, *Historical Review,* 441.

8. "Exposing Their Father's Sins," *New York Times,* January 29, 1878, 5; "The Cincinnati Will Case," *New York Times,* February 12, 1878, 1.

9. "The Kirby Will Contest: Testimony of Donn Piatt, and of Drs. Murphy and Bartholow as Experts," clipping, name of paper and date not shown, in Scrapbook 66, Castle archives.

10. "A Greenback Orator," *Indiana Progress* (Indiana, Pa.), November 20, 1879, 4. The Randolph referred to was John Randolph of Roanoke (1773–1833), longtime member of Congress from Virginia.

11. Donn Piatt, Washington, D.C., to "My dear Nephew," December 31, 1868, series IV, box 4, file 7, Castle archives.

12. Donn Piatt, Washington, D.C., to "My dear Nephew," January 9, 1869, series IV, box 4, file 7, Castle archives.

13. Donn Piatt, Mac-o-cheek, to "My dear Nephew," August 16, 1878, series IV, box 4, file 7, Castle archives.

14. Donn Piatt, Washington, D.C., to "My dear Nephew," January 20, 1879, series IV, box 4, file 7, Castle archives.

15. Piatt, "Odd Letters from Our Editor," *The Capital,* February 22, 1880, 6.

16. Miller, *Donn Piatt,* 327.

17. Clara Morris, *The Life of a Star* (New York: McClure, Phillips, 1906), 103.

18. "Donn Piatt on Conkling," *Ohio Democrat* (New Philadelphia, Ohio), January 13, 1881, 2. This was a dispatch datelined Washington, D.C., January 4, that was presumably sent to a number of newspapers.

19. Piatt, Washington, D.C., to Hassaurek, July 8, 1873, Ohio Historical Society, Columbus, Ohio.

20. Brown and Williams, *Diary of James A. Garfield,* 2:153, 166, 168.

21. Theodore Clarke Smith, *The Life and Letters of James Abram Garfield* (New Haven, Conn.: Yale University Press, 1925), 2:529.

22. For example, Piatt wrote how on the floor of the House Garfield hesitated, retreated, and refused to take a position; *The Capital,* August 30, 1874, 4, quoted in Brown and Williams, *Diary of James A. Garfield,* 1:xlvi.

23. Brown and Williams, *Diary of James A. Garfield,* 2:168.

24. Ibid., 1:xlvi-vii.

25. Ibid., 4:188–89.

26. Piatt, quoted in "Donn Piatt Defending Garfield," *Chicago Daily Tribune,* March 27, 1878, 3. For a lengthy account of the DeGolyer case, see "Gen. Garfield's Price," *Washington Post,* March 15, 1878, 3.

27. Grant, *Days of My Father,* 319.

28. "A Bad Way Out of Troubles," *New York Sun,* December 27, 1880, 2.

29. "Donn Piatt to Garfield: An Open Letter from the Noted Journalist," *Boston Globe,* November 15, 1880, 1. The text of the "open letter" is in *The Capital,* November 14, 1880, 1.

30. Piatt, Mac-o-chee, to Garfield, December 19, 1880, James A. Garfield Papers, Manuscript Division, Library of Congress.

31. Harte, as noted, was given a consulate in Germany; Hayes named Lowell minister to Spain in 1877.

32. Piatt to Hayes, June 4, 1881, Hayes Library.

33. Lincoln to Seward, March 6, 1865, Abraham Lincoln Papers, Library of Congress.

34. Ames, *Ten Years in Washington,* 159.

35. Dowler, "John James Piatt."

36. Hudson Strode, *Jefferson Davis, Tragic Hero: The Last Twenty-Five Years 1864–1889* (New York: Harcourt, Brace & World, 1964), 449.

37. It was not, of course, the first case of a Northern editor helping Davis. Horace Greeley had been one of a number of men who signed Jefferson Davis's bail bond in 1867.

38. "Personals," *The Capital,* April 20, 1873, 2.

39. William "Brother" Rogers, "Lucius Quintus Cincinnatus Lamar," *Mississippi History Now,* http://mshistory.k12.ms.us/articles/173/lucius-quintus-cincinnatus-lamar. Lamar's eulogy, which did much for postwar reconciliation between North and South, led President John F. Kennedy to include him among the eight American leaders in his book *Profiles in Courage.*

40. Morris, *Life of a Star,* 279.

41. Piatt to Davis, April 14, 1889, Alabama Department of Archives and History, Montgomery.

42. Piatt to Davis, April 20, 1889; June 22, 1889; June 28, 1889; July 8, 1889; Jefferson Davis Collection, Eleanor S. Brockenbrough Library, Museum of the Confederacy, Richmond, Va.

43. Jefferson Davis to Walter George Smith, September 10, 1889; September 25, 1889; October 17, 1889; Jefferson Davis to Piatt, September 28, 1889; Walter George Smith Papers, MC47, Philadelphia Archdiocesan Historical Research Center, Philadelphia, Pa. (hereafter PAHRC). Also see Thomas A. Bryson, "Walter George Smith and General Grant's Memoirs," *Pennsylvania Magazine of History and Biography* 94, no. 2 (April 1970): 233–44. Smith's father, Thomas Kilby Smith, had visited Mac-o-cheek at Donn Piatt's invitation and was later married there to a cousin of Donn (Walter George Smith, *Life and Letters of Thomas Kilby Smith, Brevet Major-General, United States Volunteers, 1820–1887* [New York: G.P. Putnam's Sons, 1898], 7–8).

44. Smith had wanted a legal fee of $250, but Davis said he could pay just $100. Davis wrote frankly to Smith that "my suggestion to Col. Piatt about the amt. of retainer was the result of such straitened circumstances that I have to draw upon my credit rather than upon any funds deposited, in other words to get an advance from my merchant" (Davis to Smith, September 10, 1889; Davis to Piatt, September 28, 1889; Smith Papers, PAHRC).

45. George Haven Putnam, *Memoirs of a Publisher 1865–1915* (New York: G.P. Putnam's Sons, 1915), 92–94.

46. "Specifications of the Claim of Jefferson Davis's Estate," Smith Papers, PAHRC; see also Thomas A. Bryson, "A Lawsuit Concerning the Publication of Jefferson Davis's *The Rise and Fall of the Confederate Government*," *Georgia Historical Quarterly* 54, no. 4 (Winter 1970): 540–52, and Bryson, "A Note on Jefferson Davis's Lawsuit Against Appleton Publishing Company," *Journal of Mississippi History* 33, no. 2 (May 1971): 149–66.

47. William J. Cooper Jr., *Jefferson Davis, American* (New York: Vintage Books, 2001), 663–65. Cooper (p. 667) says that despite a lack of publicity, and despite its bulk and controversial content, the book sold "astonishingly well": 22,943 copies by the year after Davis's death. One may note that in contrast, Grant's also bulky memoirs sold 325,000 copies in the first year after publication (Walter A. Friedman, *Birth of a Salesman* [Cambridge, Mass.: Harvard University Press, 2005], 49).

48. Piatt to Mrs. Jefferson Davis, December 8, 1889, Rosenstock-Davis Collection, Z/0043, Archives and Library Division, Mississippi Department of Archives and History, Jackson.

49. Miller, *Donn Piatt*, 252.

50. Brooklyn was an independent city until 1898, when it joined the other four boroughs that New York City now comprises.

51. "New York Notes: We Go to Lunch," *The Capital*, June 14, 1874. Piatt quotes Morris as saying, "You wrote me a play; it was full of fine writing, you know, and yet two little speeches out of all clung to me."

52. Sir Thomas More, "The History of King Richard III," in *The Norton Anthology of English Literature*, ed. M. H. Abrams (New York: W.W. Norton, 2000), 1B:523–24.

53. Among performances was one at Ford's Theater in Washington, a month before Abraham Lincoln's assassination, that was attended by Lincoln's assassin, John Wilkes Booth (Michael W. Kauffman, *American Brutus: John Wilkes Booth and the Lincoln Conspiracies* [New York: Random House, 2004], 179).

54. "Brooklyn Theatre," *New York Times*, October 7, 1879, 5; "Opened: The New Brooklyn Theatre to the Public," *Brooklyn Eagle*, October 7, 1879, 1; see also "Questions Answered," *Brooklyn Eagle*, December 14, 1884, 9. Morris's friendly feelings for Piatt are reflected not only in her *Life of a Star* but also in her article "A Memory of Dion Boucicault," *Cosmopolitan* 38, no. 3 (January 1905): 273–78.

55. *Chicago Tribune*, n.d., quoted in "Mr. Donn Piatt's Play," *Washington Post*, October 13, 1879, 2.

56. Undated clipping from Scranton, Pa., newspaper in Clippings scrapbook, Castle archives.

57. Morris's diaries are in the Arthur and Elizabeth Schlesinger Library, Harvard University Libraries, Cambridge, Mass. See summary of contents at http://oasis.lib.harvard. edu/oasis/deliver/~scho0742.

58. More, "History of King Richard III," 1B:524.

59. Lewis and Smith, *Oscar Wilde*, 45, 226.

60. "Chromo." Commonly used to mean a copy; short for "chromolithograph."

61. "Occasional," clipping in Scrapbook 67, Castle archives, probably from *The Capital*, datelined "Mac-o-chee, 28th February, 1882."

62. Donn Piatt, "The Great Dynamite Scare," in *The Lone Grave of the Shenandoah, and Other Tales* (New York: Belford, Clarke, 1888), 143.

63. "A New Comic Opera," *Salt Lake Daily Herald*, January 8, 1884, 6.

64. "KE-NO: A Political Opera by Donn Piatt," *Cleveland Herald*, October 22, 1883, 5.

65. Barnard, *Rutherford B. Hayes*, 402.

66. Miller, *Donn Piatt*, 287.

67. Piatt, Mac-o-check, to "Rev. Sir," probably the university's president, Thomas E. Walsh, June 1, 1882, C.S.C. CCMM 3/9, University of Notre Dame Archives, Notre Dame, Ind. Confirmation that the degree was awarded is in UDIS 130/03, Honorary Degree Data File, same archives.

68. Undated clipping from the *Marshfield Times*, Marshfield, Wis., in Castle archives. Notre Dame then had only male students; the "young ladies" were presumably students at Saint Mary's College.

69. The pages are in a ledger book in the Castle archives that also contains a number of poems by Piatt.

70. Piatt to Hayes, June 7, 1884, Hayes Library.

71. Austine Snead, Covington, Ky., to Hayes, September 17, 1882, Hayes Library.

72. Asbury, "Rutherford B. Hayes," 38.

73. "Piatt on Cleveland,," *Boston Daily Globe*, December 15, 1885, 5.

74. "A Talk with Donn Piatt," *Washington Post*, April 22, 1887, 2.

75. "Donn Piatt Barricaded," *Washington Post*, October 11, 1886, 2.

76. Adlai E. Stevenson, Office of the Postmaster General, to Piatt, August 17, 1887, Charles Deering McCormick Library, Northwestern University, Evanston, Ill. Stevenson was, after Piatt's death, vice president of the United States, in 1893–97. His grandson was the Democratic candidate for president in 1952 and 1956; his great-grandson was U.S. senator from Illinois, 1970–81.

77. "Don Piatt's Postoffice," *Washington Post*, December 18, 1886, 1.

78. Miller, *Donn Piatt*, 275.

79. Piatt to Hayes, April 20, 1884, Hayes Library.

80. The text of the Runkle Supreme Court decision (*Runkle vs. U.S.*, 122 U.S. 543 [1887]), including the text of President Hayes's 1884 order, is at http://www.45ohio.homestead.com/runklecourt.html.

81. Piatt to Hayes, June 3, 1887, Hayes Library.

82. Letter from Laura Reams, datelined Mac-O-Cheek, October 27. *Indianapolis News*, October 30, 1886, no page; Clippings scrapbook, Castle archives.

83. Piatt to Hayes, July 23, 1884, Hayes Library.

84. Piatt to Townsend, March 19, 1880, Manuscript Collection 415, George Alfred Townsend Correspondence, Special Collections, University of Delaware Library, Newark, Del.

85. The letter that Townsend returned, after making some notation on it, was found in Piatt's study after he died. "Where Donn Piatt Wrote," *Catholic Columbian,* Columbus, Ohio, February 27, 1892, no page; Clippings scrapbook, Castle archives.

86. *Westminster Review,* issue not given, quoted in Henry Howe, *Historical Collections of Ohio* (Norwalk, Ohio: Laning Printing Co., 1896), 2:114.

87. Piatt, *Men Who Saved the Union,* viii-ix.

88. Copy of Piatt letter to Dilke, dated July 24, 1887, Mac-o-chee, series IV, subseries I, box 5, Castle archives.

89. Joseph H. Barrett, *Life of Abraham Lincoln* (Mechanicsburg, Pa.: Stackpole Books, 2006; reprint of 1865 edition), 841; see also Joseph R. Nightingale, "Joseph H. Barrett and John Locke Scripps, Shapers of Lincoln's Religious Image," *Journal of the Illinois State Historical Society* 92, no. 3 (Autumn 1999).

90. "A Man for the Ohio Senatorship," *Washington Post,* December 18, 1877, 2, quoting Piatt in the *Cincinnati Enquirer,* n.d.

91. Piatt, *Men Who Saved the Union,* v.

92. Ibid., 31; see also Peter Bridges, "Lincoln and the Greatest Question of All," a review of Brian R. Dirck, ed., *Lincoln Emancipated: The President and the Politics of Race* (DeKalb: Northern Illinois University Press, 2006) in the *California Literary Review,* http://calitreview.com/208.

93. Piatt, *Men Who Saved the Union,* xxiii.

94. Ibid., 42–43.

95. Ibid., viii.

96. Ibid., 78–79.

97. Ibid., 85–86.

98. Ulysses S. Grant, *Personal Memoirs of U. S. Grant, Complete* (Teddington, England: Echo Library, 2006), 2:247.

99. Ibid., 75.

100. *Loc. cit.*

101. "An Historical Character in Need of an Historical Vindication," *Brooklyn Eagle,* May 16, 1886, 8.

102. Warden, *An Account,* 738, 742.

103. Blue, *Salmon P. Chase,* 318.

104. Piatt, *Men Who Saved the Union,* 119.

105. Goodwin, *Team of Rivals,* 563.

106. John Niven, *Salmon P. Chase: A Study in Paradox* (New York: Oxford University Press, 1995), 438.

107. Piatt, *Men Who Saved the Union,* 290.

108. Von Moltke, quoted in Piatt, *Men Who Saved the Union,* 298–99.

109. "On the Way to Europe," *New York Times,* August 8, 1886, 3.

110. Piatt, *Men Who Saved the Union,* 177–78.

111. Ibid., 186.

112. Ibid., 241.

113. "Chickamauga battle field as seen by Veterans," manuscript in Piatt's handwriting annotated "Mac-o-chee Ohio 15 May 89," series IV, subseries I, box 5, Castle archives.

114. Piatt to Davis, April 14, 1889, Department of Archives and History, State of Alabama, Montgomery.

115. Leech, *Reveille in Washington,* 268.

116. "Book Reviews and Notices," *North American Review* 135, no. 379 (September 1887), 333.

117. Both books have recently been reprinted by Kessinger Publishing Company, Whitefish, Mont.

118. Piatt, *Lone Grave,* x.

119. Edward P. Roe, *Taken Alive and Other Stories, with an Autobiography* (New York: Dodd, Mead, 1889), 29–30.

120. Edward Eggleston, *The Hoosier Schoolmaster* (New York: Grosset & Dunlap, 1892), 10.

121. Horace Traubel, *With Walt Whitman in Camden* (New York: Mitchell Kennerley, 1914), 3:23.

122. "Editorial Department: The Dude in Literature," *Belford's Magazine* 1, no. 4 (September 1888), 564.

123. "A Card from Donn Piatt," *Washington Post,* November 25, 1888, 4.

9. East Again, and Home to Stay

1. *Springfield Register,* no date or page given, quoted in advertisement by Belford, Clarke & Co. in Julian Hawthorne, *The Professor's Sister: A Romance* (New York: Belford, Clarke, 1888), 182.

2. "Our New York Letter," *Atchison Daily Globe* (Atchison, Kans.), June 20, 1888, 2.

3. Edward Bellamy, *Looking Backward* (New York: New American Library, 1960), 136.

4. U.S. Bureau of the Census, *United States Life Tables: 1890, 1901, 1910 & 1901–1910* (Washington, D.C.: Government Printing Office, 1921), 56–57.

5. "The Death of Donn Piatt," *Belford's Monthly and Democratic Review* 8, no. 43 (December 1891), 496.

6. "Gossip from the Hotels," *Washington Post,* May 12, 1888, 3.

7. There are clippings from several newspapers in Clippings scrapbook, Castle archives, all dating from February 1891, reporting a letter Piatt sent on the matter to the *New York World.*

8. The letter, dated January 5, 1889, is in the Mark Twain Papers, Bancroft Library, University of California, Berkeley; see also Barbara Schmidt, "A Closer Look at the Lives of True Williams and Alexander Belford," paper presented at the Fourth International Conference on the State of Mark Twain Studies, Elmira, New York, August 18, 2001, http://www.twainquotes.com/TWW/TWW.html.

9. Frederick Anderson, Lin Salamo, and Bernard L. Stein, eds., *Mark Twain's Notebooks & Journals* (Berkeley: University of California Press, 1975), 2:355, 418–19.

10. "When You Come to Think of It," *Science* 12, no. 306 (December 14, 1888): 297.

11. Donald Pizer, "'John Boyle's Conclusion,' An Unpublished Middle Border Story by Hamlin Garland," *American Literature* 31, no. 1 (March 1959): 59–75.

12. "Colonel Piatt as a 'Discoverer' of Genius," *Bellefontaine Examiner,* no date or page; clipping in Piatt file, Logan County Historical Society.

13. Donn Piatt, "A Roman Catholic's View," *The Arena* 14 (January 1891): 244.

14. Helen Gardener, "Sex in Brain," *Report of the International Council of Women* (Washington, D.C.: Rufus H. Darby, 1888), 369–82.

15. Henry Nash Smith, *Virgin Land,* 223.

16. Joseph Dana Miller, ed., *Single Tax Year Book* (New York: Single Tax Review Publishing, 1917), 1–11, 442–43. Henry George died after Piatt, in 1897. His popularity declined in the following century, but his ideas have influenced a number of modern writers. See http://en.wikipedia.org/wiki/Henry_George.

17. *The Capital,* 1874–78, passim; Miller, *Donn Piatt,* 318; "J.S. Moore," *New York Times,* March 7, 1892, 4. Moore wrote under a pseudonym for *The Capital,* while also contributing signed articles to the *Times.* Ida M. Tarbell describes his influence on tariff questions in Tarbell, *The Tariff in Our Times* (New York: Macmillan, 1911), 91–93.

18. Piatt, New York, to Hayes, August 4, 1888, Hayes Library.

19. Gaumer, "Mac-o-chee Valley," 468–69.

20. "Donn Piatt of Mac-o-Chee," later published in James Whitcomb Riley, *Green Fields and Running Brooks* (Indianapolis: Bobbs-Merrill, 1893), no page, http://www.gutenberg.org/dirs/1/5/0/7/15079/15079-8.txt.

21. As noted later in the text, a 1931 article said Riley's poem had been conceived there, and later visitors to the Piatt Castles were told the same thing; see http://www.dupontcastle.com/castles/piatt.htm.

22. Clippings scrapbook, Castle archives, contains clippings from various newspapers with the text of Piatt's poem. Riley's poem was first published in 1882; the author has been unable to assign a date to Piatt's. The text of Piatt's poem is in his posthumously published *Poems and Plays,* 9–10.

23. Julius Chambers, "Walks and Talks," *Brooklyn Daily Eagle,* October 13, 1915, 12. Chambers was born at Bellefontaine, Ohio, in 1847 and died in 1920 after a notable career as editor and author. An obituary is in *Cornell Alumni News,* no. 22 (February 26, 1920), 257.

24. Piatt to Riley, February 6, 1886, quoted in Elizabeth J. Van Allen, *James Whitcomb Riley: A Life* (Bloomington: Indiana University Press, 1999), 208.

25. "The Fellowcraft Club," *New York Times,* May 19, 1888, 5; "The Fellowcraft Dines," *New York Times,* March 8, 1889, 2. George Kennan (1845–1924) was an older cousin of George F. Kennan (1904–2005), the diplomatist and historian.

26. Handwritten note by Donn Piatt in Manuscripts, series IV, box 6, file 9, Castle archives.

27. Piatt to Davis, June 22, 1889, Jefferson Davis Collection, Eleanor S. Brockenbrough Library, Museum of the Confederacy, Richmond, Va.

28. Peter Hutchinson, *A Publisher's History of American Magazine Publishing,* http://themagazinist.com/uploads/Part_3_Distribution.pdf, 33.

29. Archbishop William Henry Elder to William J. Onahan, October 9, 1889, Archives, University of Notre Dame, Notre Dame, Ind. Onahan was a prominent Irish Catholic in Chicago and organizer of the forthcoming Catholic Congress.

30. "Gossip from the Hotels," *Washington Post,* May 12, 1888, 3. There had been reports in the *Post's* "City Personals" column for March 1, March 2, and April 12 that Piatt was sick at Chamberlain's.

31. "Against Cheap Literature," *Washington Post,* April 10, 1888, 2; see also Linda Cushman Schurman, "The Librarian of Congress Argues Against Cheap Novels Getting Low Postal Rates," in *Pioneers, Passionate Ladies, and Private Eyes,* ed. Larry E. Sullivan and Lydia Cushman Schurman (New York: Haworth Press, 1996), 59–72.

32. Miller, *Donn Piatt,* 304.

33. Piatt, Mac-o-cheek, to Lord, March 4, 1885, Ohio Historical Society, Columbus.

34. *Cincinnati Commercial-Gazette,* n.d., quoted in *Washington Post,* June 27, 1889, 4.

35. "Failures in Business," *New York Times,* October 24, 1889, 2.

36. Morris, *Life of a Star,* 110.

37. Brown and Williams, *Diary of James A. Garfield,* 2:398–99, 401, 405.

38. Mary Elizabeth Knowlton Mixer, *Mosaics: A Book of Poems* (Buffalo, N.Y.: Matthews-Northup Works, 1909), 71.

39. Many such articles are in a clippings scrapbook, Castle archives.

40. Donn Piatt, "Arthur Richmond and the President," *North American Review* 144, no. 362 (January 1887): 111–12.

41. "A Syndicate of Blackguards," *Atlanta Constitution,* July 15, 1889, 4; see also George Cary Eggleston, *Recollections,* 316–17.

42. Cleveland, 816 Madison Avenue, to Piatt, November 16, 1890, and December 31, 1890, series IV, box 4, file 6, Castle archives.

43. Piatt's admission that he wrote the attack on Randall is in a handwritten manuscript entitled "Donn Piatt and Arthur Richmond," dated July 24, 1889, in box 6, file 11, Castle archives.

44. "Letters to Prominent Persons No. IV—To Samuel J. Randall, M.C.," *North American Review* 143, no. 358 (September 1886): 240.

45. Ibid., 244.

46. Ari Hoogenboom, *Rutherford B. Hayes, Warrior & President* (Lawrence: University Press of Kansas, 1995), 290.

47. Piatt to Halstead, November 23, 1890, Hayes Library. Typescript; notation says original is in "Murat Halstead Collection (Mrs. Henley)." See also Curl, *Murat Halstead,* 45, 128.

48. "Murat Halstead, Editor, Is Dead," *New York Times,* July 3, 1908, 7.

49. Charles Grant Miller, undated, untitled clipping from *Cleveland Plain Dealer.* Castle archives.

50. Cist, *Army of the Cumberland,* 227.

51. Cist, Cincinnati, to Piatt, August 9, 1890, "Ella Kirby Piatt—Legal & Business" box, Castle archives.

52. Piatt, address to 25th reunion of the Army of the Cumberland. Piatt quotes Davis as writing, "Chattanooga was the key to the situation, and its loss was terrible to the Confederacy. Our only comfort was, that the people at Washington did not know what to do with it" (Piatt, *General George H. Thomas, A Critical Biography, with Concluding Chapters by Henry V. Boynton* (Cincinnati: Robert Clarke, 1893), 509.

53. Peter Cozzens, *The Shipwreck of Their Hopes: The Battles for Chattanooga* (Urbana: University of Illinois Press, 1994), 392.

54. Peter Cozzens, *This Terrible Sound: The Battle of Chickamauga* (Urbana: University of Illinois Press, 1992), 13.

55. Cozzens, *This Terrible Sound,* 9.

56. Ernest B. Furguson, "Catching up with 'Old Slow Trot,'" *Smithsonian* 37, no. 12 (March 2007): 50–58.

57. J. J. Piatt dedicated an 1877 volume of his poems to Donn Piatt as both friend and kinsman.

58. Piatt, Mac-o-cheek, to "Pres. and Directors of University of Notre Dame," January 8, 1882, UPEL 24/01, University of Notre Dame Archives, Notre Dame, Ind.

59. Piatt, "Robert Cummins Schenck," 45–53.

60. One may doubt the story, but the author knows of a more recent diplomatic appointment made with no better justification.

61. C. Vann Woodward gives a detailed account of this and other scandals during Grant's administration in "The Lowest Ebb," *American Heritage* 8, no. 3 (April 1957): 52–57.

62. Piatt, "Editor and Diplomat," *Columbia Record,* Columbia, S.C., June 12, 1890, Clippings scrapbook, Castle archives.

63. The deaths of six hundred thousand soldiers in the Civil War sent relatives to mediums who claimed they could call up the spirits of the departed. Mary Todd Lincoln consulted mediums after the Lincolns' young son Willie died in 1862, and the president himself attended one or two seances but put no credit in them. Piatt's fellow editor Horace Greeley for a time fell under the spell of a spiritualist; although Greeley claimed that he remained skeptical, he nevertheless thought there might be some sort of "magnetic telegraph" that could connect living people to the unseen world (Williams, *Horace Greeley,* 194).

64. N. B. Wolfe, *Startling Facts in Modern Spiritualism* (Chicago: Religio-Philosophical Publishing, 1875), 272–73, 353–54, 403–6, 522–26.

65. Elder to Onahan, October 9, 1889, Archives, University of Notre Dame.

66. *Official Report on the Proceedings of the Catholic Congress Held at Baltimore, Md., November 11th and 12th, 1889* (Detroit: William H. Hughes, 1889), 4, 192.

67. Miller, *Donn Piatt,* 246, 345.

68. Ibid., 246.

69. Piatt, Washington, D.C., to Ella Piatt, November 17, 1887 ("I am just in from vespers at St. Matthews. I sat in our old pew and prayed for God to bless you."), Castle archives.

70. The Protestant clergyman of the title was then named Lollypod Poundex. Why rename him Melancthon? Philip Melancthon had been Martin Luther's friend—and the Piatts owned a property on Melancthon Street in Cincinnati.

71. "Donn Piatt's Religious Novel," *Washington Post,* July 10, 1889, 7.

72. Donn Piatt, *The Reverend Melancthon Poundex* (Chicago: Robert J. Belford, 1893).

73. Clipping from the *Catholic Mirror,* Baltimore, November 21, 1891, no page, in Clippings scrapbook, Castle archives; see also "John Baptist Purcell," *Catholic Encyclopedia,* New Advent, http://www.newadvent.org/cathen/12570a.htm.

74. "Bishop Purcell's Large Debts," *New York Times,* February 24, 1879, 1. For the archbishop's obituary, see "The Death List of a Day," *New York Times,* July 6, 1883, 1.

75. Decades earlier, in an 1837 Cincinnati debate with Alexander Campbell, founder of the Disciples of Christ, Purcell had said, "No enlightened Catholic holds the Pope's infallibility to be an article of faith. I do not; and none of my brethren, that I know of, do" (Alexander Campbell and John Baptist Purcell, *The Battle of the Giants: A Debate on the Roman Catholic Religion* [Cincinnati, Ohio: C.F. Vent, 1875], 23).

76. Piatt, "A Roman Catholic's View," 246.

77. Miller, *Donn Piatt,* 377.

78. Ibid., 290.

79. "Brady's Servile Editor," *New York Times,* August 3, 1882, 5. The *Washington Post* reported on February 26, 1882 ("City Brevities," p. 4), that E. W. Brady had just become president

of the Capital Publishing Company. This may have been the E. W. Brady who was the publisher of the *Davenport Daily Times* in Davenport, Iowa, and whose sons later became publishers of *McClure's Magazine*. The author has been unable to determine whether E. W. Brady was related to Thomas J. Brady.

80. Lori Lyn Bogle and Joel I. Holwitt, "The Best Quote Jones Never Wrote," *Naval History* 18, no. 2 (April 2004): 18–23.

81. *New York Recorder,* April 14, 1891, no page; Clippings scrapbook, Castle archives.

82. "'Belford's Magazine' Is Dead," *New York World,* September 3, 1891, no page; Clippings scrapbook, Castle archives.

83. Letter from R. J. Belford, *New York World,* September 7, 1891, no page; Clippings scrapbook, Castle archives.

84. Piatt, unpublished poem in Clippings scrapbook, Castle archives.

85. One of "Donn Piatt's Maxims, Opinions, Reflections and Sentiments" in Miller, *Donn Piatt,* 354–81.

86. *Boston Herald,* August 19, 1891, no page; Clippings scrapbook, Castle archives.

87. *Chicago Post,* August 17, 1891, no page; Clippings scrapbook, Castle archives.

88. *Cleveland Plain Dealer,* August 16, 1891, no page; Clippings scrapbook, Castle archives. "Garnot" was, as Piatt wrote elsewhere (*Sunday Meditations and Selected Prose Sketches,* 426), actually Garnett—perhaps Dr. Alexander Y. P. Garnett (1819–88), a prominent physician in the Confederacy who was later professor of clinical medicine at Columbian University in Washington, D.C., and president of the American Medical Association.

89. Donn Piatt, "Garfield Dead," in *Poems and Plays* (Cincinnati: Robert Clarke, 1893), 39–43.

90. Brown and Williams, *Diary of James A. Garfield,* 2:181.

91. "The Garfield-Rosecrans Letter," *New York Times,* March 14, 1882, 1; "Garfield and Rosecrans," *New York Times,* June 12, 1882, 5.

92. "The Piatt-Garfield Chestnut," *Washington Post,* August 21, 1891, 4.

93. Piatt, "Detectives' Defects," clipping from unidentified newspaper, datelined "Mac-O-Cheek, O., July 21, 1884," in bound volume, Castle archives.

94. "The Season's Height," datelined Urbana, August 20, *Cincinnati Commercial Gazette,* August 23, 1891, no page, Clippings scrapbook, Castle archives.

95. M. P. Nolan, "Donn Piatt," *Dayton Evening News,* November 18, 1891, no page; Clippings scrapbook, Castle archives. Nolan, a Dayton resident, had commanded an Ohio regiment in the Civil War.

96. Donn Piatt, "Uncle John's Conversion," *Ladies' Repository* 29, no. 4 (July 1869): 49–54.

97. Piatt, "Memories of Washington McLean," *Belford's Magazine* 6, no. 34 (March 1889): 530–40.

98. Letter from Donn Piatt in *Cleveland Plain Dealer,* September 17, 1891, no page; copy in Castle archives.

99. "Politics Purified. . . . Col. Donn Piatt Winds Up the Campaign in a Spicy Characterization of the Men and Measures on Trial," *Cleveland Plain Dealer,* November 1, 1891, no page; Clippings scrapbook, Castle archives.

100. Piatt, October 21, 1890, to Karl Sangenbeck; copy kindly furnished to the author from Cincinnati Literary Club archives by Dale Flick, club librarian.

101. Sitting on his other side was Aaron F. Perry, a former member of Congress who had been counsel for the government in the Crédit Mobilier scandal (Piatt, Cincinnati, to Ella Piatt, November 1, 1891, series IV, box 4, file 6, Castle archives.

102. "The Late Colonel Donn Piatt," *Bismarck Daily Tribune* (Bismarck, N.D.), November 14, 1891, 4: "He . . . was so well preserved physically that until quite recently he seemed a middle-aged man, and his many readers when his death was announced heard with surprise that he was seventy-two."

103. Chambers's account of his meeting with Piatt is in "Walks and Talks," *Brooklyn Daily Eagle,* October 14, 1916, 12.

104. "McKinley, William," in *Dictionary of American Biography,* ed. Dumas Malone, vol. 6, part 1, 105.

105. Piatt in *New York World,* quoted in *Cleveland Plain Dealer,* May 10, 1891, no page, Clippings scrapbook, Castle archives. Piatt was not alone in viewing McKinley as a poseur. Vachel Lindsay would write later of "that respectable McKinley / The man without an angle or a tangle / . . . Who climbed every greasy pole, and slipped through every crack" (Lindsay, "Bryan, Bryan, Bryan, Bryan: The Campaign of Eighteen Ninety-Six, as Viewed at the Time by a Sixteen-Year Old, etc.," in *The Oxford Book of American Verse,* ed. F. O. Matthiessen (New York: Oxford University Press, 1950), 622.

106. Donn Piatt to Ella, November 1, 1891, series IV, box 4, file 6, Castle archives.

107. Donn Piatt, to "My dear John Hay," May 13, 1882, John Hay Papers, Brown University Library, Providence, R.I.

108. "The Funeral of Col. Donn Piatt," by A. H. P., *The Examiner,* November 20, 1891, no page, clipping in Castle archives.

109. *Daily Leader,* Davenport, Iowa, November 13, 1891, 1; *Daily Northwestern,* Oshkosh, Wis., November 21, 1891, 1; *Bismarck Daily Tribune,* November 14, 1891, 4; "Death of Donn Piatt," *Washington Post,* November 13, 1891, 1; "Don Piatt Dead," *New York Times,* November 13, 1891, 1.

110. "It was generally recognized [in the 1891 gubernatorial campaign] that the real stake was the presidency. Had Campbell won, he might have succeeded Benjamin Harrison as president of the United States" (Ophia D. Smith, "James E. Campbell," Ohio Fundamental Documents, Ohio Historical Society, from *The Governors of Ohio,* 2nd ed. [Columbus: Ohio Historical Society, 1969], no page, http://www.ohiohistory.org/onlinedoc/ohgovernment/governors/campbell.html).

10. Looking Back at Donn Piatt

1. "Piatt, Donn," in Johnson, *Dictionary of American Biography,* 7:556.

2. "The Meeting of the American Historical Association at Columbus," *American Historical Review* 29, no. 3 (April 1924): 428: "Miss Bessie L. Pierce, assistant professor in the University of Iowa . . . traced the history of the anti-British propaganda carried on so extensively and unscrupulously by Charles Grant Miller in the Hearst papers."

3. "Charles G. Miller, Editorial Writer, Dies," *New York Times,* October 8, 1928, 23.

4. "Washington Letter," datelined "Arlington House, December 29, 1869," *Cincinnati Commercial,* February 2, 1870, 2.

5. The correspondence between Ella Piatt, Henry Cist, and William West is in box 1, "Ella Kirby Piatt—Legal & Business," Castle archives. For a biographic sketch of West, see *New Historical Atlas of Logan County, Ohio* (Philadelphia: J.D. Stewart, 1875), xi.

6. "All War History False and Unjust," *New York World,* October 22, 1893, no page, clipping in Castle archives.

7. "Reckless Halstead," *New York Tribune,* November 10, 1893, no page; clipping in Castle archives.

8. Information on Ella's houses provided to the author by Margaret Piatt of Piatt Castles. In 1902 Ella wrote to John Dickey, secretary to James Whitcomb Riley, "I am very sorry about Mr. Riley's letters—but I have been moving around so much since Col. Piatt's death that they have [been] mislaid or lost and I do not know which" (Ella Kirby Piatt to John M. Dickey, November 26, 1902, Dickey Mss., Manuscripts Department, Lilly Library, Indiana University, Bloomington).

9. "Editorial Comment," *Atlanta Constitution,* November 20, 1891, 4.

10. Paula Bernat Bennett writes in *Palace-Burner: The Selected Poetry of Sarah Piatt* (Urbana: University of Illinois Press, 2001), xix, that Sarah Piatt "is now emerging as, after Emily Dickinson, the nineteenth-century American woman poet most appealing to readers today"; Larry Michaels calls her "an intelligent, powerful, and complex poet . . . neglected too long" (Michaels, *That New World,* 9); see also Ben Railton, *Contesting the Past, Reconstructing the Nation* (Tuscaloosa: University of Alabama Press, 2007), 154–60.

11. Mary Colum, *Life and the Dream* (Chester Springs, Pa.: Dufour Editions, 1966), 141–42. Colum was an Irish writer and the wife of another Irish writer, Padraic Colum.

12. Donn Piatt, *Stair na Gaedhilge,* quoted in Philip O'Leary, *Gaelic Prose in the Irish Free State 1922–1939* (University Park: Pennsylvania State University Press, 2004), 3.

13. O'Leary, *Gaelic Prose,* 60.

14. "Death of Donn Piatt," *Deseret News,* November 13, 1891, no page; Clippings scrapbook, Castle archives.

15. "The Mormon Female," *The Capital,* January 19, 1879, 1.

16. "The Mormon Question," *The Capital,* September 7, 1879, 4.

17. Garfield records in his diary a dinner with Piatt and Cannon on April 19, 1872 (Brown and Williams, *Diary of James A. Garfield,* 2:43). There was an 1884 account in a Washington newspaper ("On the Avenue: Small Talk About Men and Measures," *National Republican,* April 7, 1884, 4) that as a young lawyer Piatt had helped his brother Wykoff to defend Brigham Young in Cincinnati. Supposedly, Young was tried before a justice of the peace, David T. Snelbaker, convicted of horse stealing, and "consigned to the local penitentiary." Young's published journal shows that he was in Cincinnati in July 1843 but says nothing about any trouble with the law (*A Prophet's Journal: Brigham Young's Own Story in His Own Words* [Provo, Utah: Council Press, 1980], 58–59). The 1884 article quotes as its source John A. Dubble, presumably the John A. Dubble who was in the hotel business in Cincinnati for a decade beginning in 1840, and who moved to Washington in 1880 (C. M. L. Wiseman, *Centennial History of Lancaster, Ohio and Lancaster People* [Lancaster, Ohio: C.M.L. Wiseman, 1898], 129). An earlier and more likely account reported, "Don Piatt says that many years ago Brigham Young was fined ten dollars in Cincinnati for assault and battery. The quarrel originated by a young man saying that Young was a polygamist, which he resented with blows" ("Miscellaneous News Items," *Brooklyn Eagle,* February 5, 1869, 1).

18. Portraits of American statesmen and others by George P. A. Healy (1813–94) are in the collections of the National Portrait Gallery in Washington and several other museums. The author has not been able to locate Healy's portrait of Piatt, which is reproduced in Miller, facing page 110. For a Healy account of painting famous subjects (not including Piatt) see G. P. A. Healy, "Crowns and Coronets: Reminiscences of a Portrait-Painter," *North American Review* 151, no. 407 (October 1890): 432–43.

19. Clara Morris, "The Bishop's Day," *Fort Wayne Sentinel,* September 25, 1909, 1. Presumably, the article also appeared in other papers.

20. "Career of Donn Piatt," *Washington Post,* November 18, 1900, 7.

21. "Time to Call Halt," *Perry Daily Chief* (Perry, Iowa), June 1, 1902, 2.

22. "Buell, Butler, Piatt," *Washington Post,* May 29, 1904, B1.

23. Ralph M. McKenzie, *Washington Correspondents Past and Present* (New York: Newspaperdom, 1903), 11–12.

24. Paul Jacob in *Forward,* quoted in *Fitchburg Sentinel* (Fitchburg, Mass.), October 14, 1931, 10.

25. Kessinger Publishing LLC, P.O. Box 1404, Whitefish, MT 59937, http://www.kessinger.net.

26. The contemporary writer who has published most about Piatt, Mark Wahlgren Summers, has made mistakes in what he has written. For example, he claims that Piatt had "nostalgic views toward slavery" (*Press Gang,* 351, n33). He writes, "That an abolitionist could be anything but a lunatic or a sentimentalist was more than [Piatt] could accept" (ibid., 131). Piatt was never an abolitionist, as has been seen, but as a young man he defended abolitionist editors from mobs and worked hard to get his abolitionist friend, Salmon Chase, elected to the Senate. Piatt was always strongly antislavery, and his proven antislavery record begins in 1846, when he got nine hundred fellow Ohioans to sign a petition against admitting Texas to the Union as a slave state. He ran into trouble with Lincoln in part because the president wanted a more cautious course on slavery. Like most white Northerners, he did not want uneducated Southern blacks as his neighbors, but he insisted that blacks had equal rights, he urged them to move upward, and he publicized their success stories.

Summers also writes that Piatt "would edit and write until 1880" and, retiring to Ohio because of his wife's health, had faded into obscurity by the time he died (ibid., 312, 125). Ella's health may have been one reason for moving to Mac-o-cheek, but more important was Piatt's love for the quiet country. In 1887 he published his well-received *Memories of the Men Who Saved the Union;* in 1888 he moved to New York to become the editor of a national magazine; during the year before he died he wrote many articles for a major newspaper; he remained famous among both writers and readers across the country—and a throng came to his funeral.

27. These are the men placed in that category by Summers, *Era of Good Stealings,* 166.

28. Ibid., 50.

29. Ibid., 133.

30. Ibid., 121.

31. Donald A. Ritchie, *Reporting from Washington: The History of the Washington Press Corps* (New York: Oxford University Press, 2005), x.

32. Richard Norton Smith, *The Colonel: The Life and Legend of Robert R. McCormick 1880–1955* (Boston: Houghton Mifflin, 1997), 261.

33. "Etiquette in Washington," *The Capital,* March 16, 1873, 2.

34. Lloyd Lewis and Henry Justin Smith, *Oscar Wilde Discovers America* (New York: Benjamin Blom, 1967), 86–88.

35. Lately Thomas, *Sam Ward, "King of the Lobby"* (Boston: Houghton Mifflin, 1965), 396; see also Grant, *Days of My Father,* 301–2.

36. Quotations are from "Donn Piatt's Maxims, Opinions, Reflections and Sentiments," Miller, *Donn Piatt,* 357, 358, 365. Morris says in "The Bishop's Day" that "he wore a full beard to hide that detested dimple in the chin."

37. Cynthia Crossen, "Deja Vu," *Wall Street Journal,* October 30, 2006, B1.

38. "For Outgoing Mayor, an Icon to Remember the District," *Washington Post,* December 14, 2006, A1.

39. Ritchie, *Press Gallery,* 92.

40. Summers, *Press Gang,* 110.

41. Michael Burlingame, ed., *Dispatches from Lincoln's White House: The Anonymous Civil War Journalism of Presidential Secretary William O. Stoddard* (Lincoln: University of Nebraska Press, 2002).

42. "A Buzzard in the Eagle's Nest—One of Abraham Lincoln's Secretaries—How W. O. Stoddard Bargained Away Cabinet Secrets—His Telegraphic Ciphers with Gold Brokers in New York," *The Capital,* April 28, 1878, 2.

43. Donn Piatt, *Life in the Lobby: A Comedy in Five Acts* (Washington, D.C.: Judd & Detweiler, 1875). Piatt told a congressional committee, and his readers, that "as [the bank] patronized me I patronized that institution" ("Donn Piatt and the Pacific Mail," *The Capital,* January 24, 1875, 6).

44. W. E. B. Du Bois, "The Freedmen's Bureau," *Atlantic Monthly* 87, no. 521 (March 1901): 354–65.

45. John P. Diggins, *Mussolini and Fascism: The View from America* (Princeton, N.J.: Princeton University Press, 1972), 27.

46. Ralph Keyes, *The Quote Verifier* (New York: St. Martin's, 2006), 72–73;see also Peter Bridges, "The First Death Camps," *Foreign Service Journal* (January 1966): 15.

47. Upton Sinclair, quoted in Kevin Mattson, *Upton Sinclair and the Other American Century* (Hoboken, N.J.: John Wiley, 2006), 205.

48. "A Story About Donn Piatt," *Los Angeles Times,* September 10, 1885, 2.

49. "Arson as a Fee," *Washington Post,* June 19, 1910, M3, quoting George Cary Eggleston, *Recollections of a Varied Life* (New York: Henry Holt, 1910).

50. Angela J. Warye, *The Wit and Wisdom of Donn Piatt* (Dayton, Ohio: Westindorf Printing, 2000), no page.

51. H. L. Mencken, "Critics of More or Less Badness," *Smart Set* 44, no. 3 (November 1914): 153–54.

52. Richard O'Mara, "H. L. Mencken: Prose Marvel," *Virginia Quarterly Review* 79, no. 3 (June 2003): 568–78.

53. Arthur Schlesinger Jr., "History and National Stupidity," *New York Review of Books* 53, no. 7 (April 27, 2006): 14.

54. Piatt Castles, PO Box 497, West Liberty, OH 43357; phone 937–465–2821, fax 937–465–7774; www.piattcastles.org.

BIBLIOGRAPHY

Document Collections and Records

Abraham Lincoln Papers, Library of Congress.

Dickey Manuscripts, Manuscripts Department, Lilly Library, Indiana University.

Dispatches from Legation Paris, 1854 and 1855, Department of State, Records Group 59, Microfilm Publication 34, reels 9 and 40, National Archives and Records Administration, College Park, Md. (hereafter NARA).

Donn Piatt lyrics, American Sheet Music Collection, Library of Congress.

Folder, "October and November 1855, Correspondence with and concerning Donn Piatt," Department of State, Records of Foreign Service Posts, France 1853–59, RG 84, vol. 0660, NARA.

George Alfred Townsend Correspondence, Special Collections, University of Delaware Library.

George Perkins Marsh Collection, University of Vermont Library.

Hamilton Fish Papers, Manuscript Division, Library of Congress.

James A. Garfield Papers, Manuscript Division, Library of Congress.

Jefferson Davis Collection, Eleanor S. Brockenbrough Library, Museum of the Confederacy, Richmond, Va.

Jefferson Davis correspondence, Department of Archives and History, State of Alabama, Montgomery.

John Hay Papers, Brown University Library.

Joseph Holt Papers, Manuscript Division, Library of Congress.

Letterbook, vol. 1 (January 2, 1863–February 29, 1864), Middle Department and 8th Army Corps, RG 393, Part I, NARA.

Logan County Court of Common Pleas records, Logan County Genealogical Society, Bellefontaine, Ohio.

Mark Twain Papers, Bancroft Library, University of California, Berkeley.

Mason Family Papers and John Y. Mason Papers, Virginia Historical Society, Richmond.

Castle archives, Piatt Castles, West Liberty, Ohio.

Records Relating to Appointments & Commissions 1853–59, Department of State, RG 59, Microfilm Publication 967, reel 35, NARA.

Robert C. Schenck Collection, Miami University Archives, Miami, Ohio.

245

Rosenstock-Davis Collection, Archives and Library Division, Mississippi Department of Archives and History, Jackson.

Salmon P. Chase Papers, Manuscript Division, Library of Congress.

Stevenson Papers, Charles Deering McCormick Library, Northwestern University, Evanston, Ill.

University of Notre Dame Archives.

Walter George Smith Papers, Philadelphia Archdiocesan Historical Research Center.

William Henry Seward Papers, Department of Rare Books & Special Collections, Rush Rhees Library, University of Rochester, Rochester, N.Y.

William Marcy Papers, Manuscript Division, Library of Congress.

Books and Articles

Ambler, C. H. "General Robert E. Lee's Northwest Virginia Campaign." *West Virginia History* 5, no. 2 (January 1944): 101–15.

Ames, Mary Clemmer. *Ten Years in Washington.* Hartford, Conn.: A.D. Worthington, 1874.

Anderson, Frederick, Lin Salamo, and Bernard L. Stein, eds. *Mark Twain's Notebooks & Journals.* Berkeley: University of California Press, 1975. Vol. 2.

Angle, Paul M. *The Lincoln Reader.* New Brunswick, N.J.: Rutgers University Press, 1947.

Antrim, Joshua. *The History of Champaign and Logan Counties, from Their First Settlement.* Bellefontaine, Ohio: Western Pioneer Association, 1872.

Asbury, Eslie. "Rutherford B. Hayes and the Literary Club." *Queen City Heritage* 47 (Spring 1989): 32–41.

Baker, Jean H. *Mary Todd Lincoln.* New York: Norton, 1987.

Barnard, Frederick A. P., and Arnold Guyot, eds. *Johnson's New Universal Encyclopaedia.* New York: Alvin J. Johnson & Son, 1878.

Barnard, Harry. *Rutherford B. Hayes and His America.* New York: Russell & Russell, 1967.

Barnes, William, and John Heath Morgan. *The Foreign Service of the United States: Origin, Development, and Functions.* Washington, D.C.: Historical Office, Department of State, 1961.

Barrett, Joseph H. *Life of Abraham Lincoln.* Mechanicsburg, Pa.: Stackpole Books, 2006; reprint of 1865 edition.

Basler, Roy P., ed. *The Collected Works of Abraham Lincoln.* New Brunswick, N.J.: Rutgers University Press, 1953. Vols. 1, 3, 4.

Beatty, Jack. *Age of Betrayal: The Triumph of Money in America, 1865–1900.* New York: Knopf, 2007.

Beaver, Daniel R. "The U.S. War Department in the Gaslight Era: Stephen Vincent Benét at the Ordnance Department, 1870–91." *Journal of Military History* 68, no. 1 (January 2004): 105–32.

Bellamy, Edward. *Looking Backward.* New York: New American Library, 1960.

Bemis, Samuel Flagg, ed. *The American Secretaries of State and Their Diplomacy.* New York: Knopf, 1928. Vol. 6.

Bennett, Paula Bernat. *Palace-Burner: The Selected Poetry of Sarah Piatt.* Urbana: University of Illinois Press, 2001.

Berlin, Ira, ed. *Freedom: A Documentary History of Emancipation 1861–1867.* Series I, vol. 2, *The Wartime Genesis of Free Labor.* New York: Cambridge University Press, 1993.

———, ed. *Freedom: A Documentary History of Emancipation 1861–1867.* Series II, *The Black Military Experience.* New York: Cambridge University Press, 1982.

Billington, Ray Allen. *American History before 1877.* Lanham, Md.: Littlefield Adams, 1981.

Birney, William. *James G. Birney and His Times: The Genesis of the Republican Party with Some Account of Abolition Movements in the South before 1828.* New York: D. Appleton, 1890.

Blackstone, WIlliam. *Commentaries on the Laws of England.* Oxford: Clarendon Press, 1765. Book 1.

Blaine, James G. *Twenty Years of Congress: From Lincoln to Garfield.* Norwich, Conn.: Henry Bill, 1886. 2 vols.

Blue, Frederick J. *Salmon P. Chase: A Life in Politics.* Kent, Ohio: Kent State University Press, 1987.

Blum, Edward J. *Reforging the White Republic: Race, Religion, and American Nationalism, 1865–1898.* Baton Rouge: Louisiana State University Press, 2005.

Bobrick, Benson. *Master of War: The Life of General George H. Thomas.* New York: Simon & Schuster, 2009.

Bogle, Lori Lyn, and Joel I. Holwitt. "The Best Quote Jones Never Wrote." *Naval History* 18, no. 2 (April 2004): 18–23.

Booth, Bradford A. "Unpublished Letters of Bret Harte." *American Literature* 16, no. 2 (May 1944): 135–36.

Bordewich, Fergus M. *Bound for Canaan.* New York: Amistad, 2005.

Boritt, Gabor. *The Gettysburg Gospel: The Lincoln Speech That Nobody Knows.* New York: Simon & Schuster, 2006.

Boyd's Directory of the District of Columbia. Washington, D.C.: W.H. Boyd, 1873–78.

Brewer, James D., *Tom Worthington's Civil War.* Jefferson, N.C.: McFarland, 2001.

Bridges, Peter. "An Appreciation of Alvey Adee." *Diplomacy & Statecraft* 10, no. 1 (March 1999): 31–49.

———. "The First Death Camps." *Foreign Service Journal* (January 1966): 15.

———. "Lincoln and the Greatest Question of All," review of *Lincoln Emancipated: The President and the Politics of Race,* ed. Brian R. Dirck. *California Literary Review.* http://calitreview.com/208.

———. *Pen of Fire: John Moncure Daniel.* Kent, Ohio: Kent State University Press, 2002.

Brinkley, Douglas. *Wilderness Warrior: Theodore Roosevelt and the Crusade for America.* New York: HarperCollins, 2009.

Brogan, Hugh. *The Penguin History of the Unites States of America.* London: Penguin Books, 1985.

Brooks, Noah. *Washington in Lincoln's Time.* New York: Rinehart, 1958; reprint of 1895 edition.

Brown, Harry James, and Frederick D. Williams, eds. *The Diary of James A. Garfield.* Lansing: Michigan State University Press, 1967–81. 4 vols.

Brudnick, Ida A. *CRS Report for Congress: The Congressional Research Service and the American Legislative Process.* Washington, D.C.: Congressional Research Service, March 19, 2008.

Brugger, Robert J. *Maryland: A Middle Temperament, 1634–1890.* Baltimore: Johns Hopkins University Press, 1998.

Bryce, James. *The American Commonwealth.* London: Macmillan, 1890. 2 vols.

Bryson, Thomas A. "A Lawsuit Concerning the Publication of Jefferson Davis's *The Rise and Fall of the Confederate Government.*" *Georgia Historical Quarterly* 54, no. 4 (Winter 1970): 540–52.

———. "A Note on Jefferson Davis's Lawsuit Against Appleton Publishing Company." *Journal of Mississippi History* 33, no. 2 (May 1971): 149–66.

———. "Walter George Smith and General Grant's Memoirs." *Pennsylvania Magazine of History and Biography* 94, no. 2 (April 1970): 233–44.

Buckingham, James S. *The Eastern and Western States of America.* London: Fisher, Son, 1842.

Burlingame, Michael, ed. *Dispatches from Lincoln's White House: The Anonymous Civil War Journalism of Presidential Secretary William O. Stoddard.* Lincoln: University of Nebraska Press, 2002.

Calderhead, William D. "Curator's Corner: Intertwined Histories of the Supreme Court of the United States and DACOR Bacon House." *DACOR Bulletin* 58, no. 2 (February 2007).

Calhoun, Charles W. *Conceiving a New Republic: The Republican Party and the Southern Question, 1869–1900.* Lawrence: University Press of Kansas, 2006.

———, ed. *The Gilded Age: Perspectives on the Origins of Modern America.* Lanham, Md.: Rowman & Littlefield, 2007.

———. "The Political Culture: Public Life and the Conduct of Politics." In *The Gilded Age: Perspectives on the Origins of Modern America,* edited by Charles W. Calhoun, 239–40. Lanham, Md.: Rowman & Littlefield, 2007.

Cambridge History of English and American Literature. Electronic edition (2000), http://www.bartleby.com/cambridge/. Vol. 17.

Campbell, Alexander, and John Baptist Purcell. *The Battle of the Giants: A Debate on the Roman Catholic Religion.* Cincinnati, Ohio: C.F. Vent, 1875.

Carlson, Sarah-Eva. "Lincoln and the McCormick-Manny Case." *Illinois History* 48, no. 2 (February 1995): 30–31.

Carter, Clarence Edwin, ed. "The Territory of Illinois 1814–1818." In *The Territorial Papers of the United States,* edited by Clarence Edwin Carter, vol. 17. Washington, D.C.: Government Printing Office, 1950.

Cashman, Sean Dennis. *America in the Gilded Age.* New York: New York University Press, 1993.

"China Mail Service." Report of the Committee on Ways and Means, 43rd Congress, 2nd Session, House of Representatives, Report No. 268, February 27, 1875.

Cist, Henry M. *The Army of the Cumberland.* New York: Charles Scribner's Sons, 1882.

Cole, John Y. *Ainsworth Spofford: Bookman and Librarian.* Littleton, Colo.: Libraries Unlimited, 1975.

———. "Ainsworth Spofford and the 'National Library.'" PhD diss., George Washington University, 1971.

———. "The Library of Congress Becomes a World Library, 1815–2005." *Libraries and Culture* 40, no. 3 (July 2005), 385–98.

Colum, Mary. *Life and the Dream.* Chester Springs, Pa.: Dufour Editions, 1966.

Coolidge, Louis Arthur. *The Life of Ulysses S. Grant.* Boston: Houghton Mifflin, 1922.

Cooper, William J. Jr. *Jefferson Davis, American.* New York: Vintage Books, 2001.

Cottom, Robert I. Jr., and Mary Ellen Hayward. *Maryland in the Civil War: A House Divided.* Baltimore: Maryland Historical Society, 1994.

Cox, Jacob D. "How Judge Hoar Ceased to be Attorney-General." *Atlantic Monthly* 76, no. 454 (July 1895): 162–73.

Cozzens, Peter. *The Shipwreck of Their Hopes: The Battles for Chattanooga.* Urbana: University of Illinois Press, 1994.

———. *This Terrible Sound: The Battle of Chickamauga.* Urbana: University of Illinois Press, 1992.

Crane, Stephen. *The Open Boat and Other Stories.* London: William Heinemann, 1898.

Crocker, Ruth C. "Cultural and Intellectual Life in the Gilded Age." In *The Gilded Age: Perspectives on the Origins of Modern America,* edited by Charles W. Calhoun, 211–38 Lanham, Md.: Rowman & Littlefield, 2007.

Crofts, Daniel W. *Old Southampton: Politics and Society in a Virginia County, 1834–1869.* Charlottesville: University Press of Virginia, 1992.

Curl, Donald. *Murat Halstead and the Cincinnati Commercial.* Boca Raton: University Presses of Florida, 1980.

"The Death of Donn Piatt." Editorial Department, *Belford's Monthly and Democratic Review* 8, no. 43 (December 1891): 495.

Denton, Sally. *Passion and Principle.* New York: Bloomsbury USA, 2007.

DePalma, Margaret C. *Dialogue on the Frontier.* Kent, Ohio: Kent State University Press, 2004.

DeVoto, Bernard. *Mark Twain's America.* Cambridge, Mass.: Houghton Mifflin, 1932.

Dickens, Charles. *American Notes for General Circulation.* New York: D. Appleton, 1868.

Diggins, John P. *Mussolini and Fascism: The View from America.* Princeton, N.J.: Princeton University Press, 1972.

Dixon, Joan M. *National Intelligencer Newspaper Abstracts, 1834–1855.* Bowie, Md.: Heritage Books, 2000.

"Documentary: Indian Towns in Marion County." *Indiana Magazine of History* 1, no. 1 (January–March 1905): 15–17.

Dodge, N. Louise. *The Tribe of Jacob,* 3rd edition. Springfield, Mo.: Young-Stone, 1934.

Donald, David, ed. *Inside Lincoln's Cabinet: The Civil War Diaries of Salmon P. Chase.* New York: Longmans, Green, 1954.

Dowler, Clare. "John James Piatt, Representative Figure of a Momentous Period." *Ohio History* 45, no. 1 (January 1936): 7–17.

Du Bois, W. E. B. "The Freedmen's Bureau." *Atlantic Monthly* 87 (1901): 354–65.

Edwards, Rebecca Strange. *New Spirits: Americans in the Gilded Age.* New York: Oxford University Press, 2006.

Eggleston, Edward. *The Hoosier Schoolmaster.* New York: Grosset & Dunlap, 1892.

Eggleston, George Cary. *Recollections of a Varied Life.* New York: Henry Holt, 1910.

Engle, Stephen D. *Don Carlos Buell: Most Promising of All.* Chapel Hill: University of North Carolina Press, 1999.

Fink, Leon. *Workingmen's Democracy.* Urbana: University of Illinois Press, 1983.

Fischer, Victor, Michael B. Frank, and Lin Salamo, eds. *Mark Twain's Letters.* Berkeley: University of California Press, 1995. Vol. 4.

Foner, Eric. *Reconstruction.* New York: History Book Club, 2005.

Foner, Philip S. *The Great Labor Uprising of 1877.* New York: Monad Press, 1977.

Forney, John W. *Anecdotes of Public Men.* New York: Harper & Brothers, 1873.

Friedman, Walter A. *Birth of a Salesman*. Cambridge, Mass.: Harvard University Press, 2005.

Furgurson, Ernest B. "Catching up with 'Old Slow Trot.'" *Smithsonian* 37, no. 12 (March 2007): 50–58.

Gardener, Helen. "Sex in Brain." In *Report of the International Council of Women*, 369–82. Washington, D.C.: Rufus H. Darby, 1888.

Garrison, Gertrude. "Our New York Letter: As to Donn Piatt and His Life Work." *Hornellsville Weekly Tribune*, Hornellsville, N.Y., June 22, 1888.

Gaumer, Keren Jane. "Mac-o-chee Valley." *Ohio History* 26, no. 4 (October 1917).

George P. Rowell & Co's American Newspaper Directory. New York: George P. Rowell, 1872.

Gibbs, William E. "Diaz' Executive Agents and United States Foreign Policy." *Journal of Interamerican Studies and World Affairs* 20, no. 2 (May 1978): 171–73.

Gienapp, William E. *The Origins of the Republican Party 1852–1856*. New York: Oxford University Press, 1987.

Gillette, William. *Retreat from Reconstruction, 1869–1879*. Baton Rouge: Louisiana State University Press, 1979.

Goodman, Susan, and Carl Dawson. *William Dean Howells: A Writer's Life*. Berkeley: University of California Press, 2005.

Goodwin, Doris Kearns. *Team of Rivals: The Political Genius of Abraham Lincoln*. New York: Simon & Schuster, 2005.

Graham, Lawrence Otis. *The Senator and the Socialite*. New York: HarperCollins, 2006.

Grant, Jesse R. *In the Days of My Father General Grant*. New York: Harper & Brothers, 1925.

Grant, Ulysses S. *Personal Memoirs of U. S. Grant, Complete*. Teddington, England: Echo Library, 2006. Vol. 2.

Greeley, Horace. *Recollections of a Busy Life*. New York: Arno Press, 1970; reprint of 1868 edition.

Greve, Charles Theodore. *Centennial History of Cincinnati and Representative Citizens*. Chicago: Biographical Publishing, 1904.

Halker, Clark D. *For Democracy, Workers, and God*. Urbana: University of Illinois Press, 1991.

Hall, Captain Basil. *Travels in North America*. Edinburgh: Cadell, 1829. 3 vols.

Harris, Wilmer C. *Public Life of Zachariah Chandler, 1851–1875*. Ann Arbor: Michigan Historical Commission, 1917.

Harrold, Stanley. *Gamaliel Bailey and Antislavery Union*. Kent, Ohio: Kent State University Press, 1986.

Harte, Geoffrey Bret, ed. *The Letters of Bret Harte*. Boston: Houghton Mifflin, 1926.

Harwood, Herbert H. Jr. *Rails to the Blue Ridge: The Washington and Old Dominion Railroad 1847–1968*. Fairfax Station: Northern Virginia Regional Park Authority, 2000.

Hawthorne, Julian. *The Professor's Sister: A Romance*. New York: Belford, Clarke, 1888.

Hay, John, Henry Adams, and Clara Louise Hay. *Letters of John Hay and Extracts from Diary*. New York: Gordian Press, 1969.

Healy, G. P. A. "Crowns and Coronets: Reminiscences of a Portrait-Painter." *North American Review* 151, no. 407 (October 1890): 432–43.

Henig, Gerald S. *Henry Winter Davis*. New York: Twayne Publishers, 1973.

Hicken, Victor. *Illinois in the Civil War*. Urbana: University of Illinois Press, 1991.

Hinds, Asher C. *Hinds' Precedents of the House of Representatives of the United States*. Washington, D.C.: Government Printing Office, 1907. Vol. 3.

Hinsdale, Mary L. *A History of the President's Cabinet.* Ann Arbor, Mich.: George Wahr, 1911.

Hoar, George F. *Autobiography of Seventy Years.* New York: Charles Scribner's Sons, 1903. 2 vols.

Hoogenboom, Ari. *Rutherford B. Hayes, Warrior & President.* Lawrence: University Press of Kansas, 1995.

Howard, Angela Marie. "Women and Gender." In *Encyclopedia of the Gilded Age and Progressive Era,* edited by John D. Buenker and Joseph Buenker. Armonk, N.Y.: Sharpe Reference, 2005. 3 vols.

Howard, J. Q. *The Life, Public Services and Select Speeches of Rutherford B. Hayes.* Cincinnati: Robert Clarke, 1876.

Howe, Henry. *Historical Collections of Ohio.* Columbus, Ohio: Henry Howe, 1891.

——. *Historical Collections of Ohio.* Norwalk, Ohio: Laning Printing Co., 1896. 2 vols. 2

Howells, William Dean. *Years of My Youth.* New York: Harper & Brothers, 1916.

Hudson, Frederic. *Journalism in the United States from 1690 to 1872.* New York: Harper & Brothers, 1873.

Hunt, John Gabriel, ed. *The Essential Abraham Lincoln.* Avenel, N.J.: Portland House, 1996.

Hurt, R. Douglas. *The Ohio Frontier: Crucible of the Old Northwest, 1720–1830.* Bloomington: Indiana University Press, 1996.

Hutchinson, Peter. *A Publisher's History of American Magazine Publishing.* http://themagazinist.com/uploads/Part_3_Distribution.pdf.

Investigation into the Affairs of the District of Columbia, 42nd Congress, 2nd Session (1872), Report No. 72. Washington, D.C.: Government Printing Office, 1872.

"John Marshall by Hiram Powers." U.S. Senate. http://www.senate.gov/vtour/marsh.htm.

"John Sherman." Ohio History Central, Ohio Historical Society. http:www.ohiohistorycentral.org/entry.php?rec=338.

Johnson, Allen, ed. *Dictionary of American Biography.* New York: Charles Scribner's Sons, 1964. 11 vols. 1

Johnson, Robert Underwood, and Clarence Clough Buel, eds. *Battles and Leaders of the Civil War.* Edison, N.J.: Castle, 2004; reprint of 1887–88 edition. 4 vols.

Journal of the House of Representatives, 1846. Washington, D.C.: Government Printing Office, 1846.

Joyner, Fred B. "Robert Cumming Schenck, First Citizen and Statesman of the Miami Valley." *Ohio History* 58, no. 3 (July 1949): 286–97.

——. "William Cortenus Schenck, Pioneer and Statesman of Ohio." *Ohio History* 47, no. 4 (October 1938): 363–71.

Kauffman, Michael W. *American Brutus: John Wilkes Booth and the Lincoln Conspiracies.* New York: Random House, 2004.

Keller, Morton. *The Art and Politics of Thomas Nast.* New York: Oxford University Press, 1968.

Keneally, Thomas. *American Scoundrel: The Life of the Notorious Civil War General Dan Sickles.* New York: Talese/Doubleday, 2002.

Kennedy, Robert P. *The Historical Review of Logan County, Ohio.* Chicago: S.J. Clarke, 1903.

Keyes, Erasmus Darwin. *Fifty Years' Observation of Men and Events, Civil and Military.* New York: Charles Scribner's Sons, 1884.

Keyes, Ralph. *The Quote Verifier.* New York: St. Martin's Press, 2006.

Lamon, Ward Hill. *Life of Abraham Lincoln.* Lincoln: University of Nebraska Press, 1999; reprint of 1872 edition.

Landon, Melville D. *Eli Perkins: Wit, Humor and Pathos.* Chicago: Belford, Clarke, 1884.

———. *Wise, Witty, Eloquent Kings of the Platform and Pulpit.* Chicago: F.C. Smedley, 1891.

Larabee, Ann. *The Dynamite Fiend.* New York: Palgrave Macmillan, 2005.

Leahy, Christopher. "Torn Between Family and Politics: John Tyler's Struggle for Balance." *Virginia Magazine of History and Biography* 114, no. 3 (2006).

Leech, Margaret. *Reveille in Washington.* New York: Carroll & Graf, 1991.

Lessoff, Alan H. "A Handbook for Washington Historians." Review of Historical Dictionary of Washington, D.C., by Robert Benedetto, Jane Donovan, and Kathleen DuVall. Humanities and Social Sciences Net Online, June 2003. http://www.h-net.org/reviews/showrev.php?id=7722.

———. *The Nation and Its City.* Baltimore: Johns Hopkins University Press, 1994.

Lewis, Alan. "Dr. Taylor's Improved Movement Cure Institute." http://www.oocities.com/unclesamsfarm/drtaylor.htm.

Lewis, Lloyd. *Sherman: Fighting Prophet.* New York: Harcourt, Brace, 1932.

Lewis, Lloyd, and Henry Justin Smith. *Oscar Wilde Discovers America.* New York: Benjamin Blom, 1967.

The Life History of the United States. Vol. 6, *The Union Restored,* by T. Harry Williams. New York: Time-Life Books, 1974.

The Literary Club of Cincinnati 1849–1949: Centennial Book. Cincinnati: Roessler Brothers, 1949.

Logan, Celia. *Her Strange Fate.* Cincinnati: Belford, Clarke, 1888.

Lorant, Stefan. *The Glorious Burden.* Lenox, Mass.: Authors Edition, 1976.

Lowenthal, David. "'Flesh warm & nobly human!': The Impassioned Purity of Hiram Powers." Paper presented at the Hiram Powers e Firenze conference, Gabinetto Vieusseux, Florence, Italy, September 20, 2005.

Lucas, David M. "Our Grandmother of the Shawnee: Messages of a Female Deity." http://www.southern.ohiou.edu/folknography/publications/Our%20Grandmother.pdf.

Maack, Mary Niles, ed. *Historical Essays in Honor of John Y. Cole.* Washington, D.C.: Library of Congress, 2011.

Malone, Dumas, ed. *Dictionary of American Biography.* New York: Charles Scribner's Sons, 1961–64. Vols. 6, 8, 11.

Manakee, Harold R. *Maryland in the Civil War.* Baltimore: Maryland Historical Society, 1961.

Marchman, Watt P. "Rutherford B. Hayes, Attorney at Law." *Ohio History* 77, nos. 1–3 (Summer 1968), 5–32.

Marszalek, John F. *Sherman: A Soldier's Passion for Order.* New York: Free Press, 1993.

Martin, Edward Winslow [James Dabney McCabe]. *Behind the Scenes in Washington.* New York: Continental, 1873.

Matthiessen, F. O., ed. *The Oxford Book of American Verse.* New York: Oxford University Press, 1950.

Mattson, Kevin. *Upton Sinclair and the Other American Century.* Hoboken, N.J.: Wiley, 2006.

May, Robert E. *Manifest Destiny's Underworld: Filibustering in Antebellum America.* Chapel Hill: University of North Carolina Press, 2002.

McClellan, George B. *McClellan's Own Story: The War for the Union.* New York: Charles L. Webster, 1887.

McCormick, K. Todd. "A Brief History of Logan County, Ohio." http://countylogan.wheelboat.com/lchs/001/.

McDougall, Walter A. *Throes of Democracy.* New York: HarperCollins, 2008.

McFarland, R. W. "Simon Kenton." *Ohio History* 13, no. 1 (January 1904): 1–39.

McFeely, William S. *Grant: A Biography.* New York: Norton, 1981.

McKenzie, Ralph M. *Washington Correspondents Past and Present.* New York: Newspaperdom, 1903.

McKnight, George H. *English Words and Their Background.* New York: B. Appleton, 1923.

McPherson, James M. *Tried by War: Abraham Lincoln as Commander in Chief.* New York: Penguin Press, 2008.

"The Meeting of the American Historical Association at Columbus." *American Historical Review* 29, no. 3 (April 1924): 428.

Mencken, H. L. "Critics of More or Less Badness." *Smart Set* (November 1914): 153–54.

Michaels, Larry R. *That New World: Selected Poems of Sarah Piatt, 1861–1911.* Toledo, Ohio: Bihl House Publishing, 1999.

Miller, Charles Grant. *Donn Piatt: His Work and His Ways.* Cincinnati: Robert Clarke, 1893.

Miller, Joseph Dana, ed. *Single Tax Year Book.* New York: Single Tax Review Publishing, 1917.

Minot, George, and George P. Sawyer, eds. *Statutes at Large and Treaties of the United States of America from December 3, 1855, to March 3, 1859.* Boston: Little, Brown, 1859. Vol. 11.

Mitchell, Donald Grant. *Daniel Tyler: A Memorial Volume Containing His Autobiography and War Record, Some Account of His Later Years, with Various Reminiscences and the Tributes of Friends.* New Haven, Conn.: Privately printed, 1883.

Mixer, Mary Elizabeth Knowlton. *Mosaics: A Book of Poems.* Buffalo: Matthews-Northup Works, 1909.

Moore, James Bassett, ed. *The Works of James Buchanan.* Philadelphia: J.P. Lippincott, 1909. Vol. 9.

More, Sir Thomas. "The History of King Richard III." In *The Norton Anthology of English Literature,* edited by M. H. Abrams, 1B: 523–24. New York: Norton, 2000.

Morris, Caroline Piatt, and Elizabeth McCullough Smith. *A Memorial Biography of Benjamin M. Piatt and Elizabeth, His Wife.* Washington, D.C.: Gray & Clarkson, 1887.

Morris, Clara. *The Life of a Star.* New York: McClure, Phillips, 1906.

———. "A Memory of Dion Boucicault." *Cosmopolitan* 38, no. 3 (January 1905): 273–78.

Myers, Gustavus. *History of the Great American Fortunes.* Chicago: C. Kerr, 1911.

Nate, Joseph Cookman. *The History of Sigma Chi Fraternity, 1855–1925.* Chicago: Sigma Chi Fraternity, 1925.

Neely, Mark E., Jr. *The Fate of Liberty: Abraham Lincoln and Civil Liberties.* New York: Oxford University Press, 1991.

Nevins, Allan. *Hamilton Fish: The Inner History of the Grant Administration.* New York: Frederick Ungar, 1957. 2 vols.

Nevins, Allan, and Henry Steele Commager, with Jeffrey Brandon Morris. *A Pocket History of the United States.* New York: Pocket Books, 1992.

New Historical Atlas of Logan County, Ohio. Philadelphia: J.D. Stewart, 1875.

Nightingale, Joseph R. "Joseph H. Barrett and John Locke Scripps, Shapers of Lincoln's Religious Image." *Journal of the Illinois State Historical Society* 92, no. 3 (Autumn 1999): 238–73.

Nissen, Axel. *Bret Harte, Prince and Pauper.* Jackson: University of Mississippi Press, 2000.

Niven, John. *Salmon P. Chase: A Biography.* New York: Oxford University Press, 1995.

———, ed. *The Salmon P. Chase Papers.* Kent, Ohio: Kent State University Press, 1993.

Oberholtzer, Ellis Paxson. *A History of the United States Since the Civil War.* New York: Macmillan, 1926. Vol. 3.

Official Records of the Union and Confederate Armies, Additions and Corrections to Series I, Volume XVI. Washington, D.C.: Government Printing Office, 1902. Vol. 6.

Official Records of the War of the Rebellion, Series 1. Washington, D.C.: Government Printing Office, 1889. Vol. 27.

Official Report on the Proceedings of the Catholic Congress Held at Baltimore, Md., November 11th and 12th, 1889. Detroit: William H. Hughes, 1889.

O'Leary, Philip. *Gaelic Prose in the Irish Free State 1922–1939.* University Park: Pennsylvania State University Press, 2004.

O'Mara, Richard. "H. L. Mencken: Prose Marvel." *Virginia Quarterly Review* (June 2003): 568–78.

Ostendorf, Lloyd. *Mr. Lincoln Came to Dayton.* Dayton, Ohio: Otterbein Press, 1959.

Paine, Albert Bigelow. *Mark Twain: A Biography.* New York: Harper, 1935. 4 vols.

———, ed. *Mark Twain's Letters.* New York: Gabriel Wells, 1923. Vol. 1.

Papers Relating to the Foreign Relations of the United States. Washington, D.C.: Government Printing Office, 1870.

Peacock, Virginia Tatnall. *Famous American Belles of the Nineteenth Century.* Philadelphia: J.P. Lippincott, 1901.

Perrin, William Henry, and J. H. Battle. *History of Logan County and Ohio.* Chicago: O.L. Baskin, 1880.

Perry, Mark. *Grant and Twain: The Story of a Friendship that Changed America.* New York: Random House, 2004.

Piatt, Donn. "Arthur Richmond and the President." *North American Review* 144, no. 362 (January 1887): 111–12.

———. "Cuba and the Ostend Manifesto." *Harper's New Monthly Magazine* 40, no. 240 (May 1870).

———. *Extract from a Speech of Colonel Donn Piatt, on the Hon. E. M. Stanton.* Washington, D.C.: L. Towers, 1865?.

———. *General George H. Thomas, A Critical Biography, with Concluding Chapters by Henry V. Boynton.* Cincinnati: Robert Clarke, 1893.

———. *Life in the Lobby: A Comedy in Five Acts.* Washington, D.C.: Judd & Detweiler, 1875.

———. *The Lone Grave of the Shenandoah, and Other Tales.* New York: Belford, Clarke, 1888.

———. *Memories of the Men Who Saved the Union.* New York: Belford, Clarke, 1887.

———. "Memories of Washington McLean." *Belford's Magazine* 6, no. 34 (March 1889): 530–40.

———. "Our Presentation at Court." *Harper's New Monthly Magazine* 38, no. 226 (March 1869): 495–98.

———. *Poems and Plays.* Cincinnati: Robert Clarke, 1893.

———. *The Reverend Melancthon Poundex.* Chicago: Robert J. Belford, 1893.

———. "Richard Realf." *The Current,* Chicago, April 24, 1866.

———. "Robert Cummins Schenck." *Belford's Magazine* (June 1890): 46.

———. "A Roman Catholic's View." *The Arena* 14 (January 1891): 246.

———. "Some Memories of Mac-o-chee." Urbana, Ohio, newspaper (name unknown), December 21, 1889.

———. "Souvenir of Imperial Sovereigns." *The Galaxy* 11, no. 2 (February 1871): 241–46.

———. *Sunday Meditations and Selected Prose Sketches.* Cincinnati: Robert Clarke, 1893.

———. "Uncle John's Conversion." *Ladies' Repository* 29, no. 4 (July 1869): 49–54.

Piatt, Louise Kirby. *Bell Smith Abroad.* New York: J.C. Derby, 1855.

Pike, James A. *First Blows of the Civil War.* New York: American News Company, 1879.

Pizer, Donald. "'John Boyle's Conclusion': An Unpublished Middle Border Story by Hamlin Garland." *American Literature* 31, no. 1 (March 1959): 59–75.

Pletcher, David M. "Mexico Opens the Door to American Capital, 1877–1880." *The Americas* 16, no. 1 (July 1959): 1.

Poore, Benjamin Perley. *Perley's Reminiscences of Sixty Years in the National Metropolis.* Philadelphia: Hubbard Brothers, 1886. 2 vols.

Porter, Daniel R. "Governor Rutherford B. Hayes." *Ohio History* 77, nos. 1–3 (1968).

Principal Officers of the Department of State and United States Chiefs of Mission, 1778–1990. Washington, D.C.: Department of State, Office of the Historian, 1991.

Prokopowicz, Gerald J. *All for the Regiment: The Army of the Ohio, 1861–1862.* Chapel Hill: University of North Carolina Press, 2001.

Putnam, George Haven. *Memoirs of a Publisher 1865–1915.* New York: G.P. Putnam's Sons, 1915.

Railton, Ben. *Contesting the Past, Reconstructing the Nation.* Tuscaloosa: University of Alabama Press, 2007.

Rathmell, George. *A Passport to Hell: The Mystery of Richard Realf.* Lincoln, Neb.: Author's Choice Press, 2002.

Ray, Gordon N., ed. *The Letters and Private Papers of William Makepeace Thackeray.* Cambridge, Mass.: Harvard University Press, 1946. Vol. 3.

Realf, Richard. *Poems of Richard Realf.* New York: Funk & Ingalls, 1898.

"A Reception at the White House." *Harper's Bazaar* 3, no. 20 (May 14, 1870): 313.

Reid, Elizabeth, and Charles H. Coe. *Captain Mayne Reid: His Life and Adventures.* London: Greening, 1900.

Reports of Cases Argued and Determined in the Federal Courts Held in Ohio. (Norwalk, Ohio: Laning Printing, 1900. Vol. 3.

Reports of De B. Randolph Keim, Agent of the United States, etc., to the Secretary of the Treasury relating to the Condition of the Consulates of the United States. Washington, D.C.: Government Printing Office, 1871.

Rhodes, Albert. "Our Diplomates and Consuls." *Scribner's Monthly* 13, no. 2: 172.

Rice, Allen Thorndike, ed. *Reminiscences of Abraham Lincoln by Distinguished Men of His Time.* New York: North American Review, 1888.

Riley, James Whitcomb. *Green Fields and Running Brooks.* Indianapolis: Bobbs-Merrill, 1893.

"Rimensnyder Asks for New Respect for Washington's 'Boss' Shepherd." Summary of November 9, 2005, Overbeck History Lecture by Nelson Rimensnyder, sponsored by Capitol Hill Community Foundation. http://www.capitolhillhistory.org/lectures.html.

Ritchie, Donald A. *Press Gallery: Congress and the Washington Correspondents.* Cambridge, Mass.: Harvard University Press, 1991.

———. *Reporting from Washington: The History of the Washington Press Corps.* New York: Oxford University Press, 2005.

Roe, Edward P. *Taken Alive and Other Stories, with an Autobiography.* New York: Dodd, Mead, 1889.

———. *The Works of E. P. Roe.* New York: P.F. Collier & Son, 1902. Vol. 11.

Rogers, William "Brother." "Lucius Quintus Cincinnatus Lamar." *Mississippi History Now.* http://mshistory.k12.ms.us/articles/173/lucius-quintus-cincinnatus-lamar.

Ross, Steven J. "We Who Built the Queen City." *Queen City Heritage* 47, no. 1 (Summer 1989).

Rossinow, Douglas Charles. *Visions of Progress.* Philadelphia: University of Pennsylvania Press, 2008.

Rothman, David J. *Politics and Power: the United States Senate 1869–1901.* Cambridge, Mass.: Harvard University Press, 1966.

Rovelstad, Mathilde V. "The Library of Congress, a 19th-Century Neo-Baroque Monument." *Libri* 49 (1999): 243–54.

Russell, William Howard. *My Diary North and South.* Boston: T.O.H.P. Burnham, 1863.

Salamo, Lin, and Harriet Elinor Smith, eds. *Mark Twain's Letters.* Berkeley: University of California Press, 1997. Vol. 5.

Samuels, Ernest, ed. *The Education of Henry Adams.* Boston: Houghton Mifflin, 1974.

Sandburg, Carl. *Abraham Lincoln: The Prairie Years.* New York: Harcourt, Brace, 1926. Vol. 2.

———. *Abraham Lincoln: The War Years.* New York: Harcourt, Brace, 1939. Vol. 1.

Saum, Lewis O. *The Popular Mood of America, 1860–1890.* Lincoln: University of Nebraska Press, 1990.

Sawrey, Robert D. *Dubious Victory: The Reconstruction Debate in Ohio.* Lexington: University Press of Kentucky, 1992.

Schlesinger, Arthur M. Jr. *The Age of Jackson.* Boston: Little, Brown, 1953.

———. "History and National Stupidity." *New York Review of Books* 53, no. 7 (April 27, 2006): 14.

Schmidt, Barbara. "A Closer Look at the Lives of True Williams and Alexander Belford." Paper presented at the Fourth International Conference on the State of Mark Twain Studies, Elmira, N.Y., August 18, 2001. http:// www.twainquotes.com/TWW/TWW.html.

Schurman, Linda Cushman. "The Librarian of Congress Argues Against Cheap Novels Getting Low Postal Rates." In *Pioneers, Passionate Ladies, and Private Eyes,* edited by Larry E. Sullivan and Lydia Cushman Schurman. New York: Haworth Press, 1996.

Schutz, Noel Jr. "The Study of Shawnee Myth in an Ethnographic and Ethnohistorical Perspective." PhD diss., Indiana University, 1975.

Schuyler, Eugene. *American Diplomacy and the Furtherance of Commerce.* New York: Charles Scribner's Sons, 1886.

Scott, Frank W. "Newspapers Since 1860." In *The Cambridge History of American Literature,* edited by William Peterfield Trent et al., 324. New York: G.P. Putnam's Sons, 1921. Vol. 3.

Sherman, John. *Recollections of Forty Years in the House, Senate and Cabinet.* Chicago: Werner, 1896.

Simon, John Y., ed. *The Papers of Ulysses S. Grant.* Carbondale: Southern Illinois University Press, 2005. Vols. 26, 28.

Simon, John Y., and Michael E. Stevens, eds. *New Perspectives on the Civil War.* Madison, Wis.: Madison House, 1998.

Simpson, Brooks D., and Jean V. Berlin, eds. *Sherman's Civil War: Selected Correspondence of William T. Sherman 1860–1865.* Chapel Hill: University of North Carolina Press, 1999.

Smith, Elizabeth B. "Some Remarkable Kentucky Converts." *Catholic World* 59, no. 351 (June 1894).

Smith, Henry Nash. *Virgin Land: The American West as Symbol and Myth.* New York: Vintage Books, 1950.

Smith, Jean Edward. *Grant.* New York: Simon & Schuster, 2001.

Smith, Ophia D. "James E. Campbell." *Ohio Fundamental Documents,* Ohio Historical Society [from The Governors of Ohio (Columbus: Ohio Historical Society, 1969, 2nd ed., no page no.]. http://www.ohiohistory.org/onlinedoc/ohgovernment/governors/campbell.html.

Smith, Richard Norton. *The Colonel: The Life and Legend of Robert R. McCormick 1880–1955.* Boston: Houghton Mifflin, 1997.

Smith, Theodore Clarke. *The Life and Letters of James Abram Garfield.* New Haven, Conn.: Yale University Press, 1925. Vol. 2.

Smith, Walter George. *Life and Letters of Thomas Kilby Smith, Brevet Major-General, United States Volunteers, 1820–1887.* New York: G.P. Putnam's Sons, 1898.

"So Ho! Don!" *Vanity Fair* 2 (December 8, 1860): 289.

Stampp, Kenneth M. *Indiana Politics During the Civil War.* Indianapolis: Indiana Historical Bureau, 1949.

Starr, Paul. *The Creation of the Media.* New York: Basic Books, 2004.

The Statistics of the Population of the United States. Vol. 1, Ninth Census. Washington, D.C.: Government Printing Office, 1872.

Steele, Joan. *Captain Mayne Reid.* Boston: Twayne Publishers, 1978.

Stoddard, William O. *Inside the White House in War Time.* Lincoln: University of Nebraska Press, 2000; reprint of 1890 edition.

Stoddard, William O. Jr., ed. *Lincoln's Third Secretary: The Memoirs of William O. Stoddard.* New York: Exposition Press, 1955.

Stover, John F. *History of the Baltimore and Ohio Railroad.* West Lafayette, Ind.: Purdue University Press, 1987.

Strode, Hudson. *Jefferson Davis, Tragic Hero: The Last Twenty-Five Years 1864–1889.* New York: Harcourt, Brace & World, 1964.

Summers, Mark Wahlgren. *The Era of Good Stealings.* New York: Oxford University Press, 1993.

———. *Party Games.* Chapel Hill: University of North Carolina Press, 2004.

———. *The Press Gang.* Chapel Hill: University of North Carolina Press, 1994.

Tap, Bruce. *Over Lincoln's Shoulder: The Committee on the Conduct of the War.* Lawrence: University of Kansas Press, 1998.

Tarbell, Ida M. *The Life of Abraham Lincoln.* New York: Macmillan, 1928.

———. *The Tariff in Our Times.* New York: Macmillan, 1911.

Teillard, Dorothy Lamon, ed. *Recollections of Abraham Lincoln.* Lincoln: University of Nebraska Press, 1994; revision of 1895 edition.

"Testimony Regarding the Contracts with Cowles & Brega for the Extermination of Moths in Army Clothing." Report of the Committee on Expenditures in the War Department, 44th Congress, 1st Session, House of Representatives, Report No. 799, August 5, 1876.

"They Lived Long on the Land." Family Farm Project brochure. West Liberty, Ohio: Piatt Castles, 2007.

Thomas, Benjamin P., ed. *Three Years with Grant as Recalled by War Correspondent Sylvanus Cadwallader.* Lincoln: University of Nebraska Press, 1996.

Thomas, Benjamin, and Harold M. Hyman. *Stanton: The Life and Times of Lincoln's Secretary of War.* New York: Knopf, 1962.

Thomas, Lately. *Sam Ward, "King of the Lobby."* Boston: Houghton Mifflin, 1965.

Thompson, Margaret Susan. *The "Spider Web": Congress and Lobbying in the Age of Grant.* Ithaca, N.Y.: Cornell University Press, 1985.

Traubel, Horace. *With Walt Whitman in Camden.* New York: Mitchell Kennerley, 1914. Vol. 3.

Trent, William Peterfield et al., eds. *Cambridge History of American Literature.* New York: G.P. Putnam's Sons, 1921.

Trollope, Mrs. [Frances Milton]. *Domestic Manners of the Americans.* London: Whittaker, Treacher, 1832.

Turner, Justin G., and Linda Levitt Turner. *Mary Todd Lincoln: Her Life and Letters.* New York: Knopf, 1972.

Twain, Mark. "Memoranda." *Galaxy* 11, no. 4 (April 1871): 615.

Twain, Mark, and Charles Dudley Warner. *The Gilded Age.* New York: Oxford University Press, 1996; reprint of 1873 edition.

"Unpublished Letters of Bret Harte." *American Literature* 16, no. 2 (May 1944): 135–36.

Van Allen, Elizabeth J. *James Whitcomb Riley: A Life.* Bloomington: Indiana University Press, 1999.

Van Deusen, Glyndon G. *Horace Greeley, Nineteenth-Century Crusader.* Philadelphia: University of Pennsylvania Press, 1953.

Villard, Harold G., and Oswald Garrison Villard, eds. *Lincoln on the Eve of '61: A Journalist's Story by Henry Villard.* New York: Knopf, 1941.

Wagandt, Charles L. "The Army versus Maryland Slavery, 1862–1864." *Civil War History* 10 (June 1964): 141–48.

"Wall Street in War Time." *Harper's New Monthly Magazine* 30, no. 179 (April 1865), 615–16.

Wallace, Lew. *An Autobiography.* New York: Harper & Brothers, 1906. 2 vols.

"War Notes." *Virginia Magazine of History and Biography* 27, no. 1 (January 1919): 78.

Warden, Robert Bruce. *An Account of the Private Life and Public Services of Salmon Portland Chase.* Cincinnati: Wilstach, Baldwin, 1874.

Warye, Angela J., ed. *The Wit and Wisdom of Donn Piatt.* Dayton, Ohio: Westindorf Printing, 2000.

Watterson, Henry. *"Marse Henry," an Autobiography.* New York: George H. Doran, 1919. 2 vols.

Weeks, Philip. *Buckeye Presidents: Ohioans in the White House.* Kent, Ohio: Kent State University Press, 2003.

Weisenburger, Francis P. "Lincoln and His Ohio Friends." *Ohio History* 68, no. 3 (July 1959): 242–45.

West, Richard Samuel. *The Political Cartoons of Joseph Keppler.* Champaign: University of Illinois Press, 1988.

White, Andrew Dickson. "Russia in War-Time." *Century Illustrated Magazine* 58, no. 4 (August 1904): 601–6.

Whyte, James H. *The Uncivil War: Washington During the Reconstruction, 1865–1878.* New York: Twayne, 1958.

Williams, Charles Richard, ed. *Diary and Letters of Rutherford B. Hayes.* Columbus: Ohio State Archaeological and Historical Society, 1922–1926. 5 vols.

Williams, Robert C. *Horace Greeley: Champion of American Freedom.* New York: New York University Press, 2006.

Wilson, A. N. *The Victorians.* London: Arrow Books, 2003.

Wilson, David L., and John Y. Simon, eds. *Ulysses S. Grant: Essays and Documents.* Carbondale: Southern Illinois University Press, 1981.

Wilson, Douglas L., and Rodney O. Davis, eds. *Herndon's Informants: Letters, Interviews and Statements about Abraham Lincoln*. Urbana: University of Illinois Press, 1998.

Wiseman, C. M. L. *Centennial History of Lancaster, Ohio and Lancaster People*. Lancaster, Ohio: C.M.L. Wiseman, 1898.

Wittke, Carl, ed. *History of the State of Ohio*. Vol. 3, *The Passing of the Frontier 1825–1850*, by Francis P. Weisenburger. Columbus: Ohio State Archaeological and Historical Society, 1941.

Wolfe, N. B. *Startling Facts in Modern Spiritualism*. Chicago: Religio-Philosophical Publishing, 1875.

Woodward, C. Van. "The Lowest Ebb." *American Heritage* 8, no. 3 (April 1957): 52–57.

Wortham, Thomas, ed. *The Early Prose Writings of William Dean Howells*. Athens: Ohio University Press, 1990.

Young, Brigham. *A Prophet's Journal: Brigham Young's Own Story in His Own Words*. Provo, Utah: Council Press, 1980.

Zimring, Franklin E., and Gordon Hawkins. *The Search for Rational Drug Control*. New York: Cambridge University Press, 1992.

INDEX